Nelson Secondary
Maths

Nelson

Thomas Nelson and Sons Ltd
Nelson House Mayfield Road
Walton-on-Thames Surrey
KT12 5PL UK

Thomas Nelson Australia
102 Dodds Street
South Melbourne
Victoria 3205 Australia

Nelson Canada
1120 Birchmount Road
Scarborough Ontario
MIK 5G4 Canada

First published by Thomas Nelson and Sons Ltd 1996
I(T)P Thomas Nelson is an International Thomson Publishing Company
I(T)P is used under licence

ISBN 0-17-431455-8
NPN 9 8 7 6 5 4 3 2 1

Printed in Spain

Nelson Secondary Maths 3 is written by:

Jim Noonan (Series Coordinator)
Paula Barker
Terry Bevis
Gay Cain
Brian Martin
Christine Mitchell
Robert Powell
Gwen Wood

The authors are grateful for advice received from schools in Avon, Birmingham, Cornwall, Cumbria, Essex, Gloucestershire, Gwent, Hampshire, Hereford & Worcester, Nottingham, Salford, South Glamorgan, Tyneside and Wiltshire involved in trials of material for this series.

Aknowledgements
The publishers are grateful to the following for permission to reproduce their material.
Ordnance Survey, pages 11 and 12; Sharon Rudd, page 10.

Contents

Preface

This book forms part of the Nelson Secondary Maths series, designed to cover the Programme of Study for Key Stages 3 and 4 of the National Curriculum in England and Wales. The Scottish 5–14 Guidelines and Northern Ireland Curriculum are also referenced.

Starting points at the beginning of each chapter give an indication of the background knowledge and skills needed to tackle the chapter content. Assignments covering all aspects of 'Using and Applying Mathematics' occur as separate tasks and as parts of many exercises. These exercises give plenty of opportunity for consolidation and practice of work in Number; Algebra; Shape, Space and Measures and Handling Data. Each chapter ends with a review of the work covered.

The material is designed to support you in acquiring skills and knowledge on the pathway to gaining a better understanding of mathematics.

Fair proportions

In this chapter you will learn:

- → to use ratio
- → to use map scales
- → to divide in a given ratio
- → to work with similar shapes

Starting points

Before starting this chapter you will need to know how to

- simplify fractions
- find a fraction of a quantity
- make a simple scale drawing
- round to the nearest whole number.

Exercise 1

1 Copy and complete these equivalent fractions.

$\frac{1}{2} = \frac{\square}{4} = \frac{5}{\square} = \frac{12}{\square}$

2 Simplify these fractions.

(a) $\frac{6}{8}$ (b) $\frac{7}{21}$ (c) $\frac{10}{12}$ (d) $\frac{9}{15}$

3 Calculate these fractional amounts.

(a) $\frac{1}{4}$ of £10 (b) $\frac{1}{8}$ of 58 m

(c) $\frac{2}{3}$ of £24 (d) $\frac{3}{5}$ of 128 litres

4 Round these numbers to the nearest whole number.

(a) 3.78 (b) 12.24

(c) 136.54 (d) 57.45

(e) 89.91

5 This picture is drawn on 1-cm square paper.

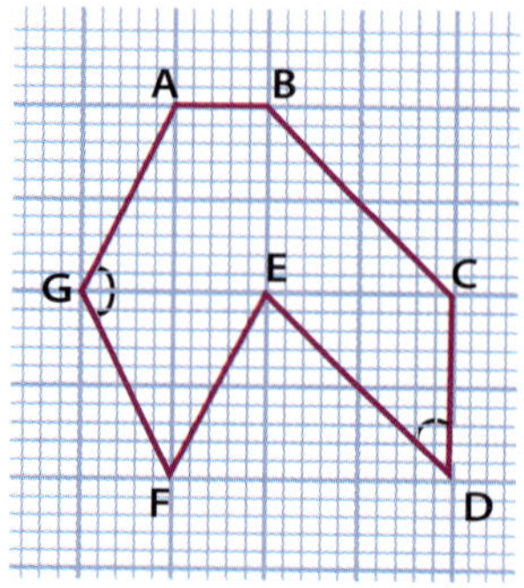

(a) Make an enlarged copy of the shape on 3-cm square paper.

(b) Measure the lengths AB, CD and FG on the original and on the enlarged pictures.

(c) Write down what you notice.

(d) Measure the marked angles at D and G on the original and the enlarged pictures.

(e) Write down what you notice.

6 (a) Measure the length and width of your classroom in centimetres.

(b) Make a scale drawing of the room using 1 cm on your drawing to represent 100 cm in the classroom.

(c) Mark on your plan approximately where you are sitting and the position of the teacher's desk.

Key fact

Ratio is the relationship between two quantities or measures.

Introducing ratios

The bus is 8 metres long and 2 metres wide.

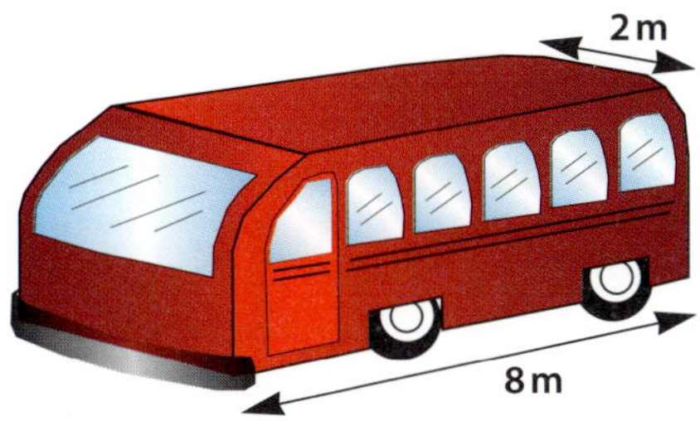

The ratio of its width to its length is 2 to 8.
2:8 is the same as 1:4.

: means 'to'
1 to 100
is written as 1:100

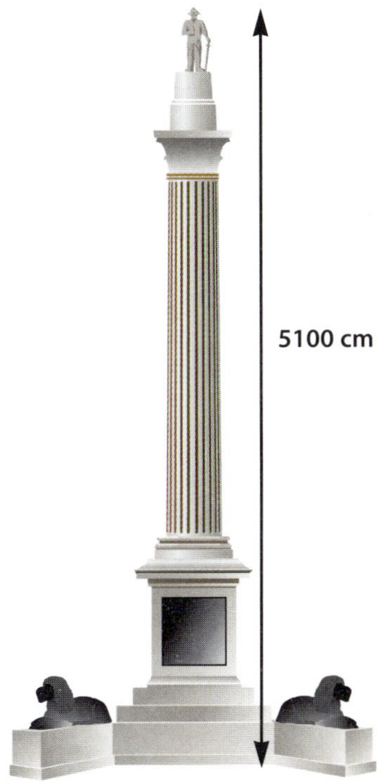

Nelson's column is about 5100 cm tall.

If a model is to be 100 times smaller, the scale of the model would be 1:100.

This means 100 cm on Nelson's column would be 1cm on the model.

The model would be 5100 ÷ 100 cm tall, which is 51 cm.

51:5100 is the same as 1:100.

The scale of the picture of the elephant is 1:40.

The length of the real elephant would be 6 cm × 40 = 240 cm.
6:240 is the same as 1:40.

Exercise 2

1 Write the relationship of these pairs of quantities as ratios.

(a) 2 kg, 5 kg (b) 1 tonne, 4 tonnes

(c) 3 shovels, 1 shovel (d) 7 buckets, 2 buckets

(e) 3 tons, 5 tons (f) 9 kg, 4 kg

Both parts of the ratio must be in the same units.

2 Convert these quantities to the same units and then write them as ratios.

(a) 1 cm, 50 cm (b) 2 m, 1 cm

(c) 1 m, 5 km (d) 1 g, 1 kg

(e) 1p, £3 (f) £7.50, 1p

3 Orange squash has to be mixed with water in the ratio 1:4. That is 1 part squash to 4 parts water.

fl oz means fluid ounces

How much water would you need to mix with these quantities of orange squash?

(a) 1 litre (b) 2 ml (c) 10 ml

(d) 3 pints (e) 4 litres (f) 6 fl oz

How much squash would you need to mix with these quantities of water?

(g) 4 pints (h) 20 ml (i) 28 fl oz

(j) 100 ml (k) 10 litres (l) 60 ml

4 Mortar can be made by mixing 1 bucket of cement with 5 buckets of sand.

The ratio of cement to sand is 1:5.

How much sand would you need to mix with the following quantities of cement to make mortar?

(a) 2 buckets (b) 5 shovels (c) 7 kg

(d) 10 tonnes (e) 15 tons (f) 23 kg

How much cement would you need to mix with these quantities of sand?

(g) 5 kg (h) 15 tonnes (i) 25 buckets

(j) 35 shovels (k) 235 kg (l) 12 buckets

Simplifying ratios

Here are 4 squares and 6 circles.

The ratio of squares to circles is 4:6.

These shapes can be rearranged into two groups of 2 squares and 3 circles.

So the ratio of each group is 2:3.

The ratio in each group is the same as the ratio in the whole pattern.

The ratio 4:6 is the same as the ratio 2:3.

The ratio of squares to circles is simplified from 4:6 to 2:3.

Notice that the ratio of circles to squares is 3:2.

**Ratios can be simplified like fractions.
2:4 and 3:6 are the same as 1:2**

Exercise 3

1 Write these as ratios, as simply as possible.

(a) **a**s to **z**s

aaaaaaaa **zzzz**

(b) **O**s to **X**s

OOOO **XXXXXXXXXXXX**

(c) s to  s

> Remember to make sure that the units are the same before writing a ratio.

(d) 24:36 (e) 28:42 (f) 54:18

(g) 36:90 (h) 25 mm to 2 m (i) 150 g to 3 kg

(j) £2 to 75p (k) 250 m to 0.5 km (l) 80p to £1.25

Cooking with ratios

COTTAGE CHEESE AND CHIVE FILLING

(Fills 4 sandwiches)

50 g butter, softened	2 oz butter, softened
125 g cottage cheese	4 oz cottage cheese
1 × 5 ml spoon chopped fresh chives	1 teaspoon chopped fresh chives

Cream the butter, cottage cheese and chives thoroughly together and chill before using.

Using this recipe you would have enough ingredients to make four sandwiches.

If you need to make more or fewer sandwiches you have to adjust the recipe.

Example

To make 2 sandwiches you would need to use half as much of each ingredient:

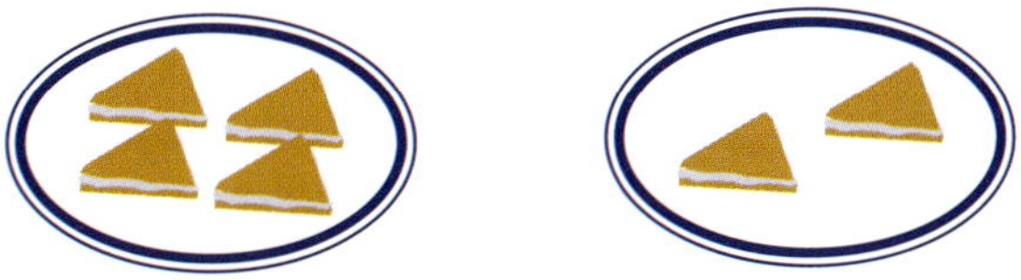

In Imperial measures this is:

1 oz butter
2 oz cottage cheese
$\frac{1}{2}$ teaspoon chopped fresh chives

To make 12 sandwiches you would need to use 3 times the quantity of ingredients.

To make enough filling for 15 sandwiches you could first work out how much filling makes 1 sandwich and then decide how much makes 15 sandwiches.

In metric measures:

Butter needed for 1 sandwich:	$50\text{ g} \div 4 = 12.5\text{ g}$
Butter needed for 15 sandwiches:	$12.5\text{ g} \times 15 = 625\text{ g}$

Assignment 1 Recipe cards

Write out the recipe card again in both metric and Imperial measures to give you enough filling for:

- 20 sandwiches
- 6 sandwiches.

Exercise 4

The questions in this exercise refer to this recipe.

18TH CENTURY LEMON CHEESE PIE

(Serves 6 people)

PASTRY	FILLING
100 g plain flour	4 eggs
50 g butter	100 g castor sugar
50 g castor sugar	10 g plain flour
1 egg yolk	juice of 2 lemons
1 × 15 ml spoon cold water	300 g cottage cheese

1 How much plain flour would you need to make enough pastry for 12 people?

2 How much butter would you need to make pastry for 15 people?

3 How many egg yolks would you need to make pastry for 20 people?
Explain your answer

4 How many 15-ml spoons of water would you need to make pastry for

(a) 12 people? (b) 15 people? (c) 21 people?

5 How much cottage cheese would you need for the filling for 9 people?

6 How many lemons would you need to make the pie for 21 people?

7 Castor sugar is used in both the pastry and the filling.

How much castor sugar would you need altogether to make the pie for 21 people?
(Assume you have more than enough of all the other ingredients.)

8 Flour is used in both the pastry and the filling.

How much plain flour would you need altogether to make the pie for 21 people?
(Assume you have more than enough of all the other ingredients.)

9 If you had 1 kg of cottage cheese, for how many people could you make the pie?

(Assume you have more than enough of all the other ingredients.)

10 Eggs are used in both the pastry andd the filling.

For how many people could you make the pie if you had 20 eggs and plenty of the other ingredients?
(Assume you have more than enough of all the other ingredients.)

11 Half a kilogram of castor sugar would be enough to make the pie for how many people?
(Assume you have more than enough of all the other ingredients.)

12

(a) Choose a recipe for biscuits or small cakes.

(b) Adjust your recipe so that you would have enough ingredients to give everybody in your class one cake or biscuit.

(c) Find out the cost of the ingredients.

(d) Calculate how much it would cost to make the recipe for the whole class.

(Do not forget a small charge for the cost of the gas or electricity to bake the cakes.)

(e) If you wanted to sell the cakes and make 10% profit, how much would you charge for each cake?

Maps and ratios

Numbers written in ratios must always be in the same units.

Always try to write the ratio as 1:? if possible.

Scales used on maps are often written as ratios.

If 1 cm on the map is used to represent 1 km on the ground then the ratio is written 1:100 000.

Real World

Map

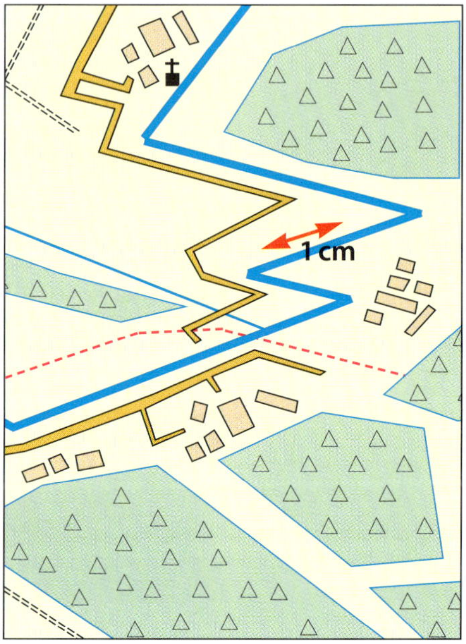

Exercise 5

Copy and complete this table.

Distance on the map (cm)	Distance on the ground (km)	Ratio
1	2	1:200 000
1	1.5	
1	2.5	
1	10	
2	1	
10	2	
1		1:350 000
1		1:75 000

Assignment 2 Using scales in York

The scale used on this map is 1:50 000.

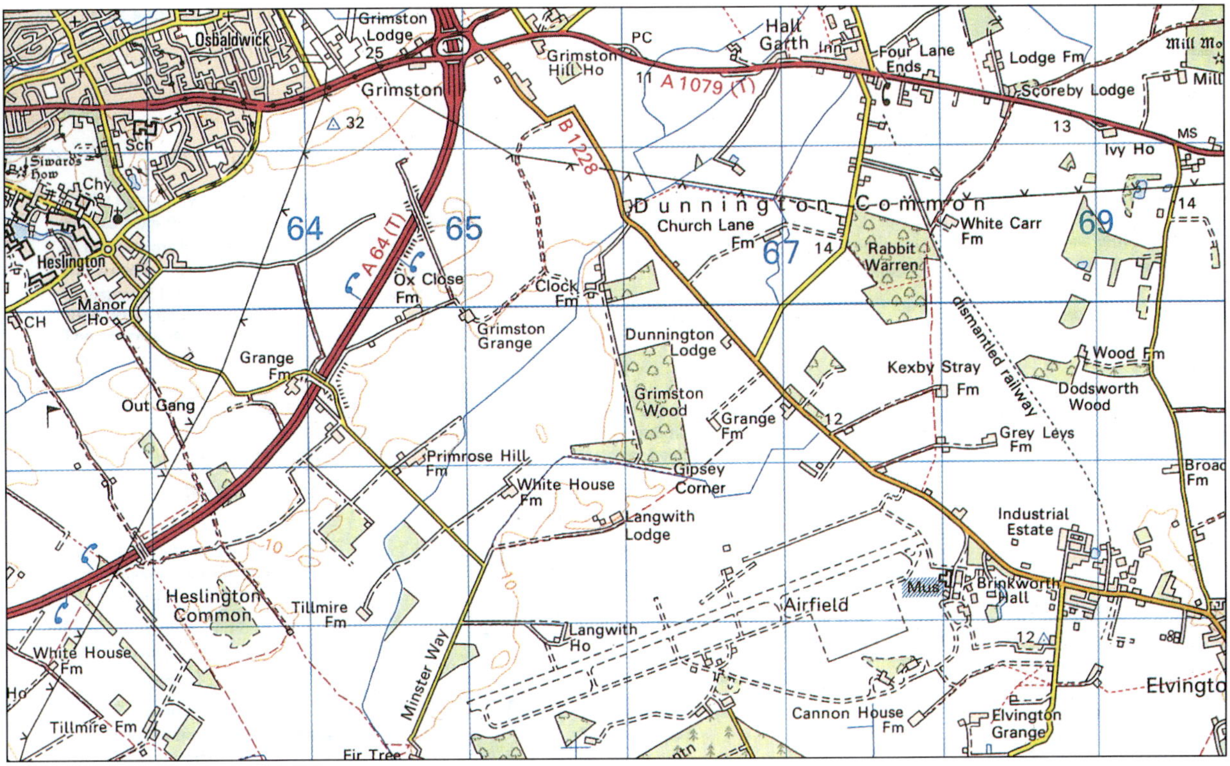

If the distance is not straight, use a piece of string to measure the route.

- How long is the airfield?
- How far is Cannon House Farm from the nearest road?
- What is the distance from the roundabout at Grimston to the bridge at Grange Farm?
- How long is the road B1228 from Grimston to the industrial estate?
- How far is it from Clock Farm to White Carr Farm as the crow flies?
- How much farther is it to travel between these two farms by road?
- What is the total area covered by this section of the map?
- Approximately what is the area of Grimston Wood?

Assignment 3 Using scales in Manchester

The scale used on this map is 1:25 000.

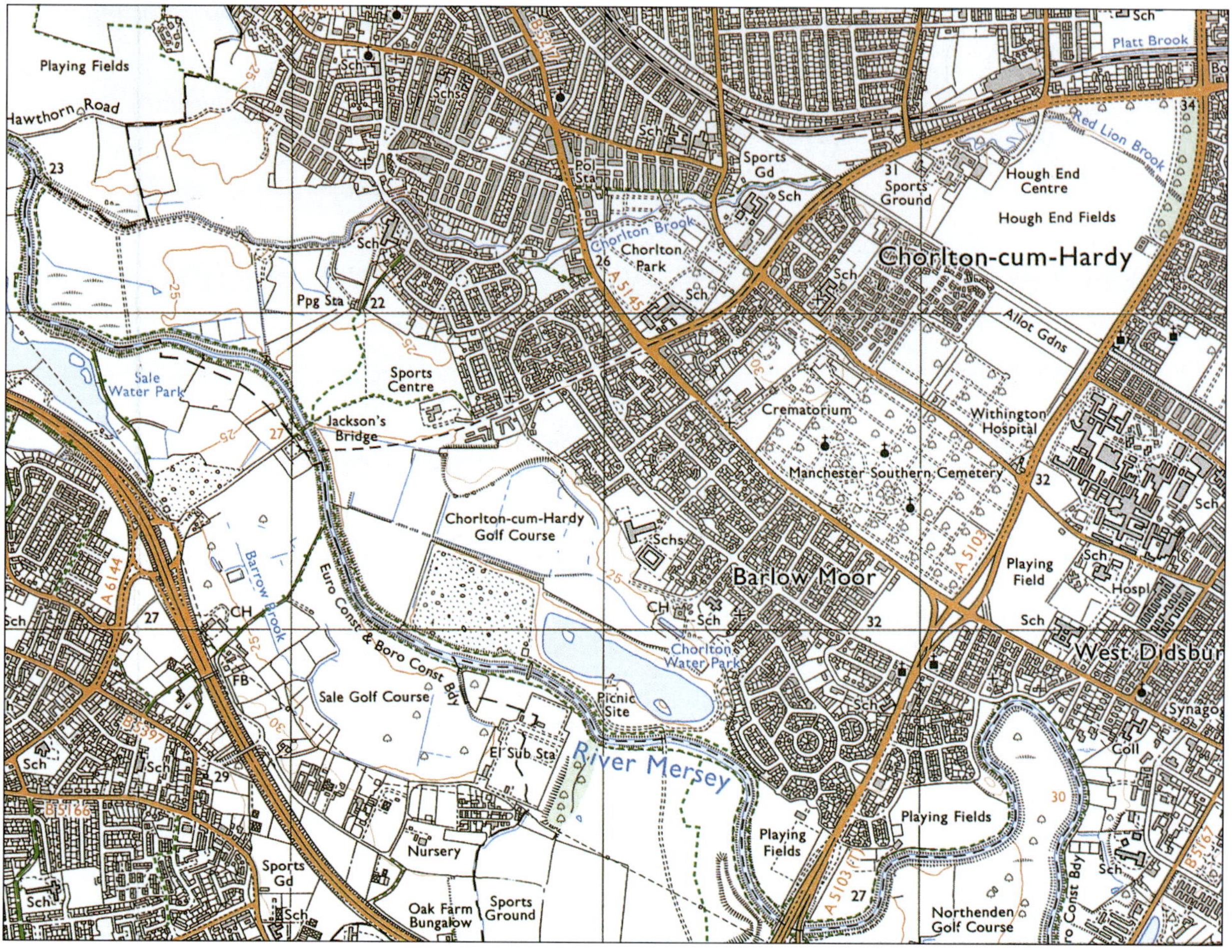

- How long is the section of the River Mersey seen on this map?
- How long is the Chorlton Water Park?
- You leave the college on the A5145 and take the shortest route to the sports centre.
  How long is the journey?
- What is the area of the Manchester Southern Cemetery?
- What is the total area covered by this section of the map?
- Find a map of your own district.
  Use it to work out four distances that you have to travel frequently.

Dividing a line in a given ratio

This green line is 3 cm long.

The arrow divides the line in the ratio 1:2.

There is 1 centimetre on the left and there are 2 centimetres on the right.

This purple line is 4 times as long as the green line. It is 12 cm long.

When a 12-cm line is divided in the ratio 1:2, it has 4 cm on the left of the arrow and 8 cm on the right.

Exercise 6

1 Draw these lines and then divide them in the ratio given.

Write the length of each part alongside the lines.

(a) A line 10 cm long, divided in the ratio 1:4.

(b) A line 9 cm long, divided in the ratio 1:2.

(c) A line 8 cm long, divided in the ratio 1:3.

(d) A line 10 cm long, divided in the ratio 2:3.

(e) A line 10 cm long, divided in the ratio 3:1:1.

(f) A line 7 cm long, divided in the ratio 2:5.

(g) A line 14 cm long, divided in the ratio 2:3:2.

(h) A line 10 cm long, divided in the ratio 3:1.

(i) A line 10 cm long, divided in the ratio 3:5.

(j) A line 12 cm long, divided in the ratio 4:1:3.

2 Without drawing the lines, write down the length of the parts when these are divided in the ratio given.

(a) A line 2 m long, divided in the ratio 3:2.

(b) A line 15 m long, divided in the ratio 5:3:2.

2 : 3

2 × 5 : 3 × 5
10 : 15

2 × 7 : 3 × 7
14 : 21

Calculating with ratios – 1

The ratio of boys to girls in a class was 2:3.

For every 2 boys in the class, there were 3 girls.

If there were 10 boys (5 × 2) in the class, there would be 15 girls (5 × 3).

If there were 14 boys (7 × 2) in the class, there would be 21 girls (7 × 3).

Exercise 7

1. The ratio of pupils present to pupils absent in a school is 28:1.
   There were 15 pupils absent.
   How many pupils were present?
2. A sum of money was shared out in the ratio of 5:7.
   The person receiving the larger amount was given £21.
   How much did the other person receive?
3. The ratio of the length of a room to its width is 5:4.
   The width of the room is 3.6 m.
   What is its length?
4. Flour and butter are used to make fruit cake in the ratio of 5:2.
   How much flour is needed for 35 g of butter?
5. At a football match, the ratio of police to spectators is 1:37.
   There were 78 852 tickets sold for the cup final.
   Approximately how many members of the police force would be there?
   Explain your answer.

6 Champagne can be bought in several different sized bottles.

The Jeroboam contains the same as 4 normal-sized bottles.

The Methuselah, the Salmanezah and the Nebuchadnezzar are even larger.

The ratio of the number of normal-sized bottles contained in the Jeroboam, the Methuselah, the Salmanezah and the Nebuchadnezzar is 1:2:3:5.

(a) How many normal-sized bottles are contained in:

(i) the Methuselah?

(ii) the Salmanezah?

(iii) the Nebuchadnezzar?

(b) The cost of a Jeroboam is about £100.
How much would you expect the other sizes of bottles to cost?
Explain your answer.

Calculating with ratios – 2

> For every 2 people watching BBC, there were 3 people watching ITV.

50 000 people were surveyed.

The ratio of the number people watching BBC to the number watching ITV at a particular time was 2:3.

To find out how many had watched BBC:

$\frac{2}{5}$ of 50 000 = 20 000

> 'of' is used instead of multiply

To find out how many had watched ITV:

$\frac{3}{5}$ of 50 000 = 30 000

Sometimes ratios involve more than two measures or quantities.

Example

> The ratio 2:3:5 means 10 parts are needed.

£10 is to be shared between three friends in the ratio of 2:3:5.

The first person gets $\frac{2}{10}$ of £10 = £2.

The second person gets $\frac{3}{10}$ of £10 = £3.

The third person gets $\frac{5}{10}$ of £10 = £5.

To check, add the three amounts: £2 + £3 + £5 = £10

Exercise 8

For Questions 1 to 10, divide the quantities in the ratios shown.

1	£100	3:7	**2**	£20	2:3
3	£35	5:2	**4**	£15	1:1
5	£12.80	5:3	**6**	£10.80	2:3:4
7	18 kg	1:3:5	**8**	54 m	2:3:1
9	144 kg	5:1:6	**10**	40.5 m	4:2:3

11 The pupils of a school are surveyed about travel to school.
The ratio of walkers to cyclists is 4:5.
If there are 1530 pupils in the school, how many walk and how many cycle?

12 An alloy is made from copper and tin in the ratio of 4:3.
How much of each metal is there in 17.5 kg of alloy?

13 A particular shade of pink paint can be made by mixing red paint and white paint in the ratio of 5:3.
If you needed 28 litres of pink paint, how many litres of red paint and white paint would you need?

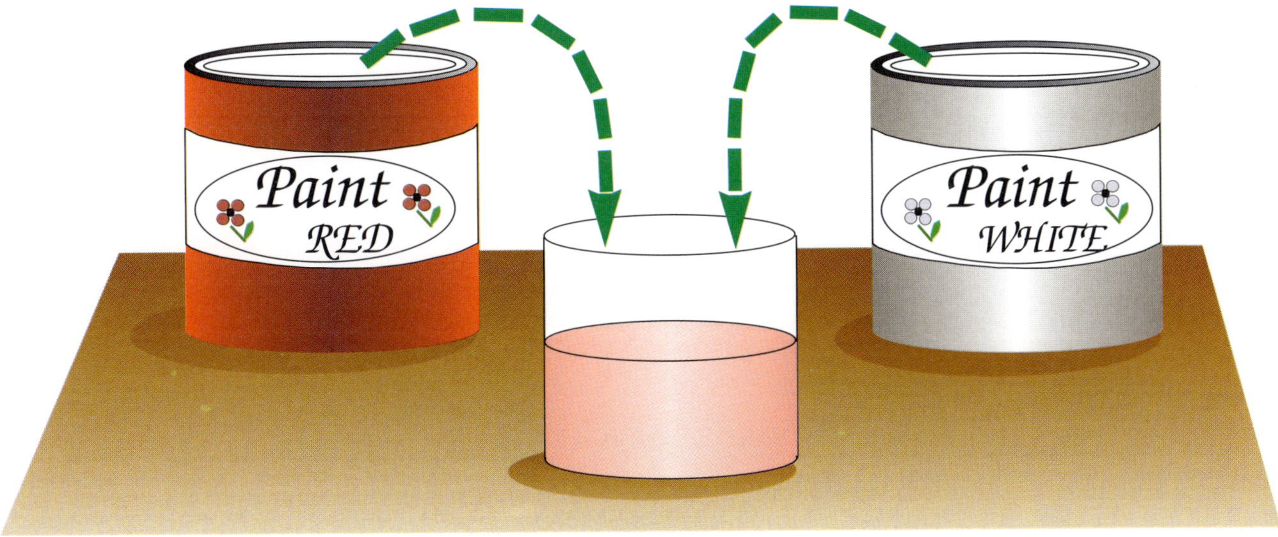

14 A machine produces plastic toys.
The ratio of faulty toys to good ones is 1:32.
If the machine produces 48 000 toys in a week, how many faulty toys would it be expected to produce?

15 Three people buy a lottery ticket between them.
One pays 40p, the second pays 35p and the third pays 25p.
They decide to share the winnings in the same ratio.
How much would they each get if they won in total:

(a) £10? (b) £75? (c) £32 500?

(d) £254 635.65? (e) £8642 483.24? (f) £18 887 123.90?

Key fact

Shapes which are similar have corresponding sides in the same ratio.
The shapes are enlargements of each other.

Similar shapes

Here are two similar triangles.

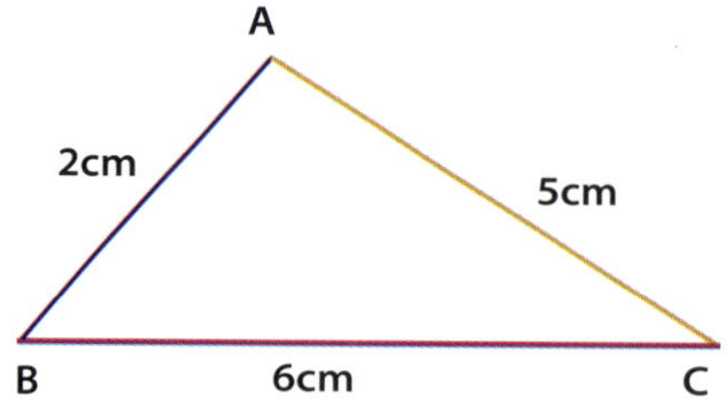

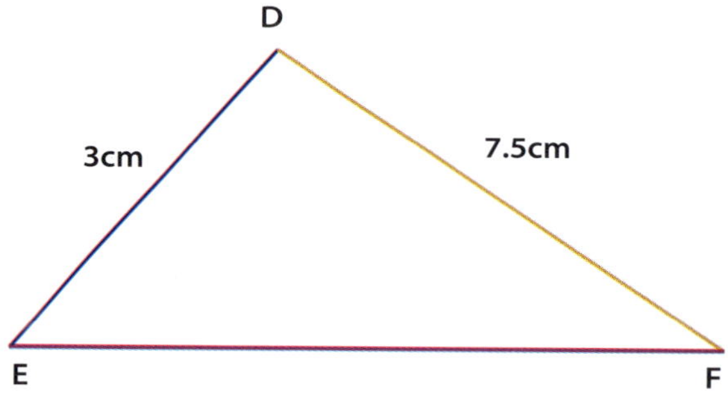

The side joining vertex A to vertex B is called AB.

The ratio of sides DE:AB is 3:2.

The ratio of sides DF:AC is 7.5:5.
This ratio will simplify to 3:2.

So the ratio of EF:BC is also 3:2.

Example

To calculate the length of side EF, use the length of side BC and the ratio of the sides.

$$\frac{\text{Length of EF}}{\text{Length of BC}} = \frac{3}{2}$$

$$\begin{aligned}\text{Length of EF} &= \text{length of BC} \times \tfrac{3}{2} \\ &= 6\,\text{cm} \times \tfrac{3}{2} \\ &= 9\,\text{cm}\end{aligned}$$

If BC is 6 cm long then EF must be 9 cm long.

Assignment 4 Similar shapes

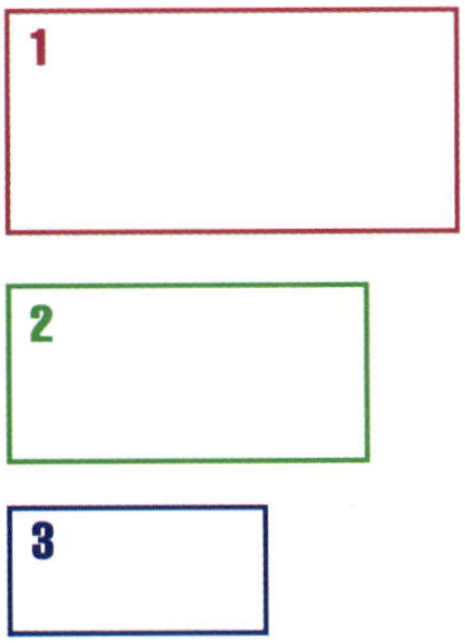

- Draw three different sized rectangles where the ratio of the length to the width of each is 2:1. Label these rectangles 1, 2 and 3.
- Mark on each diagram the length and the width you have used.
- Write down the ratio of the width of rectangle 1 to the width of rectangle 2.

  Write down the ratio of the widths for rectangle 1 and rectangle 3.
- Write down the ratio of the length of rectangle 1 to the length of rectangle 2.

  Write down the ratio of the lengths for rectangle 1 and rectangle 3.
- Work out the perimeters of each of the rectangles.

  Write down the ratio of the perimeter of rectangle 1 to the perimeter of rectangle 2.

  Again write down the same ratio for rectangle 1 and rectangle 3.
- What do you notice about the ratios?
- Compare the areas of the rectangles by considering the ratios and write down what you notice.

Exercise 9

1 These two shapes are similar.

What is the length of the side labelled *a*?

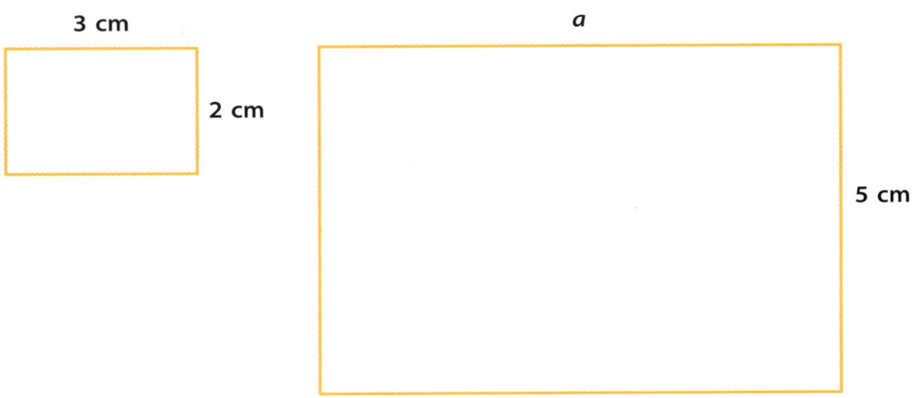

2 These two shapes are similar.

What are the values of *b* and *c*?

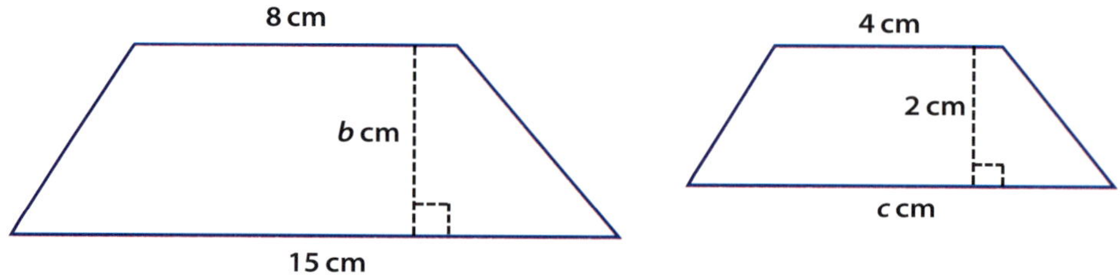

3 These three shapes are similar.

Calculate the values of *d*, *e*, *f* and *g*.

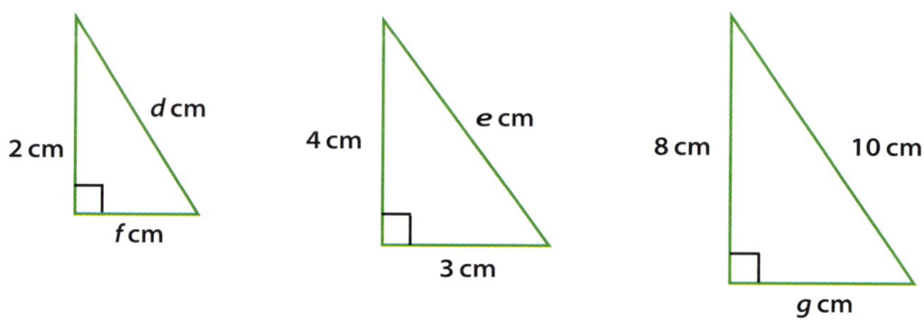

4 Calculate the area of each of the triangles in Question 3.
Write down the ratio of the three areas.
Make sure all the numbers in your ratio are whole numbers.

Assignment 5 Rectangles

- Look around the classroom and at home for rectangles.
- Measure the length and width of at least ten rectangles.
- Work out the ratio of the width to the length of each one.
  Write the ratio as 1:? in each case.

Metric paper

The ratio of the sides which makes this possible is approximately 1:1.4 – known as the golden ratio

The most common size of paper used around the world is known as A4.

Two sheets of A4, combined together, produce a similar rectangle which is known as A3.

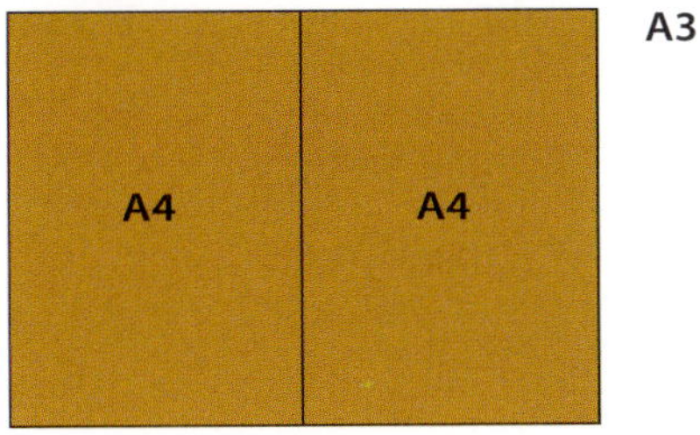

If this process is continued a sheet with an area of 1 square metre is produced known as A0.

This diagram shows a piece of A0 paper divided into the other sizes.

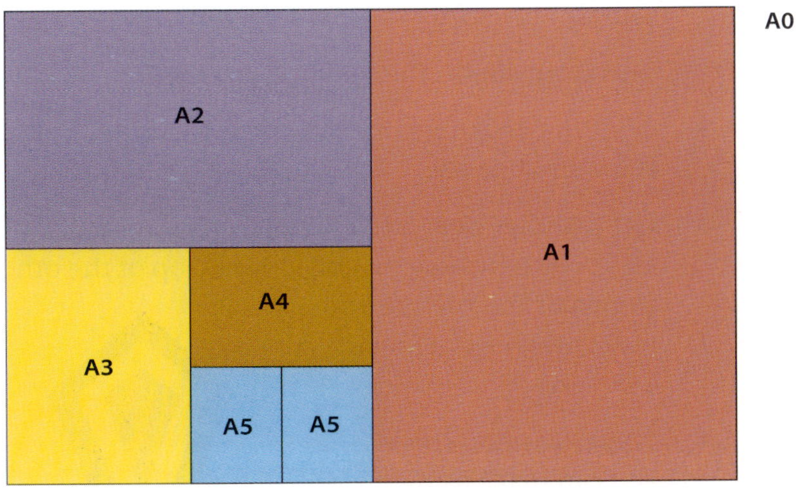

A piece of A4 paper can be folded in two to produce a similar rectangle, A5 and so on.

Assignment 6 Having fun with metric paper!

- Start with an A4 piece of coloured paper.

  Cut it in half, to produce two A5 pieces.

- Take one A5 piece and fold it to make a kite using the diagrams below.

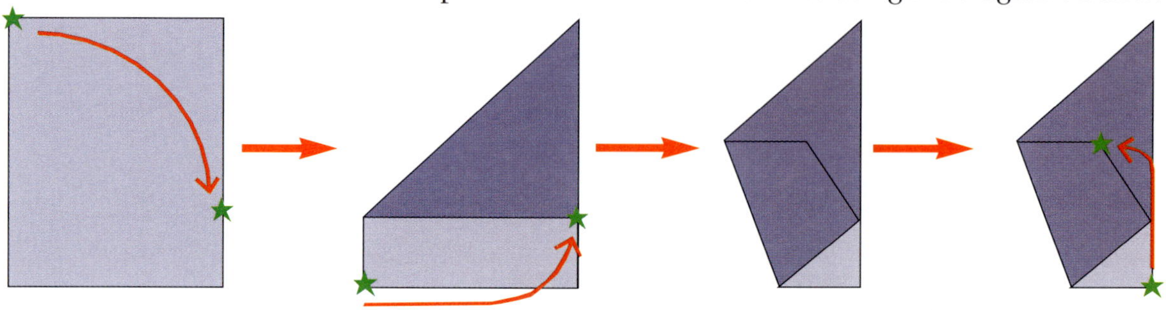

Fold the paper to join the stars.

Turn the kite over before using it.

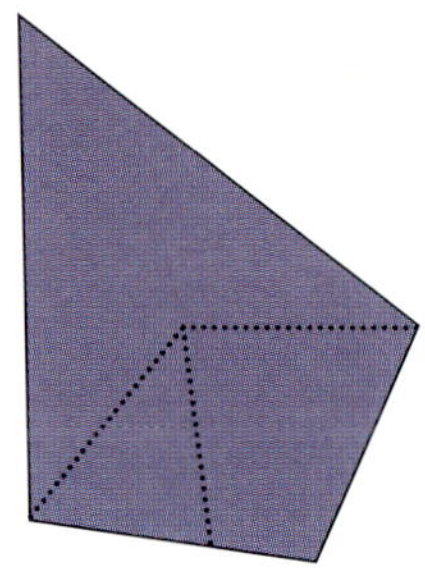

- Take the other piece of A5 and cut it into two pieces of A6.

  Use one piece of A6 to produce another kite in the same way as before.

  This is **similar** to the first one you made.

- Continue making kites and cutting the other piece until the paper is too small to use.
- Get together with other people who have made different coloured kites. Nest them by placing one on top of the other centrally as shown in this picture and tessellate them to make a pattern.

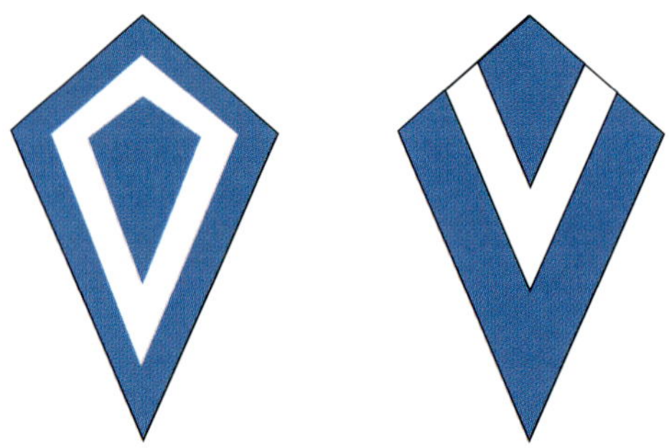

- There are other shapes that you can make using metric paper in this way, which will produce very attractive patterns.

Review Exercise

1 Write these ratios in their simplest form.

(a) 1 cm, 30 cm (b) 5 cm, 25 cm

(c) 15 tonnes, 6 tonnes (d) 20p, £5

2 (a) These shapes are similar.

What is the length of the side marked *a*?

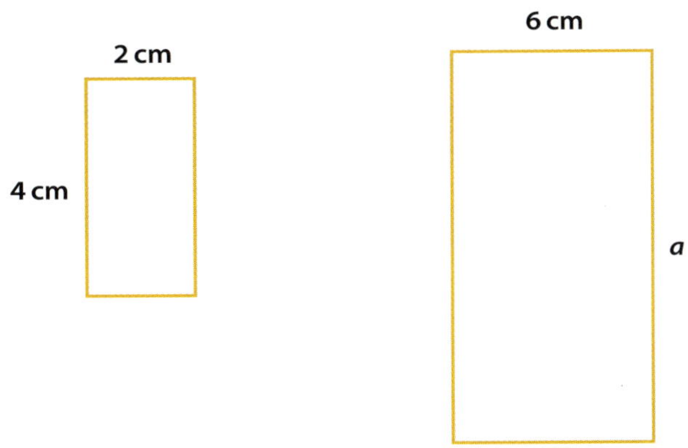

(b) These shapes are similar.

What are the lengths of the sides marked *b* and *c*?

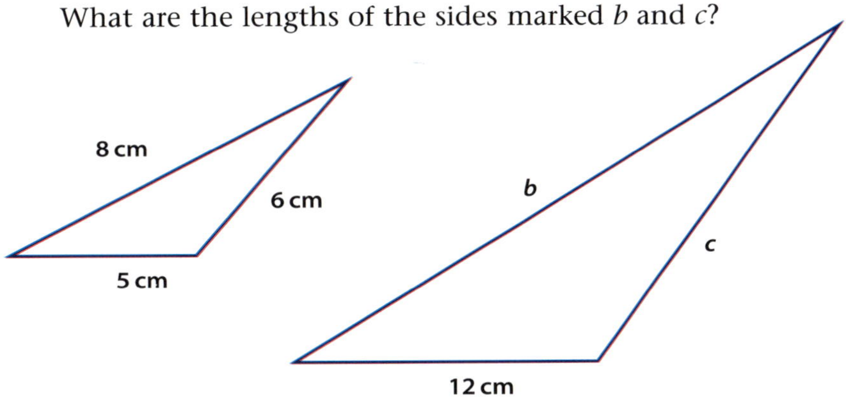

3 A sum of money was shared out in the ratio of 4:5.
The person receiving the smaller amount was given £26.
How much did the other person receive?

4 A recipe uses 100 g of butter and 150 g of rolled oats to make 16 flapjacks.
How much of each ingredient would be needed for 40 flapjacks?

5 The scale on an Ordnance survey map is 1:500 000.

(a) What are the distances on the ground in kilometres for these distances measured on the map?

(i) 1 cm (ii) 5 cm (iii) 10 cm

(iv) 12.5 cm (v) 13.8 cm (vi) 9.7 cm

(b) On the same map, a rectangular park measures 1.6 cm by 2.3 cm. What is the actual area of the park in square kilometres?

6 A survey of a town showed that the ratio of the number of homes without television to the number with television was 1:46.
There were five homes on an estate without television.
How many homes would you expect to have television?

7 Draw the following lines and divide them in the ratio indicated.

(a) 12 cm 1:2 (b) 15 cm 5:1

8 A tropical fish keeper wants to have angel fish, loaches and neon tetras in the ratio of 5:1:10.
The keeper wants to have 96 fish in total in the tank.
How many of each variety of fish should there be?

9 There are many ratios related to the human body.

(a) Collect these measurements from the pupils in your class.
- (i) height
- (ii) fathom (fingertip to fingertip when the arms are extended)
- (iii) distance around the head
- (iv) waist
- (v) distance around the neck
- (vi) distance from elbow to finger tips
- (vii) handspan
- (viii) foot length
- (ix) distance around the wrist

(b) Investigate the ratio of
- (i) the distance around the head to height
- (ii) the waist measurement to the distance round the neck
- (iii) the foot length and the height
- (iv) the fathom and the height.

(c) Can you find other relationships in body measurements?

Trial and improvement

In this chapter you will learn:

- ➜ **more about approximations and decimal places**
- ➜ **about significant figures**
- ➜ **about using sensible guesses to solve problems**
- ➜ **how to improve the accuracy of an answer**

Starting points

Before starting this chapter you will need to know:

- the meaning of the position of a digit in a number
- how to add, subtract, multiply and divide with decimal numbers.

Exercise 1

1 Which number is half way between:

(a) 10 and 20? (b) 12 and 16?
(c) 100 and 200? (d) 22 and 24?
(e) 18 and 19? (f) 70 and 75?
(g) 8.2 and 8.3? (h) 2.4 and 2.5?
(i) 4.32 and 4.33?

2 What is the value of the digit 2 in these numbers?

(a) 24.6 (b) 428 (c) 48.2
(d) 12.4 (e) 9.24 (f) 1.02

3 Calculate:

(a) $4.2 + 8$ (b) $3.5 + 4.8$ (c) $12.8 + 5.2$
(d) $9.8 - 4$ (e) $3.7 - 2.4$ (f) $12.2 - 9.8$
(g) $28.3 + 4.02 + 11$ (h) $112.4 - 73.6$

4 Work out these without using a calculator.

(a) 3.6×100 (b) 7.2×10

(c) 13.4×100 (d) $45.2 \div 10$

(e) $12.8 \div 100$ (f) $0.67 \div 10$

(g) $28 \div 100$ (h) 0.03×1000

Sensible answers

Calculators will give accurate answers to many problems, but the most accurate answer is not *always* a helpful or sensible answer.

Consider sharing £120 among seven people.

Using a calculator, gives an answer with many decimal places.

$120 \div 7 = 17.142\ 857\ 14 \ldots$

The calculator answer is *not* the most sensible one for this problem.

Each of the seven people would probably agree to receive £17.14.

Use your calculator to work out the answer to each of these questions in the next exercise.

Consider what is likely to be a sensible answer, and record your decision.

Exercise 2

1 Divide £100 000 fairly among nine people.

2 Pencils are boxed so that each box holds a dozen pencils. How many boxes can be filled with 230 pencils?

3 Share £250 among three people.

4 A sale advertises EVERYTHING HALF PRICE.

What are you likely to pay for an item originally priced at £11.95?

5 50 satsumas are shared among six children.
How many will each receive?

6 Ribbon is cut into 50-cm lengths.
How many lengths can be cut from 3.2 metres of ribbon?

7 (a) Find the price of an article, labelled £21.99 if 10% discount is allowed.

(b) If the label price of the article, is increased by 10%, what will the new price be?

Working to approximate values

In some situations, an answer rounded to the nearest unit, or to the nearest ten, is good enough.

Example

$12.3 \times 1.4 = 17.22$

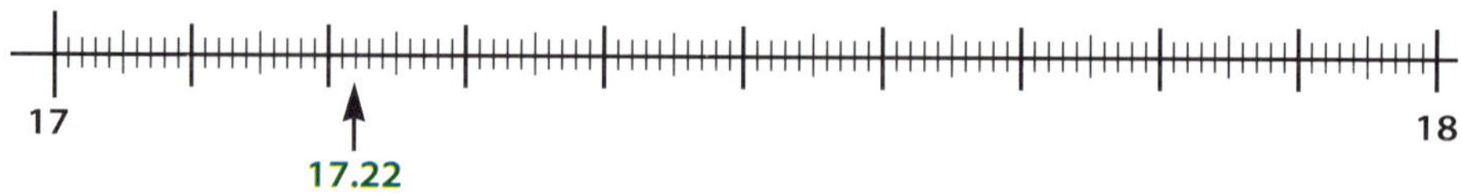

17.22 is closer to 17 than 18.

The answer **to the nearest whole number** is 17.

Example

$36.4 \times 9.5 = 345.8$

345.8 is closer to 350 than 340.

The answer **to the nearest ten** is 360.

Example

$248 \times 1.6 = 396.8$

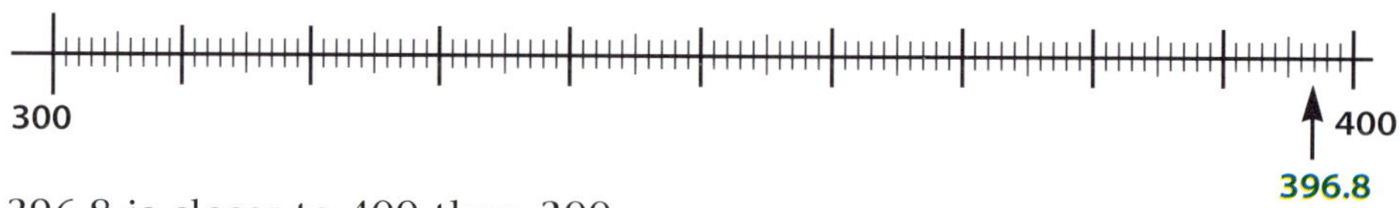

396.8 is closer to 400 than 300.

The answer **to the nearest hundred** is 400.

Example

$47 \times 5 = 235$

The answer is exactly half way between 230 and 240.

When a value is **exactly half way**,you take the higher value.

The answer given to the nearest ten is 240.

Key fact

For values exactly halfway, take the higher value, e.g. 235 is written as 240 (to the nearest 10).

Exercise 3

1 Use a calculator to work out these.
Give your answers to the nearest whole number.

(a) 3.4×4.8 (b) $270 \div 17$

(c) $13.6 + 29.3 - 2.8$ (d) $3.4 \times 5.9 \times 1.2$

(e) $12.8 \times 4.5 \div 0.8$

2 Use a calculator to work out these.
Give your answers to the nearest ten.

(a) 32.6×4.8 (b) 45.8×23.9

(c) $2748 \div 12.5$ (d) $12.7 \times 45.8 \times 3.9$

(e) $114 \times 92.5 \div 15.2$

3 Use a calculator to work out these.
Give your answers to the nearest hundred.

(a) 48.2×36.2 (b) 145.6×35.7

(c) $395.5 \div 9.2$ (d) $58.9 \times 3.9 \times 62.4$

(e) $115 + 1385 + 4047$

Assignment 1 The answer is …

Make up five questions which give these answers when approximated:

- 452 to the nearest unit
- 140 to the nearest ten
- 3200 to the nearest hundred
- 13 to the nearest unit
- 400 to the nearest hundred
- 400 to the nearest ten

> **2 d.p. means the number is given correct to 2 decimal places.**

Decimal places

Another way of approximating is to give an answer correct to a certain number of decimal places.

To write a number correct to one decimal place means that all digits after the decimal point should be replaced by only one digit.

Look carefully at the second digit after the decimal point to help you to decide whether to round the first digit after the decimal point up or down.

Example

Look at the 6 in 13.468 to see if 13.468 is closer to 13.4 or 13.5.

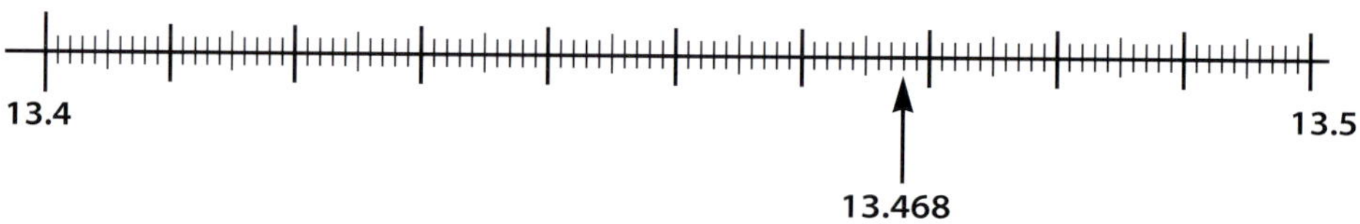

13.468 is written as 13.5 (correct to 1 decimal place) because 13.468 is closer to 13.5 than to 13.4.

Similarly,	13.468
can be written as	13.47 (correct to 2 decimal places)
or as	13 (to the nearest whole number).

Example

146.529 becomes 146.53 (correct to 2 d.p.)

146.529 becomes 146.5 (correct to 1 d.p.)

146.529 becomes 147 (to the nearest unit)

> **Remember – when exactly half way, round to the higher value.**

Exercise 4

Copy and complete this table.

	To 1 decimal place	To 2 decimal places
256.27		
24.846		
152.964		
342.05		
4471.522		
2.5066		
0.3456		
3059.555		
34.0363		
3.3690		
62.008		
40.999		

Assignment 2 — Match the numbers

Look at these questions and answers.

Each answer matches one of the questions, though not always exactly.

Questions	Answers
15.7×4.55	$= 82.717$
$164 \div 12.8$	$= 11500$
$98 \times 3.4 \times 0.6$	$= 39300$
5.05×0.79	$= 81.8$
$6.7 \times 259 \div 11$	$= 71$
$999 \div 23$	$= 12.813$
$98.2 \times 0.68 + 15$	$= 4.0$
$45 \times (217 + 38)$	$= 157.8$
$34 \times 34 \times 34$	$= 200$
$49.465 \div 0.598$	$= 43.43$

(An arrow joins 15.7×4.55 to $= 71$.)

- Find all the matches. (The first one is done for you)
- Write down how accurate you think each answer is.

Estimating and accuracy

When estimating values, it is important to consider sensible accuracy levels.

Consider estimating the answer to this calculation.

24×48

1000	is a sensible estimate because $20 \times 50 = 1000$.
1200	is a better estimate because $24 \times 50 = 1200$, but is harder to work out without using a calculator.
1152	is the accurate answer to the question, but is unlikely to be an estimate.

Consider estimating other values, such as distance.

The distance between two towns might be estimated to the nearest kilometre if they are quite close to each other.

However, if they are a long way apart, it might be more sensible to give an estimate to the nearest 100km.

Exercise 5

1 In each of these problems, decide which of the answers offered give a sensible estimate. Explain your answers.

(a) 216×52 is about:

(i) 1100 (ii) 110 (iii) 11000

(b) 73×73 is about:

(i) 5000 (ii) 4900 (iii) 6000

(c) $\sqrt{1000}$ is about:

(i) 15 (ii) 30 (iii) 40

(d) $27560 \div 310$ is about:

(i) 900 (ii) 9 (iii) 90

(e) 0.456×24.8 is about:

(i) 12 (ii) 11.3 (iii) 0.8

(f) $1710 \div 93$ is about:

(i) 200 (ii) 20 (iii) 2

2 Which of these estimates would you consider to be most reasonable? Explain your answers.

(a) The length of the M1 motorway is:

(i) 190 miles

(ii) 200 miles

(iii) 188.78 miles

(b) The distance to the Moon is:

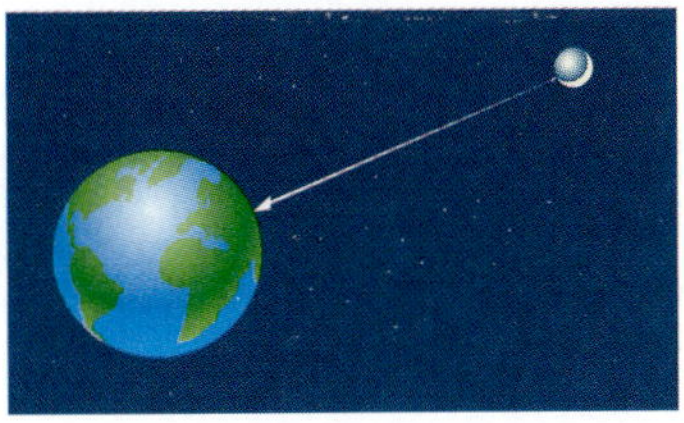

(i) 400 000 km

(ii) 356 000 km

(iii) 356 413.8 km

(c) The price of a loaf of bread is:

(i) 45p

(ii) 11.82p

(iii) £0.425

(d) The distance around the Earth is:

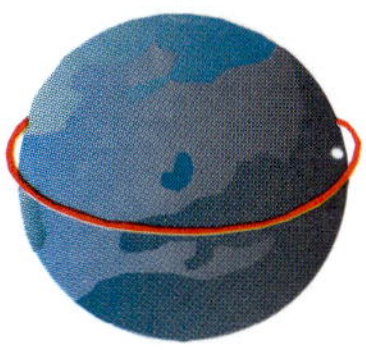

(i) 400 km

(ii) 40 000 km

(iii) 40 152 km

(e) The population of the UK is:

(i) 60 million

(ii) 30 million

(iii) 57 478 331

Assignment 3 Agreeing estimates

- Share your results from Question 2 in Exercise 5 with two or three others.
- Discuss your decisions, and amend any if necessary.

Significant figures

The cards in this diagram are face down.

Face up they will provide a good estimate of the size.
If you could choose just one digit to give you the best idea of the size of the Moon's diameter, which would it be?

The digit with the highest place value is the most significant in telling you a value.

The value of the card in the thousands column for the diameter of the moon is 3.

So, you might estimate that the Moon's diameter is about 3000 km.

Turning over all the cards gives:

3 4 7 3

The diameter of the moon:

- to one significant figure is 3000 km
- to two significant figures is 3500 km
- to three significant figures is 3470 km
- to four significant figures is 3473 km.

Notice that the result to two significant figures is recorded as 3500 km.
This is because 3473 is closer to 3500 than to 3400.

Exercise 6

1 (a) Which of the cards is the most important in giving the height of Everest?

THE HEIGHT OF EVEREST IS:

A B C D metres

The cards are turned over to reveal:

8 8 4 8

(b) What is the height to one significant figure?

(c) What is the height to two significant figures?

(d) What is the height to three significant figures?

2

The number regarded as attending a concert was: 1 0 5 9 2

How many attended:

(a) to one significant figure?

(b) to two significant figures?

(c) to three significant figures?

3 Write each of these numbers to one significant figure.

(a) 34800 (b) 4332 (c) 76409 (d) 894

4 Write each of these numbers to two significant figures.

(a) 14920 (b) 334 (c) 509842 (d) 2745

sig.fig. is short for significant figures

More significant figures

Consider the number 1375.2.

To write this number correct to 3 sig.fig., look carefully at the fourth digit in 1375.2.

1375.2 ≃ 1380 (3 sig.fig.)

To write 1375.2 correct to 2 sig.fig., look carefully at the third digit: 1375.2.

So 1375.2 ≃ 1400 (2 sig.fig.)

Exercise 7

1 Copy and complete this table.

		3 sig. fig.	2 sig. fig.	1 sig. fig.
a	128.5			100
b	28.464	28.5		
c	1079.0		1100	
d	2.959			
e	120689			100000
f	36.889			
g	10.005			
h	7.0404	7.04		
i	290.8			
j	2591			

4^2 is read as 4 squared

$\sqrt{16}$ is read as square root of 16

2 Copy and complete this table.
Use your calculator to find these values, but record them to the given approximations.

		To nearest unit	To 1 d.p.	To 2 sig. fig.
a	23^2			
b	7.8^2			
c	52^2			
d	1.4^2			
e	12.5^2			
f	$\sqrt{450}$			
g	$\sqrt{59}$			
h	$\sqrt{200}$			
i	$\sqrt{789}$			
j	$\sqrt{34}$			

Assignment 4 Maximum and minimum

These three measurements are given together with the level of accuracy used.

A length of wood is 34 cm (to the nearest centimetre).

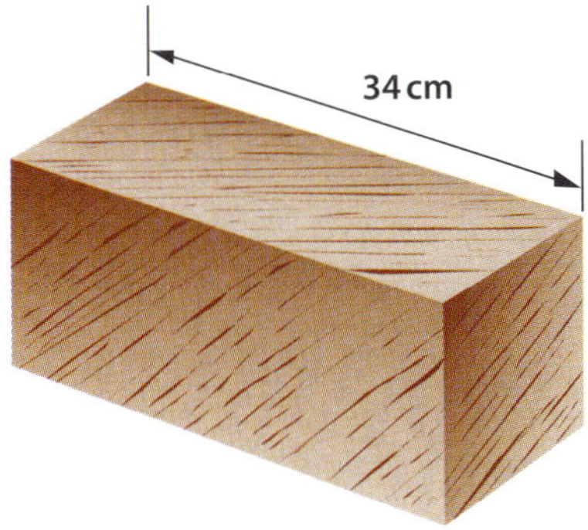

The weight of a cat is 5.4 kg (to the nearest 100 grams).

An estimation of the population of Europe in 2000AD is 861 000 000 (to 3 sig.fig.).

- For each case, give three measurements which would still fit the description.
  For example, you could write the length of wood is 34.2 cm which is 34 cm to the nearest centimetre.
- In each case, what would the smallest possible measurement be?
- In each case, what would the largest possible measurement be?

Good guessing

A good guess can be a quick and sensible way to solve some problems. With further information about how close the guess is, it may be improved.

Assignment 5 Guess my number

You need a partner for this guessing game.

- Think of a number between 1 and 100, and record it so that your partner will not see it. Your partner has to try to guess this number.
- Copy this table. Your partner records a guess and you note if it is too big, or too small.

Guess number	Guess	Too big or too small
1st		
2nd		
3rd		
4th		

- When your partner has guessed your number, change around.
- Repeat this activity, guessing five numbers each.
- Count the number of guesses needed in all to find the numbers. The person who has the fewer guesses wins.

Assignment 6 Find me

Record your guesses on a table like this.

Guess number	Guess	Result	Too big/too small
1st			
2nd			
3rd			

See how many guesses it takes you to find these numbers:

- A palindromic number whose square is between 100 and 200
- A prime number whose square is between 300 and 400
- An even number whose square is between 1000 and 1100
- A whole number whose square is between 5400 and 5500
- A number whose square is between 530 and 540
- A number whose square is between 2050 and 2100

Trial and improvement

The process of guessing and improving your guess used in Assignments 5 and 6 is called trial and improvement.

Here is a model or flow chart of the method:

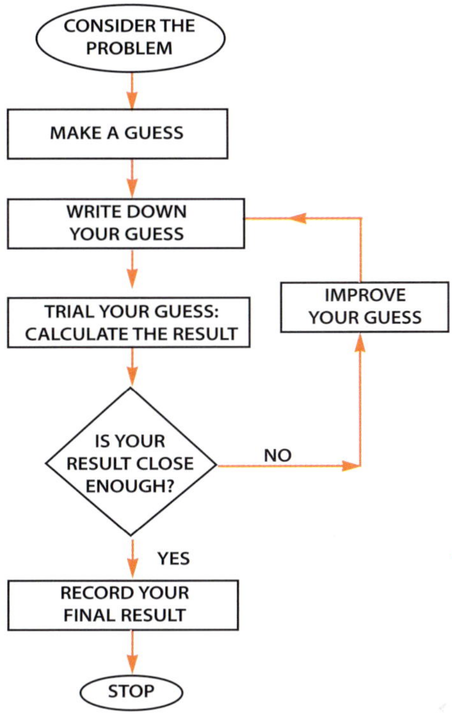

Here is another example of using trial and improvement:

Example

A book is lying open, showing two pages. Each page number is squared, then the two answers are added together and give 545. What are the page numbers?

The page numbers must follow each other, so the first guess must be two consecutive numbers.

The pages are 16 and 17.

Guess	Trial	Comment
11 and 12	$11^2 + 12^2 = 265$	Too small
14 and 15	$14^2 + 15^2 = 421$	Too small
17 and 18	$17^2 + 18^2 = 613$	Too big
16 and 17	$16^2 + 17^2 = 545$	Correct

Use the trial-and-improvement method to help you to solve the problems in the next exercise.

Exercise 8

1 Two whole numbers are added together to give 118.
The difference between them is 36.
What are the two numbers?

2 Look at this diagram.

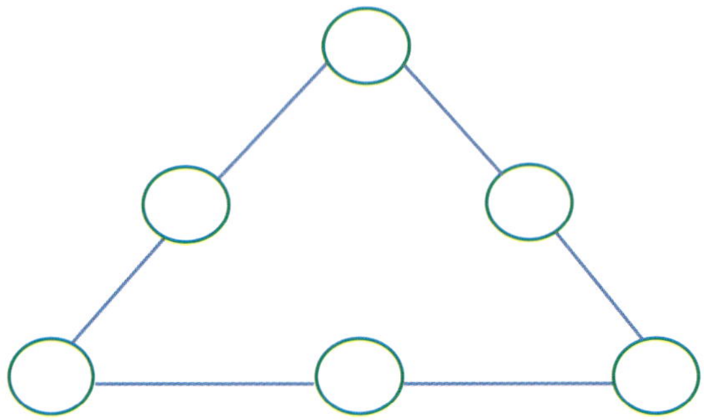

(a) Place the numbers 1 to 6 into a copy of this diagram so that each side of the triangle adds to 10.

(b) Place the numbers 1 to 6 into another copy of the diagram so that each side of the triangle adds to 11.

(c) Place the numbers 1 to 6 into another copy of the diagram so that each side of the triangle adds to 12.

3 Two numbers add together to give 45, and multiply together to give 486.
What are the two numbers?

4 Two numbers add together to give 215.
They have a difference of 37.
Find the two numbers.

5 The sum of £1.85 is made up of 13 coins.
Some are 20p pieces, and the rest are all 5p pieces.
How many of each coin is there?

6 The difference between two whole numbers is 75.
When one is divided by the other the result is 3.7 (correct to 1 d.p.).
What are the two numbers?

7 Which year was the last year which was an exact square number?

Using the trial-and-improvement method to find square roots

Example

Find the square root of 112.

$10 \times 10 = 100$ and $11 \times 11 = 121$.
112 is between 100 and 121 so the first guess for the square root of 112 must be between 10 and 11.

Guess	Result	Too big/too small
10.5	$10.5^2 = 110.25$	too small
10.7	$10.7^2 = 114.49$	too big
10.6	$10.6^2 = 112.36$	too big
10.55	$10.55^2 = 111.3025$	too small

From the results so far, the answer must be between 10.55 and 10.6.
Writing either of these, correct to one decimal place, gives 10.6. So,
$\sqrt{112} = 10.6$ (correct to one decimal place)
With more trials, a more accurate answer could be found.

Exercise 9

1 On a copy of this table, use the trial and improvement method for finding the square root of each number without using the $\sqrt{\ }$ button on your calculator.

Give your answers correct to one decimal place.

Guess	Result	Too big/too small

(a) $\sqrt{10}$ (b) $\sqrt{35}$ (c) $\sqrt{42}$ (d) $\sqrt{120}$ (e) $\sqrt{70}$ (f) $\sqrt{2}$

2 For a greater challenge, find answers to Question 1, correct to two decimal places.

Assignment 7 Chain

- Choose a start number.
  Divide it by 5 and then add 2.
  The result is your new start number.

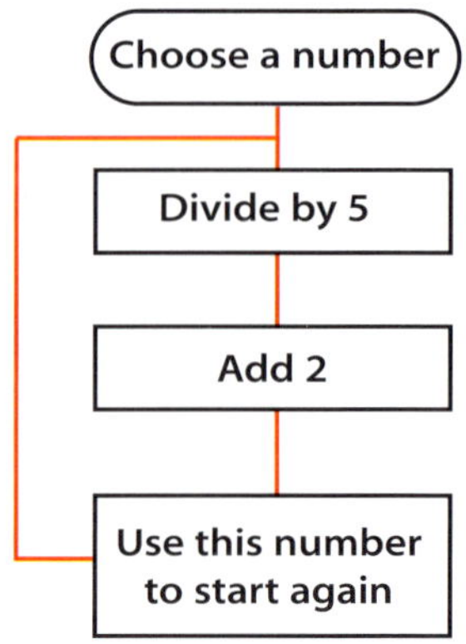

- Repeat the instructions and keep going!
- Record your results carefully each time.
- What do you notice?
- What happens if you change the start number?
- What happens if you swap the instructions around?
  For example, add 2 and *then* divide by 5.
- Try different numbers in the instructions.

Exercise 10

Use the trial-and-improvement method to help you to solve these problems.

1 A square has an area of $20\,cm^2$.
Find the length of its side correct to 1 decimal place.

2 A cube has a volume of $150\,cm^3$.
Find the length of its side correct to 1 decimal place.

3 Find the square root of 24, correct to 2 decimal places.

4 Find the cube root of 100, correct to 2 decimal places.

5 A square has an area of $30\,cm^2$.
Find its perimeter, correct to 2 decimal places.

Ending with the starting number

Sometimes the end number is the same as the start number.

For example:

START NUMBER → SQUARE → TAKE AWAY 20 → END NUMBER

One number which works here is 5 because $5 \times 5 - 20 = 5$. You start with 5 and end with 5.

Exercise 11

1 Find starting numbers which have the same end numbers for these:

(a) START NUMBER → SQUARE → TAKE AWAY 30 → END NUMBER

(b) START NUMBER → SQUARE → TAKE AWAY 6 → END NUMBER

(c) START NUMBER → SQUARE → TAKE AWAY 56 → END NUMBER

(d) START NUMBER → SQUARE → TAKE AWAY 12 → END NUMBER

(e) START NUMBER → SQUARE → TAKE AWAY 90 → END NUMBER

(f) START NUMBER → SQUARE → TAKE AWAY 72 → END NUMBER

(g) START NUMBER → SQUARE → TAKE AWAY 2 → END NUMBER

2 In each of the above, there are two starting numbers which will work.
Find both of them.

3 What do you notice about your answers to Questions 1 and 2?

Assignment 8 Keep going!

Follow this chart.

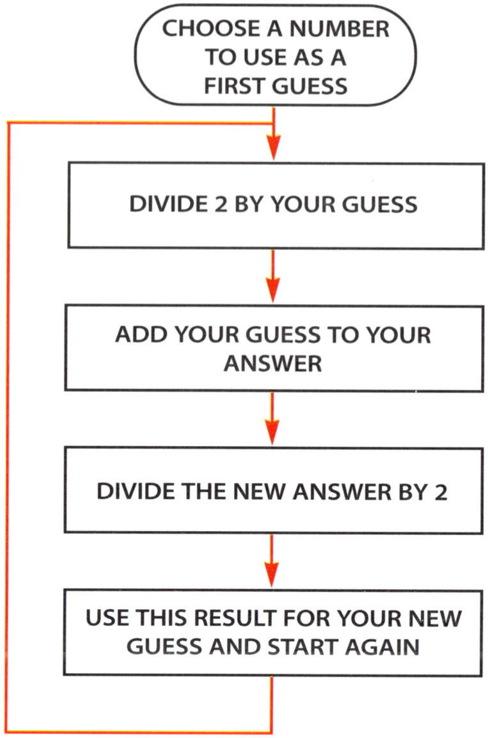

- If you start with the number 12, this is what you get.

Guess	Result
12	6.08
6.08	3.21
3.21	1.91
1.91	

- Copy and complete the table. Record your results correct to 2 decimal places.

  What do you notice about your results?
- Try a different starting number.
- What is the answer giving you?
- Can you explain why?

Review Exercise

1 Copy and complete this table.

Number	To nearest ten	Correct to 2 d.p	Correct to 2 sig.fig
348.556			
24.922			
2.6439			
92.064			

2 Jenny adds her age to her brother's age and gets 24.
She is 6 years older than her brother. What is her age?

3 Copy and complete this table

Problem	To nearest unit	Correct to 1 d.p	Correct to 1 sig.fig
$38 \times 42 \div 9$			
$984 \div 23$			
$1096 \div 0.7$			
$17 \times 17 \times 17$			

4 23 coins include only 2p pieces and 5p pieces.
The total amount of money they make up is 79 pence.
How many of each coin is there?

5 Find the values of these without using the $\sqrt{\ }$ button on your calculator:

(a) $\sqrt{5}$ (b) $\sqrt{26}$ (c) $\sqrt{250}$ (d) $\sqrt{3420}$

6 Two consecutive numbers are multiplied together to give 3422.
What are the two numbers?

7 Which numbers do not change when you square them, and then take away 42?

8 The area of a square is $70\,\text{cm}^2$.
Find the length of its side, correct to 2 decimal places.

9 The volume of a cube is $70\,\text{cm}^3$.
Find the length of its side, correct to 2 decimal places.

Statistical diagrams

In this chapter you will learn:

- → **how to select appropriate statistical diagrams**
- → **how to graph continuous data**
- → **how to use frequency diagrams**
- → **how to construct pie charts**
- → **how to analyse data**

Starting points

Before starting this chapter, you will need to know how to:

- calculate the mode, median, mean and range of a set of data
- use different types of average
- read information from line graphs
- read information from and draw simple pie charts.

Key fact
The set of values that information is taken from is called a population.

Gathering data

When you collect data, you will either look at *all* the possible data available or a **representative** part of the data.

Collecting data from a population is called **sampling**. A population can be sampled in different ways.

Example

A **population** could be *all* the recordings in the music charts in a particular year.

A **sample** taken from this population might be those made by female artists.

A different sample might be recordings that reached number 1 in the charts.

The type of data you collect will affect how the data is displayed.

Exercise 1

1 Imagine you have to collect the required data in each of these populations.
Would you investigate the whole population or only a sample?

	Population	*Data you require*
(a)	Pupils in your class	their birthdays
(b)	Trees in a park	their heights
(c)	Cars on the road	the number of passengers
(d)	Passengers on a train	the cost of their tickets
(e)	Cars on the car park	their ages

Key fact

A random sample is one which is not affected by outside influences.

Key fact

A biased sample is affected by outside influences.

Samples

A sample can be **random** or **biased**.

Exercise 2

1 Which of these samples are biased? Which are random? Explain your answers.

(a) A survey asking which is the best football club in the country taken outside a Premier League ground at the end of a match

(b) A survey of people's favourite types of music taken outside a Symphony Hall at the end of a classical concert

(c) Measuring the speeds of cars passing through a large town between 7 a.m. and 9 a.m.

(d) Choosing six numbers for a lottery

(e) Asking pupils which lesson they prefer during a Maths lesson

(f) The results of rolling a fair dice

2 A pupil is doing a survey of whether boys or girls do more homework.

(a) To avoid bias, how should the question be asked?

(b) How many people should be asked?

(c) What do you think might affect people's answers?

Using a questionnaire to collect data

Designing a good questionnaire is not as easy as it sounds.

- When you design a questionnaire you should include sufficient choices to cover all possible answers.
- The information on the questionnaire must be clear and have only one possible meaning.
- Answers should be short.
- When you plan the collection of your data, you should be aware of things which might affect or change your results.

To design a good questionnaire you should think about these things:

- Be clear about which information you require.

  Write down what you want.
- Decide who you will survey.

  Why have you chosen this group?
- Decide when and where you will carry out your survey.

  Why have you chosen this time and place?
- Are there factors which might affect your results?

  Is there anything you could do to avoid this?
- How are you going to record the data?
- How are you going to display the data you are collecting?

Exercise 3

1 This is a question from a pupil's questionnaire.

> **What type of TV programme do you prefer?**
>
> ____

(a) How would you answer this question?

Write down your answer.

(b) Ask some other pupils what their answers would be.

Make a list of their answers.

(c) What is wrong with the way this question is asked?

Suggest a better way of asking this question.

Here is one different way of asking the same question.

> **What is your favourite type of TV programme?**
>
> | | | | |
> |---|---|---|---|
> | Music | ☐ | Soap | ☐ |
> | Films | ☐ | Other | ☐ |
> | Comedy | ☐ | | |

(d) How would you answer this question?

(e) Do you think it easier to answer this question?

If so, explain why.

(f) Suggest ways in which you could record the answers to this question.

(g) Ask a number of people the same question and record their answers.

(h) Make suggestions to improve the question even more.

2 (a) What is this questionnaire designed to survey?

> **Questionnaire**
>
> 1. How often do you shop? ______________
> 2. Which shop do you use? ______________
> 3. Why do you use this shop? ______________
> 4. How much do you spend? ______________
> 5. How far is the shop? ______________
> 6. How do you get to the shop? ______________

(b) Explain why the results of this survey would be difficult to record.

(c) Rewrite this questionnaire so that it can be completed more easily.

3 Explain what is wrong with each of these questions.
Rewrite each question so that it can be answered more easily.

(a) What time do you go to bed?

(b) Are you tall, average height or small?

(c) Do pupils in your class prefer CDs, tapes or records?

(d) Where do you like to go on holiday?

(e) Do you have a cooked breakfast, toast, cereals, or nothing to eat before you come to school?

(f) Which colour cars do you prefer?

Assignment 1 Questionnaires

Design a questionnaire to sample data on one of these topics:

- Parents give boys more freedom than girls.
- Boys read less than girls.
- Girls get more pocket money than boys.
- Boys prefer playing sports to watching TV.

Gathering data by observation

When you are gathering data by observation, you must take these factors into account:

- What do you want to survey?
- How is data to be recorded?
- For how long will you continue to record the data?
- When is the data to be recorded?
- Who is going to record the data?
- How you are going to present your data?

Exercise 4

1 What would you need to do to sample the following data by observation?

(a) A survey of the ages of supermarket customers

(b) A survey to investigate the numbers of people travelling in cars

(c) A survey of pupils cycling to school

(d) A survey of the type of weather

2 You decide to carry out a survey of the age of customers using a post office. You wait outside the local post office at 10 a.m. on a Monday morning.

Your results indicate that the majority of people who use this local post office are pensioners.

Explain why your results may not be accurate.

3 Design a data collection sheet to sample data from one of the surveys described in Question 1.

Gathering data by experiment

When you are gathering data by experiment you need to:

- be sure the experiment does test the theory you are trying to test
- carry out sufficient experiments to produce results which reflect what is really happening.

Exercise 5

1 (a) How could you record the results of an experiment to investigate whether a drawing pin usually lands point up?

(b) How many times do you think you would have to repeat this experiment?
Explain your answer.

2 Carry out experiments to test the hypothesis that drawing pins are more likely to land point up than point down.

Displaying different types of data

The type of data affects the way that data should be displayed.

Discrete data is gathered by counting.

Discrete data, like 'colour of car' gathered by counting, can be displayed in a **bar chart**.

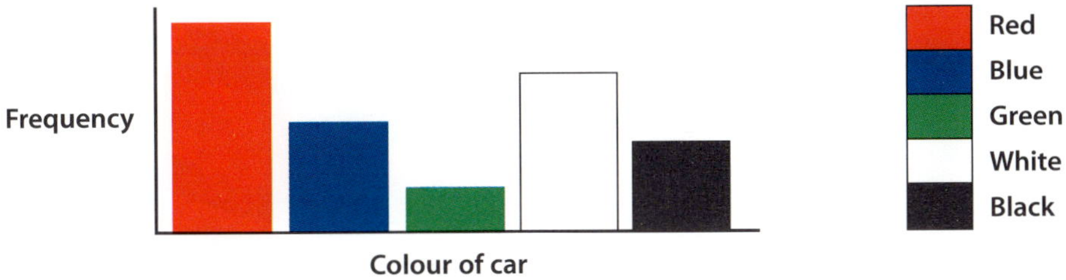

Notice that the bars are separate.

The labels can appear under each bar, or in a key as shown above.

A bar chart is used to display discrete data.

Discrete data can also be displayed in a **pictogram**.

Continuous data is gathered by measuring.

Continuous data, like 'a car length' gathered by measuring, can be recorded on a **histogram**.

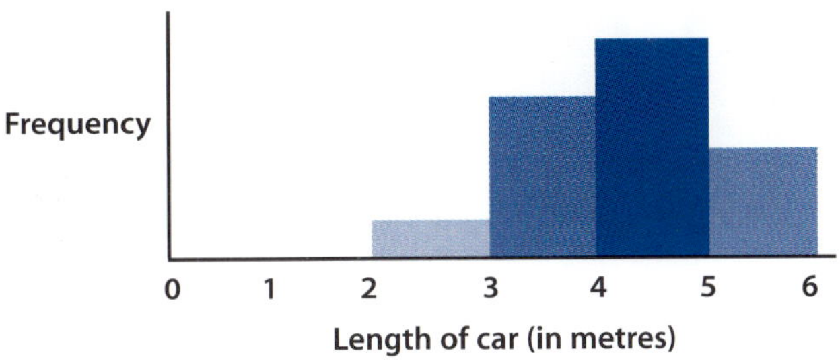

A histogram is used to display continuous data.

Notice that the bars are joined, and that the labels appear at the joins.

Exercise 6

1 Which of these are examples of continuous data and which are examples of discrete data?
Explain your answers.

(a) The time to run 100 metres

(b) A child's shoe size

(c) Your age in years

(d) The volume of sales of CDs

(e) The temperature during the day

(f) The number of people on a bus

(g) The amount of petrol in a car

(h) The height of pupils

(i) The number of people travelling in a car

2 A group of pupils carried out a survey of the lengths of songs and obtained these results.

Time (in minutes)	Frequency
0–2	2
2–4	86
4–6	57
6–8	17
8–10	5
	Total 167

(a) What is this type of statistical diagram called?

(b) Is the grouped data discrete or continuous?

(c) Where should a result of exactly 2 minutes be placed in the table?

(d) What factors might have affected this data?

(e) Use this information to draw a bar chart (if the data is discrete) or a histogram (if the data is continuous).

3 A second group of pupils records the number of single CDs, album CDs, tapes and LPs bought by a group of people in one month.

Type of recording		Frequency
Single CD	卌 卌 卌 卌 卌 卌 卌 卌 III	43
Album CD	卌 卌 卌 II	17
Tape	卌 卌 卌 卌 卌 III	28
LP record	II	2
	Total	

(a) What is this type of statistical diagram called?

(b) How many people were surveyed in this sample?

(c) Is this data discrete or continuous?

(d) What factors might have affected this survey?

(e) Use the information to draw either a bar chart or histogram.

4 A third group of pupils carried out a similar survey about the number of single CD, album CD, tapes and LP records bought by a group of people in one month. Here are their results.

Type of recording		Frequency
Single CD	III	3
Album CD	卌 卌 卌 卌 卌 卌 卌 卌 卌 卌 III	53
Tape	卌 卌 卌 卌 II	22
LP record	卌 卌 II	12
	Total	90

(a) Draw a single bar chart to illustrate both this data and the data from Question 3.

(b) The sample taken by this group of pupils resulted in data which is different from the previous group.
Write down reasons to explain how this might have happened.

5 One group of pupils uses a database to collect data on record sales since 1985.

This group records the sale of singles since 1985.

Year	85	86	87	88	89	90	91	92	93	94	95	96	97
Sales in millions	73	70	66	63	62	60	57	54	50	47	45	46	42

(a) Is the sales data discrete or continuous?

(b) Draw a bar chart or histogram to illustrate this sales data.

(c) Using a suitable scale, illustrate the sales data using a pictogram.

The pupils go on to find the sales of CDs over the same period.

Year	85	86	87	88	89	90	91	92	93	94	95	96	97
Sales in millions	3	10	22	33	46	48	53	64	72	78	82	86	90

(d) Draw a single bar chart to display both sets of data.

Comparing data using line graphs

The data in Question 5 is discrete and therefore a line graph drawn with a solid line is meaningless.

However, because sales happen continuously over the period of time, often this type of data is shown on a line graph.

In this case, a dotted line is used.

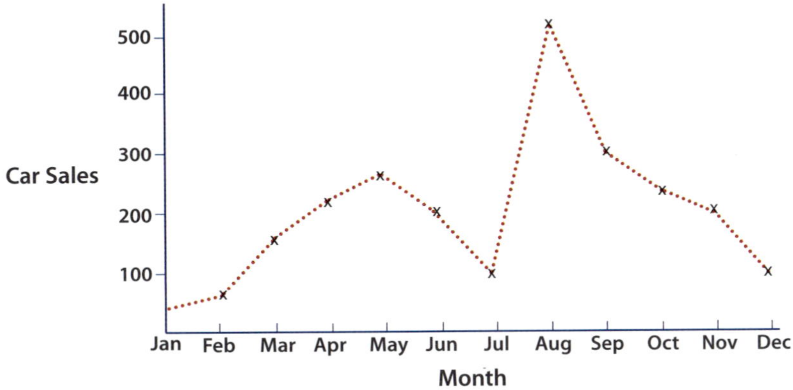

Exercise 7

1 Over a two-week period, pupils recorded the maximum and minimum temperature each day and recorded them in this table.

Day	M	Tu	W	Th	F	Sa	Su	M	Tu	W	Th	F	Sa	Su
Max temp °C	19	18	12	10	11	13	15	17	19	20	18	21	17	15
Min temp °C	6	5	4	3	2	4	6	7	4	3	6	5	8	3

Draw a line graph to show the rise and fall of the temperatures over this period.
(If you decide the data is discrete, your line should be dotted.)

2 This table shows how much is left in a bank account at the end of each month.

Month	Jan	Feb	Mar	Apr	May	Jun	Jul	Aug	Sept	Oct	Nov	Dec
Amount £	50	75	34	12	58	86	96	70	35	5	13	25

Draw a line graph to show the rise and fall in this bank account.
(If you decide the data is discrete, your line should be dotted.)

Key fact

In a frequency polygon, the line between the fixed points has no meaning.

Frequency polygons

One way to compare discrete or continuous data is to draw a frequency polygon.

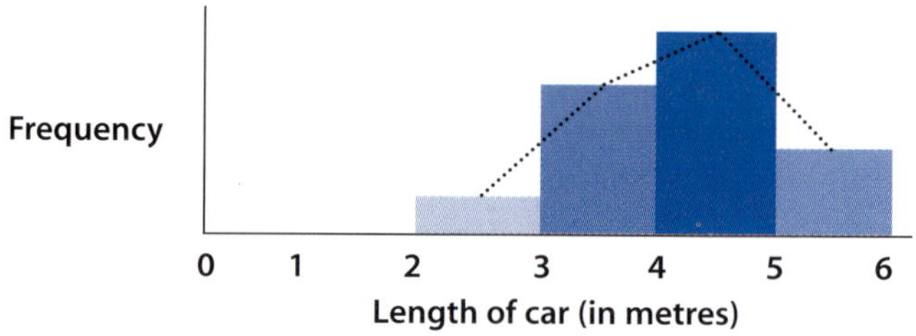

A frequency polygon links the midpoints at the top of each column representing a section of data.

Exercise 8

1 These frequency polygons represent sales of single records and CDs since 1985.

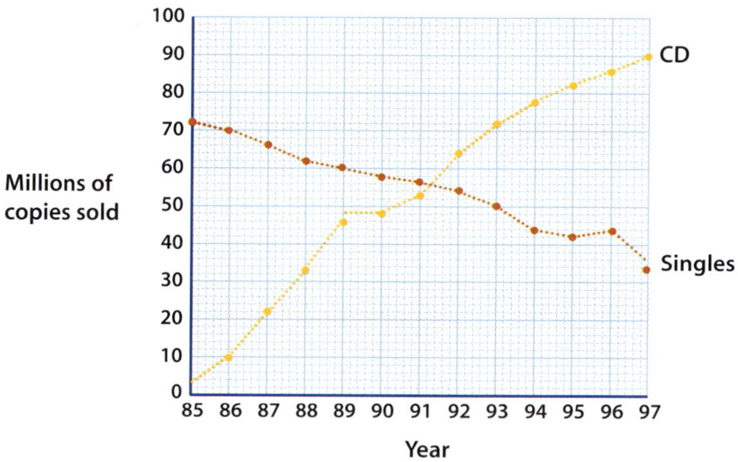

(a) What were the sales of single records in 1985?

(b) When did sales fall below 70 million copies a year?

(c) How many were sold in 1990?

(d) What can you say about the number of CDs sold in 1985?

(e) In which year did the sale of CDs go over 40 million?

(f) When did the sale of CDs become greater than the sale of singles?

2 This table shows the sales of CDs and LP records since 1985.

Year	85	86	87	88	98	90	91	92	93	94	95	96	97
CD Sales (in millions)	3	10	22	33	46	48	53	64	72	78	82	86	90
LP Sales (in millions)	57	56	54	50	48	44	30	26	20	16	14	12	10

(a) On a copy of the axes drawn in Question 1, draw frequency polygons of the CD and LP sales between 1985 and 1997.

(b) When did the sales of LP records begin to fall most quickly?

(c) In which year did the sales of CDs become greater than the sales of LP records?

3 This table shows the sales of CDs and audio tapes over the same period.

Year	85	86	87	88	98	90	91	92	93	94	95	96	97
CD Sales (in millions)	3	10	22	33	46	48	53	64	72	78	82	86	90
LP Sales (in millions)	48	64	72	80	74	72	65	55	48	45	43	38	36

(a) On a copy of the axes drawn in Question 1, draw frequency polygons of the CD and tapes sales between 1985 and 1997.

(b) In which year did tape sales begin to fall?

(c) In which year did the sales of CDs become greater than the sales of audio tapes?

4 Using the two sets of frequency polygons you have drawn in Questions 2 and 3, explain which method of music sales has been affected most by the introduction of the CD in the mid 1980s.

Assignment 2 Record sales

- Design a questionnaire to find why people buy their music on CD, tape or record.

  (Remember to be aware of things that may affect your results: cost, the age of people surveyed, etc.)

- Use your questionnaire to carry out a survey.
- Record your results using suitable diagrams.

Frequency polygons of grouped data

If data is collected from many people, it makes sense to group the data.

Example

In a survey of 70 boys in Year 7, their heights were measured in centimetres. Here are the results:

132	134	139	141	141	142	142	142	142	142
144	145	146	146	146	147	147	148	148	148
148	149	151	151	152	152	152	152	152	153
154	154	154	154	154	155	155	155	156	156
157	157	158	158	158	158	158	159	159	159
159	159	161	161	161	161	161	162	162	163
164	165	165	165	165	166	168	169	172	174

This data is grouped from 130 cm to 140 cm, from 140 cm to 150 cm and so on.

Before you can draw a frequency polygon, you must calculate the middle value in each group of data.

Each group is represented by the mid-range value for that group.

For the group of data from 130 cm to 140 cm, the midpoint will be 135 cm.

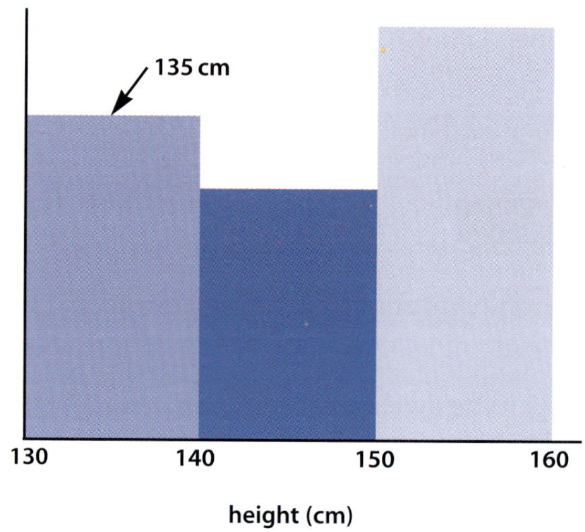

Exercise 9

1 A survey was carried out of the heights of 70 boys and 70 girls in Year 7 as they arrived at their secondary school. This table shows heights of the 70 boys surveyed.

Height (cm)	Frequency	Mid group value
130–140	3	135
140–150	19	
150–160	30	
160–170	16	
170–180	2	
Total	70	

(a) Draw a histogram to illustrate the frequency of the heights of the boys in Year 7.

(b) Copy the table and complete the missing mid-group values.

(c) Draw a frequency polygon on top of your histogram.

2 Here are the heights of the 70 girls in Year 7 surveyed.

Height (cm)	Frequency	Mid group value
130–140	1	
140–150	13	
150–160	25	
160–170	25	
170–180	6	
Total	70	

(a) Copy and complete the table of the heights of Year 7 girls.

(b) Draw a frequency polygon of the heights of the girls in Year 7.

(c) Using the data from Question 1, draw the frequency polygon of the heights of the boys in Year 7 on this diagram as well.

(d) What do the frequency polygons of the pupils in Year 7 tell you about the heights of the boys and the girls in Year 7?

(e) What may be wrong with the data?

3 A survey of the same pupils, carried out when they were in Year 9, produced these results.

Year 9 Boys

Height (cm)	Frequency	Mid group value
140–150	1	
150–160	12	
160–170	21	
170–180	25	
180–190	8	
190–200	2	
Total	70	

Year 9 Girls

Height (cm)	Frequency	Mid group value
140–150	0	
150–160	9	
160–170	28	
170–180	24	
180–190	8	
190–200	1	
Total	70	

(a) Copy and complete the tables.

(b) On one pair of axes, draw frequency polygons to compare the heights of boys in Year 7 and in Year 9.

(c) Draw frequency polygons to compare the heights of girls in Year 7 and in Year 9.

(d) Write down any conclusions you can draw from the differences between the two pairs of frequency polygons.

(e) On one pair of axes, draw frequency polygons to compare the heights of boys and girls in Year 9.

(f) Compare these frequency polygons to those drawn for Question 1. Write down what you notice.

Using a pie chart to compare data

Pie charts are another way to illustrate data. They show comparisons between data.

These are the results of a survey of the favourite TV programmes of 180 pupils.

Favourite TV programmes	Frequency	Pie chart angle
Music	30	60°
Films	23	
Comedy	12	
Soap	56	
Cartoon	34	
Other	25	
Sample size	180	

To calculate the angle per pupil, divide the degrees in the circle by the number of pupils (sample size).

For example, $360° \div 180 = 2°$ per pupil

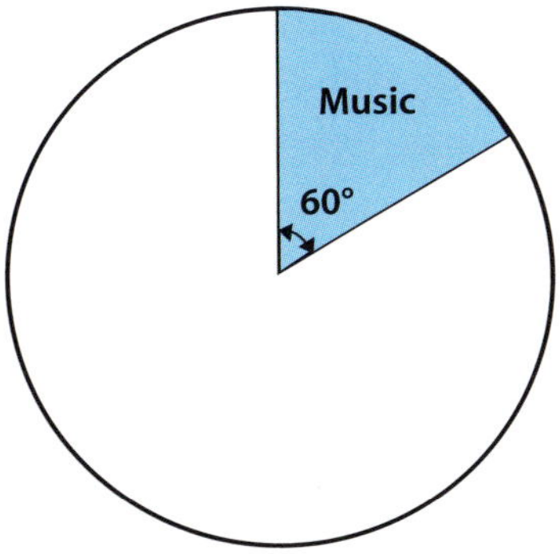

For Music: $30 \times 2° = 60°$

In a pie chart the 360° of the whole circle represents all the data.

Assignment 3 TV pie chart

- Copy and complete the frequency table above.
- Copy the pie chart.
- Mark in the angle representing Music.
- Continue around the circle marking in the angles for each programme type until the circle is full.

Exercise 10

1 A class in Year 8 were asked their favourite type of TV programme.

Favourite TV programmes	Frequency	Pie chart angle
Music	8	80°
Films	3	
Comedy	6	
Soap	12	
Cartoon	6	
Other	1	
Sample size		

(a) How many pupils were surveyed?

(b) Calculate the multiplier needed to work out the angle of each sector.

(c) Copy the table and complete the angles in the third column. The first angle has been calculated for you.

(d) Use the information in your table to draw a pie chart.

2 Here are the results of the same class, surveyed again in Year 9.

Favourite TV programmes	Frequency	Pie chart angle
Music	12	
Films	3	
Comedy	7	
Soap	9	
Cartoon	2	
Other	3	
Sample size	36	

(a) Copy the table and complete the angles in the third column.

(b) Use the information in your table to draw a pie chart.

(c) Write down the differences displayed by this pie chart and the one drawn for Question 1.

3 Pupils carry out surveys of the favourite types of music in two Year 9 groups. These are the results.

Year Group 9A

Favourite music	Frequency	Angle of sector
Pop	10	120°
Rock	5	60°
Soul	4	48°
Reggae	2	24°
Heavy metal	9	108°
Sample size	30	360°

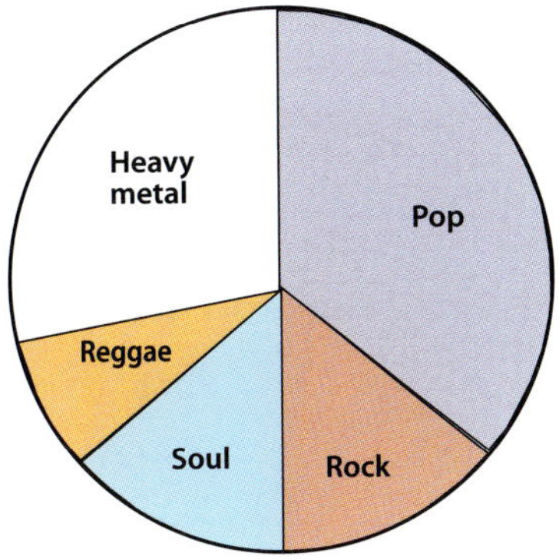

Year Group 9B

Favourite music	Frequency	Angle of sector
Pop	10	90°
Rock	5	45°
Soul	7	63°
Reggae	6	54°
Heavy metal	12	108°
Sample size	40	360°

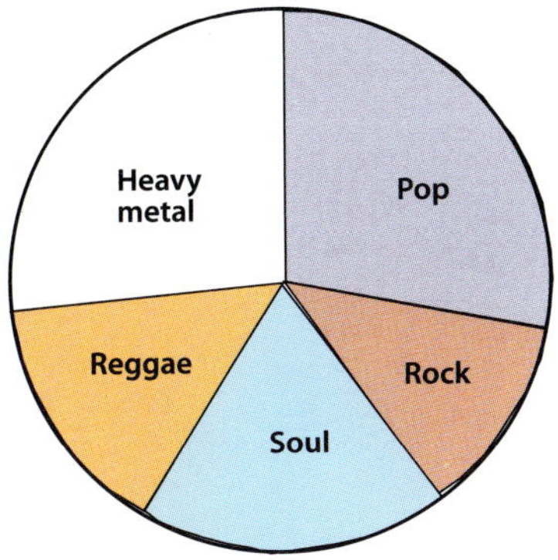

These are the conclusions reached by the pupils.

(a) Pop music is more popular in Year Group 9A than in Year Group 9B.

(b) More people like rock music in Year Group 9A than in Year Group 9B.

(c) The same number of people like 'heavy metal' music in both groups.

Explain why each of these conclusions is incorrect.

Pie charts for more difficult numbers

In real situations, the size of the sample of data collected is not usually a factor of 360°.

In this case, you may need to use a calculator to find the multiplier which gives the angle.

Example

Here are the results of another survey.

This time, there are 32 pupils.

First, to calculate the sector angles, divide by the size of the sample:

$360 \div 32 = 11.25$

Then, use 11.25 as the multiplier.

For Pop: $4 \times 11.25 = 45$

For Rock: $9 \times 11.25 = 101.25$

The angle 101.25° will be too accurate. Round your answers to the nearest whole number of degrees.

For Rock: $9 \times 11.25 = 101.25 \simeq 101$

For Soul: $6 \times 11.25 = 67.5 \simeq 68$

For Reggae $5 \times 11.25 = 56.25 \simeq 56$

For Heavy metal: $8 \times 11.25 = 90$

Round angles up or down to nearest whole number.

Favourite	Frequency music	Angle of sector
Pop	4	45°
Rock	9	(101.25 ≃) 101°
Soul	6	(67.5 ≃) 68°
Reggae	5	(56.25 ≃) 56°
Heavy metal	8	90°
Sample size	32	360°

Total should equal 360°.

Check that the angles add up to 360°.

$45 + 101 + 68 + 56 + 90 = 360$

Exercise 11

1 This table shows the results of a survey of the number of pupils in the dining hall during lunch.

Year group	Number of pupils	Sector angle
7	78	
8	66	
9	58	
10	42	
11	52	
Sample size		360

(a) Calculate the sample size (number of pupils).

(b) Use your answer to part (a) to work out the multiplier which will give you the sector angles.

(c) Use this to copy and complete the table.
(Remember you may have to round your answers.)

(d) Draw a pie chart to illustrate the survey results.

Assignment 4 Tops

- Plan and carry out one of these surveys using the pupils in your class:

    Favourite music

    Favourite TV programme

    Favourite pop stars

    Favourite football teams

  or, you may choose a survey of your own.

- Illustrate the results of your survey using the methods discussed in this chapter.

Review Exercise

1 During one week, a survey is to be carried out to find out how pupils get to school.

Design a questionnaire to gather this data.

2 These are the results of a survey done last term.

Day	Mon	Tue	Wed	Thur	Fri
Walk	436	440	450	430	425
Bus	163	150	155	163	168
Car	44	48	38	52	49
Bicycle	23	25	30	15	20

(a) Is this data discrete or continuous?

(b) Draw either a bar chart or histogram to illustrate the number of pupils travelling to school by car.

(c) Draw a pictograph to illustrate the number of pupils cycling to school each day.

(d) Draw pie charts of the ways in which pupils get to school on a Monday and a Friday.

(e) Draw a frequency polygon showing the numbers of pupils cycling and coming to school by car each day.

(f) If the table includes the whole sample of children in school each day, on which day were most children in school?

3 (a) Use your questionnaire from Question 1 to carry out a survey of how the people in your class come to school each day.

(b) Using the diagrams you think best, write a report of your findings.

(c) Explain what might have affected your results.

Describing patterns in numbers

In this chapter you will learn:

- → **how to explore number patterns**
- → **how to describe and generate patterns using algebra**
- → **how to find and use algebraic expressions and formulae**

Starting points

Before starting this chapter you will need to know how to:

- continue patterns and sequences
- describe patterns and sequences in words.

Exercise 1

1 What is missing from each of these sequences?
Describe, in your own words, how you worked it out.

(a) A, D, G, ?, M, P

(b) 1, 3, 6, 10, ?, 21

(c) December, October, ?, June

(d)

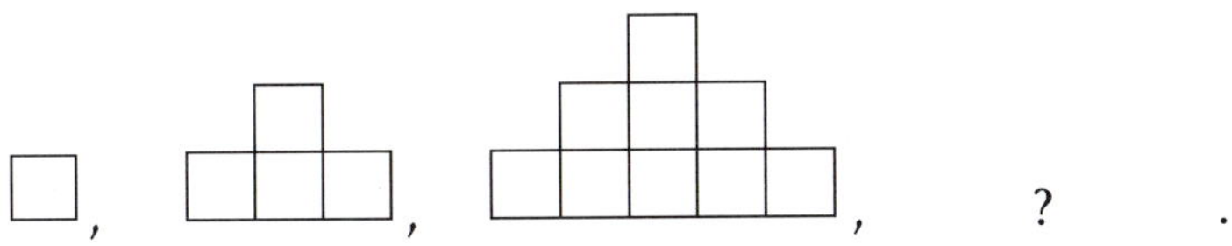

A number sequence is a list of numbers which is made by following a rule.

2 Copy these number sequences and continue them for three more terms. Describe, in your own words, how you worked them out.

(a) 1, 3, 5, 7, ...

(b) 3, 6, 9, 12, ...

(c) 2, 3, 5, 8, 12, ...

(d) 1, 2, 4, 8, ...

(e) 160, 80, 40, 20, ...

(f) 20, 19, 17, 14, ...

3 This hexagon has six edges.

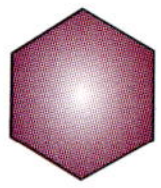

Two hexagons together have eleven edges.

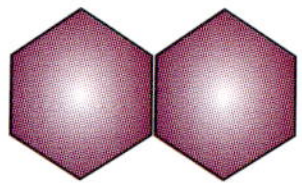

Three hexagons together have sixteen edges.

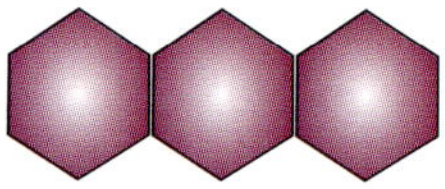

(a) Copy the sequence above and continue it for three more terms.

(b) Copy this table and complete it to show the number of hexagons and the number of edges.

Number of hexagons	Number of edges
1	6
2	11
3	16
4	
5	
6	
7	
8	
9	
10	

You will need to predict the number of edges for 7, 8, 9 and 10 hexagons

(c) Describe the growing pattern in the table.

(d) Describe, in your own words, the relationship between the number of hexagons and the number of edges.

(e) Work out the number of edges in a pattern of 20 hexagons.

Assignment 1 Spelling MATHS

You may have met this type of problem before.

How many different routes can be taken which spell MATHS?

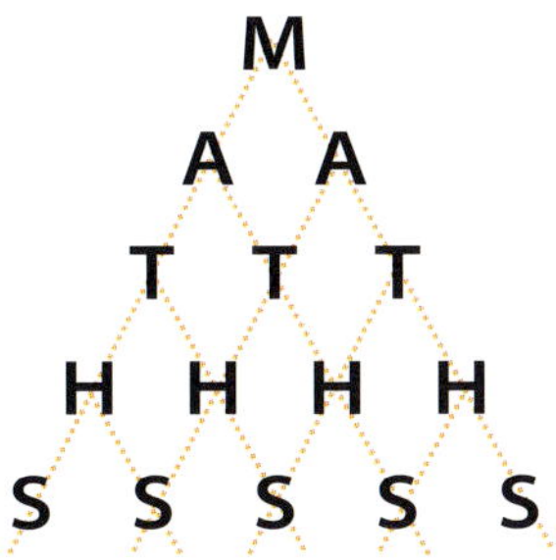

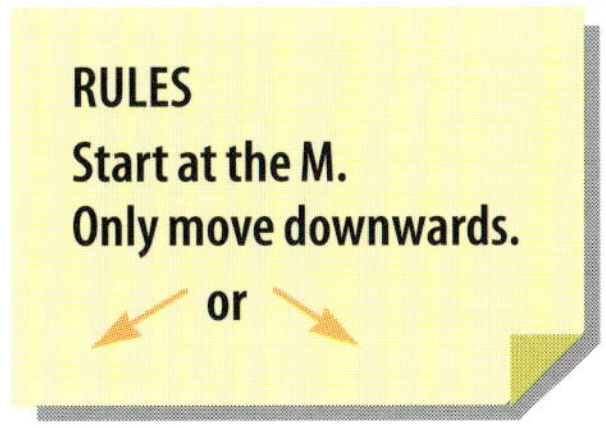

(If you want to try this on your own first, do not read on.)

For the letter M, there is obviously only one possible route!

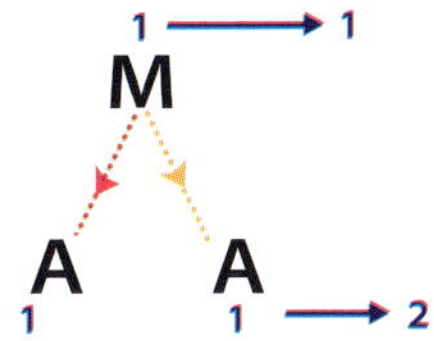

But to spell MA, there are two routes:
from M to the left A or
from M to the right A.

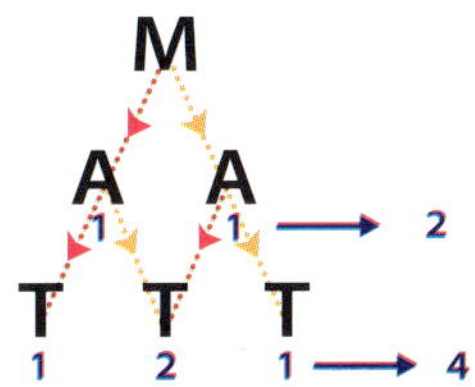

To spell MAT, from each A there are two routes:
left or right.
There are two As, so altogether there are four ways to spell MAT.

- Copy the first three steps above.

  Continue the process to help you to solve the problem.

  Write down any patterns that you notice.

- Use what you have found to predict how many routes spell PATTERN.

- Design a puzzle of your own.

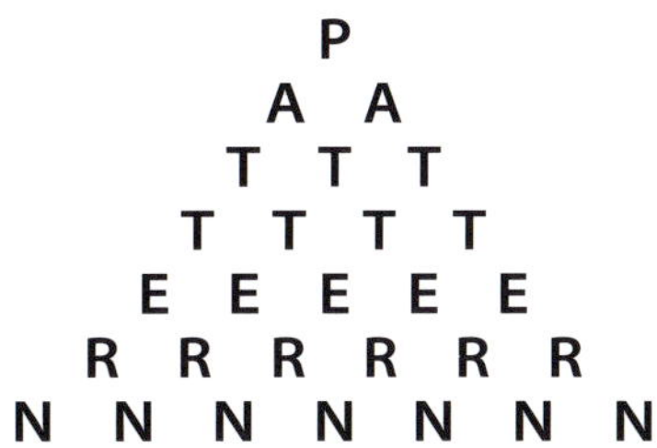

Pascal's triangle

In Assignment 1, the actual words or letters used was not important. It is more important to consider the number of routes to each letter.

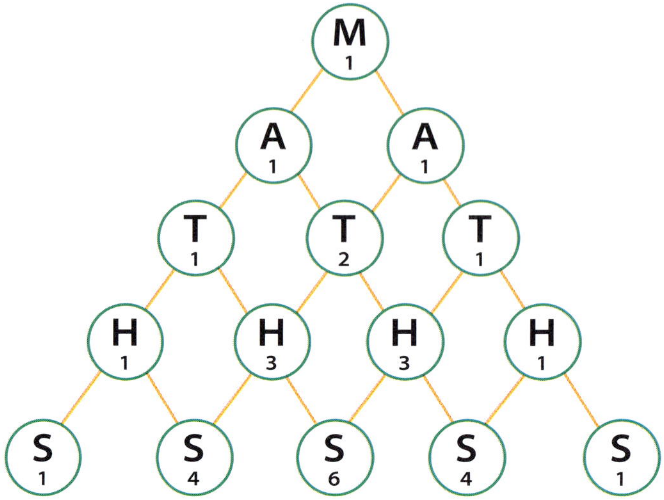

If the number of routes are written on their own, this triangle of numbers is obtained.

1

1 1

1 2 1

1 3 3 1

1 4 6 4 1

1 5 10 10 5 1

1 6 15 20 15 6 1

The next two rows

This pattern of numbers was known to the Chinese in about 1300AD, but it was named after Blaise Pascal (1623–1662). He was a Frenchman who spent a lot of time investigating the number patterns within this triangle.

Exercise 2

1 The diagram on page 72 shows the first seven rows of Pascal's triangle.

Describe how the numbers in each row are obtained from the previous row.

2 Make a copy of Pascal's triangle and add the next three rows.

Counting numbers are the numbers 1, 2, 3, 4, ...

3 On your copy of Pascal's triangle, draw in the line of symmetry.

4 On your copy of Pascal's triangle, using a blue crayon or blue felt-tip pen, circle the set of counting numbers where they occur in order.

Write down any patterns that you notice.

5 On your copy of Pascal's triangle, using a red crayon or red felt-tip pen, circle the set of triangle numbers where they occur in order.

Write down any patterns that you notice.

6 Make another copy of Pascal's triangle, this time with ten rows.

(a) Where are the odd numbers?

(b) Where are the even numbers?

7 Write down any pattern that you notice.

Make another copy of Pascal's triangle, again with ten rows.

(a) Where are the multiples of 3?

(b) Where are the multiples of 4?

(c) Where are the multiples of 5?

Write down any other patterns that you notice.

Assignment 2 Snack machines

A school snack machine accepts only 10p and 20p coins.

There is only one way to pay for a 10p sweet.

A 30p snack can be paid for in three different ways:

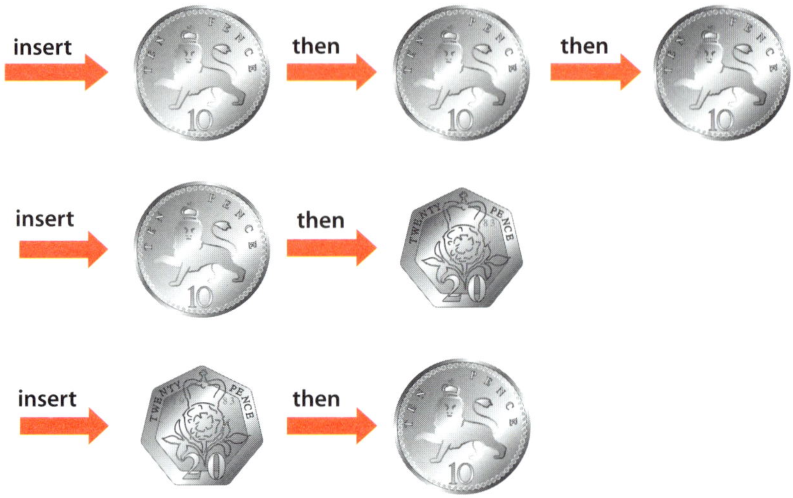

10p followed by 20p is different from 20p followed by 10p.

- Find the number of different ways of paying for items which cost 10p, 20p, 30p, 40p and 50p.
- It may be useful to put your results into a table.

Cost of item	Number of ways of inserting coins
10p	1
20p	
30p	3
40p	
50p	

- Can you see how the pattern is growing? If so, describe it.

If you cannot see how the pattern is growing ask your teacher for a clue.

- Use the pattern to continue the table for items costing up to 100p.

The Fibonacci sequence

The sequence obtained in Assignment 2 is part of the sequence known as the Fibonacci sequence.
Although it was known about over 2000 years ago, it owes its name to the Italian mathematician Fibonacci (1175–1230).
Each term is found by adding together the two previous terms.

Notice that the first two terms are 1.

The first seven terms of the sequence are:

1 1 2 3 5 8 13

Exercise 3

1 Copy and complete this table to show the first fifteen terms of the Fibonacci sequence.

Term	1st	2nd	3rd	4th	5th	6th	7th	8th	...	15th
Sequence	1	1	2	3	5	8	13			

2 This diagram shows some of the numbers in the sequence which are multiples of 2.

Term	1st	2nd	3rd	4th	5th	6th	7th	8th	...	15th
Sequence	1	1	(2)	3	5	(8)	13			

(a) On your copy of the table, mark all numbers in the sequence which are multiples of 2.

(b) Using a different colour or symbol, mark all numbers in the sequence which are multiples of 3.

(c) Using a third colour or symbol, mark all numbers in the sequence which are multiples of 4.

(d) Make a new copy of the table, and use different colours or symbols to mark all numbers in the sequence which are multiples of 5, 6 or 7.

(e) Make another copy of the table. This time, mark all numbers in the sequence which are multiples of 8, 9 or 10.

3 (a) Using your results from Question 2, copy and complete this table.
(You may wish to consider terms higher than the fifteenth term of the Fibonacci sequence.)

Multiple	Terms
2	3rd, 6th, …
3	4th, …
4	
5	
6	
7	
8	
9	
10	

(b) Use any patterns you have noticed to continue writing terms up to the 30th term.

(c) Read these five statements and write down which are true and which are false.

A: The 20th term is a multiple of 2.

B: The 20th term is a multiple of 3.

C: The 20th term is a multiple of 5.

D: The 30th term is a multiple of 2, 3, 4 and 5.

E: The 24th term is a multiple of 6, 7, 8 and 9.

4 Square any term of the Fibonacci sequence.
What is the connection between this result and the terms on either side of the chosen term?
Try other terms.

'Square' means 'multiply by itself'.

Consecutive terms follow each other.

5 Square and add any two consecutive terms of the Fibonacci sequence.
Write down what you notice.
Does this work for other consecutive pairs?

6 Which term of the Fibonacci sequence is obtained by adding the squares of:

(a) the 4th and 5th terms?

(b) the 10th and 11th terms?

(c) the nth and $(n + 1)$th terms?

Assignment 3 Steps

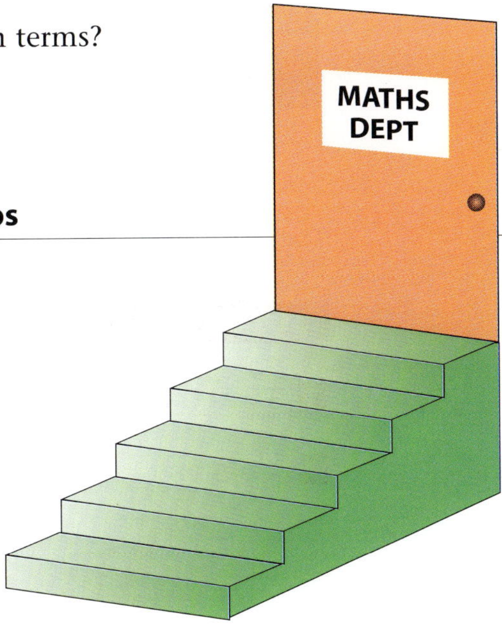

Imagine that you are about to go up a five-step staircase leading to a Maths department.

However, you are only able to take one step or two steps at a time.

Here are some possible ways of going up the five steps.

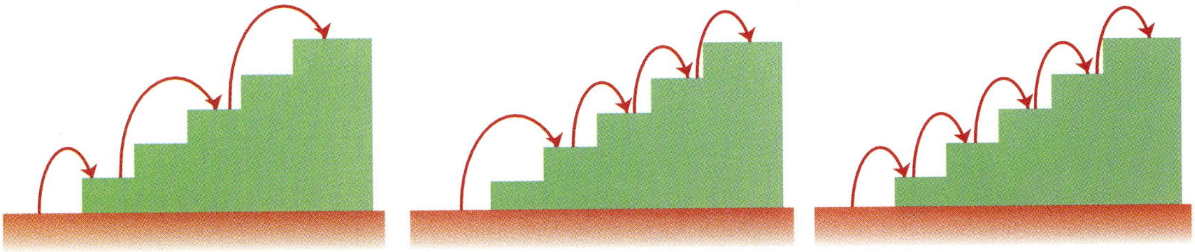

- How many different ways are there altogether?
- Investigate staircases of different sizes.
- Can you find a pattern to help you to predict the number of different ways of going up a staircase of any size?
- What if you are able to take one step, two steps or three steps at a time?
  What about other combinations?

Tile patterns

These tile patterns were made using a rule.

The questions in the next exercise are all about this rule.

Exercise 4

1 Draw three other tile patterns that follow the same rule.

2 Copy and complete this table.

Number of yellow tiles	Number of blue tiles
1	
2	16
3	
4	
5	
6	

If you need help, ask your teacher for a clue.

3 Write down in words how to work out the number of blue tiles if you know the number of yellow tiles.

4 Copy this flow diagram and fill in the boxes.

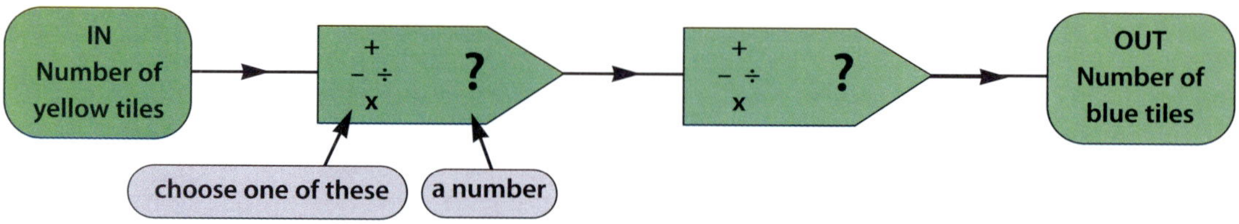

5 The flow diagram in Question 4 gives a rule for working out the number of blue tiles. If y stands for the number of yellow tiles and b stands for the number of blue tiles, use the rule to find b if:

(a) $y = 7$ (b) $y = 12$ (c) $y = 18$.

Exercise 5

1 Copy these tile patterns and make a table to show the numbers of green and yellow tiles.

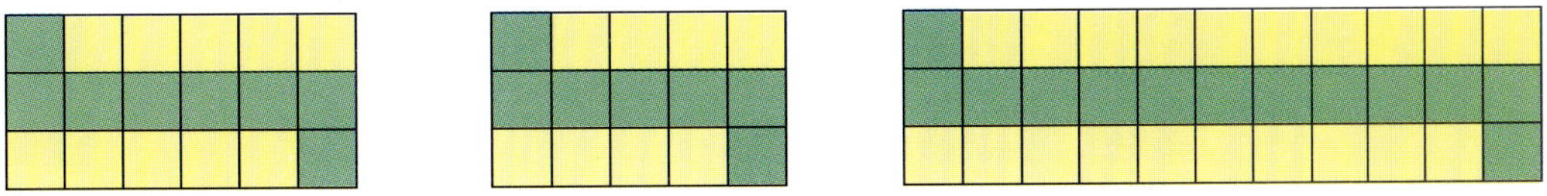

2 Draw some more tile patterns like those in Question 1. Add the results to your table.

3 Use your table from Question 2 to copy and complete this flow diagram.

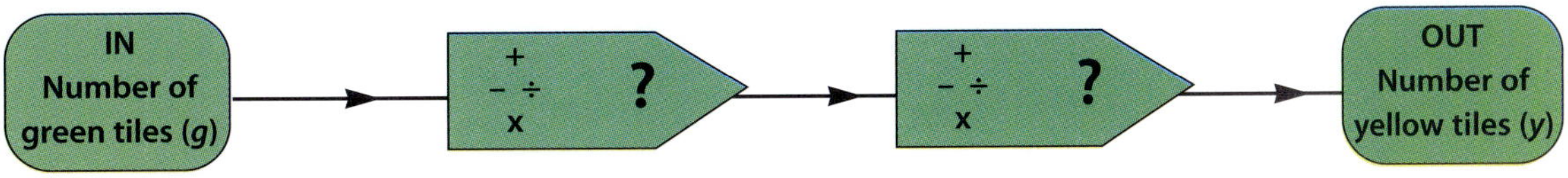

4 The flow diagram in Question 3 gives a rule for working out the number of yellow tiles. Use your flow diagram to find y when:

(a) $g = 5$ (b) $g = 10$ (c) $g = 20$.

5 If you know the number of yellow tiles, can you use the flow diagram in Question 3 to work out the number of green tiles? Find g when $y = 12$.
Explain how you obtained your answer.

6 (a) Make up your own set of tile patterns.

(b) Make a table of results.

(c) Draw the flow diagram for your pattern.

'Systematically' means 'in an order'.

Using algebra

Consider these tile patterns again.

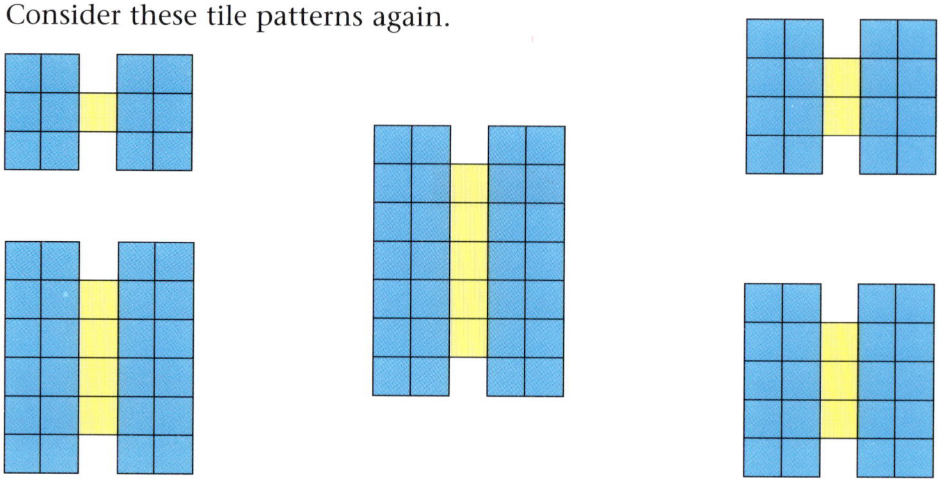

When diagrams are arranged systematically, it often helps in identifying the mathematical pattern.

Pattern 1 Pattern 2 Pattern 3

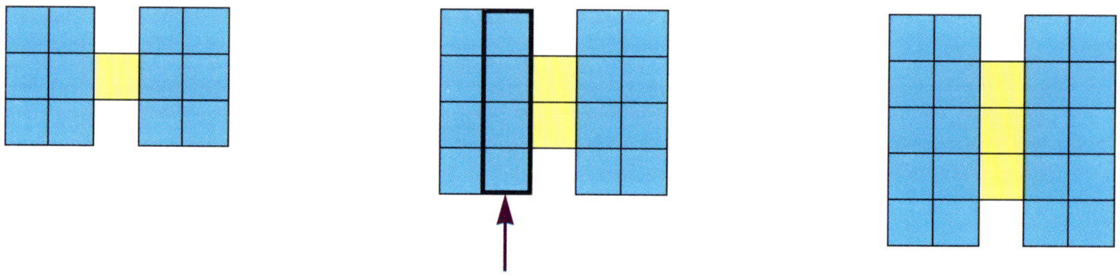

This single line of blue tiles contains the same number as yellow tiles plus 2.

Using algebra, this relationship can be written as $y + 2$ where y is the number of yellow tiles.

As there are four such lines, the total number of blue tiles is

$4 \times (y + 2) = 4y + 8$

Writing this pattern in a flow diagram gives:

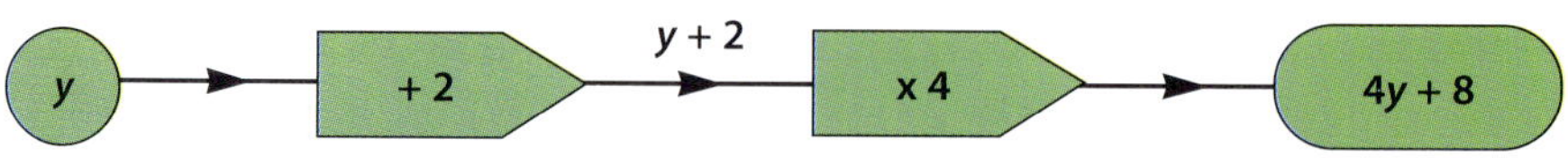

So, the number of blue tiles is found from the **algebraic expression** $4y + 8$.

Exercise 6

1 Look at these tile patterns.

(a)

(b)

(c)

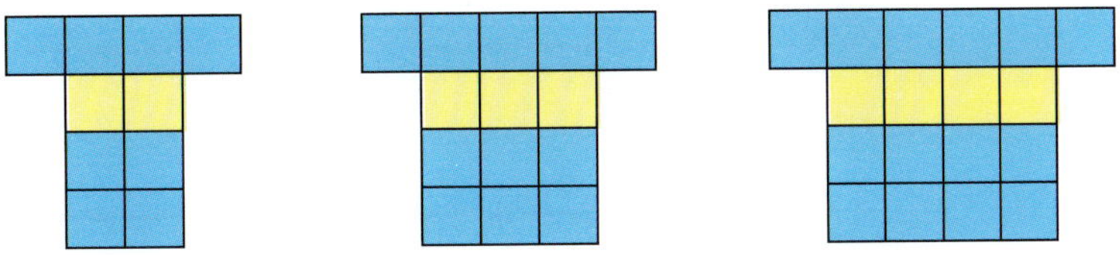

(d)

(e)

(f)

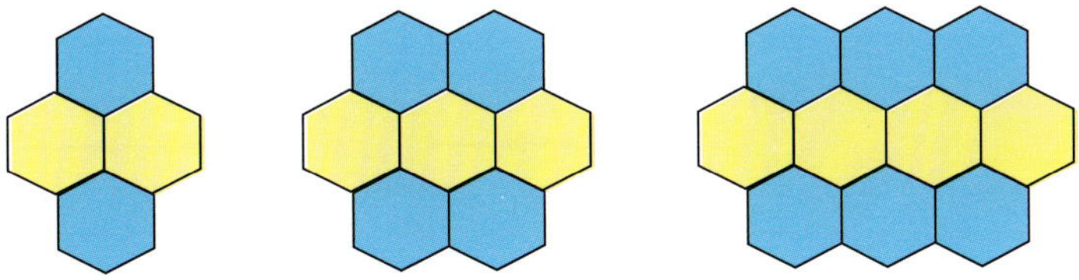

For each tile pattern, write an algebraic expression to find b, the number of blue tiles in terms of y, the number of yellow tiles.

Exercise 7

1 Here are the flow diagrams for some different yellow and blue tile patterns.

(a)

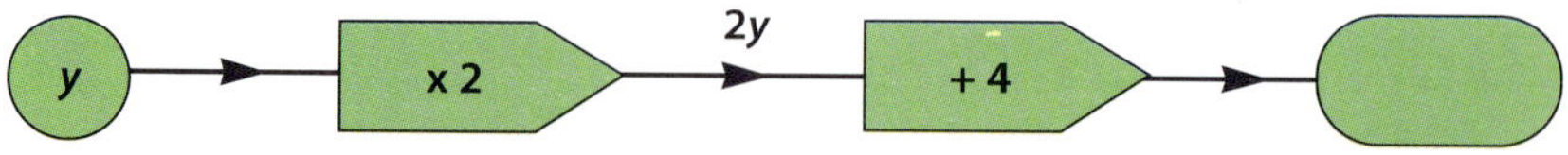

(b)

(c)

(d)

(e)

(f)

For each tile pattern:

(i) copy the flow diagram

(ii) write an algebraic expression for obtaining the number of blue tiles given the number of yellow tiles, y.

2 Copy and complete these flow diagrams.

(a)

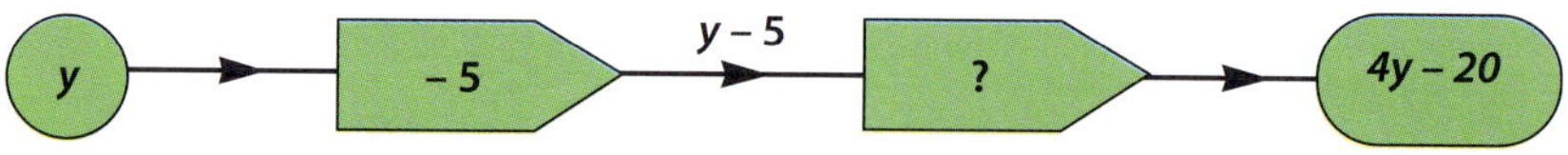

(b)

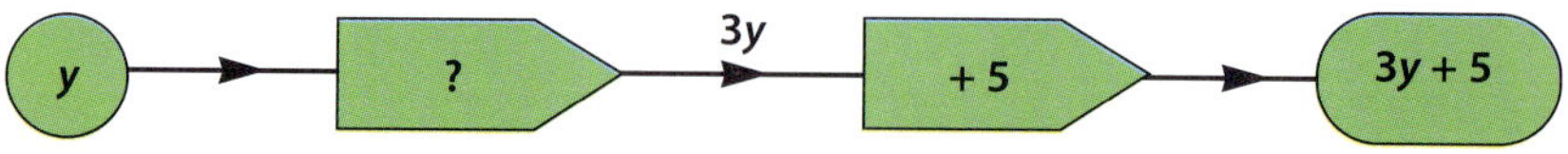

(c)

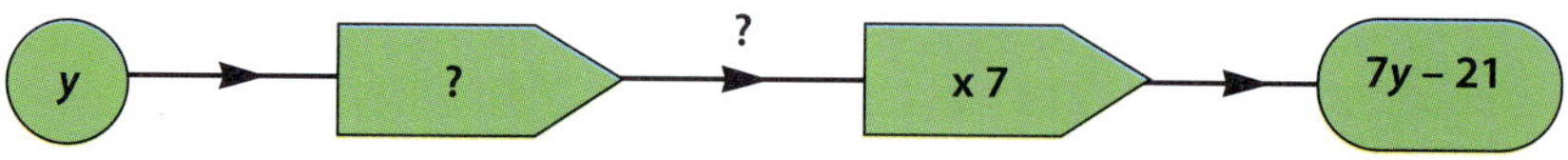

(d)

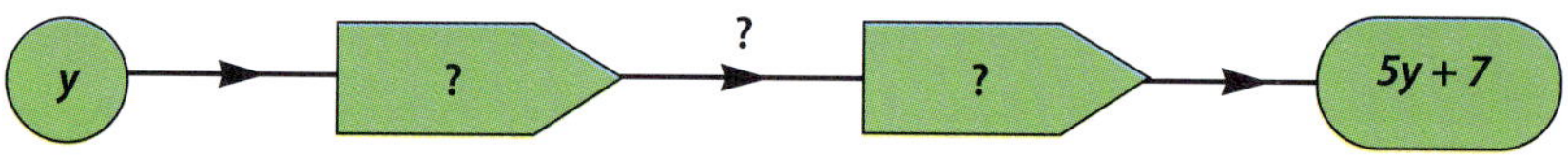

Formulae is the plural of formula.

Formulae

Consider this tile pattern again.

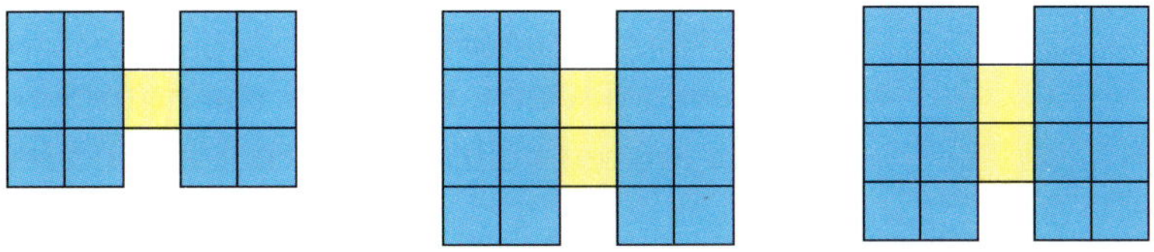

Let y stand for the number of yellow tiles and b stand for the number of blue tiles.

Key fact
A formula is a general rule which describes a pattern.

The number of blue tiles can be found from the algebraic expression $4y + 8$.

This expression can be related to the number of blue tiles like this:

$b = 4y + 8$

This is called a *formula*.

Key fact
Variables are the values (numbers) in a formula which can be altered.

Variables

y and b are called *variables*.

Substituting 10 for y in the formula will give the number of blue tiles when there are 10 yellow tiles.

$b = 4y + 8$

$b = 4 \times (10) + 8$

$b = 40 + 8$

$b = 48$

Example

In a tile pattern, the formula connecting the number (r) of red tiles to the number (g) of green tiles is $r = 5g - 10$.

Find r when $g = 5$.

$r = 5g - 10$

$r = 5 \times (5) - 10$

$r = 25 - 10$

$r = 15$

Find r when $g = 12$.

$r = 5g - 10$

$r = 5 \times (12) - 10$

$r = 60 - 10$

$r = 50$

Exercise 8

1 (i) Look at your answers to parts (a) to (f) in Question 1 of Exercise 6. For each one, write the algebraic expression as a formula connecting b to y.

(ii) For each pattern, work out the number of blue tiles when there are ten yellow tiles (that is, find b when $y = 10$).

2 The formula connecting the number (y) of yellow tiles to the number (b) of blue tiles is $y = 2b + 5$.

Find y when:

(a) $b = 2$

(b) $b = 8$

(c) $b = 35$.

3 The formula connecting the number (p) of purple tiles to the number (r) of red tiles is $p = 7r + 12$.

Find p when:

(a) $r = 2$

(b) $r = 9$

(c) $r = 25$.

4 A scientific experiment is described by the formula $t = 4\frac{1}{2}c - 3$.

Find t when:

(a) $c = 2$

(b) $c = 10$

(c) $c = 7$.

5 A straight line is described by the equation (formula) $y = 3x + 2$.

(a) Find y when $x = 5$.

(b) Find y when $x = ^{-}4$.

(c) Find x when $y = 35$. Explain how you worked this out.

Assignment 4 Swimming pools

This diagram shows a square swimming pool. It measures 3 by 3.

It is surrounded with square patio slabs. There are 16 slabs.

- Investigate the number of slabs needed for square pools of different sizes.
- Try to *predict* the number of slabs needed for a 10 by 10 pool.
- Try to find a formula connecting s, the number of slabs, with l, the length of a side of the pool.
- What about 2 layers of slabs around the pool, or 3 layers or more?
- How about different shaped pools?

More sequences

Many of the patterns met in this chapter give sequences which go up (or go down) by the same amount each time.

Consider this sequence:

3 5 7 9 11 13 15 17 19 …

The sequence begins with 3 and there is a difference of 2 between consecutive terms. (It keeps adding 2.)

+2 +2 +2 +2

3 5 7 9 11 13 15 17 19 …

By the 5th term, 2 will have been added (5 – 1) times.

So the 5th term can be written as 3 + 2(5 – 1) which is equal to 11.

So, the nth term is $3 + 2(n - 1) = 3 + 2n - 2$

$= 2n + 1$

The letter n is used to denote any term (the general term).

Exercise 9

1 Copy these sequences.

(a) 2, 5, 8, 11, 14, ... (b) 1, 3, 5, 7, 9, ...

(c) 8, 13, 18, 23, 28, ... (d) 15, 13, 11, 9, 7, ...

(e) 5, 1, −3, −7, −11, ... (f) 4, $4\frac{1}{2}$, 5, $5\frac{1}{2}$, 6, ...

For each sequence, find

(i) the difference between consecutive terms

(ii) the next two terms

(iii) the nth term.

2 A salary starts at £7500 per year. Each year, it increases by £500. Find the expression for the salary after n years.

3 The nth term of a sequence is $5n + 1$. By putting $n = 1$ and $n = 2$, find the first term and the difference between consecutive terms.

4 These are the nth terms of three different sequences.

(a) $3n + 5$ (b) $4n - 3$ (c) $12 - 2n$.

For each sequence, find the first term and the difference between two consecutive terms of the sequence.

More formulae

Here are two tables of results connecting the number (y) of yellow tiles to the number (b) of blue tiles.

y is called a variable. The value of *y* varies.

Number of yellow tiles (y)	Number of blue tiles (b)	
1	12	
		+4
2	16	
		+4
3	20	
		+4
4	24	
		+4
...	...	

$b = 4y + 8$

y	b	
1	16	
		−3
2	13	
		−3
3	10	
		−3
4	7	
		−3
...	...	

$b = 19 - 3y$

The method used for obtaining the nth term of a sequence can be used to find the formulae connecting y and b.

Exercise 10

1 Find the formula connecting each of these pairs of variables.

(a)

y	*b*
1	9
2	11
3	13
4	15
…	…

(b)

g	*r*
1	5
2	10
3	15
4	20
…	…

(c)

x	*y*
1	6
2	11
3	16
4	21
…	…

(d)

p	*q*
1	7
2	8
3	9
4	10
…	…

(e)

c	*d*
1	3
2	7
3	11
4	15
…	…

(f)

r	*t*
1	⁻4
2	⁻1
3	2
4	5
…	…

(g)

a	*b*
1	9
2	8
3	7
4	6
…	…

(h)

m	*n*
1	18
2	16
3	14
4	12
…	…

Review Exercise

1 This number triangle is made in a similar manner to Pascal's triangle.

```
        1
      1   2
    1   3   2
  1   4   5   2
1   5   9   7   2
```

(a) Copy the triangle of numbers and add five more rows to it.

(b) Add together the numbers in each row.
Write down what you notice.

(c) What is the sum of the numbers in the 10th row?

(d) What is the sum of the numbers in the 15th row?

2 (a) Write out the first ten terms of the Fibonacci sequence (page 75).

(b) Choose any four consecutive terms. For example,

…, 2, 3, [5, 8, 13, 21,] 34, 55, …

Multiply the two outside numbers.

Multiply the two inside numbers.

Write down your answers.

(c) Repeat this for other groups of four consecutive numbers.
What do you notice?

3 Look at these two tile patterns.

Pattern A

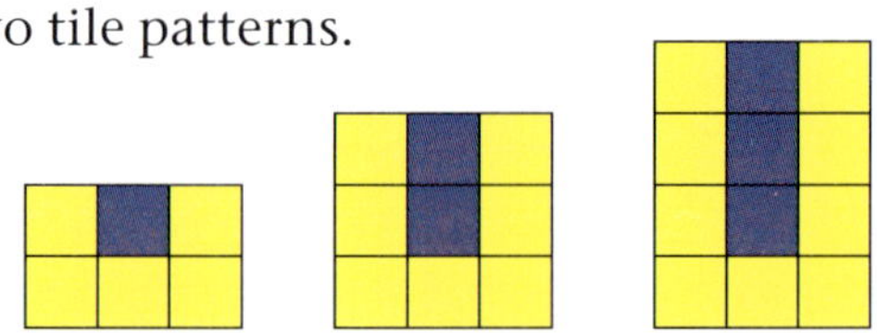

Pattern B

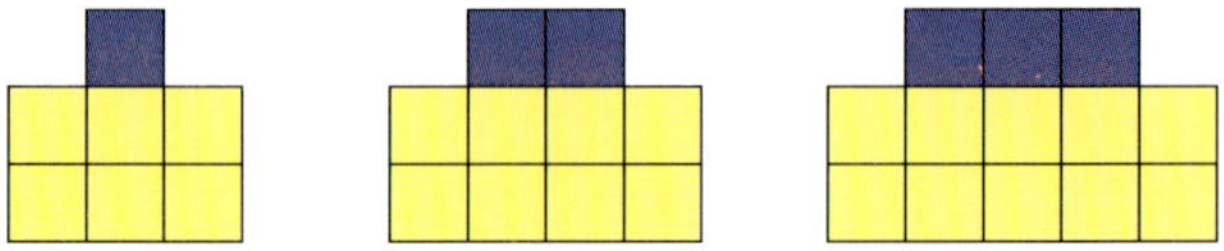

(a) For each pattern, if b is the number of blue tiles, write an algebraic expression for obtaining the number of yellow tiles.

(b) Write a formula for each pattern connecting y, the number of yellow tiles to b, the number of blue tiles.

4 The formula connecting the number (r) of red tiles to the number (b) of blue tiles is $r = 4b - 3$.

(a) Find r when:

(i) $b = 2$

(ii) $b = 8$

(iii) $b = 15$.

(b) Find b when $r = 17$.

5 Copy these sequences.

(a) 4, 7, 10, 13, 16, ...

(b) 20, 18, 16, 14, 12, ...

(c) $1\frac{1}{2}$, 2, $2\frac{1}{2}$, 3, $3\frac{1}{2}$, ...

For each sequence, find:

(i) the difference between consecutive terms

(ii) the next two terms

(iii) the nth term.

6 For each of these pairs of variables, find the formula connecting them.

(a)

b	w
1	10
2	13
3	16
4	19
...	...

(b)

x	y
1	−3
2	−1
3	1
4	3
...	...

(c)

g	r
1	6
2	4
3	2
4	0
...	...

Calculating area and volume

In this chapter you will learn:

- → **how to find the area of simple shapes using a formula**
- → **how to find the volume of simple solids and prisms using formulae**
- → **how to find surface area of these shapes**

Starting points

Before starting this chapter you will need to

- recognise these terms: triangle, square, rectangle, parallelogram, trapezium, kite and pentagon
- know the meaning of the terms equilateral and isosceles.

Assignment 1 Tangrams

- A square is divided into seven pieces, labelled A to G.

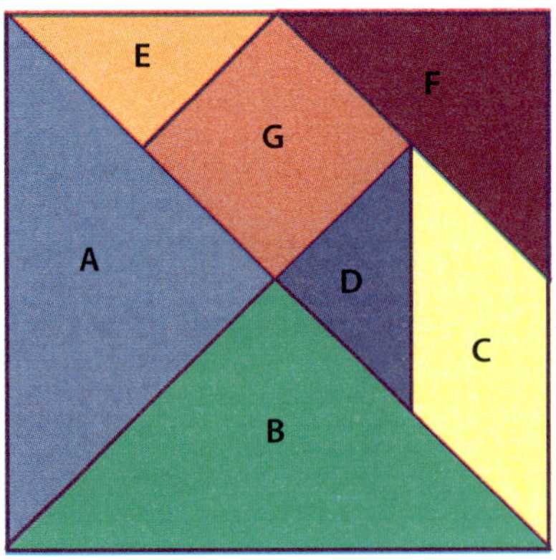

- What name is given to each of the seven pieces of the tangram?

  Which pieces are the same shape?
- Make an exact copy of the tangram on centimetre-square paper and cut out the pieces.

- What name is given to these three shapes?

- Now make these three shapes using *exactly* five pieces for each one. Pieces must *not* overlap but they may be turned over.
- Use all seven pieces of the tangram to make this shape.

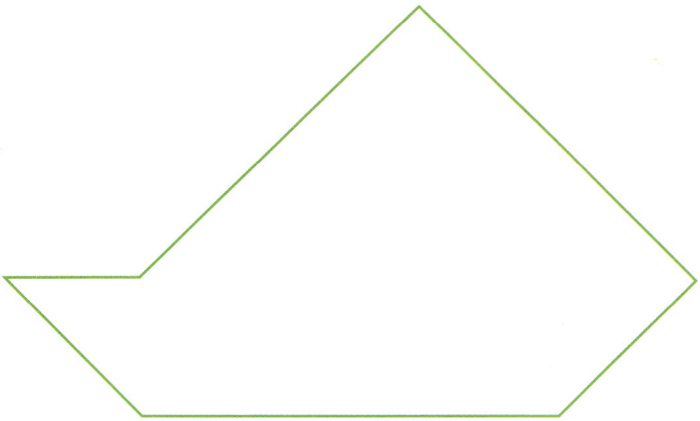

- Now make up some more shapes using all seven pieces of the tangram.

  Draw them on squared paper.

Exercise 1

1 Choose the correct name for each of these shapes from this list:

parallelogram square rectangle kite trapezium

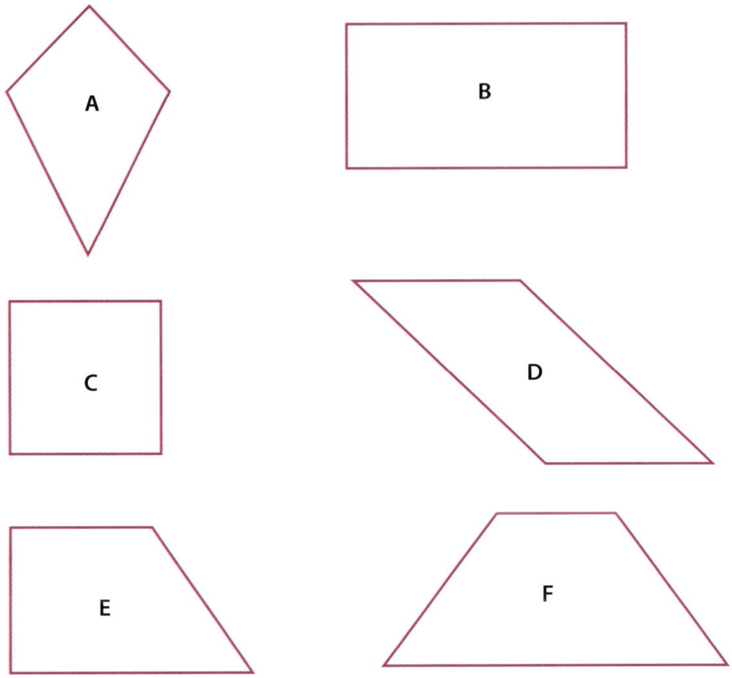

2 Identify each of these triangles as isosceles, right-angled or equilateral.

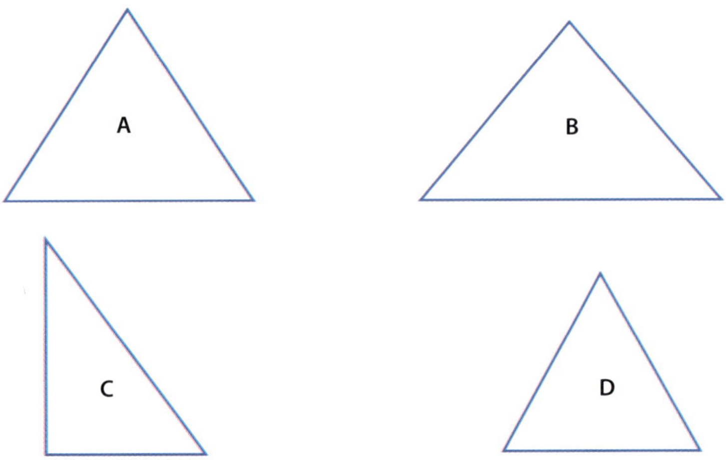

Area is the space within a 2D shape.

Area

Assignment 2 Rectangular areas

Check the dimensions of this rectangle are 9 cm by 4 cm.

The dimensions of a rectangle are its length and its width.

- What is the area of this rectangle?
- Draw other rectangles with the same area.
- Write down the dimensions of each of your rectangles.
- Write down how to use the dimensions to find the area.

Area is measured in square units: cm^2 or m^2.

Exercise 2

1 Find the area of these rectangles.

(a)

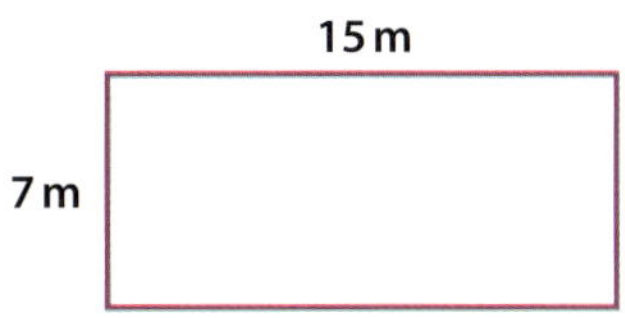

(b)

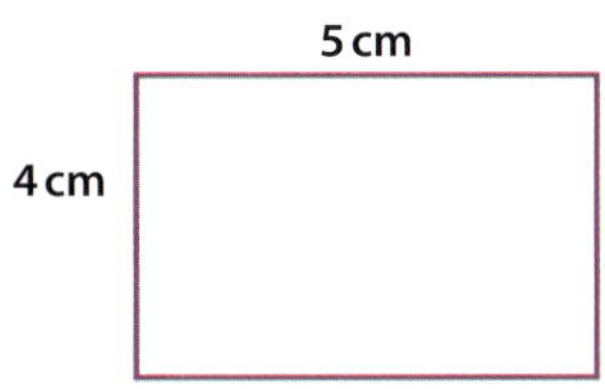

(c)

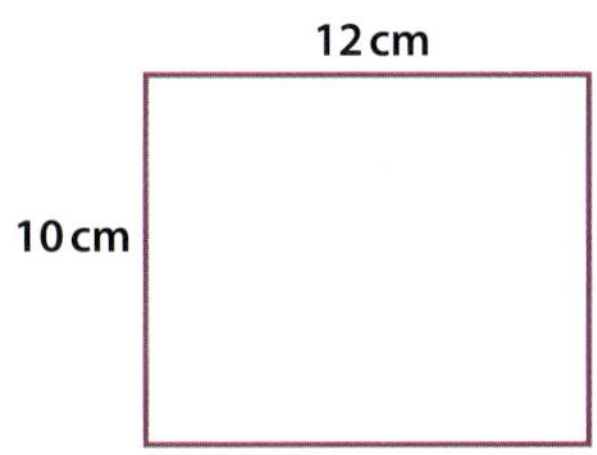

(d)

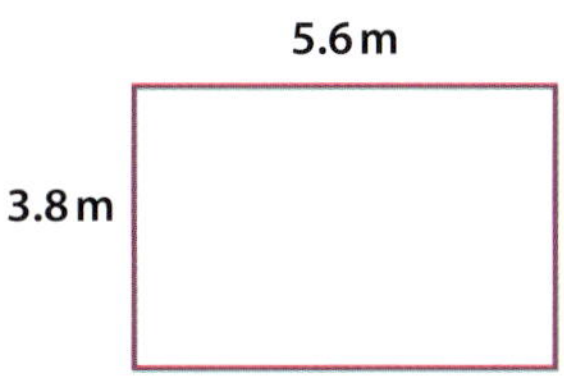

(e)

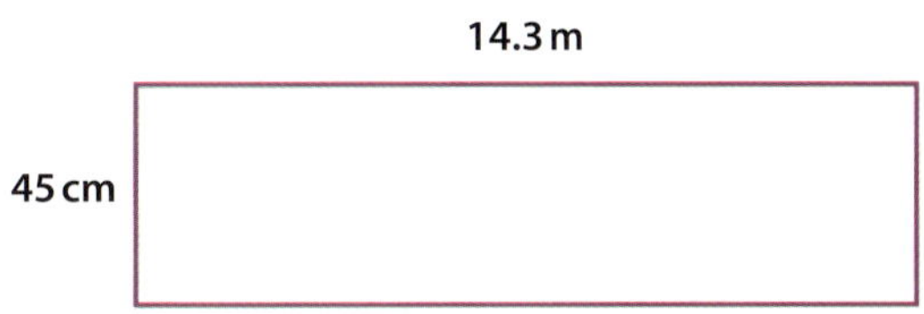

The units in part (e) include cm and m.

2 A garden plot is to have two flower beds planted in it as shown:

What area of land will be left for lawn?

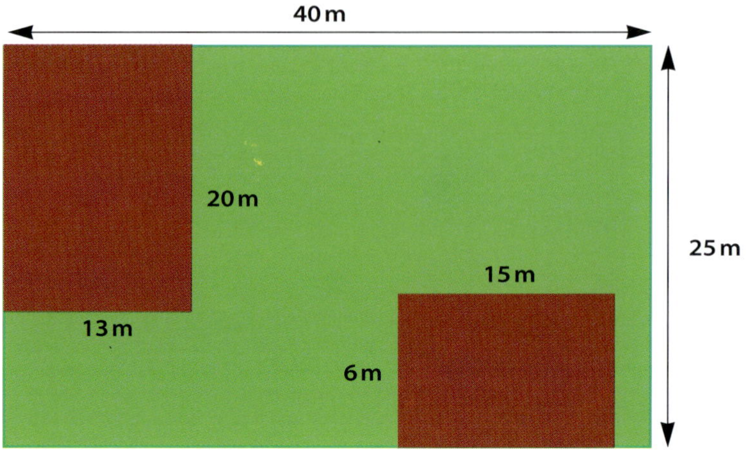

3 A wood block floor 5 m by 3 m is covered with tiles 25 cm by 12 cm.

(a) What is the area of one tile?

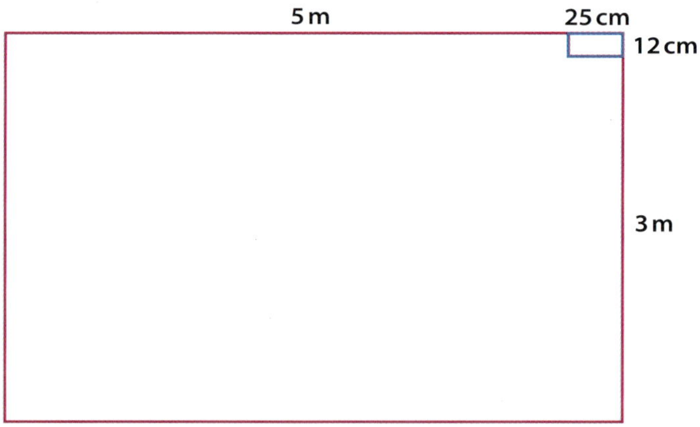

1 m = 100 cm

(b) How many tiles would be needed to cover the floor of a room 5 m by 3 m?

Assignment 3 Open chains

- Copy these diagrams on to squared paper and draw a box around the outside of each one. The first one has been done for you.

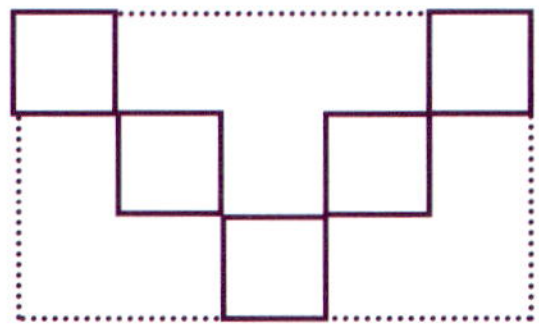

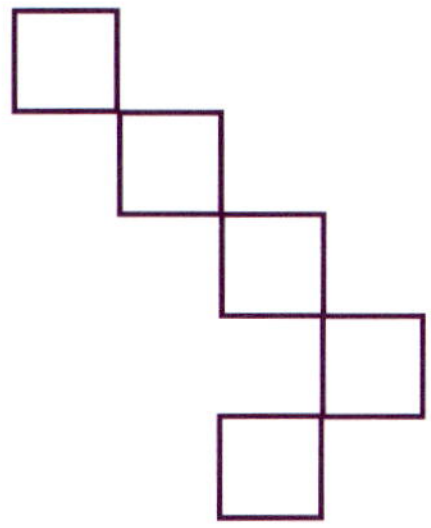

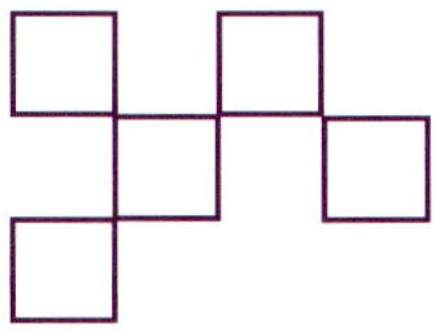

The perimeter is the distance around the box.

- What is the perimeter of the box you have formed?
- What is the area of the box you have formed?
- What is the rule for joining the squares?
- Try to find other arrangements for joining five squares together using the same rule.
- Investigate how to join five squares to make the largest and smallest perimeters possible.
- Investigate how to join five squares to make the largest and smallest areas possible.
- Investigate for other numbers of squares and find the largest and smallest areas and perimeters for 8, 17, 23, 55, 100 and n squares.

Compound shapes

Sometimes a shape is made from more than one rectangle.

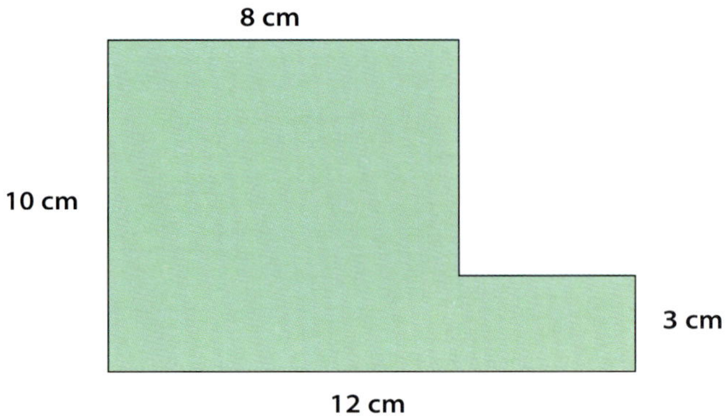

To find the area you need to divide the shape up into smaller rectangles.

This could be done in two different ways.

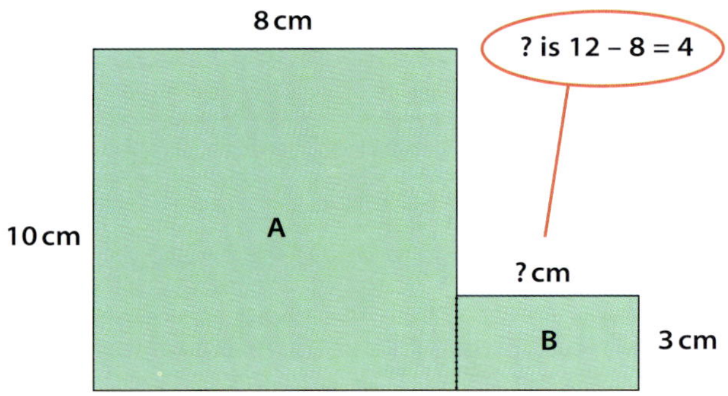

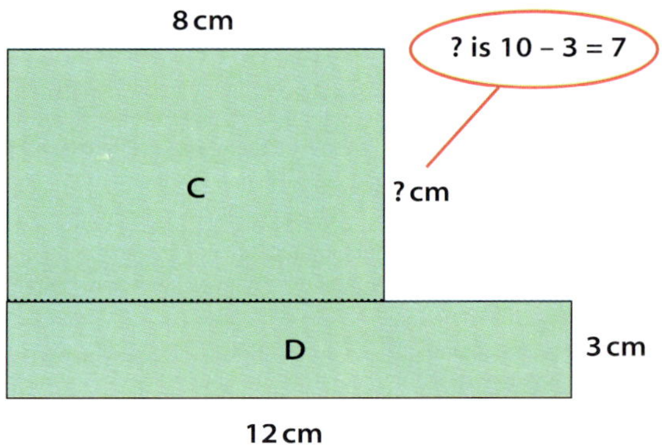

Area of A = 10 cm × 8 cm = 80 cm^2

Area of B = 4 cm × 3 cm = 12 cm^2

Total area = 80 cm^2 + 12 cm^2 = 92 cm^2

Area of C = 7 cm × 8 cm = 56 cm^2

Area of D = 12 cm × 3 cm = 36 cm^2

Total area = 56 cm^2 + 36 cm^2 = 92 cm^2

Exercise 3

1 For each of these shapes, find two ways of working out the area. (All measurements are in centimetres.)

(a)

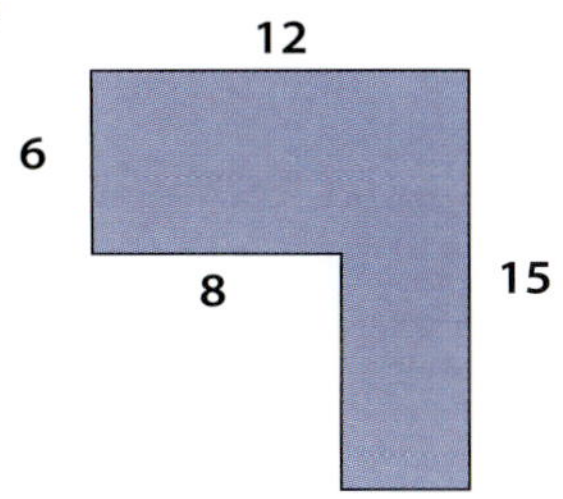

(b)

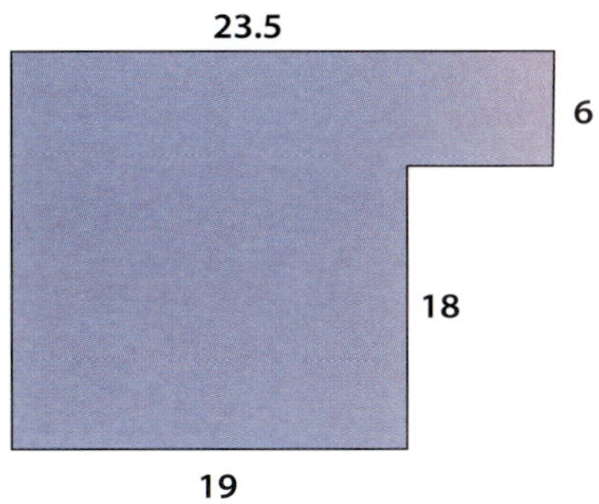

(c)

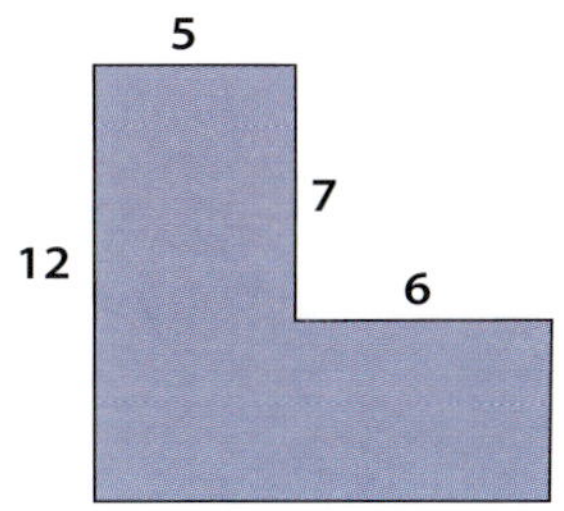

(d)

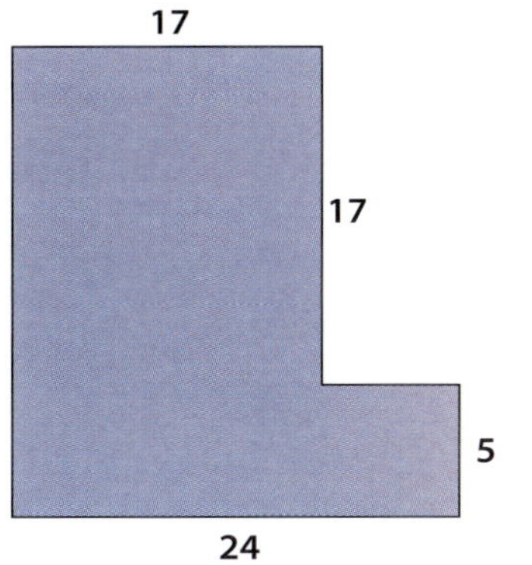

(e)

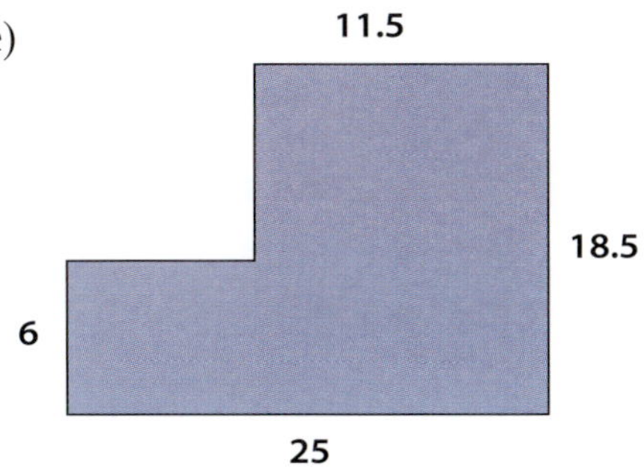

2 Find the areas of these three shapes.
(All measurements are in metres.)

(a)

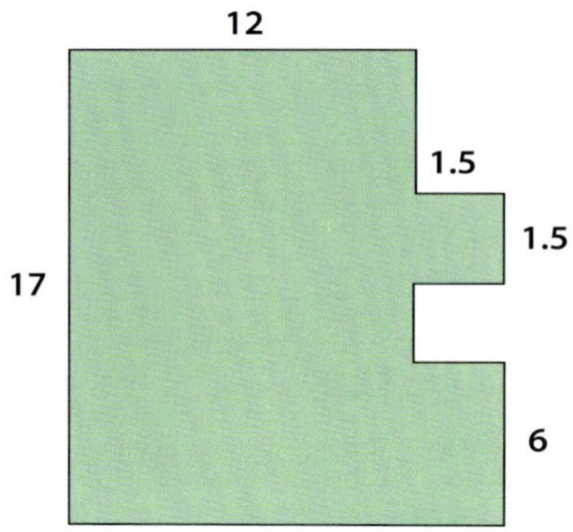

(b)

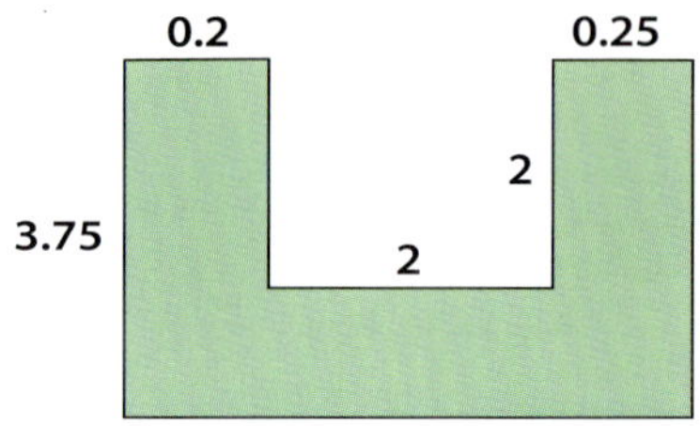

(c)

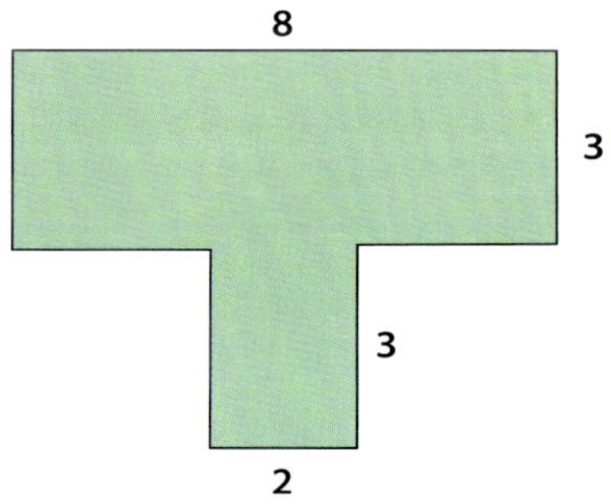

(d)

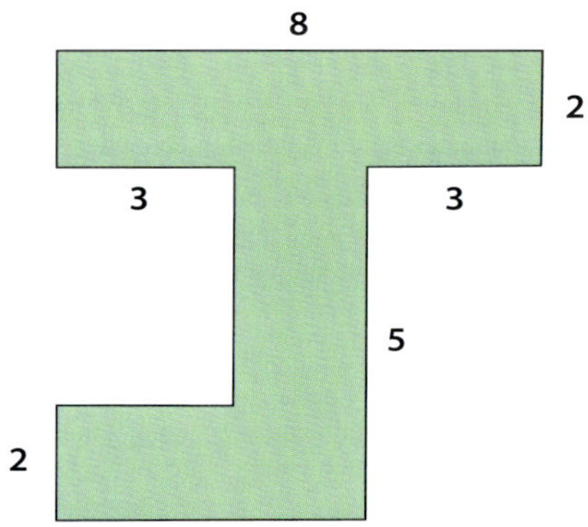

Assignment 4 The same area

- Draw as many shapes as possible which have an area of 24 cm^2.
- Find the perimeter of each of your shapes.
- Record your results in a table.

  Write down what you notice.
- What is the largest perimeter?

  What is the smallest perimeter?

Assignment 5 Parallelograms

- Draw this shape on square dotty paper. Cut it out.

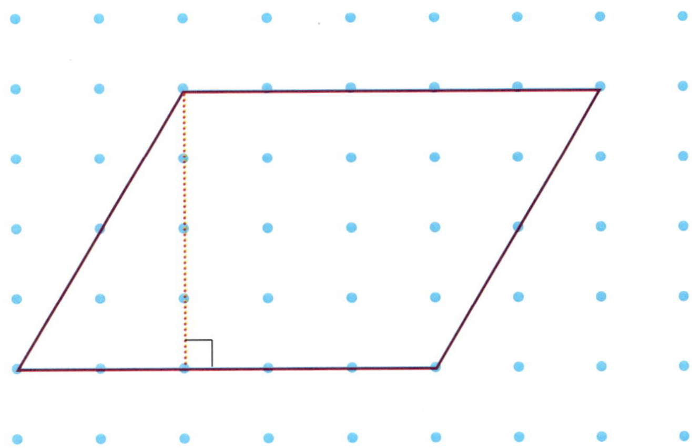

- Draw in the perpendicular height and cut off the triangle.
- Put the triangle on the other side of the shape.

  Stick these two pieces into your book.
- What shape have you made? What is its area?
- Describe how you would find the area of the parallelogram *without* cutting it up.
- Write a rule for the area of the parallelogram.

Exercise 4

Key fact

Area of parallelogram = length × perpendicular height

1 Calculate the area of each of these parallelograms.

(a)

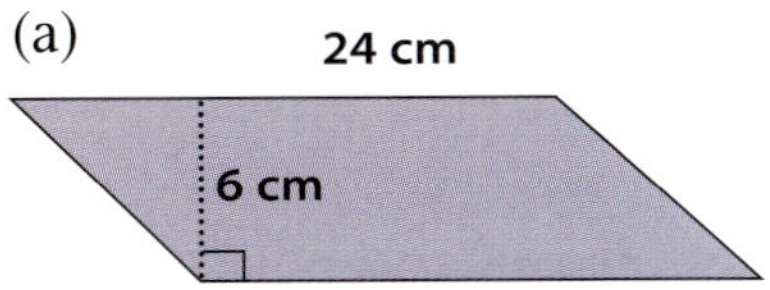

(b)

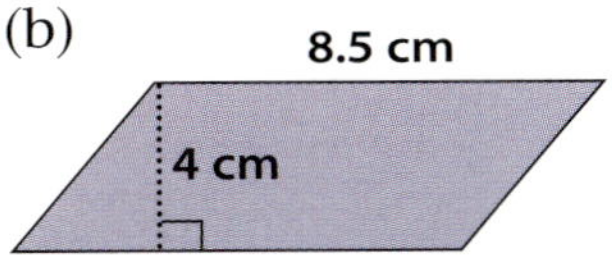

(c)

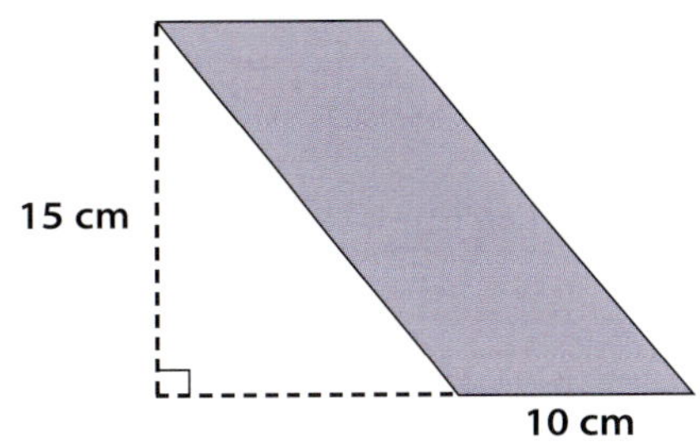

Triangles

A right-angled triangle is half a rectangle.

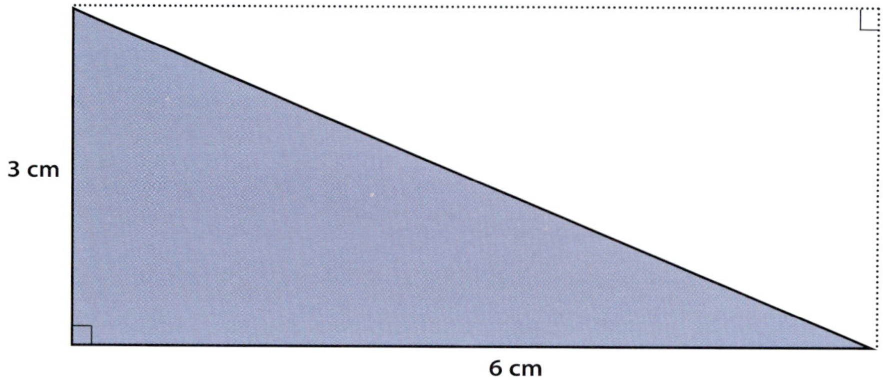

The area of the rectangle is $6\,\text{cm} \times 3\,\text{cm} = 18\,\text{cm}^2$

The area of the triangle is *half* the area of the rectangle.

Therefore, the area of the triangle is $\frac{1}{2}$ of $18\,\text{cm}^2 = 9\,\text{cm}^2$

A rectangle can be drawn around *any* triangle.

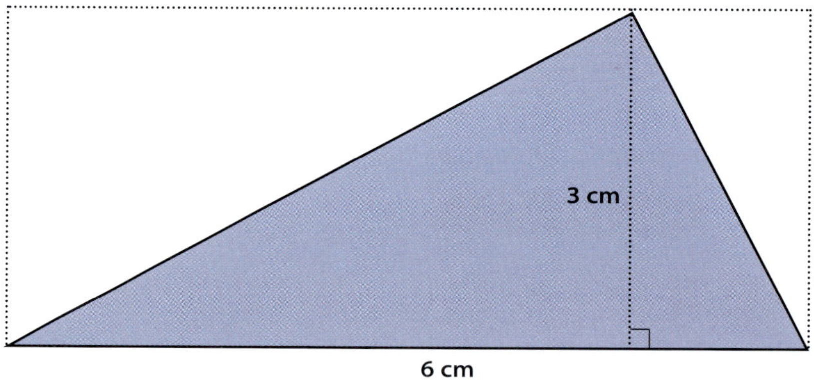

The length of the rectangle is the same as the base of the triangle.

The height of the triangle and rectangle are both the same.

The area of the rectangle is $6\,\text{cm} \times 3\,\text{cm} = 18\,\text{cm}^2$

The area of the triangle is half the area of the rectangle.

Therefore, the area of the triangle is $\frac{1}{2}$ of $18\,\text{cm}^2 = 9\,\text{cm}^2$

Key fact

Area of triangle = $\frac{1}{2}$ base $\times$ height

Exercise 5

1 Find the area of these triangles.

(a)

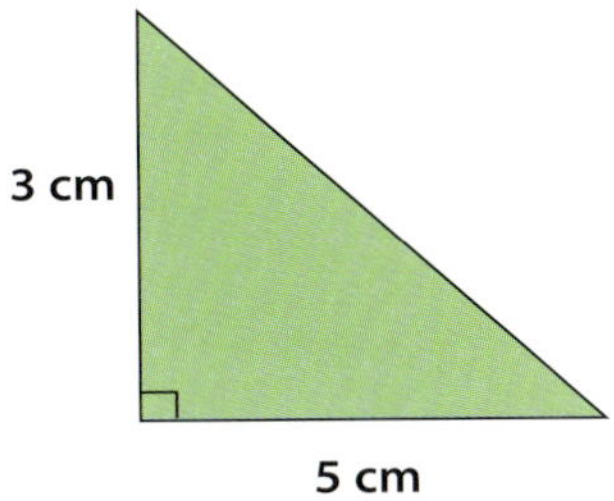

(b)

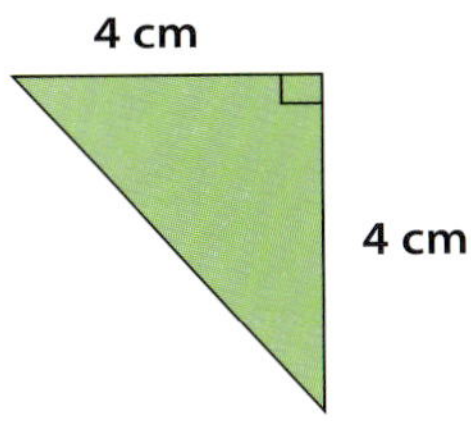

(c)

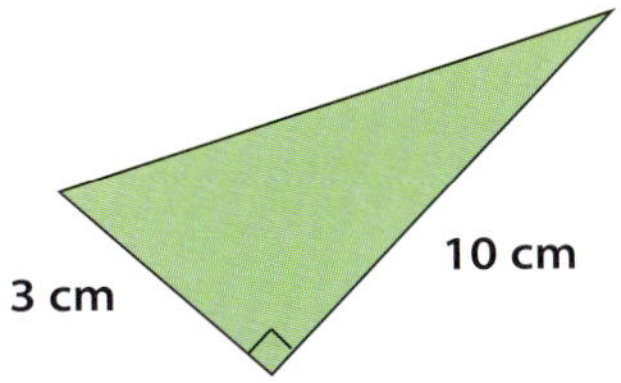

(d)

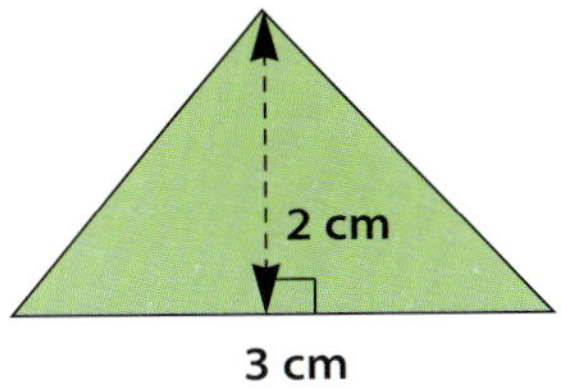

(e)

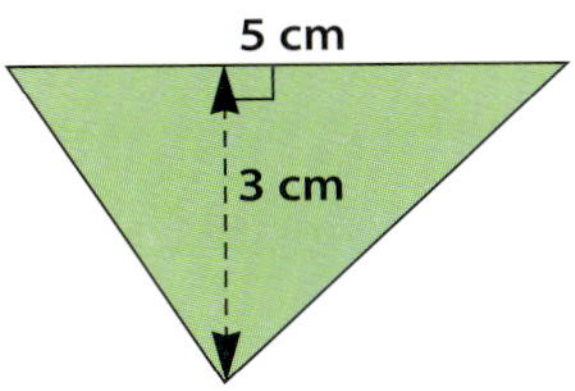

(f)

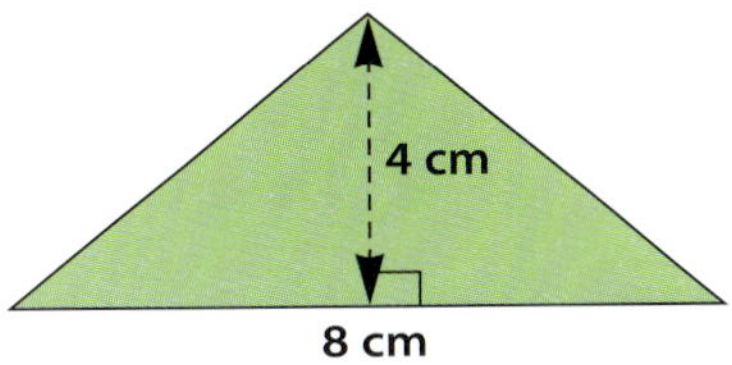

2 Find the area of the pattern coloured in red.

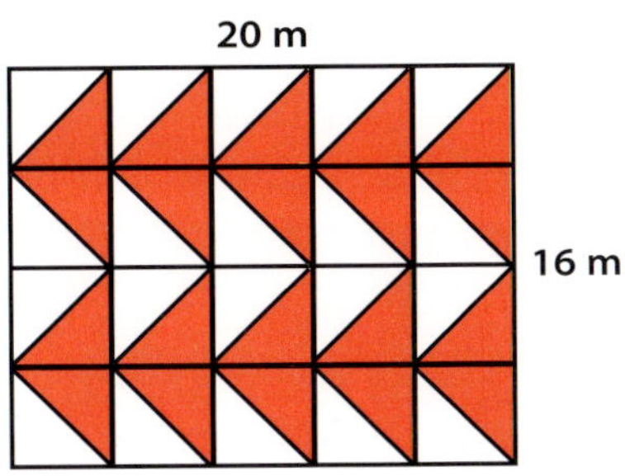

Assignment 6 Triangles from parallelograms

- Cut out a copy of this parallelogram.

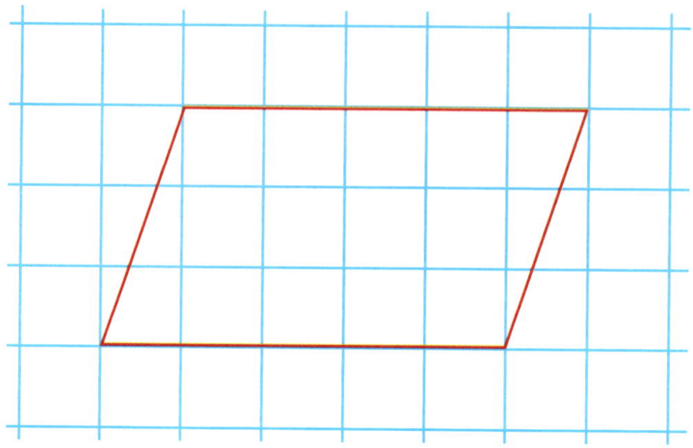

- What is the perpendicular height of the parallelogram?
- What is the area of the parallelogram?
- Draw in a diagonal and cut the parallelogram into two triangles.
- Place your two triangles on top of one another.

  They should be exactly the same.

  The area of one triangle is half the area of the parallelogram.
- The area of the parallelogram is

  $5\,\text{cm} \times 3\,\text{cm} = 15\,\text{cm}^2$
- The area of each triangle is

  $\frac{1}{2}$ of $15\,\text{cm}^2 = 7\frac{1}{2}\,\text{cm}^2$
- Stick your two triangles into your book to show that they form a parallelogram.

Exercise 6

1 Calculate the area of each of these shapes. Show all your working.

(a)

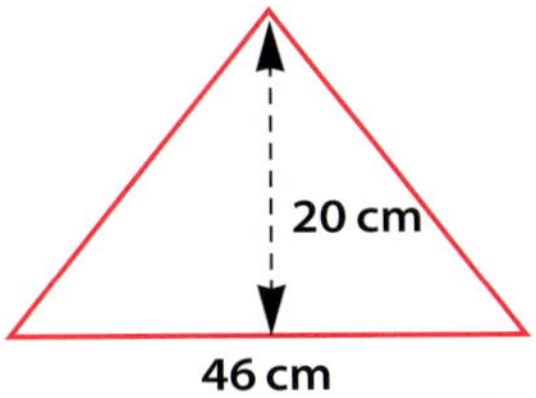

(b)

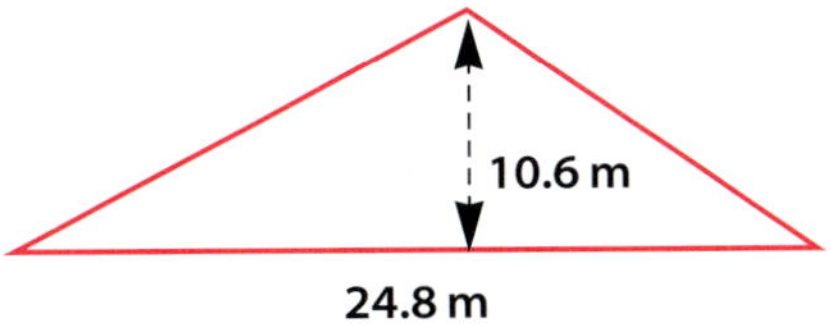

(c)

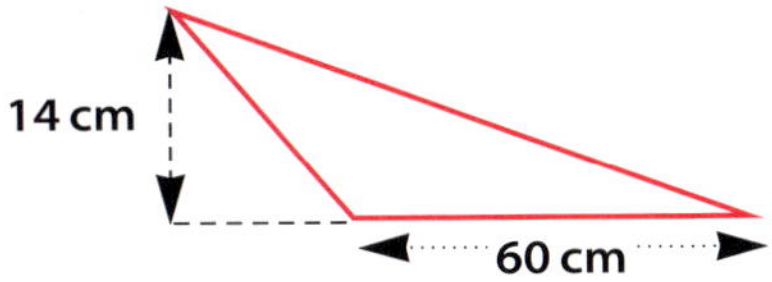

(d)

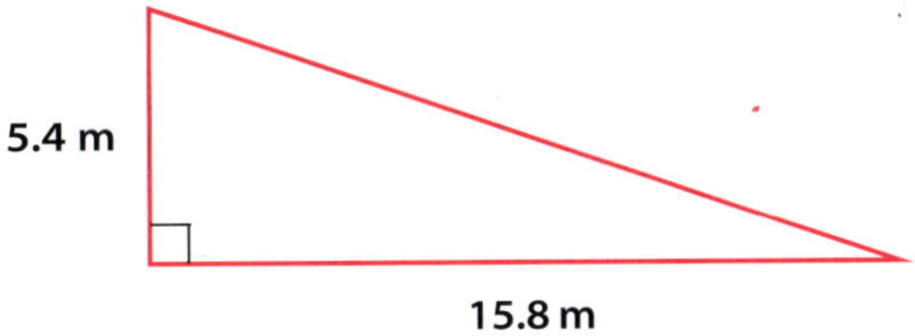

(e)

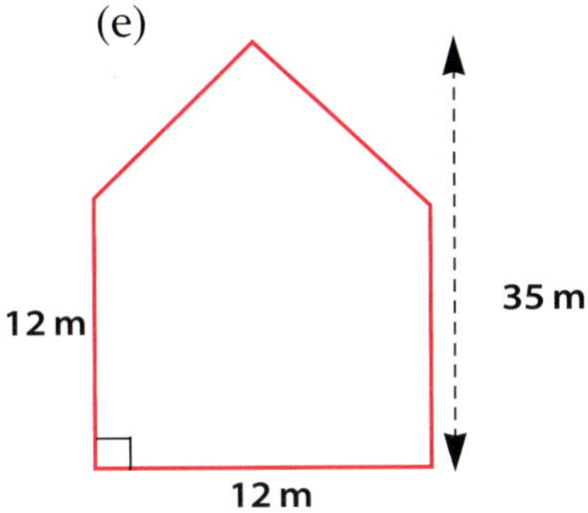

(f)

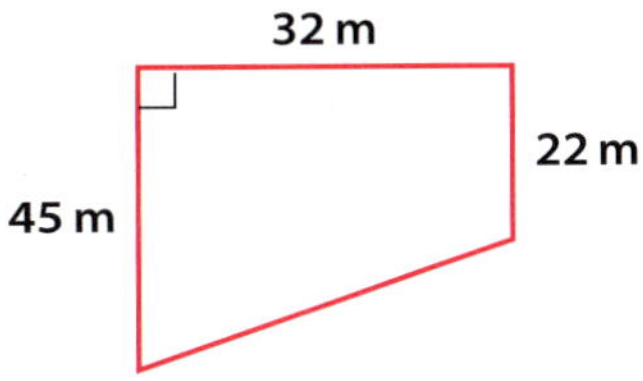

1 By dividing this shape into separate shapes, find its area. (All measurements are in centimetres.)

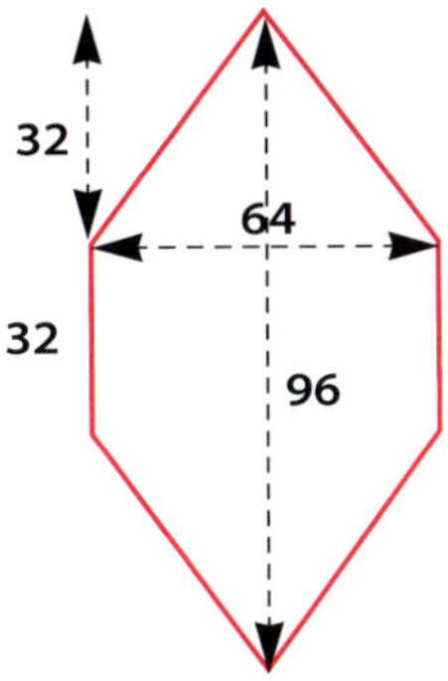

Assignment 7 Dotty shapes

This shape has 4 dots on the perimeter, no dots on the inside, and an area of 1 square.

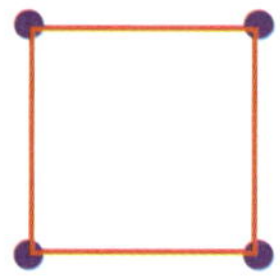

This shape has 3 dots and an area of $\frac{1}{2}$ square.

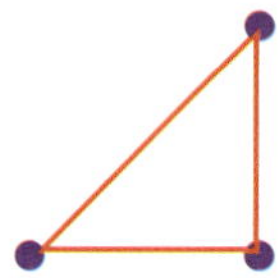

What about this shape?

Notice that none of the shapes drawn have dots on the inside.

- Draw some more shapes which have 4, 5, 6 and 7 dots on the outside but no dots on the inside.
- For each diagram, record the number of dots on the outside of the shape and the area of the shape.

  Record your results in a table.
- Write down what you notice.
- What will the area be for 15, 20 or n dots on the perimeter?
- What happens if there is 1 dot on the inside?
- What happens if there are 2, 3, 4 or more dots on the inside?

Trapezia is the plural of trapezium.

Assignment 8 Trapezia

- Draw two of these shapes on squared paper. Cut them out.

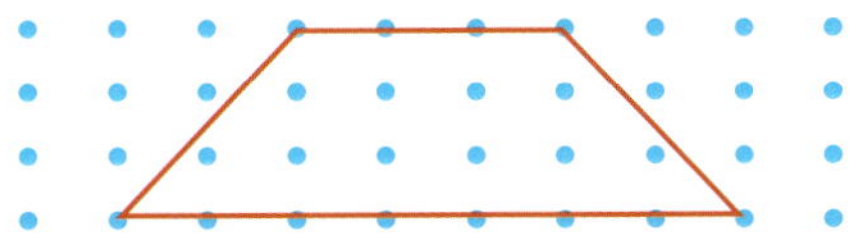

- Turn one shape over and place it to the right of the other to make one complete shape with no gaps.

  What shape have you made? What is the area of this new shape?

  What is the area of one trapezium?

- Now draw two more trapezia, both the same as each other, on plain paper.

  Turn one over and place them together as before to make one shape.

  What shape have you made? What is the area of this new shape?

  What is the area of one trapezium?

The area of a trapezium

A parallelogram can be formed using two copies of one trapezium.

The length of the parallelogram is the sum of the parallel sides of the trapezium.

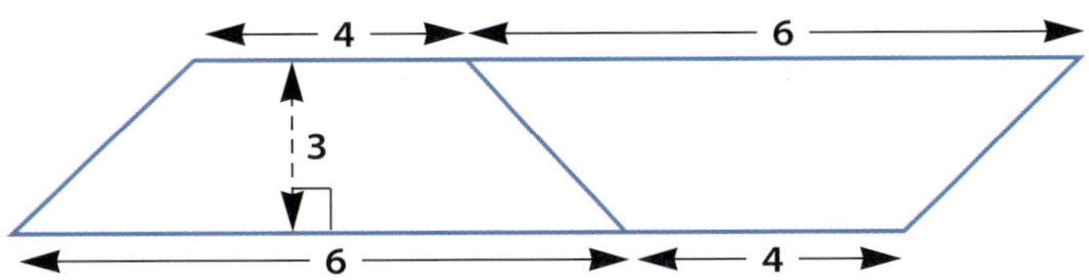

The height of the parallelogram is the same as the height of the trapezium.

The area of the parallelogram is calculated as length × height.
$(4\,\text{cm} + 6\,\text{cm}) \times 3\,\text{cm} = 30\,\text{cm}^2$

The area of each trapezium is half the area of the parallelogram.
$\frac{1}{2}$ of $30\,\text{cm}^2 = 15\,\text{cm}^2$

This is the rule for the area of a trapezium:

area of trapezium = $\frac{1}{2}$ sum of parallel sides × perpendicular height

$\frac{1}{2}(6\,\text{cm} + 4\,\text{cm}) \times 3\,\text{cm} = 15\,\text{cm}^2$

Key fact

area of trapezium = $\frac{1}{2}(a + b) \times h$ (where a and b are the parallel sides)

Key fact

area of kite = $\frac{1}{2}$ product of diagonals

Assignment 9 Kites

The stays (diagonals) of this kite are 12 cm and 20 cm.

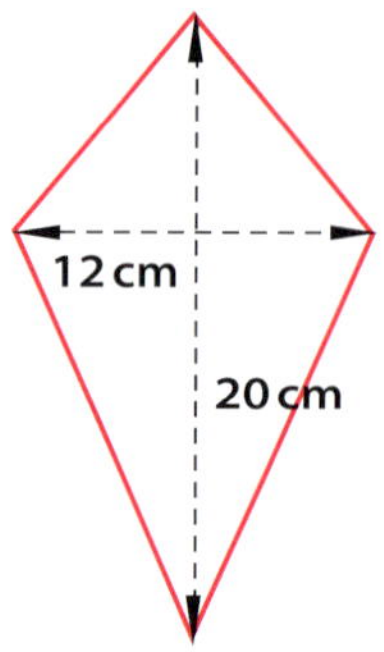

- By dividing the kite into two triangles, find its area.
- Do the same for a kite with diagonals 20 cm and 45 cm.
- What is the rule for the area of the kite?

Exercise 7

1 Calculate the area of each of these shapes.
(All measurements are in centimetres.)

(a)

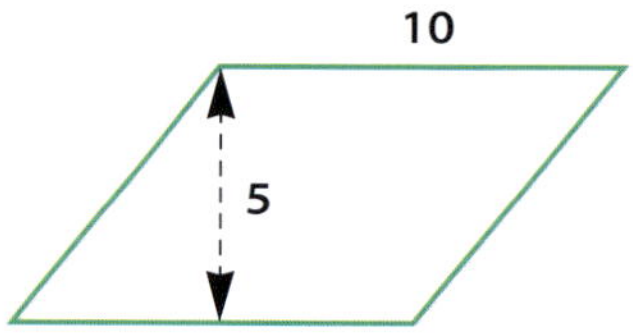

(b)

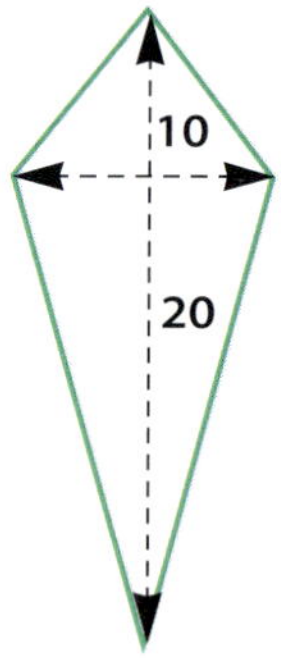

(c)

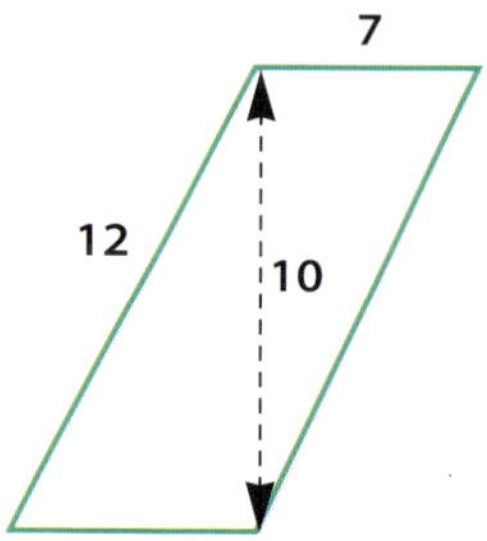

(d)

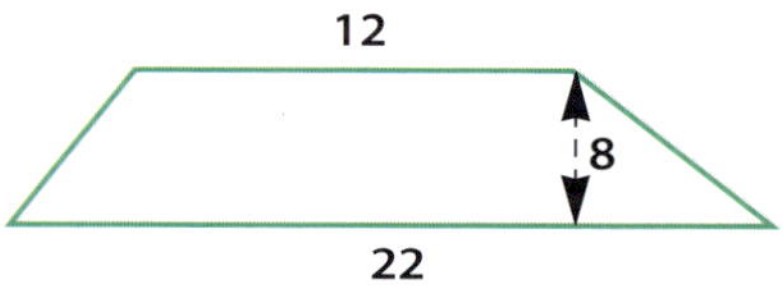

2 Calculate the area of each of these shapes.
(All measurements are in metres.)

(a)

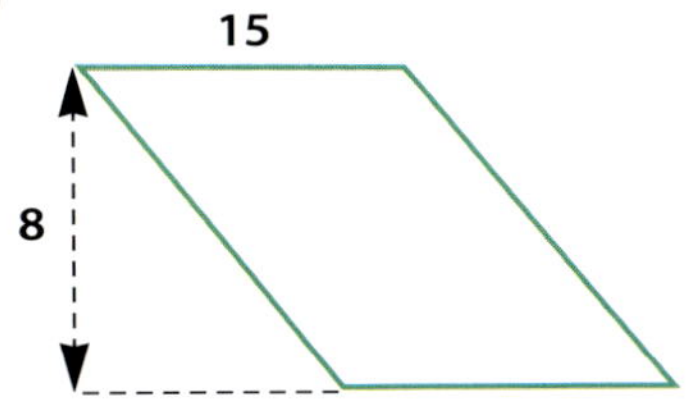

(b)

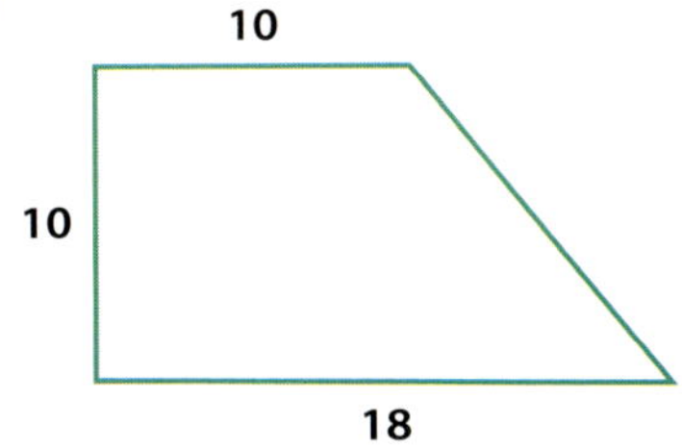

(c)

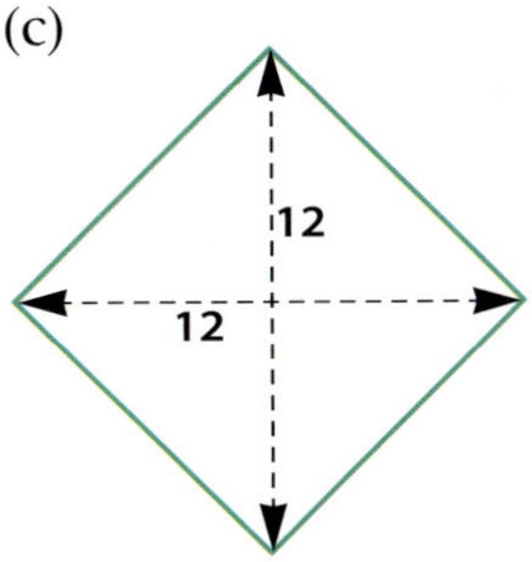

(d)

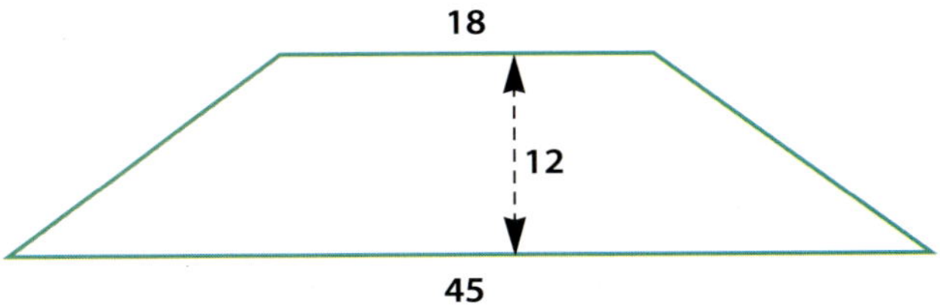

3 Calculate the area of the parts shaded in each of these diagrams.
(All measurements are in centimetres.)

(a)

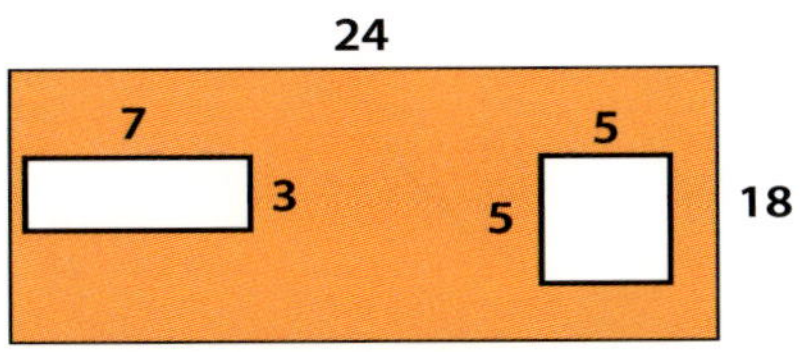

(b)

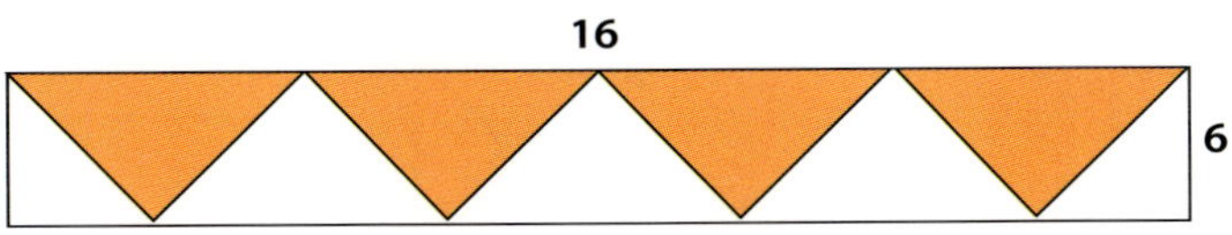

(c)

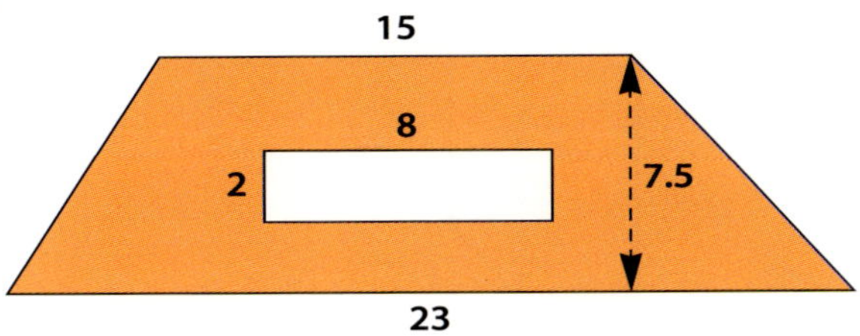

Volumes

Assignment 10 Volumes

You could work in pairs for this assignment.

- Make as many different cuboids as you can using 24 cubes. Draw them on isometric paper.
- How many different ones can you make?
- What is the volume of each of your cuboids?
- Write down the dimensions of each of your cuboids.
- Write down how to use the dimensions of a cuboid to find its volume.

Key fact

volume of cuboid = length × width × height

Exercise 8

1 Find the volume of each of these cuboids.
(All measurements are in centimetres.)

(a)

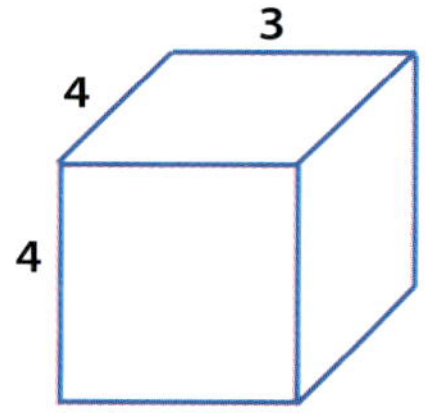

(b)

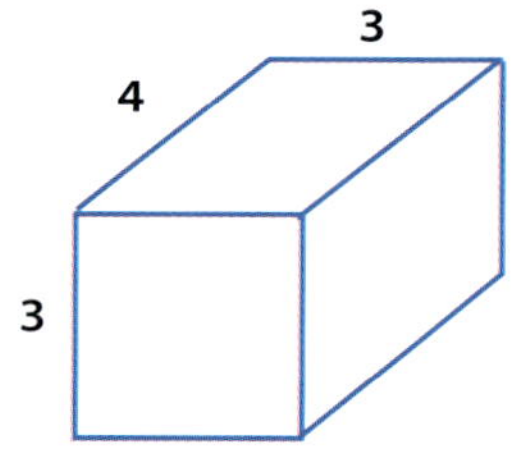

(c)

(d)

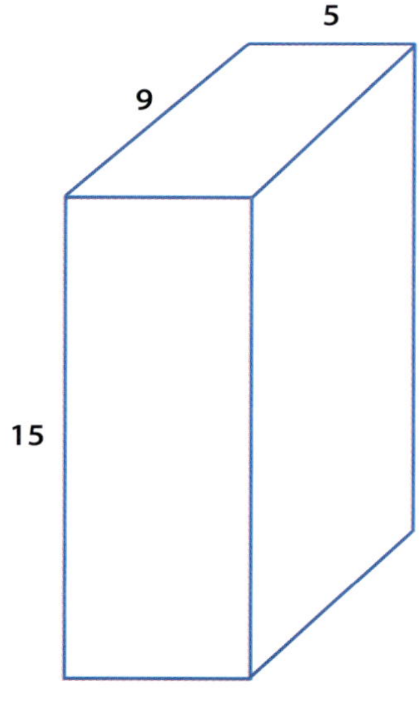

Assignment 11 Locker problem

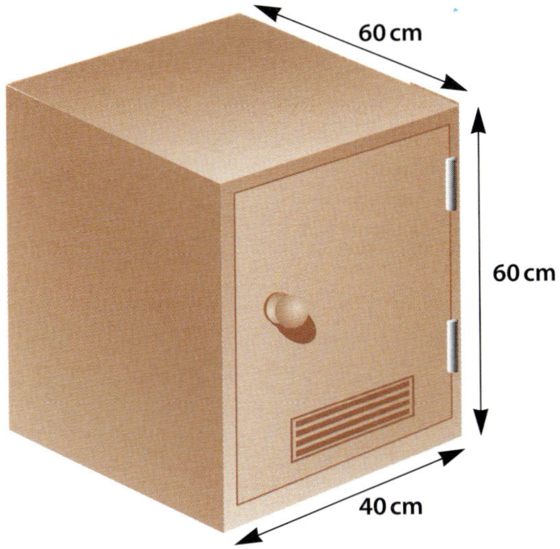

A company is purchasing a new set of lockers for the staff room.

Each locker is 60 cm × 40 cm × 60 cm.

There are 24 of these lockers and the management have to decide on the best way to arrange them.

Once they have decided on the arrangement, they will have to paint each face which is visible.

The cost of painting is 75p per face.

- How many different ways could you arrange the lockers?
- Draw these on paper and calculate the cost of painting each of your designs.
- Which arrangement would be the cheapest?

Splitting volumes

The cuboids in Exercise 8 were quite straightforward.

In the next exercise, the shapes are more complicated.

They are built using two or more separate cuboids.

As with area, you sometimes have to split the shapes up to calculate volumes.
Do this for the shapes in Exercise 9.

Exercise 9

1 Calculate the volume of each of these shapes.
(All measurements are in centimetres.)
Show your working.

(a)

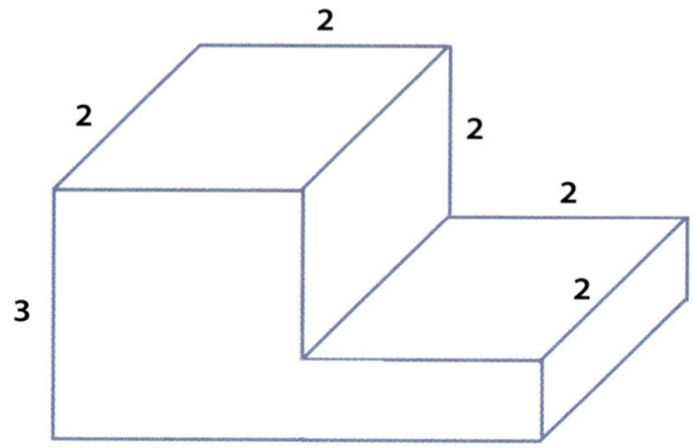

(b)

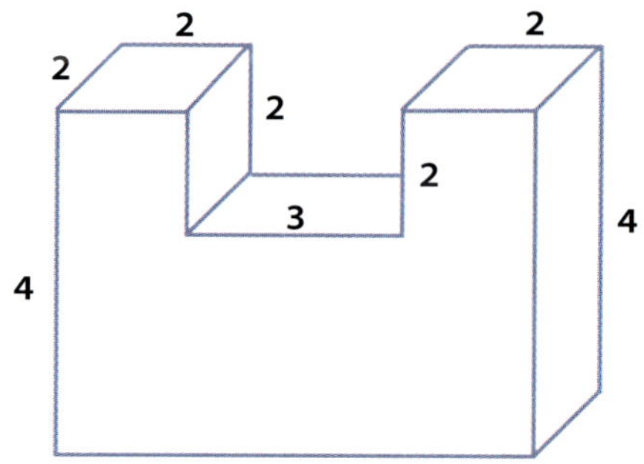

(c)

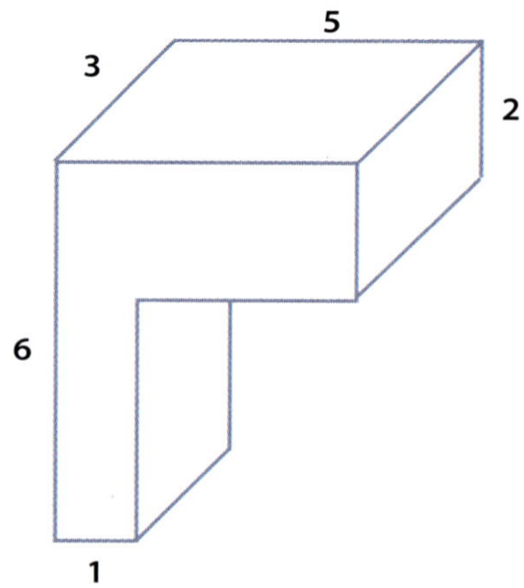

Prisms

A prism has a uniform cross-section.

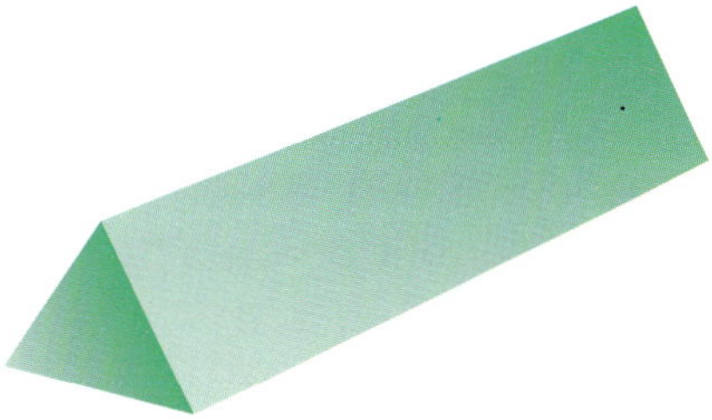

Each slice through is the same.

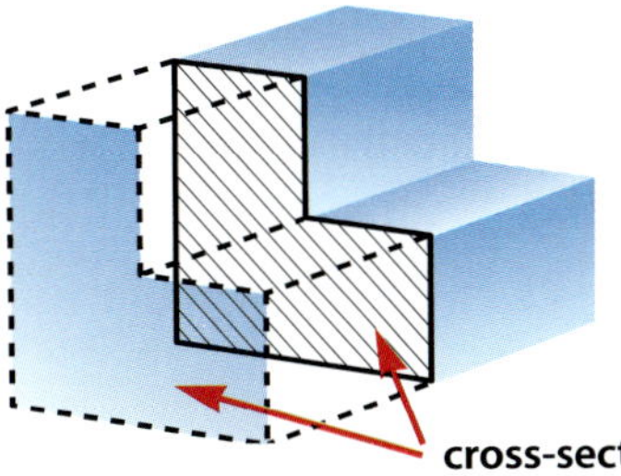

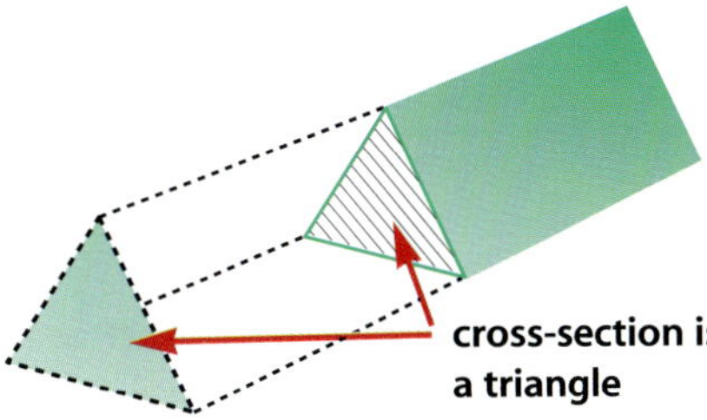

Exercise 10

1 Which of these shapes is a prism?

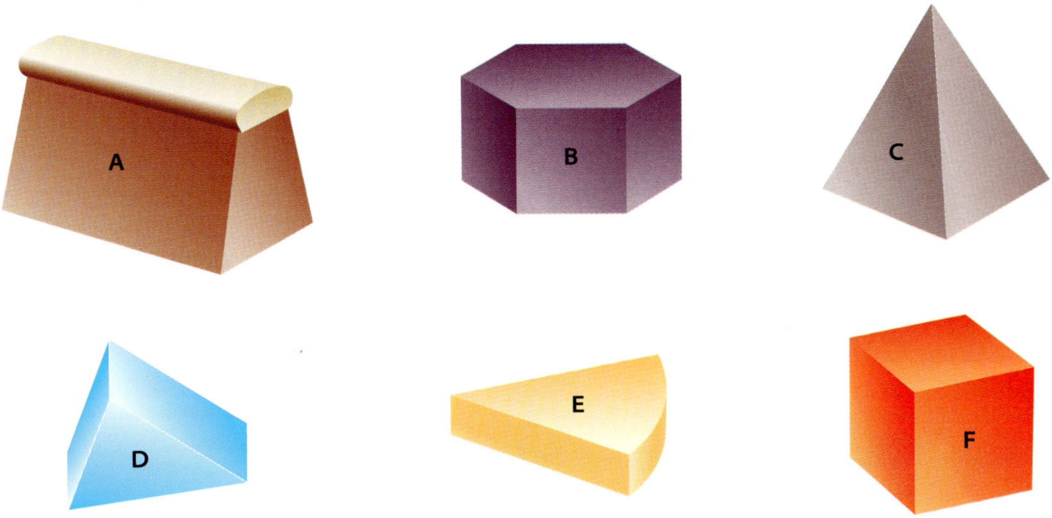

Calculating the volume of a prism

The volume of a prism is made up of many
slices of the same shape.

If you can find the area of one slice, multiply this by the length to find the volume.

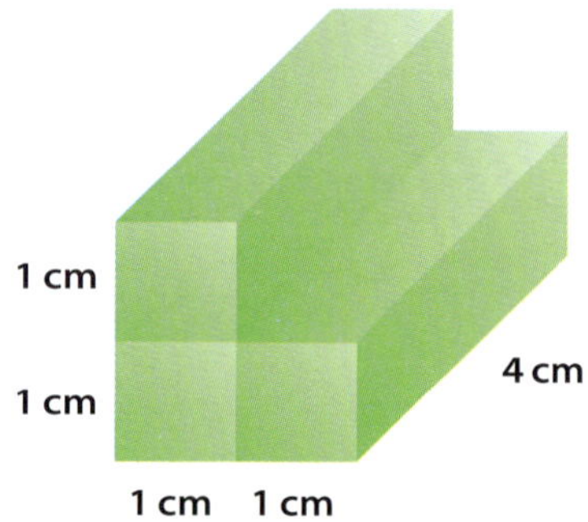

The cross-section at the end of this prism has area 3 square units.

It is 4 units long, so the volume is 12 cubic units.

For a triangular prism, the cross-section is a triangle.

Volume of prism = area of cross-section × length

For a triangular prism, this is

area of triangular end × length

Exercise 11

Key fact
Volume of prism = area of cross-section × length

1 Calculate the volume of each of these prisms.

(a)

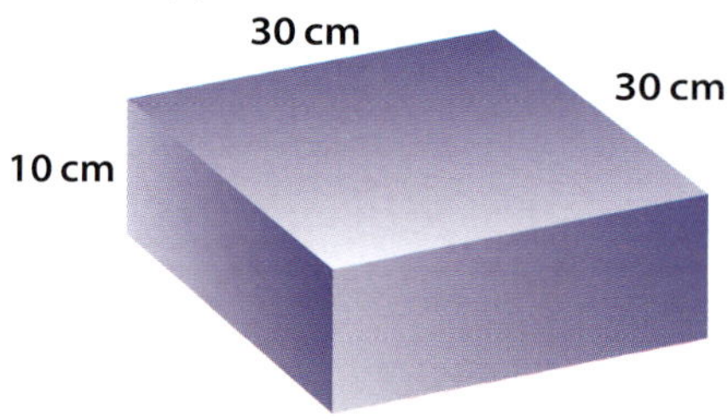

(b)

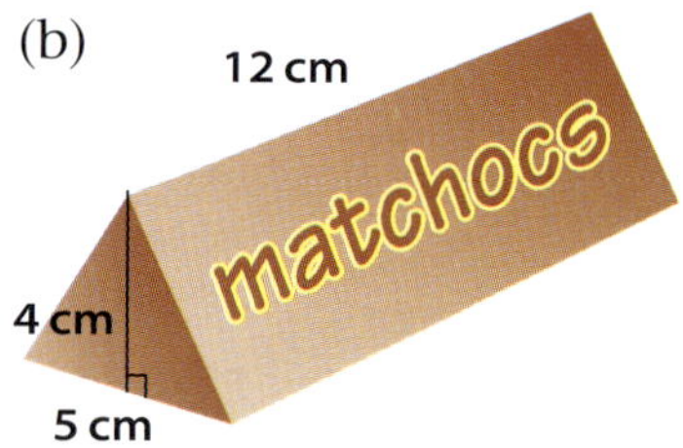

(c)

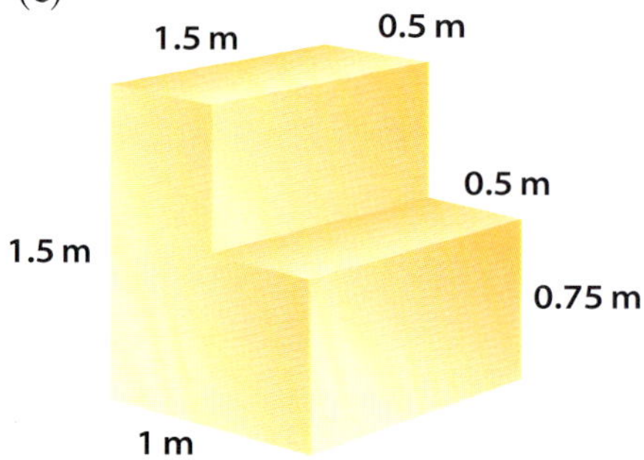

(d)

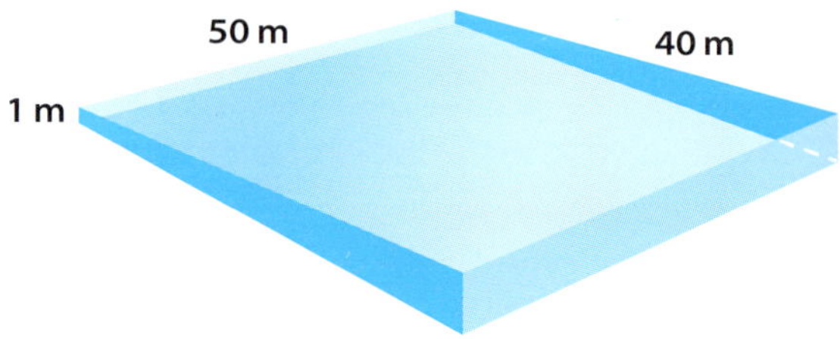

Review Exercise

1 Calculate the area of each of these shapes.

(a)

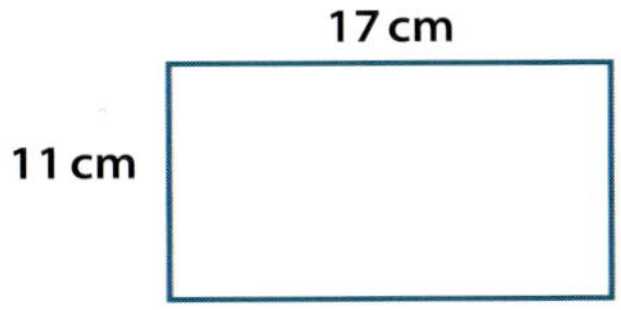

(b)

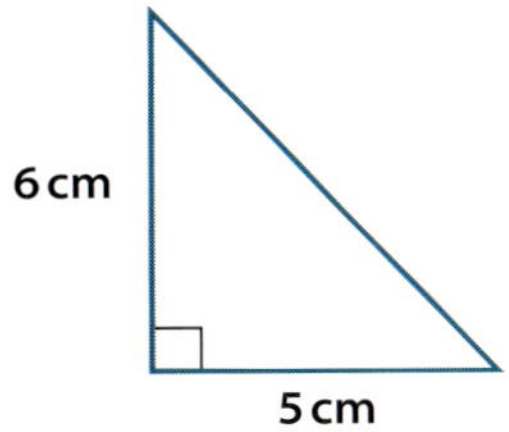

(c)

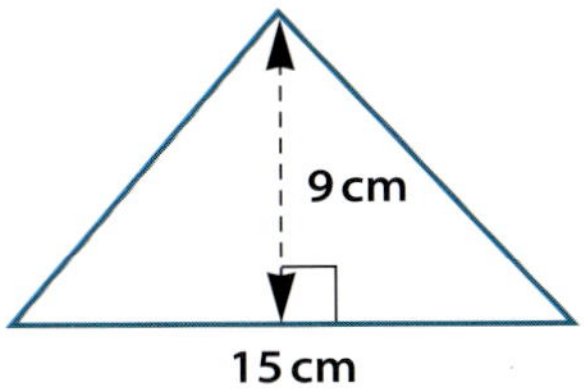

(d)

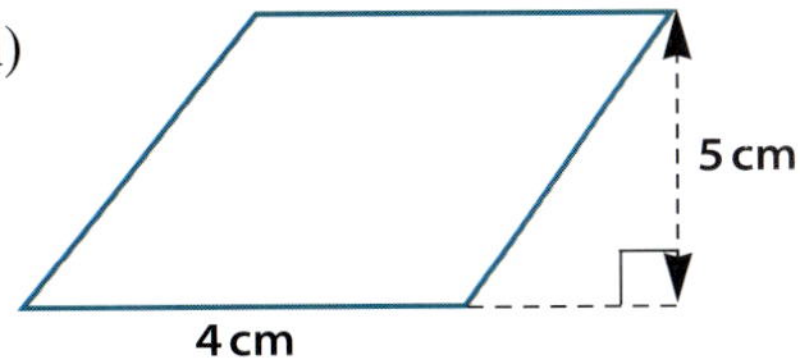

2 Find the area of each of these letter shapes.
(All measurements are in centimetres.)

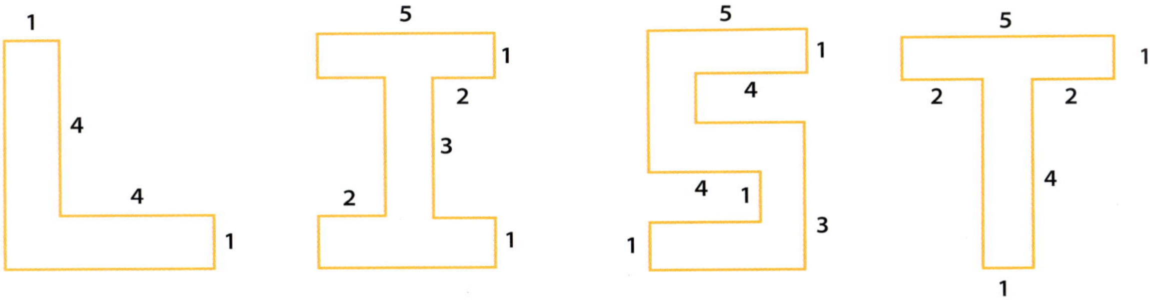

3 This picture shows a garden with a path around it.

The garden is 16 m × 11 m and the outside is 20 m × 15 m.

What is the area of the path?

4 Calculate the volume of each of these solids.

(a)

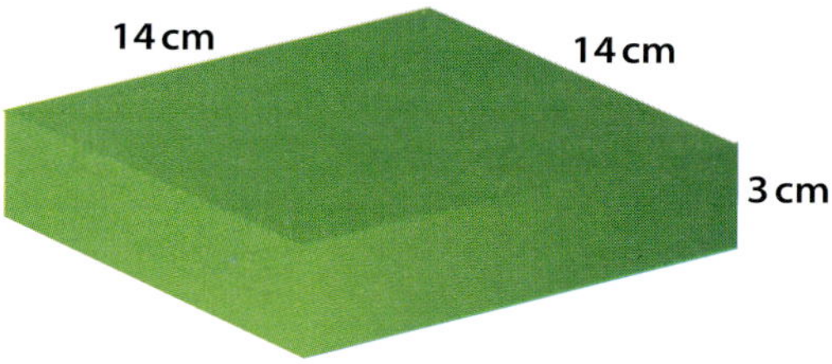

(b)

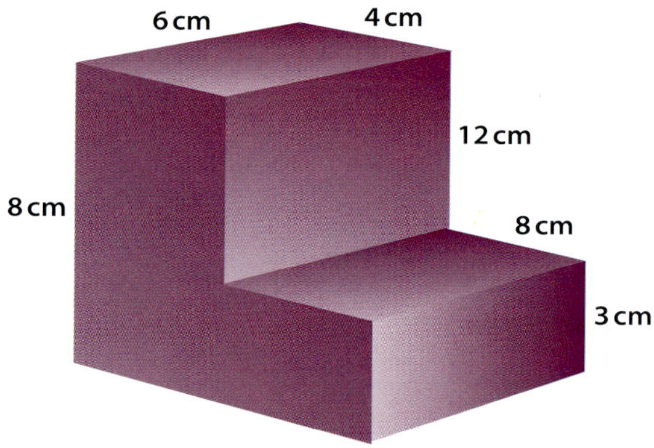

(c)

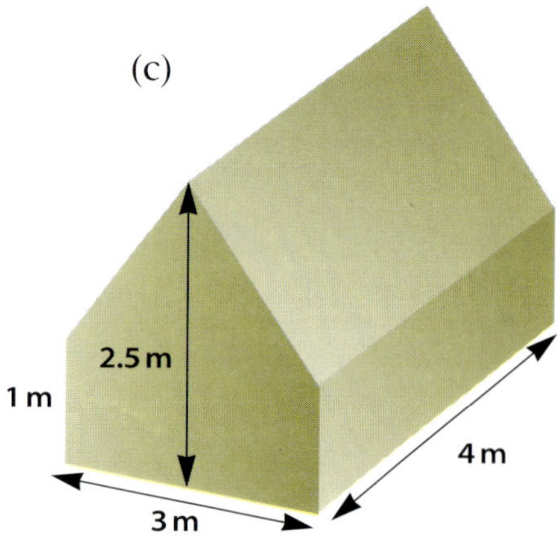

Extending probability

In this chapter you will learn:

- → **how to list outcomes for two events**
- → **how to create probability / sample space**
- → **the sum of probability outcomes**
- → **how to display probability**

Starting points

Before starting this chapter you will need to be able to:

- work with simple fractions
- organise and record results
- use a probability scale from 0 to 1.

Exercise 1

1 From this list of fractions, select all the equivalent pairs you can find.

$\frac{3}{6}$ $\frac{3}{12}$ $\frac{1}{2}$ $\frac{6}{18}$ $\frac{3}{36}$ $\frac{1}{4}$

$\frac{3}{8}$ $\frac{10}{15}$ $\frac{3}{33}$ $\frac{2}{3}$ $\frac{1}{12}$

2 Copy and complete the following.

(a) $\frac{2}{5} + \frac{1}{5}$ (b) $\frac{1}{6} + \frac{5}{6}$

(c) $\frac{1}{7} + \frac{2}{7} + \frac{3}{7}$ (d) $\frac{1}{3} + \frac{5}{12} + \frac{1}{12}$

(e) $\frac{1}{3} + \frac{2}{5}$ (f) $\frac{1}{4} + \frac{1}{2}$

3 A vending machine gives three types of hot drink:

Coffee Tea Chocolate

Each drink costs the same. You have enough money to buy only two drinks.

Write down all the possible outcomes.

4 Make a probability scale by drawing a line 10 cm long. Mark on it the points 0 and 1.

On this probability scale, mark the approximate position of probability of:

(a) getting a head when you spin a fair coin

(b) throwing a six on a normal dice

(c) selecting a diamond card from an ordinary pack of playing cards.

5 Small tiles with letters on them were used to make the word Birmingham.

B I R M I N G H A M

The tiles were put into an envelope and one was taken out, without looking.

Write down the probability that the letter chosen was:

(a) a letter 'G' (b) a letter 'M'

(c) any vowel (d) any consonant

> **The probability of choosing the letter I is written p(I).**
> **$p(I) = \frac{2}{10} = \frac{1}{5}$**

Combined outcomes

Assignment 1 River race

Twelve boats are entered for a river race.

The boats all begin on the start line and move one square forward each time the total of the two dice equals their number.
The winner is the first boat to complete the course.

Here is a race in progress.

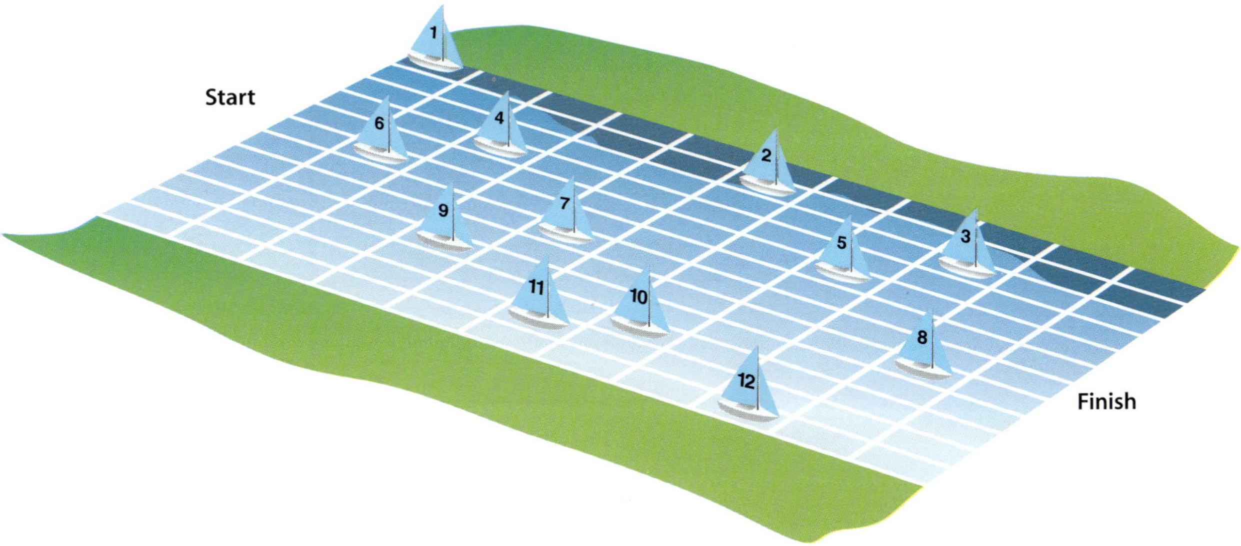

You will need two dice.

- Roll two dice to race the boats.
  On a copy of the race grid, record their positions during the race.
- Repeat this task, recording the results of each throw until one boat wins.

Try to predict, giving your reasons:

- which boat will win the next race
- which boat will *not* win the race
- which boats are *less likely* to win the race
- which boats are *most* likely to win the race
- a possible finishing order for the twelve boats.

Exercise 2

1 Two dice are thrown and their scores added together. On a copy of this table, record the totals that can be obtained. (It has been started for you.)

		1st dice					
	+	1	2	3	4	5	6
2nd dice	1	2	3				
	2						
	3						
	4						
	5						
	6						

Use your table to answer these questions.

(a) How many ways can the two dice fall?

(b) List the number of different totals, and how many ways each total can be made.

(c) Write down the probability of scoring:

(i) 3 (ii) 7

(iii) 10 (iv) 1

2 Using the table from Question 1 state the probability of throwing:

(a) a double

(b) a score greater than 7

(c) a score less than 5

(d) at least one 6.

A 'double' is when the two dice each show the same number.

3 Draw a table to show all the outcomes from spinning two 10p coins.

(a) State the probability of getting two heads.

(b) State the probability of getting two tails.

(c) State the probability of getting a double.

(d) State the probability of getting a head and a tail.

> **A 'double' is two heads or two tails.**

4 A drawer contains four different coloured tops and two different coloured trousers.

You take a top and a pair of trousers from the drawer without looking.

Draw a table to show all the possible outcomes.

Use your table to state the probability that:

(a) a pair of blue items are chosen

(b) a pair of red items are chosen

(c) a pair of the same colour are chosen

(d) a pair of odd items are chosen.

Assignment 2 Plus Bingo

For this game of Bingo, you need to work in a group.

Each person needs to draw a 3 × 4 grid like this to make a game card.

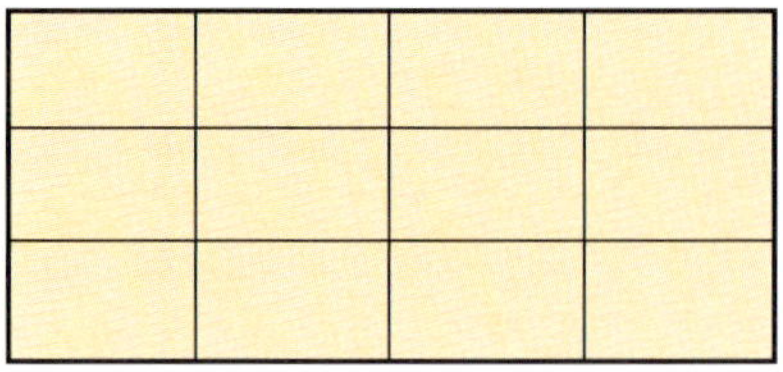

- First, prepare your game card.

  During the game you are going to take it in turns to roll two dice, and anyone who has the sum of the two numbers on the dice on their game card will cross out that number.

  The winner will be the first person to cross out all their numbers.

  You are allowed to have the same number appearing on your card more than once, but you can only cross out one square for each throw of the dice.

  Decide what numbers to use, and write a number into each space on your game card.

- Now, play Bingo, taking it in turns to roll the two dice.
  Cross out the sum of the two numbers if it appears on your card.
  Continue until one player wins.
- Play the game several times, using a fresh game card each time.
- Discuss in your group which are the best numbers to put on to the card.
- As a group, design a card to use in a game with the rest of the class.

Sum means the result of adding.

Choose numbers from 2 to 12.

Assignment 3 Product Bingo

- For this game of Bingo, cross out the product of the two numbers on the dice.
- Design a game card for this game.
- Test it by playing the game with your group.

Product means the result of multiplying.

Assignment 4 Difference Bingo

- For this game of Bingo, cross out the difference between the numbers on the dice.
- Design a game card for this game.
- Test it by playing the game with your group.

Key fact

A possibility space is a grid showing all possible outcomes.

Possibility spaces

In Exercise 2, you met a method for recording all the possible outcomes of a situation.

A grid showing all the outcomes is called a **possibility space**.

Here is the grid used for Questions 1 and 2 in Exercise 2.

1st dice

2nd dice

+	1	2	3	4	5	6
1						
2						
3						
4						
5						
6						

Here are two spinners. Each spinner is divided into four sections.

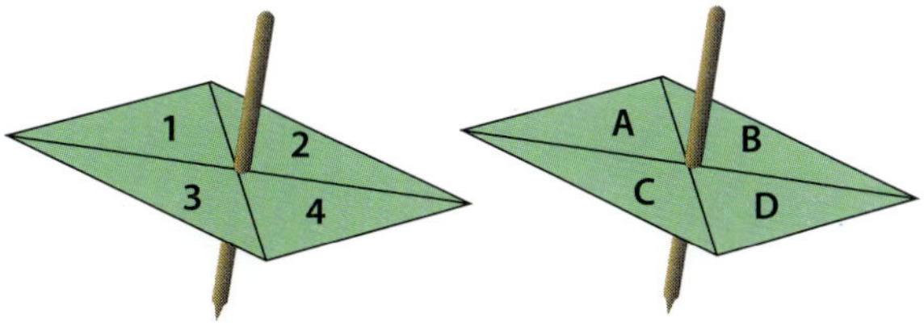

One spinner is numbered 1 to 4; the other is lettered A to D.

Some of the possible outcomes are shown on this possibility space.

	1	2	3	4
A				
B			3B	
C				
D		2D		

A possibility space is also called a sample space.

Exercise 3

1 (a) Make a copy of the possibility space for the two spinners.

Complete all the possible outcomes.

(b) How many different results are there?

(c) How many of the results include the number 1?

(d) What is the probability of getting the number 1 with these spinners?

(e) How many of the results include the letter B?

(f) What is the probability of getting the letter B with these spinners?

(g) What is the probability of getting C2?

2 A coin and a dice are thrown.

(a) Copy this grid and complete the possibility space.

		Dice					
		1	2	3	4	5	6
Coin	H						
	T						

(b) What is the probability of getting a head with a number greater than 4?

3 A canteen offers a drink and a bag of crisps at break time.

(a) Draw a possibility space to show all the possible break-time combinations.

(b) How many combinations include a 'cola' drink?

(c) What is the probability of including a packet of salt'n'vinegar crisps?

Assignment 5 Experimental work

Key fact

Experimental probability is calculated from the results of experiments.

- Working in pairs or on your own, take two ordinary dice.

  Roll the dice together and add the scores. Record the result.
- Repeat the activity 20 times.
- From your own experimental results, find the probability of getting each score.
- Enter your results on to the class recording sheet or a database.

  Use the results of the whole class to find the probability of getting each score.

  Add all the probabilities from the whole class's results together, and write down what you notice.
- Compare the probabilities of obtaining each of these scores with the probabilities of obtaining each of the scores in your experiment. Write down what you notice.

Key fact

Theoretical probability is calculated from a possibility space.

- Copy and complete this possibility space for throwing two dice to show all possible outcomes, using your results from Question 1 in Exercise 2.

1st dice

2nd dice

+	1	2	3	4	5	6
1						
2						
3						
4						
5						
6						

  Use this possibilty space to calculate the probability of getting each result.

  Add all these probabilities together and write down what you notice.
- Compare the probabilities you obtained in the experiment with those from the possibility space. Write down what you notice.

Assignment 6 Experimental and theoretical probabilities

In groups of two or three, carry out at least one of these activities.

Activity 1

Drawing two counters from a bag one at a time and returning each counter to the bag

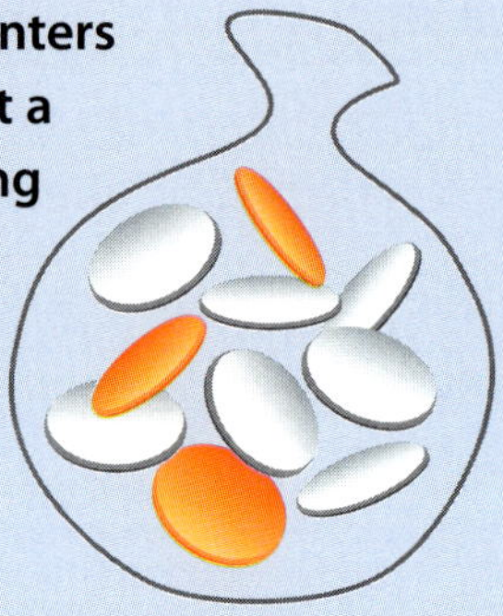

win is 2 reds

Activity 2

The totals of two different dice

win is a score of ten

Activity 3

The combination of a coin and a dice

win is an even number with a head

In each case:

- decide what is the winning outcome and record your decision
- decide how you are going to record your results
- repeat the activity a number of times and record your results
- calculate your experimental probabilities for the events occurring
- construct possibility spaces and calculate your theoretical probabilities
- compare your results.

Key fact
The sum of the probabilities of the outcomes always equals one.

Checking probabilities

When you spin a coin, there are two equally likely outcomes.

$p(\text{head}) = \frac{1}{2} \quad p(\text{tail}) = \frac{1}{2}$

$p(\text{head or tail}) = \frac{1}{2} + \frac{1}{2} = 1$

When you throw a dice, there are six equally likely outcomes.

$p(1) = p(2) = p(3) = p(4) = p(5) = p(6) = \frac{1}{6}$

$p(\text{throwing 1 or 2 or 3 or 4 or 5 or 6}) = \frac{1}{6} + \frac{1}{6} + \frac{1}{6} + \frac{1}{6} + \frac{1}{6} + \frac{1}{6} = 1$

Exercise 4

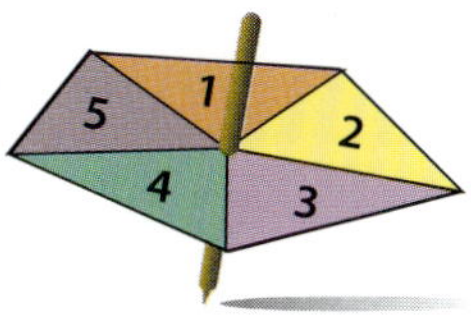

1 Two spinners are used in a game.

(a) Copy and complete this possibility space.

	1	2	3	4	5
red					
black					

(b) To win you need to get a red and an even number.
On the possibility space, shade in the winning results.

(c) What is the probability of winning?

(d) What is the probability of losing?

(e) Add your answers from (c) and (d) together and write down what you notice about the total.

$\frac{10}{10}$ is the same as 1.

(f) What is the probability of getting a black with any number?

Explain your answer.

2 The probability of winning another activity is $\frac{1}{4}$.

What is the probability of losing?

3 The probability that it will snow on the 25th December is $\frac{1}{100}$.

What is the probability that it will *not* snow?

Assignment 7 Routes

This is a diagram of a game you may have seen.

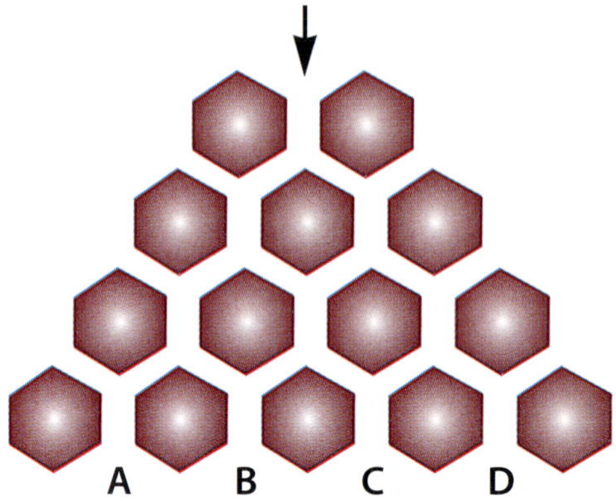

A ball is dropped into the top and rolls down the channels.

- Do you think the ball is more likely to come out of exit A or B or C or D?

  Write down your answer, giving your reasons.

- Here is a way to see if you were right.

  It is not necessary to draw the diagram in so much detail.

  It could be drawn like this.

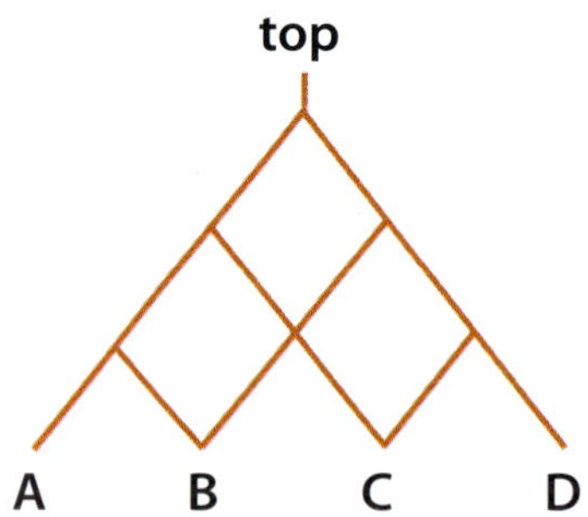

When the ball comes to a junction, it has to go either left or right.

The probability of it going left (L) is $\frac{1}{2}$.

The probability of it going right (R) is also $\frac{1}{2}$.

- This diagram shows how the ball could reach some of the junctions.

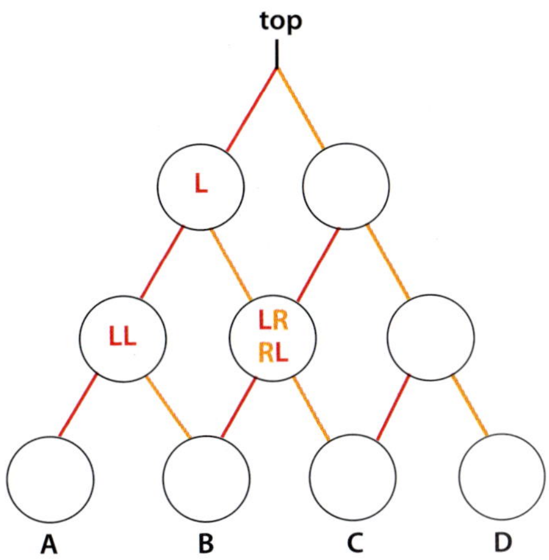

- Copy the diagram and show all the ways that the ball could reach each junction.
- Using the results from your previous diagram to help you, copy this diagram and fill in the probability fraction for each exit.

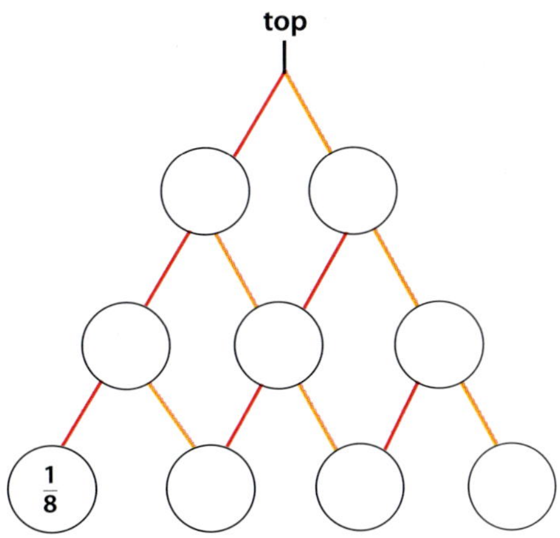

- Write down the sum of the four fractions.

  Write a comment about this answer.

  For instance, is it what you expected?

Review Exercise

1 This Bingo game involves rolling two dice and adding the scores obtained.

Look at each of these cards for the Bingo game.

(a)

1	2	3	4
5	6	7	8
9	10	11	12

(b)

7	7	7	7
7	6	6	6
6	5	5	5

(c)

3	3	4	4
5	5	6	6
7	7	8	8

(d)

7	7	7	7
6	6	6	6
5	5	5	5

(e)

5	6	6	6
7	7	7	7
8	8	8	9

(f)

2	3	4	5
6	7	7	8
9	10	11	12

Write down which ones you would choose to use and which ones you would not choose to use.

Give reasons for your decisions.

2 Draw a possibility space to show all the outcomes obtained from these spinners.

A win is achieved by getting the same colour on both spinners.

What is the probability of winning?

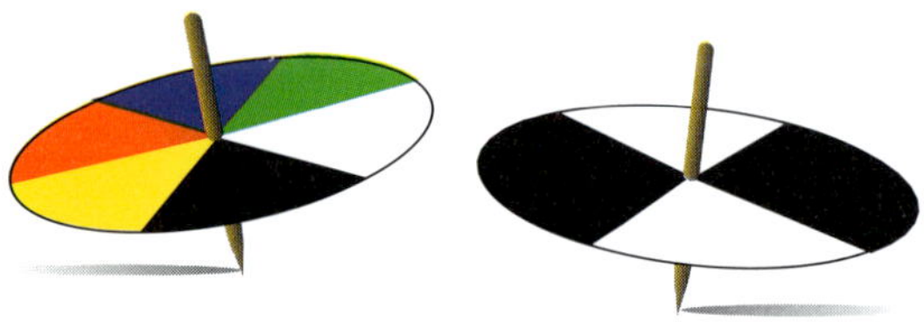

3 In an experiment, two dice are thrown 360 times and the scores added. The results are recorded on this bar chart.

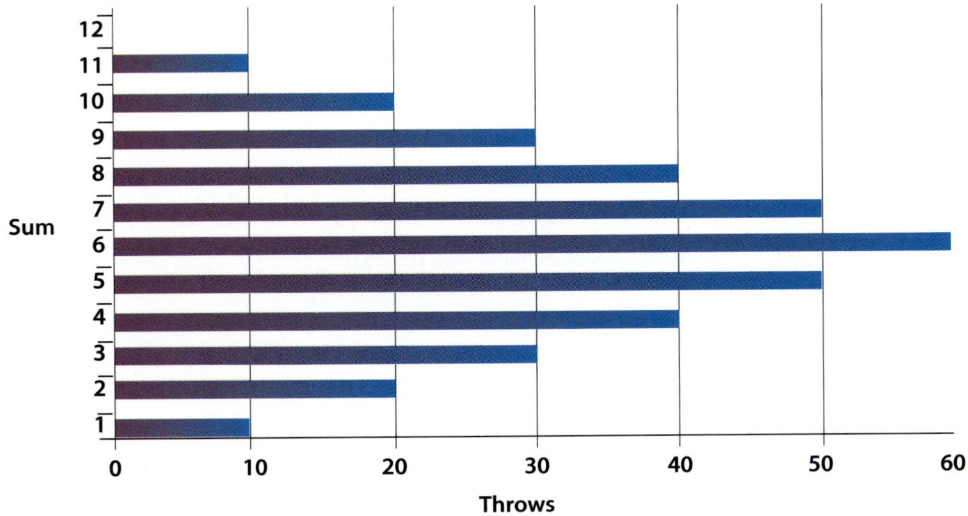

You suspect that one of the dice is not marked with the numbers 1 to 6.

Use the information from the results to help you to decide whether your suspicions are correct.

Explain how you arrive at your conclusions.

4 Three coins are spun. You need two heads and a tail to win.

(a) Design a possibility space for this activity to show all the possible outcomes.

(b) What is the probability of winning?

5 You have three identical tin cans with no labels.

One contains cat food, one contains peaches and the third contains rice pudding.

(a) What is the probability of you opening only one tin and it containing peaches?

(b) What is the probability of you opening the tin that does *not* contain peaches?

Quadrilaterals and other polygons

In this chapter you will learn:

- → how to identify different quadrilaterals from their properties
- → how different quadrilaterals are related
- → how to solve problems using the properties of polygons

Starting points

Before starting this chapter you will need to remember

- the meaning of the terms acute, obtuse and reflex
- the names of the different quadrilaterals and polygons
- angle properties of polygons.

Exercise 1

1 Copy and complete the table to name the angles in this shape.

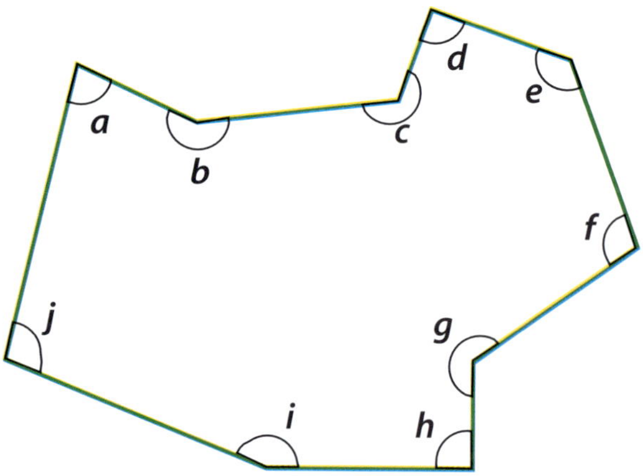

	acute	obtuse	reflex	right angle
a				
b				
c				
d				
e				
f				
g				
h				
i				
j				

2 Write down which of these shapes are rectangles.

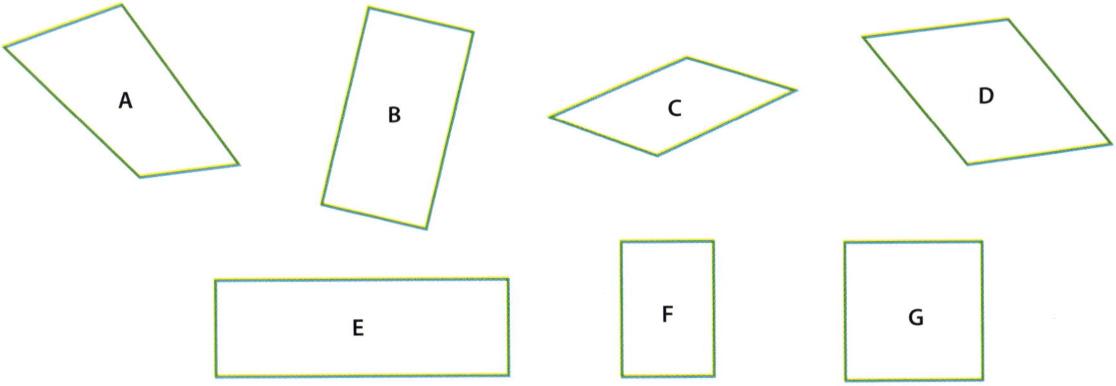

3 Write down which of these shapes are squares.

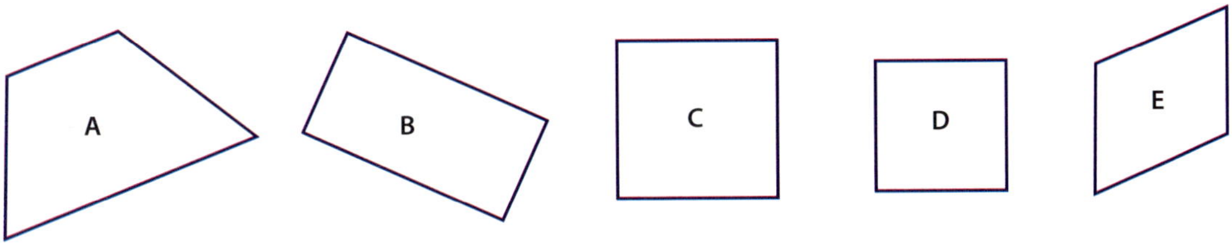

4 Write down which of these shapes are parallelograms.

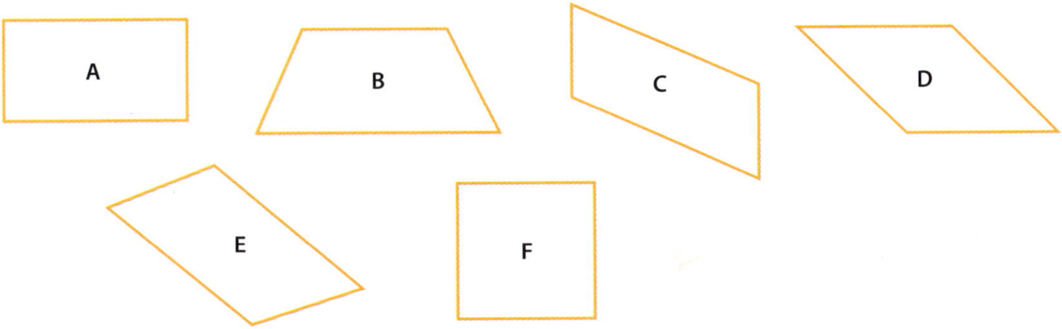

5 Write down the special name given to each of these quadrilaterals.

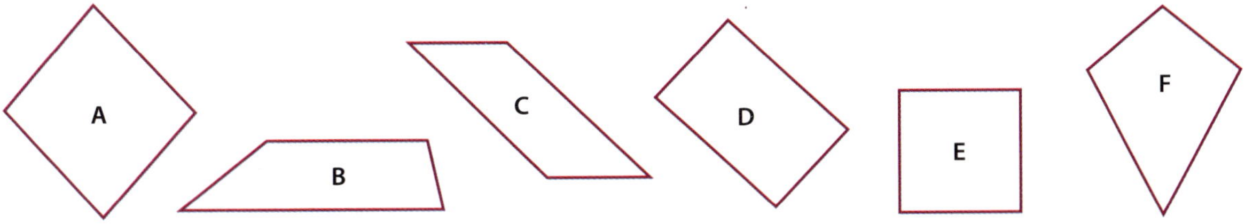

6 Look at these shapes.

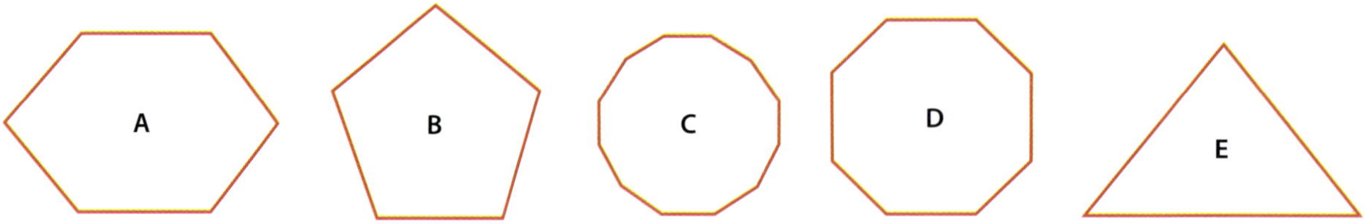

(i) Write down the name of each of these shapes.

(ii) Write down which of these shapes are 'regular'.

(iii) Write down exactly how you decide whether a shape is regular.

7 Write down the number of sides and the size of the angles inside each of these regular polygons.

(a) Pentagon

(b) Hexagon

(c) Octagon

(d) Decagon

(e) Dodecagon

Properties of quadrilaterals

Exercise 2

1 Write down exactly how you decide whether a shape is a rectangle.

2 Write down exactly how you decide whether a shape is a square.

3 Write down exactly how you decide whether a shape is a parallelogram.

4 A quadrilateral has four equal angles.
Explain why these must be four right angles.

5 Look at these shapes. (They have not been drawn accurately.)

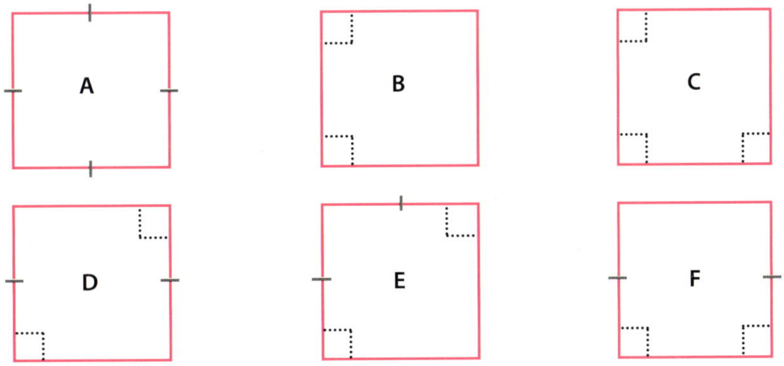

The short lines show equal lengths.

For each shape:

(a) write down whether the shape *must* be a square

(b) explain how you came to your decision.

6 Look at these shapes. (They have not been drawn accurately.)

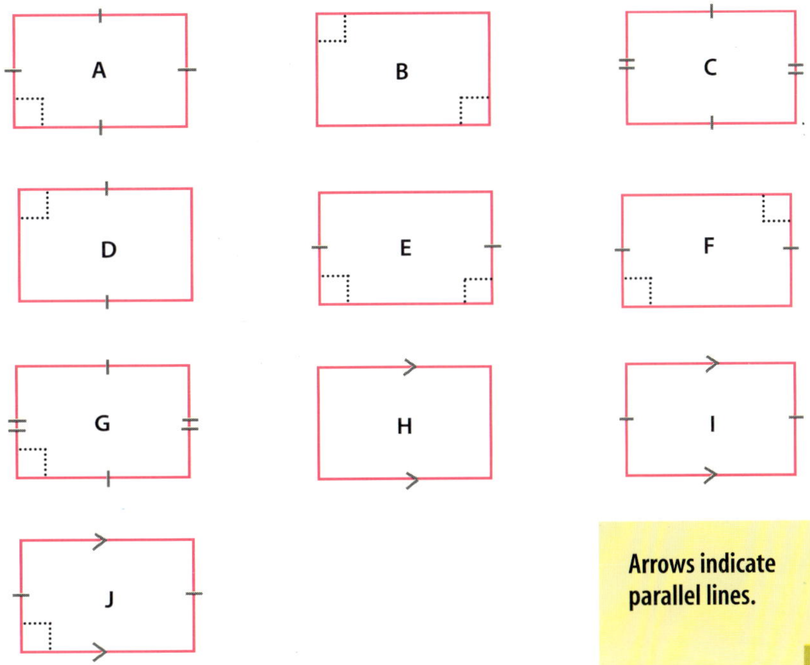

Arrows indicate parallel lines.

For each shape:

(a) write down whether the shape *must* be a rectangle

(b) explain how you came to your decision.

7 Look at these shapes. (They have not been drawn accurately.)

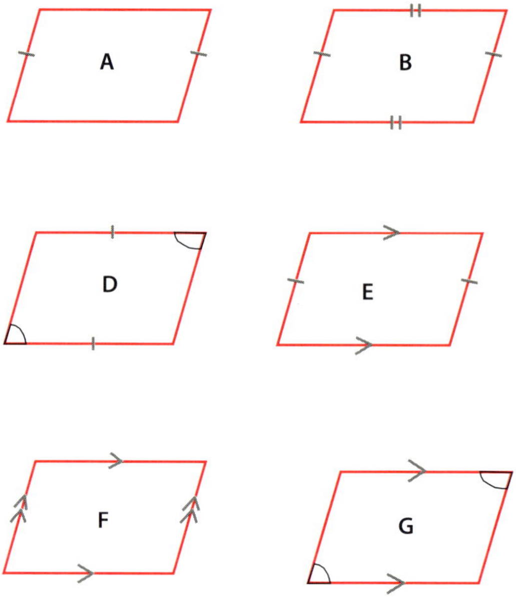

The curved arcs show equal angles.

For each shape:

(a) write down whether the shape *must* be a parallelogram

(b) explain how you came to your decision.

8 (a) Draw a quadrilateral with four equal sides.

(b) Write down the name of this quadrilateral.

(c) Draw another quadrilateral with four equal sides which has a different name.

(d) Write down the name of this quadrilateral.

(e) Try to draw a different quadrilateral with four equal sides.

9 (a) Draw a quadrilateral with two pairs of equal sides.

(b) Write down the name of this quadrilateral.

(c) Draw a different quadrilateral with two pairs of equal sides.

(d) Write down the name of this quadrilateral.

(e) Draw and name as many other quadrilaterals as you can with two pairs of equal sides.

10 Copy this table.

Property	Quadrilaterals
4 right angles	rectangle, square
2 lines of equal length	
4 lines of equal lengths	
2 pairs of equal length lines	
1 pair of parallel lines	
2 pairs of parallel lines	

Write the names of all quadrilaterals from this list which *must* have the property shown.
rectangle square rhombus kite parallelogram trapezium
(The first line has been completed for you.)

Diagonals of quadrilaterals

A diagonal is a line joining any two vertices of a polygon which are not already connected by a side.

Exercise 3

1 (a) Draw a square.

(b) Draw both diagonals of the square.

(c) Measure carefully the length of both diagonals.

(d) Write down the length of the diagonals.

(e) Repeat this for at least three different squares.

(f) Write down a conclusion which compares the length of the two diagonals of a square.

2 (a) Draw a rhombus.

(b) Draw both diagonals of the rhombus.

(c) Measure carefully the length of both diagonals.

(d) Write down the length of the diagonals.

(e) Repeat this for at least three different rhombuses.

(f) Write down a conclusion which compares the length of the two diagonals of a rhombus.

3 Use a similar method to the one used in Questions 1 and 2 to demonstrate whether the diagonals of a parallelogram are equal or not.

4 Use a similar method to the one used in Questions 1 and 2 to demonstrate whether the diagonals of a rectangle, a trapezium and a kite are equal or not.

5 (a) On plain paper, use a compass and ruler to construct a rectangle which measures 10 cm by 6 cm.

(b) Draw one diagonal of the rectangle.

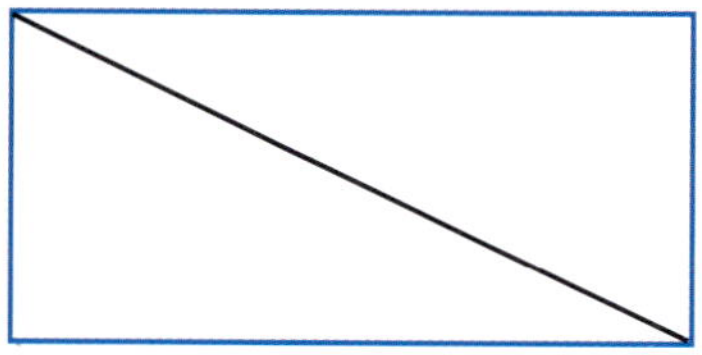

'To bisect' means 'to cut in half'.

(c) Use a compass and ruler to bisect the diagonal. Mark the point A.

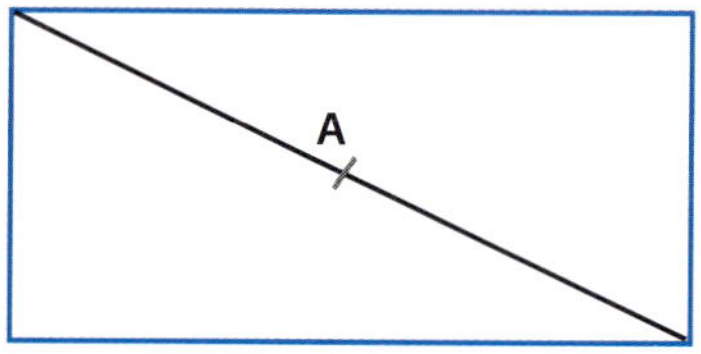

(d) Draw the other diagonal of the rectangle. It should pass through point A.

(e) Repeat this activity starting with the other diagonal.

(f) Repeat the activity for another rectangle.

(g) This activity shows that the diagonals of a rectangle bisect each other.

Repeat the activity for a square, a parallelogram, a trapezium, a rhombus and a kite.

Write down which quadrilaterals have diagonals which bisect each other.

6 (a) Draw a rectangle.

(b) Draw the diagonals of the rectangle.

(c) Measure the angles formed between the diagonals.

(d) Write down whether the diagonals of a rectangle cross at right angles.

(e) Draw a square, a rhombus, a trapezium, a kite and a parallelogram.

(f) Draw the diagonals of each quadrilateral.

(g) Measure the angles formed by the diagonals.

(h) Write down which quadrilaterals have diagonals which cross at right angles.

7 These are the shapes you have been using in this exercise.

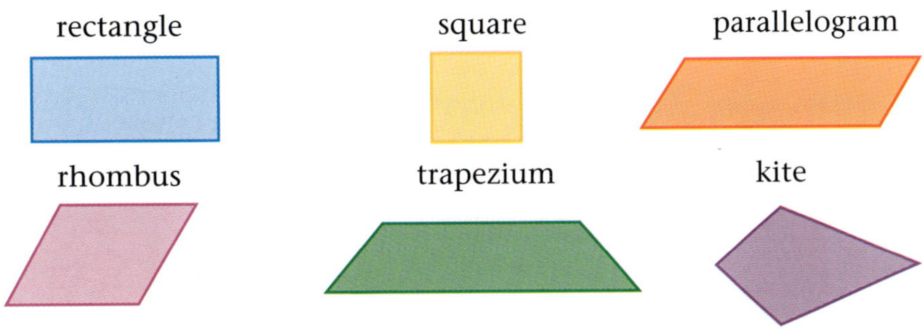

Copy this table.

	Diagonals equal	**Diagonals bisect**	**Diagonals cross at right angles**
Rectangle	✓	✓	
Square			
Parallelogram			
Rhombus			
Trapezium			
Kite			

Use your answers from the earlier questions in this exercise to complete the table by placing a tick in the appropriate boxes. (The line for rectangle has been completed for you.)

The family tree for quadrilaterals

Exercise 4

1. A square is a special type of rectangle.

   Write down the names of the other quadrilaterals of which a square is a special type.

2. Write down which quadrilaterals are special types of parallelogram.

3. Write down which quadrilaterals are special types of kite.

4. Write down which quadrilaterals are special types of trapezium.

Assignment 1 The family of quadrilaterals

- Create a poster showing each of these four-sided shapes.

trapezium | square | rectangle | kite

parallelogram | quadrilateral | rhombus

- Make it clear where some shapes are special types of others. For instance, part of your poster may look like this,

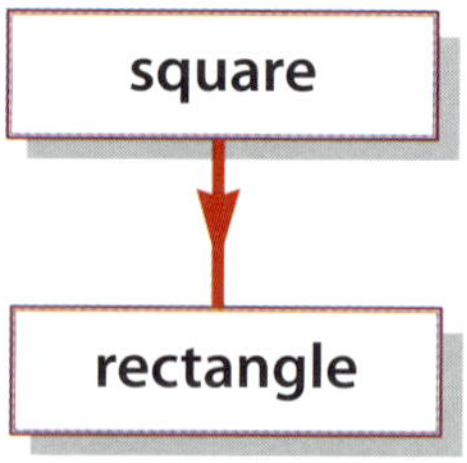

using the arrow to show 'is a special type of'.

Flow diagrams to identify a quadrilateral

Exercise 5

1 This flow diagram helps you to decide the name of a quadrilateral.

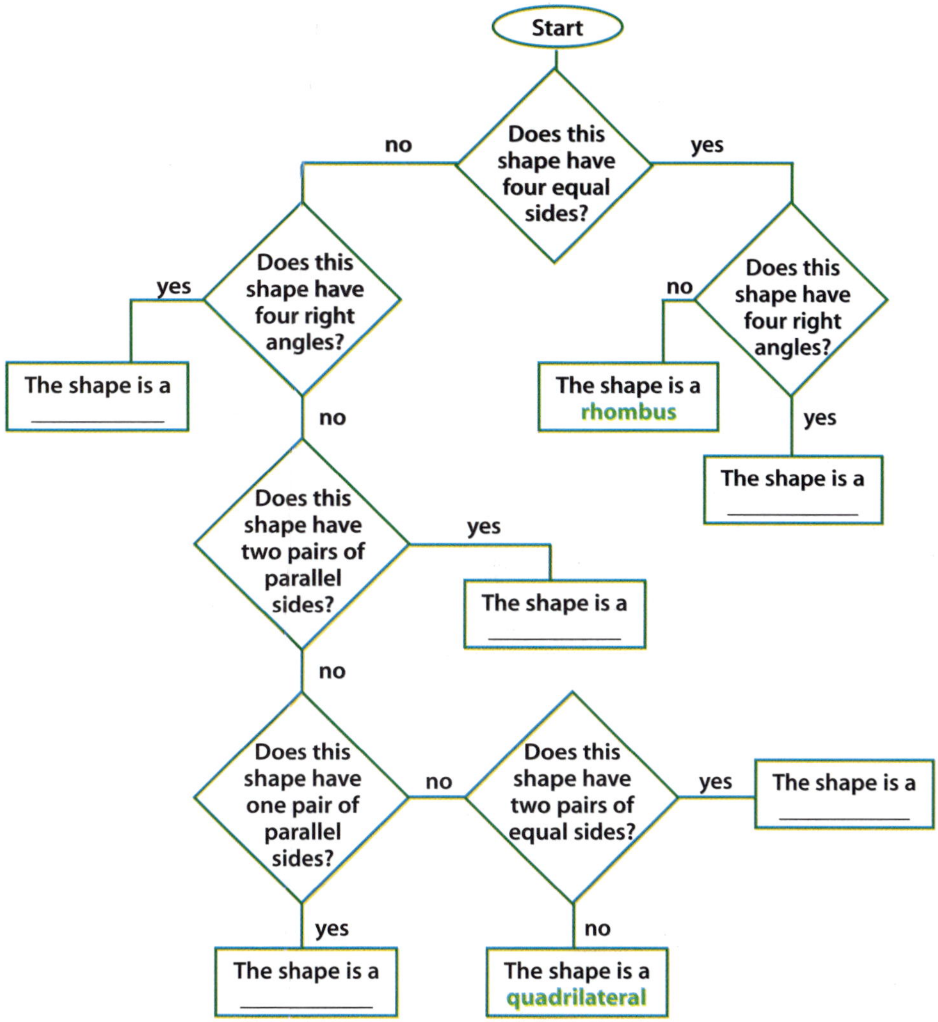

On a copy of the flow diagram, fill in the names which have been left out.

2 Look at these four quadrilaterals.

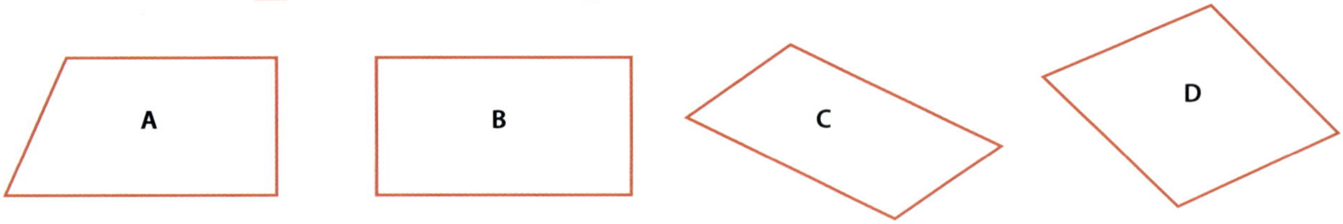

(a) Use your flow diagram to identify the quadrilaterals.

(b) Write down the answer to each question box you work through.

For example, if the shape was a square you would write:

yes, yes, square

3 This flow diagram uses the properties of the diagonals to name a quadrilateral.

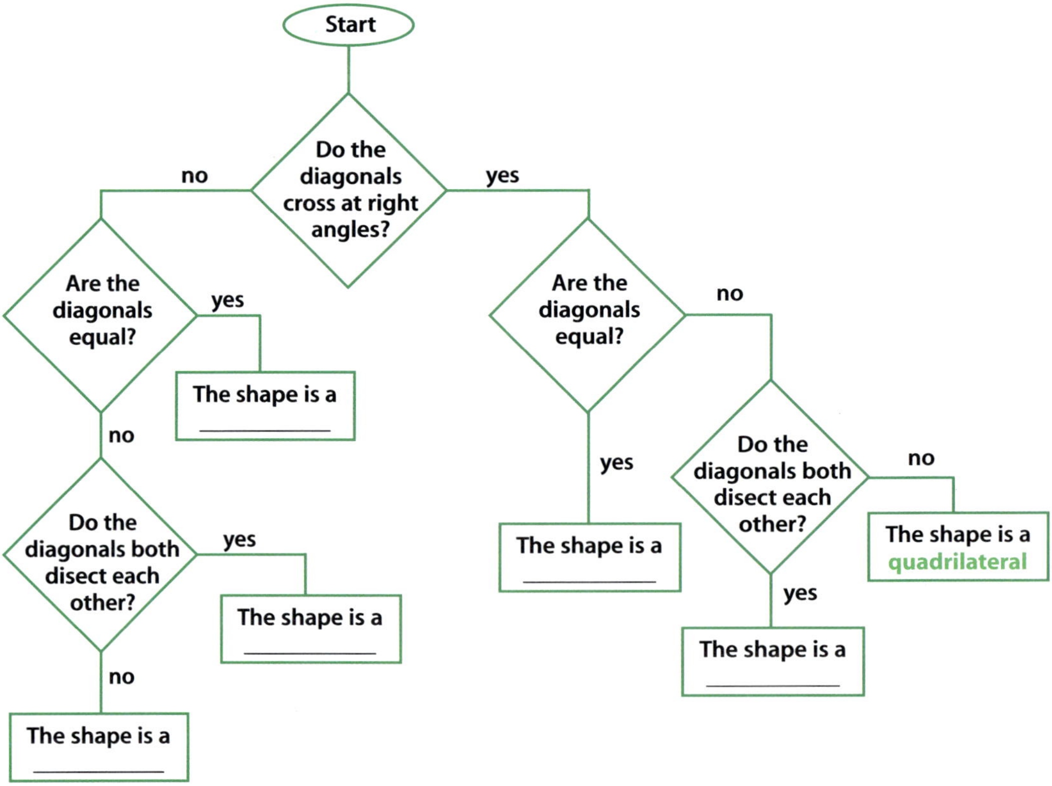

On a copy of the diagram, fill in the names which have been missed out.

4 These six diagrams show the diagonals of some quadrilaterals. (They have not been drawn accurately.)

(a)

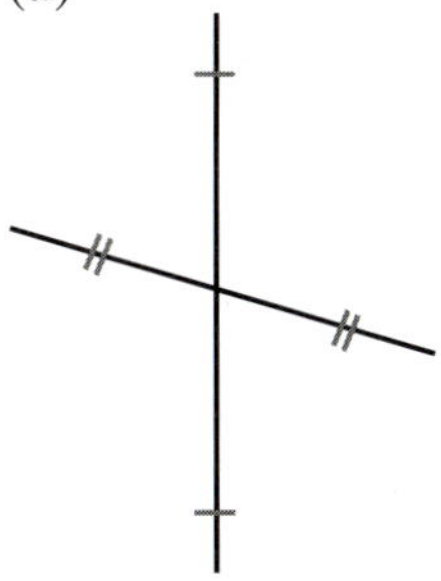

(b)

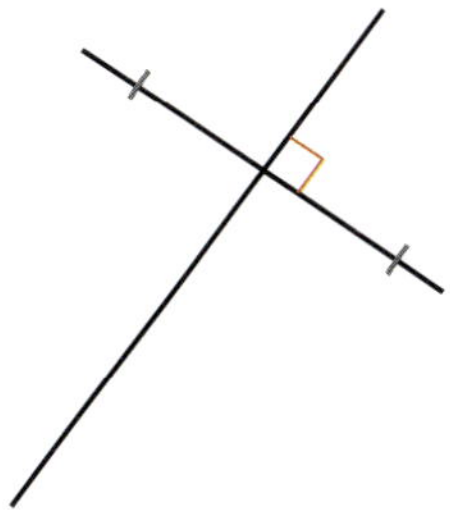

(c)

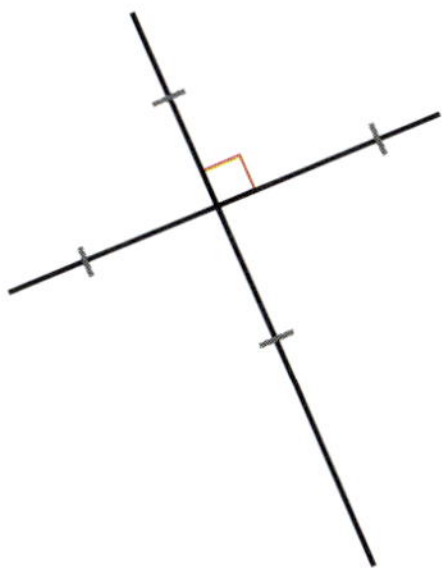

(d)

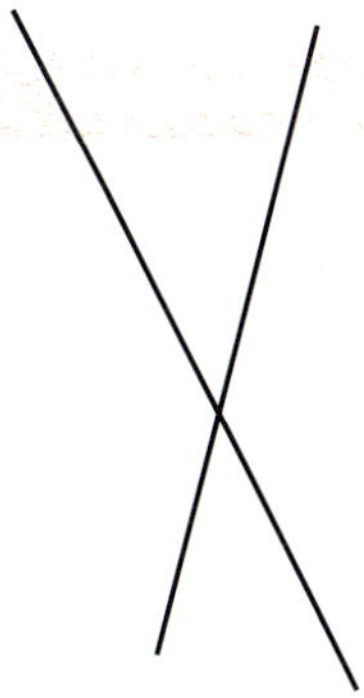

(e)

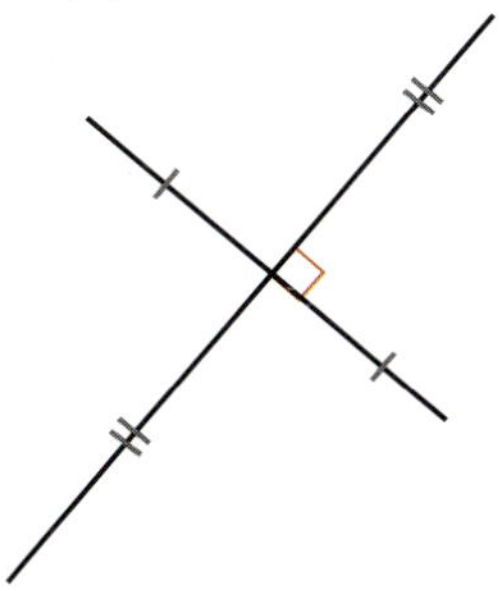

(f)

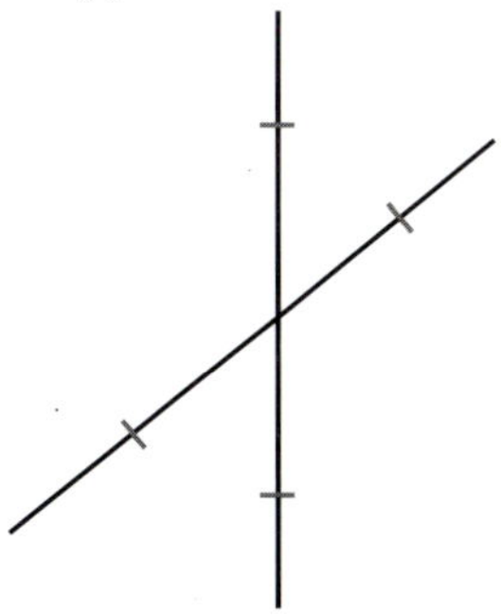

(i) Use your flow diagram to identify these six quadrilaterals.

Write down the answer to each question box you work through, as well as the name of the quadrilateral.

(ii) Copy each diagram accurately and draw in the quadrilateral to check that your answer is correct.

Minimum information needed to identify a quadrilateral

This next exercise looks at the *minimum* information needed to identify these particular quadrilaterals:

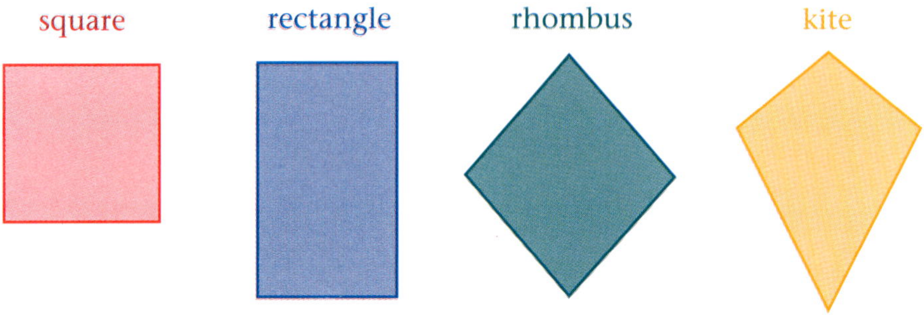

Exercise 6

1 A square has all six of these properties:

A: four equal sides

B: four equal angles

C: two pairs of parallel sides

D: equal diagonals

E: diagonals bisect each other

F: diagonals cross at right angles

(a) Draw six different quadrilaterals, which are *not* squares, each one having one of the properties A–F.

(b) Now take the properties in pairs: A with B, A with C, A with D, A with E, A with F, B with C, and so on.
Which pairs can *only* be drawn in a square?

Where it is possible to draw a quadrilateral which is *not* a square with two of the properties, draw it and name it.

(c) Is it possible to draw a quadrilateral which has three of the properties A–F, but which is *not* a square?

If so, draw it and name it.
If not, explain why.

2 A rectangle has all five of these properties:

A: two pairs of equal sides

B: four equal angles

C: two pairs of parallel sides

D: equal diagonals

E: diagonals bisect each other

(a) Which of these five properties can be drawn in a quadrilateral which is *not* a rectangle?

Where it is possible to draw a quadrilateral which is *not* a rectangle with one of the properties, draw it.

(b) Which pairs of these five properties can be drawn in a quadrilateral which is *not* a rectangle?

Draw the quadrilateral and name it.

(c) Is it possible to draw a quadrilateral which has three of the properties A–E, but which is *not* a rectangle?

If so, draw it and name it. If not, explain why.

3 A rhombus has all four of these properties:

A: four equal sides

B: two pairs of parallel sides

C: diagonals bisect each other

D: diagonals cross at right angles.

Take each property in turn.

Draw four different quadrilaterals, which are *not* rhombuses, each one having one of the properties A–D.

4 A kite has all three of these properties:

A: two pairs of adjacent sides equal

B: one diagonal is bisected

C: diagonals cross at right angles.

'adjacent' means 'next to'

How many of these properties are needed to be *certain* that the quadrilateral is a kite?

Write down the properties you think are needed.

Assignment 2 Using LOGO

- Write LOGO procedures to construct a square, a rectangle, a rhombus and a parallelogram.
- Show how the procedures use the properties of the quadrilateral.
- Try to write a procedure for a trapezium and another for a kite.

Assignment 3 Using flow diagrams

If you follow the instructions in this flow diagram, you will draw a square.

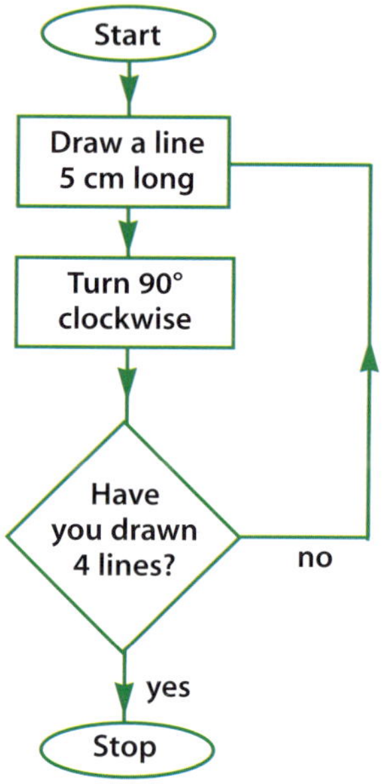

This LOGO procedure also draws a square:

```
TO SQUARE
REPEAT 4 [FORWARD 50 RIGHT 90]
END
```

- Compare the flow diagram with the procedure.
- Look at your procedure to draw a rectangle in Assignment 2.
- Use that procedure to help you to write a flow diagram to draw a rectangle.
- Write a flow diagram to draw a rhombus and a parallelogram.
- Some quadrilaterals have properties which you construct, such as parallel lines. Now write different flow diagrams for some of these quadrilaterals.

Assignment 4 Drawing quadrilaterals

- Use a computer package such as CABRI GEOMETRE or GEOMETERS SKETCHPAD to construct some of the quadrilaterals in such a way that, however they are moved, they keep the properties of the quadrilateral.
- Ask your partner to test your quadrilaterals and identify which ones they are.
- To make it more challenging, make all of the quadrilaterals look like squares when your partner first sees them.

Other polygons

Assignment 5 Family tree of triangles

In Assignment 1, you worked with the family tree for quadrilaterals. Use this list of different triangles to form a family tree of triangles.

- equilateral triangle
- right-angled triangle
- isosceles triangle
- right isosceles triangle
- scalene triangle

Assignment 6 Flow diagrams for triangles

On a copy of this diagram, write questions in the empty spaces to make the flow diagram identify triangles correctly.
(The first question has been filled in for you.)

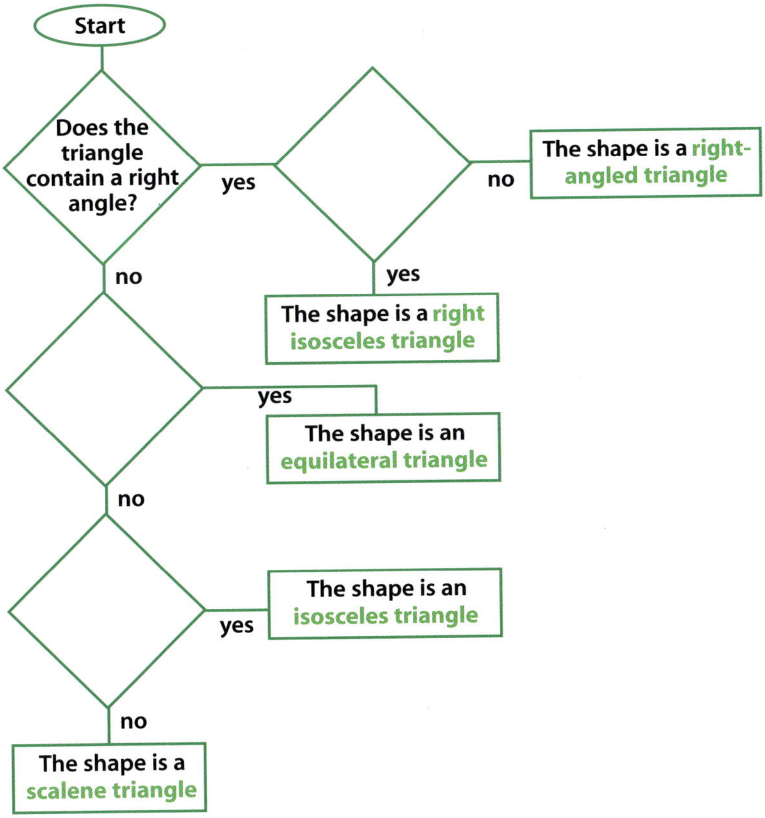

Exercise 7

1 (a) Draw a regular hexagon.
Draw all the diagonals of the hexagon which pass through the centre.

(b) Name the shapes formed.

(c) Write down the properties of this shape which enabled you to decide the name of the shape.

2 (a) Draw a regular octagon.
Draw all the diagonals of the octagon which pass through the centre.

(b) Name the shapes formed.

(c) Write down the properties of this shape which enabled you to decide the name of the shape.

'Vertex' is another word for corner. Vertices is the plural.

3 (a) Draw a regular hexagon.

(b) Number the vertices from 1 to 6.

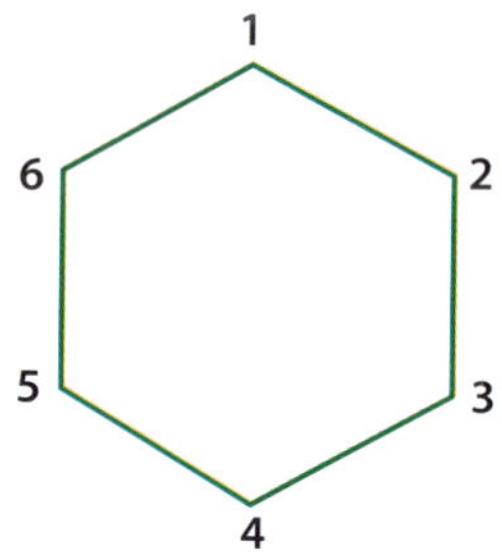

(c) Draw a line between vertex 1 and vertex 3.

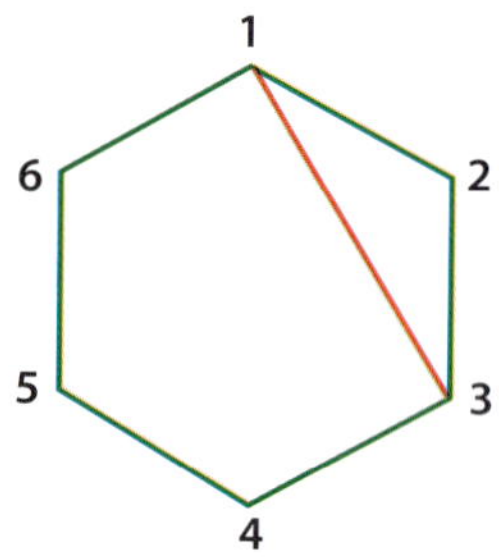

(d) Draw a second line between vertex 4 and vertex 6.

(e) Name the shapes you have created inside the hexagon.

(f) Write down the properties of these shapes which you used to identify it.

4 (a) Construct a regular hexagon. Number the vertices from 1 to 6.

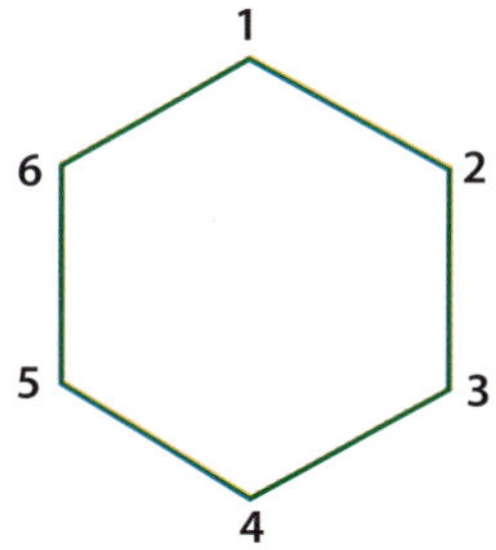

(b) Draw a line from vertex 1 to vertex 4.

(c) Name the two shapes formed.

(d) Write down the properties which you used to identify the shape.

5 (a) Construct a regular octagon. Number the vertices from 1 to 8.

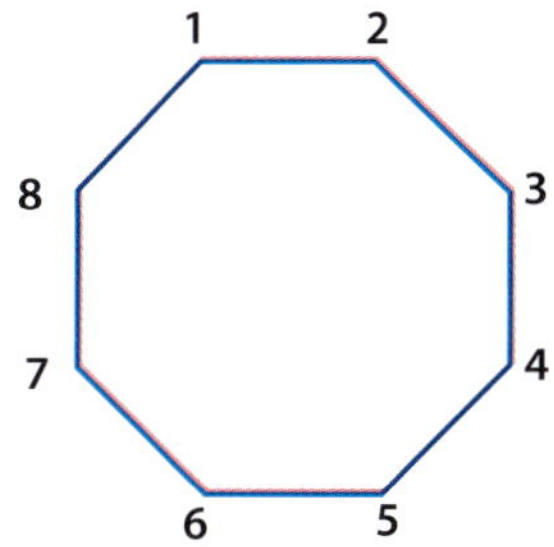

(b) Join vertex 1 to vertex 6, vertex 2 to vertex 5, vertex 3 to vertex 8 and vertex 4 to vertex 7.

(c) Name all the shapes formed.

(d) Write down the properties of the shapes which you used to identify them.

6 (a) Construct a regular octagon. Number the vertices from 1 to 8.

(b) Join all pairs of vertices whose sum is 9.

(c) Name all the shapes formed.

(d) Write down the properties of the shapes which you used to identify them.

7 (a) Construct a regular octagon. Number the vertices from 1 to 8.

(b) Join alternate vertices.

(c) Name all the shapes formed.

(d) Write down the properties of the shapes which you used to identify them.

Assignment 7 Angles in a quadrilateral

- Draw a circle.
- Mark any four points on the circumference of the circle.

  Join the points to form a quadrilateral.
- Measure the angles of the quadrilateral and record them.
- Draw several quadrilaterals in circles and record the size of their angles.
- Add together the size of the angles on opposite sides of the quadrilateral.

  Write down what you see from these results.
- Use a computer package such as CABRI GEOMETRE or GEOMETERS SKETCHPAD to confirm your conclusion.

Assignment 8 Opposite angles in a quadrilateral

- Draw a circle.
  Draw the diameter of the circle.
- Mark two points on the circumference, one on each side of the diameter.
- Join each point to each end of the diameter to form a quadrilateral.

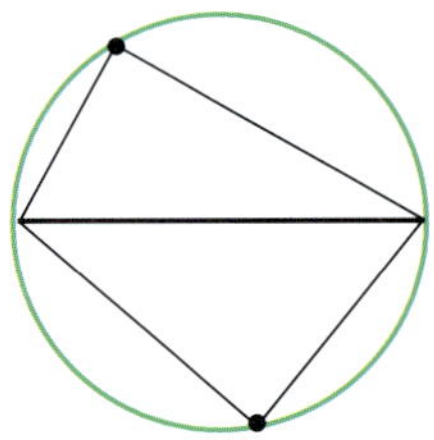

- Measure and write down the angles of the quadrilateral at the two points which you marked on the circumference.
- Repeat this for several other quadrilaterals formed in the same way. Write down what you see from these results.
- Use a computer package such as CABRI GEOMETRE or GEOMETERS SKETCHPAD to confirm your conclusion.

Assignment 9 Shapes in a regular octagon

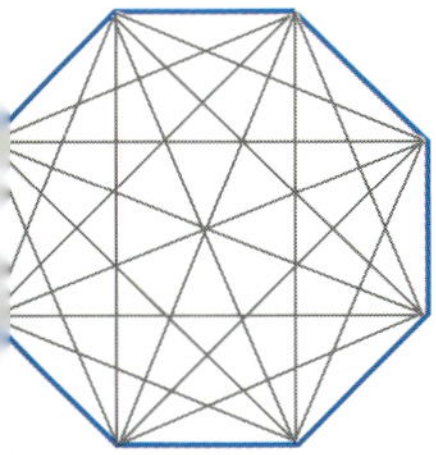

- Draw all the diagonals in a regular octagon.
- Use coloured pencils to show the position of:
  - (i) a square
  - (ii) a rectangle
  - (iii) a parallelogram
  - (iv) a trapezium with two pairs of equal angles
  - (v) a trapezium with no equal angles
  - (vi) a kite.
- On a new copy of the diagram, use coloured pencils to show the position of:
  - (i) a right-angled triangle
  - (ii) a right isosceles triangle
  - (iii) an isosceles triangle without a right angle.

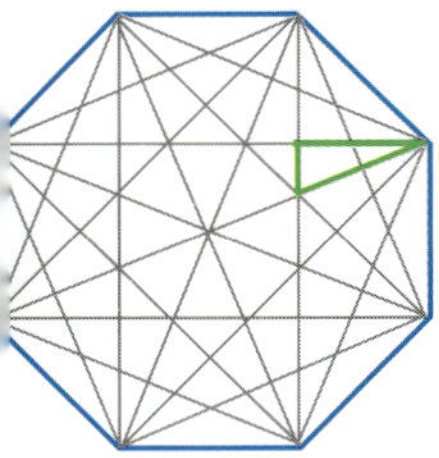

- This diagram shows a triangle outlined in green.

  How many triangles can you find which are congruent to the green triangle?

  How many triangles can you find which are similar to the green triangle?

Assignment 10 Shapes in an irregular octagon

- Draw an octagon which has equal angles but does not have equal sides.
- Draw all the diagonals.
- Show the position of as many different triangles as possible.
- Show the position of as many different quadrilaterals as possible.
- Choose and outline a shape.
- How many shapes can you find which are congruent to your shape?
- How many shapes can you find which are similar to your shape?
- Find your own way to extend this assignment.

Review Exercise

1 Write down the names of each of these quadrilaterals.

(a)

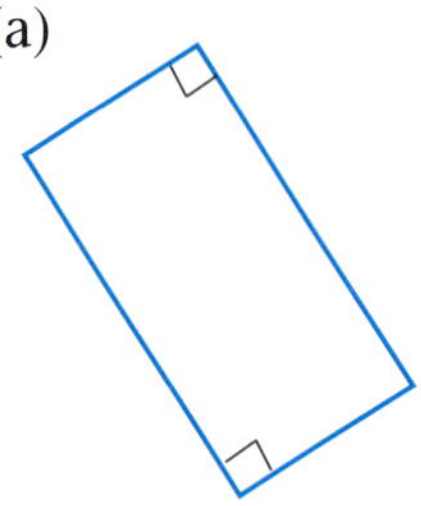

(b)

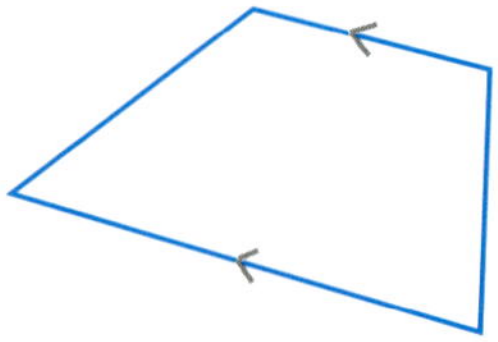

(c)

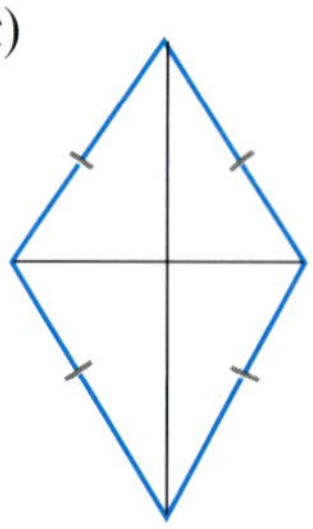

(d)

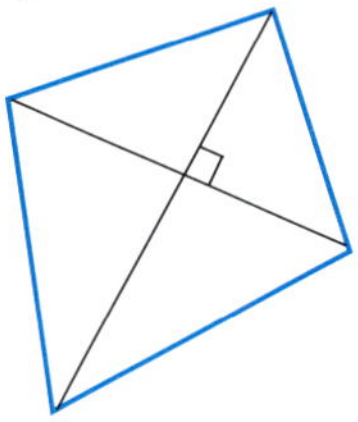

(e)

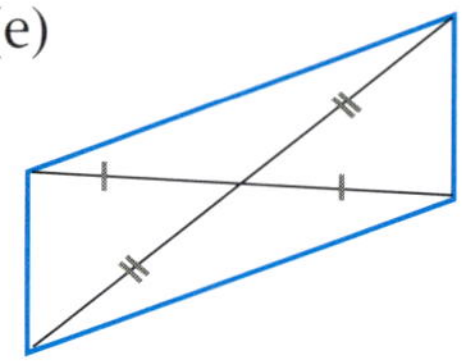

2 Write down as many quadrilaterals as possible which have four equal sides.

3 Write down as many quadrilaterals as possible which have four right angles.

4 Write down as many quadrilaterals as possible which have at least one pair of parallel sides.

5 Write down as many quadrilaterals as possible which have at least one pair of opposite angles equal.

6 Write down as many quadrilaterals as possible which have two pairs of adjacent sides equal.

7 Write down as many quadrilaterals as possible which have diagonals of equal length.

8 Write down as many quadrilaterals as possible which have diagonals which cross at right angles.

9 Write down as many quadrilaterals as possible which have diagonals which bisect each other.

10 Write down as many quadrilaterals as possible which have diagonals which bisect at right angles.

11 Write down as many quadrilaterals as possible which have diagonals which are equal in length and bisect each other at right angles.

12 Write down as few properties as possible which are needed to describe a rhombus.

13 Write down as few properties as possible which are needed to describe a parallelogram.

14 Write down as few properties as possible which are needed to describe a kite.

15 Write down as few properties as possible which are needed to describe a square.

16 Write down the names of all the types of triangle which can contain a right angle.

Assignment 11 Quadrilaterals in a circle

- Draw a circle. Mark both ends of a diameter.
- Mark a point on the circumference on each side of the diameter.

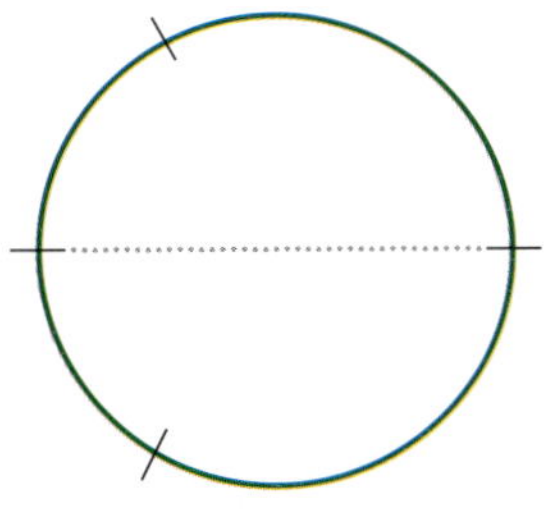

- Join the four points to form a quadrilateral.
- Which quadrilaterals can be formed in this way?
- Write down the name of the quadrilateral and construct it accurately.

Correlation

In this chapter you will learn:

- → how to plot scatter diagrams
- → about correlation
- → how to draw and use lines of best fit
- → how to test hypotheses

Starting points

Before starting this chapter you will need to know how to:

- identify and use a range of measures
- plot ordered pairs on a grid.

An ordered pair is like a coordinate (x,y); it has to be plotted in a certain order.

Exercise 1

1 Pair up each of the measurements on the left with the items listed on the right.

For example, 1 (150 cm) with i (Height of a pupil).

Measurement		Item or feature	
1	150 cm	a	Weight of a bus
2	35 km	b	Amount of petrol in a car
3	32 kg	c	Height of a table
4	28 litres	d	Thickness of a compact disc
5	1 mm	e	Weight of an insect
6	40 m	f	Length of a garden
7	8 tonnes	g	Distance between two towns
8	15 g	h	Weight of a large dog
9	225 ml	i	Height of a pupil
10	800 mm	j	Amount of coffee in a mug

2 This grid shows the weights and heights of five pupils.

Pupil A can be recorded as the ordered pair: (60 kg, 160 cm).

Write down the ordered pairs for pupils B, C, D and E.

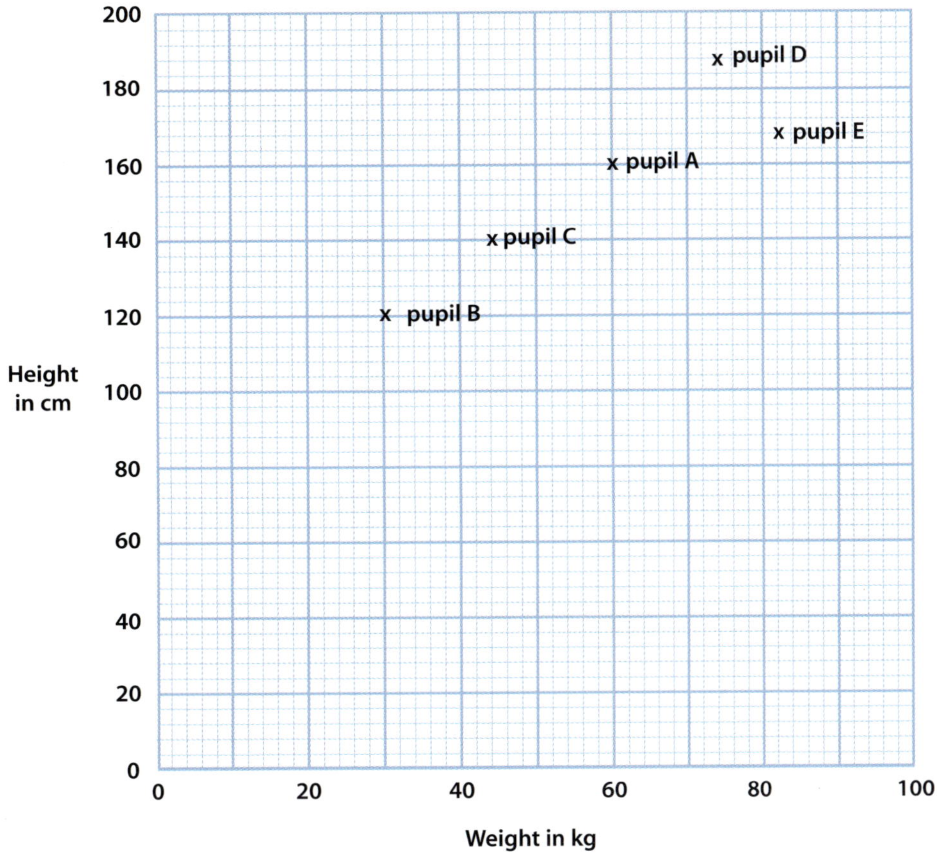

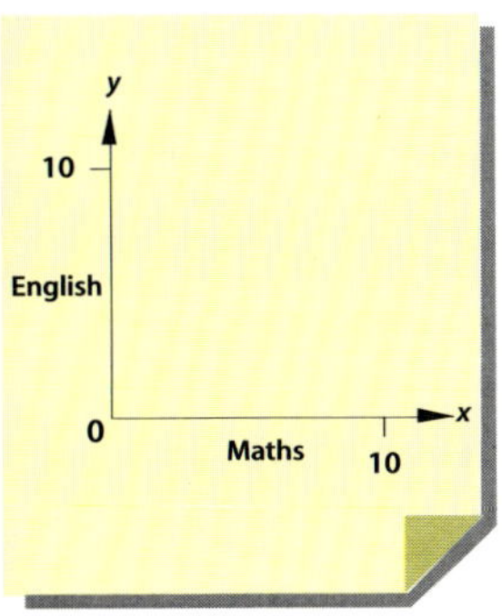

3 This table shows the marks obtained by six pupils in both a Maths test and an English test.

Pupil	A	B	C	D	E	F
Maths (x)	2	5	4	9	10	7
English (y)	7	5	9	8	6	4

Plot these results as ordered pairs on a grid.
You will need to number the axes from 0 to 10.

Scatter diagrams and correlation

Twelve pupils were chosen to do two Maths test papers.
Here are their marks.

Pupil	A	B	C	D	E	F	G	H	I	J	K	L
Paper 1 (mark out of 50)	25	44	12	50	15	30	6	38	34	20	47	10
Paper 2 (mark out of 120)	60	108	38	112	40	70	24	86	80	58	102	26

If you look at the table, it is not easy to see if there is any connection between the two sets of results.

When you measure two things together, you can see if there is any connection between them by plotting the values on a graph.

This type of graph is called a **scatter diagram**.

Key fact

On a scatter diagram each point represents two values. One set of values is plotted along the horizontal axis; the other set is plotted up the vertical axis.

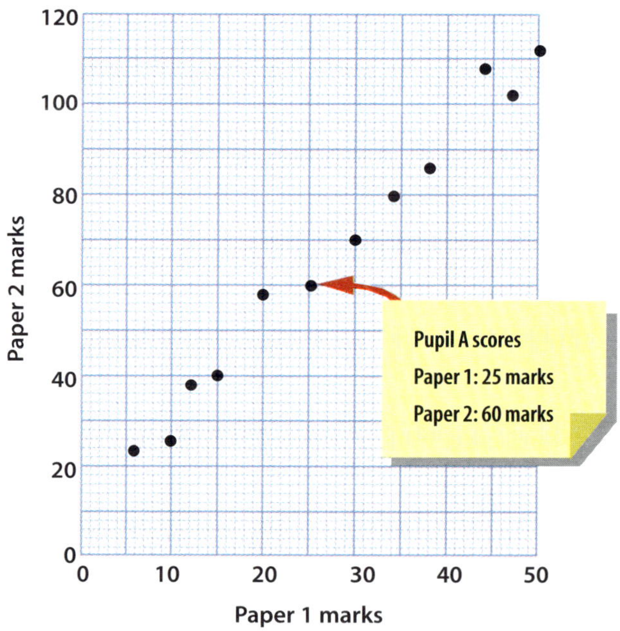

The scatter diagram shows that there *is* a connection between the two sets of results.

In general, the higher the score on Paper 1, the higher is the score on Paper 2.

The connection between the two sets of results is called the **correlation**.

There is a good correlation between the marks gained on Paper 1 and the marks gained on Paper 2.

Exercise 2

1 Read these ten statements.

A: The taller a person is, the longer their legs are.

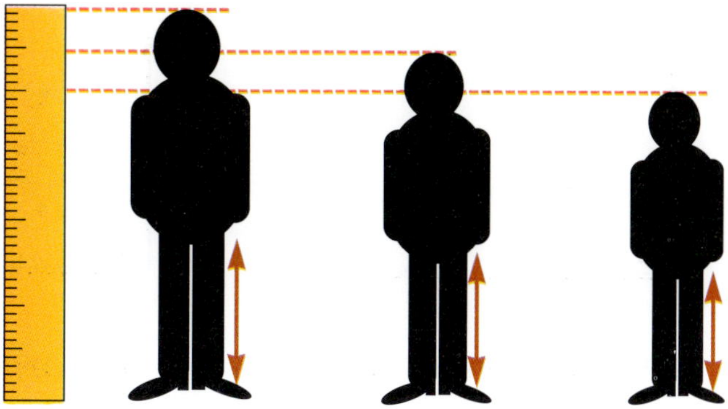

B: The higher the scores obtained in a Maths test, the higher the scores obtained in an English test.

C: The older the pupil is, the more pocket money he or she gets.

D: The nearer to the Equator a place is, the hotter the weather is.

E: The higher the scores obtained in a Maths test, the higher the scores obtained in a Science test.

F: The longer a car, the faster speed at which it can travel.

G: The heavier a person is, the stronger he or she is.

H: The larger the circumference of the head, the more intelligent the person.

I: The more hours doing homework, the less hours spent watching TV.

J: The older a pupil is, the taller he or she is.

For each statement A–J, write down whether you think that:

(i) there is a good correlation

(ii) there may be some correlation

(iii) there is no correlation between the two situations.

The circumference is the length around the outside of a shape.

The types of correlation

These two diagrams both show a **positive correlation**.

As one quantity increases, so does the other.

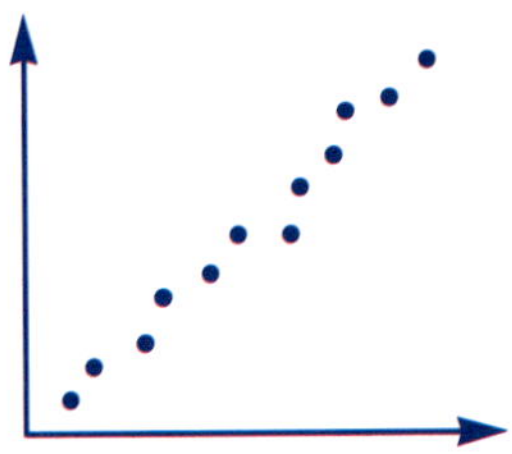

Good or strong positive correlation

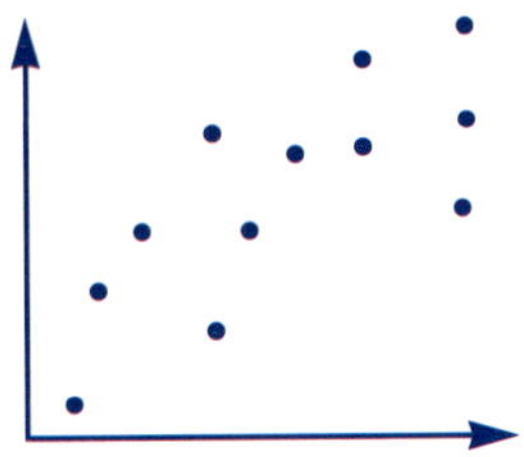

Weak positive correlation

Examples of positive correlation are:

- *Ice cream sales* going up with *Temperature*
- *Number of pages* in a book and *Time taken to read* it.

This diagram shows a **negative correlation**.

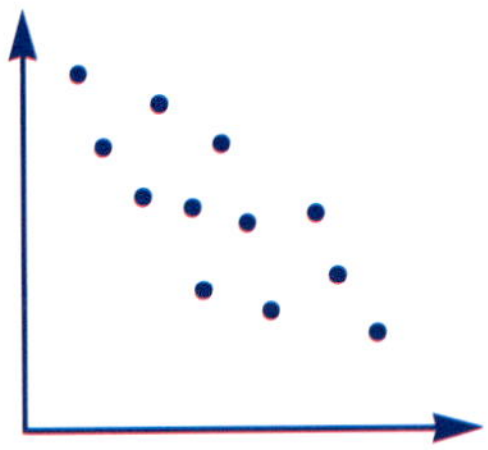

As one quantity increases, the other decreases.

Examples of negative correlation are:

- A goalkeeper's *Skill* compared with the number of *Goals let in*
- *Size of car engine* and the *Number of miles* travelled on a litre of fuel.

This diagram shows **no correlation.**

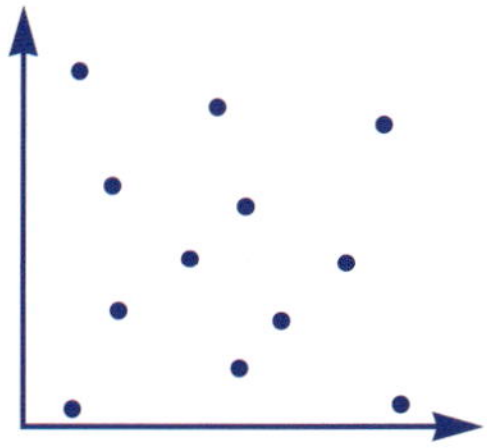

There appears to be *no* connection between the sets of values plotted on the two axes.

Examples of no correlation are:

- *Intelligence* compared with *Height*
- *Pupils' ages* compared with the *Number of hours spent watching TV*.

Assignment 1 Types of correlation

- Look again at the ten statements from Exercise 2.

  A: The taller a person is, the longer their legs are.

  B: The higher the scores obtained in a Maths test, the higher the scores obtained in an English test.

  C: The older the pupil is, the more pocket money he or she gets.

  D: The nearer to the Equator a place is, the hotter the weather is.

  E: The higher the scores obtained in a Maths test, the higher the scores obtained in a Science test.

  F: The longer a car, the faster speed at which it can travel.

  G: The heavier a person is, the stronger he or she is.

  H: The larger the circumference of the head, the more intelligent the person.

  I: The more hours doing homework, the less hours spent watching TV.

  J: The older a pupil is, the taller he or she is.

- Decide for each if there is positive or negative correlation.
  Is the correlation strong or weak?
  For which statements is there no correlation?

- Write down more examples of the different types of correlation.

Exercise 3

1 This table shows the marks obtained by ten pupils in a Maths test and a French test.

For example, pupil A scored 17 in Maths and 6 in French.

Pupil	A	B	C	D	E	F	G	H	I	J
Maths	17	12	15	5	1	14	13	10	19	7
French	6	11	5	17	20	12	8	14	4	13

(a) Which pupil scored five marks in Maths?

(b) Add the Maths and French marks for each pupil. Which pupil gained the highest overall total?

(c) Plot a scatter diagram.
(Use a scale of 1cm to 2 marks along each axis.)

(d) Describe the type of correlation obtained.

2 Eight pupils took part in a gymnastics competition.

Points were awarded by two judges: Judge P and Judge Q.
The winner was the gymnast with the highest total points.

This table shows the points given by each judge.

Pupil	A	B	C	D	E	F	G	H
Judge P	9	9	5	3	3	7	1	6
Judge Q	5	8	8	9	3	2	0	10

(a) Which pupil scored zero points from one judge?

(b) Which pupil won the competition?

(c) Use the data in the results table to plot a scatter diagram.
(Use a scale of 1cm to 1 point along each axis.)

(d) Describe the type of correlation obtained.

3 This table shows the weight in kilograms and the waist measurement in centimetres of 12 pupils.

Pupil	A	B	C	D	E	F	G	H	I	J	K	L
Weight (kg)	46	84	70	82	74	38	90	68	70	54	66	92
Waist (cm)	56	90	64	80	74	54	92	70	84	60	76	96

(a) Which pupil was heaviest?

(b) Which pupil had the smallest waist?

(c) Plot a scatter diagram.
(Use a scale of 1cm to 10 units along each axis.)

(d) Describe the type of correlation obtained.

4 This table shows the size of engine in cc of eight different motorcycles.

Also included is the petrol consumption for each in miles per litre.

cc stands for cubic centimetre (or cm^3)

Motorcycle	A	B	C	D	E	F	G	H
Engine size (cc)	50	125	150	200	250	350	400	500
Petrol consumption	44	36	35	31	21	14	9	11

(a) Plot a scatter diagram.
(Use a scale of 1 cm to 50 cc along the horizontal axis and 1 cm to 5 miles per litre along the vertical axis.)

(b) Describe the type of correlation obtained.

5 This table shows the sales per day of canned drinks from a school vending machine.
The temperature in °C for each day is also shown.

Day	M	Tu	W	Th	F	M	Tu	W	Th	F
Temperature (°C)	20	24	25	23	21	17	16	14	14	18
N° drinks sold	70	96	98	82	80	48	52	38	42	64

(a) Plot a scatter diagram. (Use a suitable scale for each axis.)

(b) Describe the type of correlation obtained.

Line of best fit

This scatter diagram shows the marks obtained by eight pupils in a Maths test and a Science test.

It can be seen that there is a good correlation between the two tests.

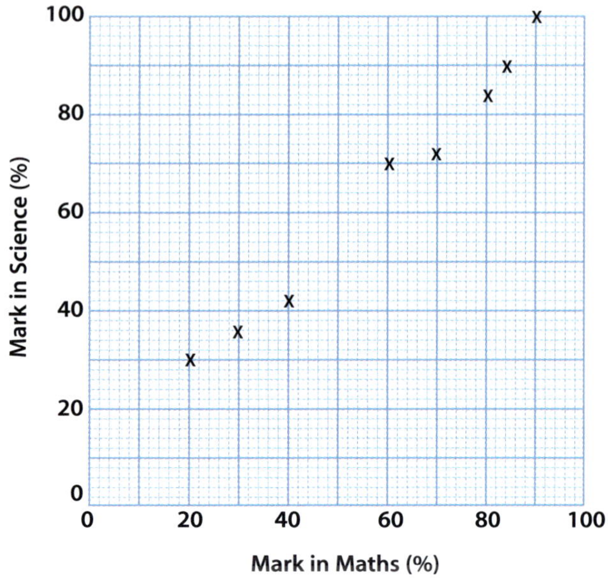

Key fact

The 'line of best fit' is the line that best fits nearly all the points.

A straight line could be drawn so that it nearly fits all of the points. This line is called the **line of best fit**.

Note that the number of points above the line is about the same as the number of points below the line, and the distance of the points above and below the line balance out.

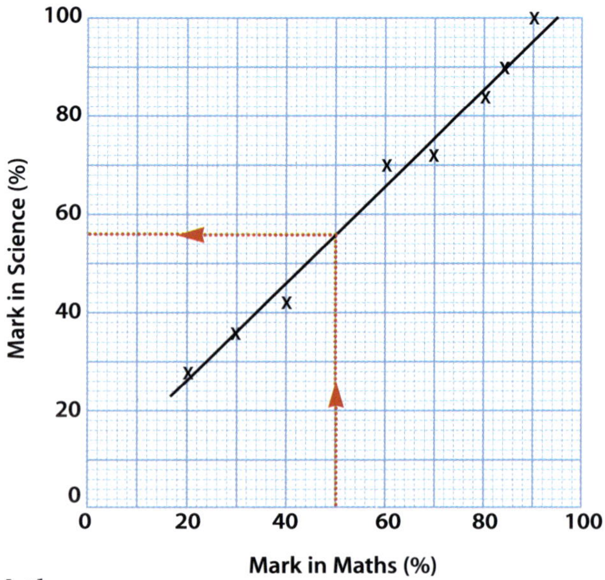

If a pupil took the Maths test only, the line of best fit could be used to predict the mark he or she might have got in the Science test, and vice versa.

If this pupil scored 50% in Maths, the expected score in Science would be 56%.

Exercise 4

1 This table shows the marks obtained by eight pupils in a French test and a German test.

Pupil	A	B	C	D	E	F	G	H
French	6	4	16	8	20	12	18	2
German	6	6	13	9	14	10	12	5

(a) Plot a scatter diagram.
(Use a scale of 1cm to 2 marks along each axis.)

(b) Describe the type of correlation shown.

(c) Draw a line of best fit.

(d) A pupil was ill and missed the German test.
He obtained 10 marks in his French test.
Use your graph to estimate his likely score in the German test.

(e) Another pupil missed her French test.
She obtained 11 marks in her German test.
What is her likely score in the French test?

2 This table shows the temperatures in °C of eight places.
Also shown are the latitudes in degrees North.

Place	A	B	C	D	E	F	G	H
Temperature (°C)	10	17	20	25	30	32	35	40
Latitude (°N)	49	40	35	27	21	19	10	5

(a) Plot a scatter diagram.
(Use a scale of 1cm to 5 units along each axis.)

(b) Describe the type of correlation shown.

(c) Draw a line of best fit.

(d) The temperature of a city is 15°C.
What would you expect its latitude to be?

(e) A village is on the Equator (that is, latitude 0°).
Estimate the temperature in °C.

3 This table shows the percentages obtained by ten pupils in a Maths test and a Science test.

Pupil	A	B	C	D	E	F	G	H	I	J
Maths	34	40	84	64	80	50	90	74	60	46
Science	10	20	80	60	68	34	86	66	48	32

(a) Plot a scatter diagram.
(Use a scale of 1cm to 10 marks along each axis.)

(b) Describe the type of correlation shown.

(c) Draw a line of best fit.

(d) A pupil missed his Science test.
However, he obtained 70% in his Maths test.
Use the graph to estimate his likely score in the Science test.

(e) Another pupil missed her Maths test. She obtained 42% in her Science test. What is her likely score in the Maths test?

4 This table shows the age (in years) and the price (in £) of eight cars of the same make and model.

Car	A	B	C	D	E	F	G	H
Age	2	8	7	4	10	6	1	3
Price	9200	3000	4800	8000	2600	6000	10000	8000

(a) Plot a scatter diagram. (Use a scale of 1cm to 1 year along the horizontal axis and 1cm to £1000 up the vertical axis.)

(b) Describe the type of correlation shown.

(c) Draw a line of best fit.

(d) How much would you expect to pay for 5-year-old model?

(e) You have £4000.
What would be the age of the car you could expect to buy?

(f) Estimate the cost of a brand new car.
Explain how you got your answer.

(g) A $2\frac{1}{2}$-year-old model is advertised for sale at £5000. Plot this point on your scatter diagram. Comment on this, and give a possible explanation.

Hypothesis testing

Hypotheses is the plural of hypothesis.

An hypothesis is a theory or a statement about something.

Here are some possible hypotheses:

- The taller a person, the heavier he or she is.
- The taller a person, the larger his or her shoe size is.

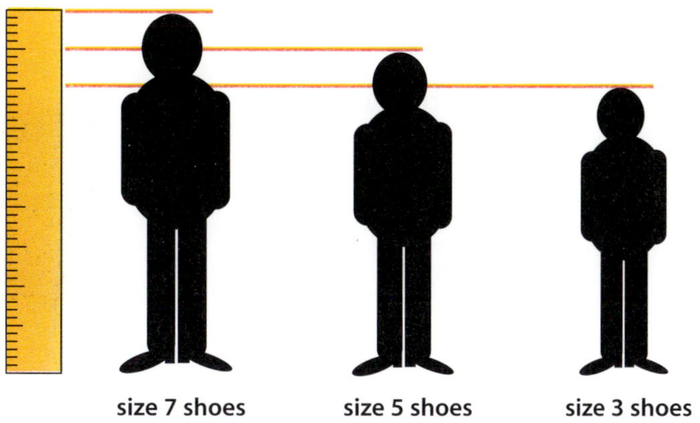

- The taller a person, the longer his or her arm is.
- The taller a person, the larger his or her waist measurement is.
- The longer a person's leg, the faster he or she can run.
- The longer a person's leg, the further he or she can jump.
- The longer a person's arm, the further he or she can throw.
- The larger the size of a person's hand span, the larger his or her feet are.
- The slower a person's pulse rate, the faster his or her reaction time is.
- The heavier a person, the faster his or her pulse rate is.
- The heavier a person was at birth, the taller he or she is now.

An hypothesis can be tested so that it can be proved or disproved.

In the next assignment you are going to test an hypothesis, and you will need to work with one or two other pupils.

You can choose your hypothesis from the list above, or you may choose your own hypothesis *but* see your teacher first.

Assignment 2 Hypothesis testing

Data are facts and figures.

- Form your working group.
- Choose your hypothesis to test.
  (Some ideas are given on page 163.)
- Collect the data for your test.
  This is called a **survey**.

  To do this, design a suitable recording sheet.

  Then check what equipment you need and either take the measurements yourselves or obtain the information from a computer database.

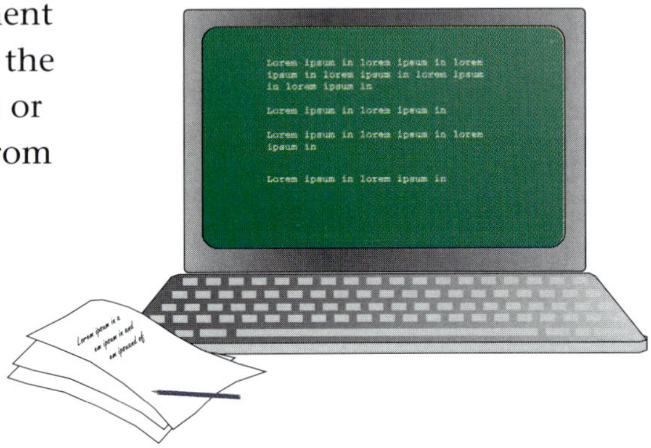

- Record the results that you have collected.

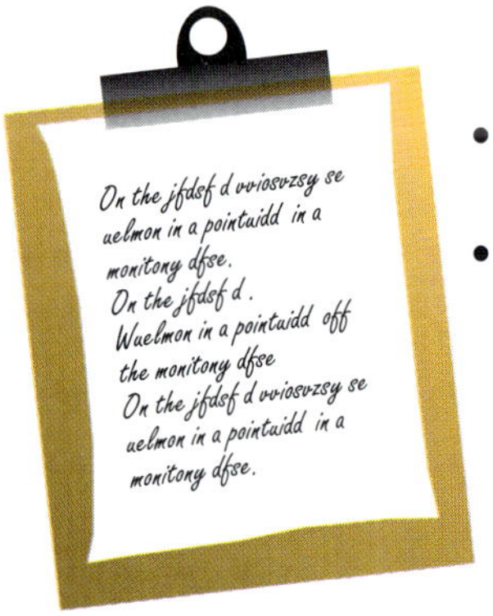

- Analyse your results.
- At each stage of your work, discuss your findings and come to some conclusions. Write down your findings.
  Present your survey report.

> SURVEY REPORT (example)
>
> 1. INTRODUCTION
> 2. HOW I CONDUCTED MY SURVEY
> 3. TABLE OF RESULTS
> 4. MY ANALYSIS
> 5. RESULTS PRESENTATION
> 6. CONCLUSIONS

The next page of notes on presentation and analysis of data will help you to produce the correct material.

Presentation and analysis of data

Information and results are often collected using rough notes.

It is very important that the final presentation of your survey includes the following items.

- An **introduction**:
  - describing the hypothesis
  - perhaps noting what you expect the outcome to be
  - how you prepared for the task.

- A description of **how you conducted the survey**:
  - who you worked with
  - the materials or equipment used
  - any problems or difficulties encountered.

- A **table of results**.
  - how your samples were chosen
  - how you found the results.

- An **analysis** of the results:
  - the range
  - mode, median and mean averages.

- The **presentation of results**.
  Where appropriate this could include:
  - histograms or bar charts
  - pie charts
  - scatter diagrams
  - computer generated graphs.

- A **conclusion**:
  - summarising your findings
  - predicting outcomes of data not obtained
  - giving details on how you could possibly have made improvements to the testing.

Review Exercise

1 Read these four statements.

A: The height of a person compared with the amount of money they earn

B: The scores obtained in an English test compared with the scores obtained in a History test

C: The number of builders compared with the time taken to build a house

D: The speed of typing on a computer compared with the number of books read per year

For each of the statements A–D, write down whether:

(i) there is a good correlation

(ii) there may be some correlation

(iii) there is no correlation between the two situations.

2 (a) Describe the type of correlation shown by each of these graphs.

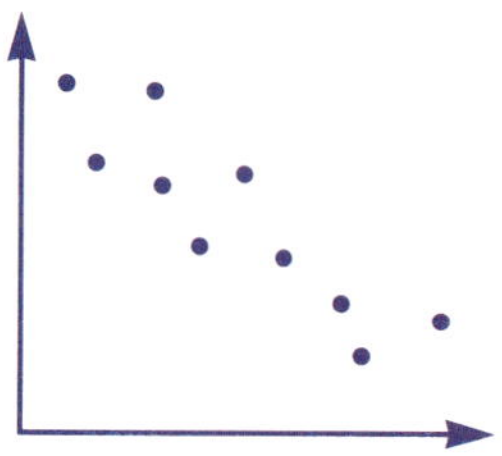

Graph P

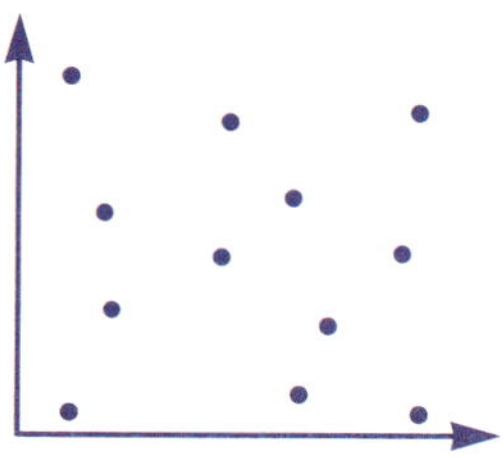

Graph Q

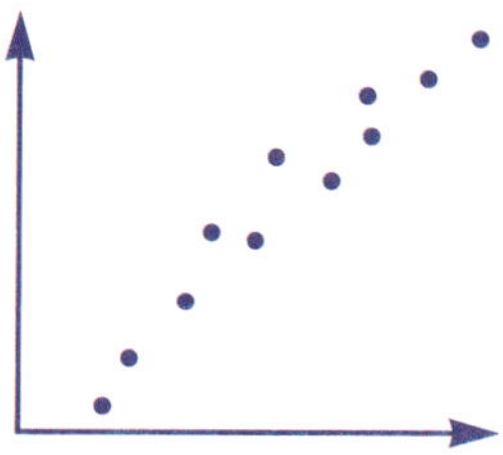

Graph R

(b) Match the graphs P, Q and R to these situations:

(i) The size of feet and the marks obtained in a Maths test

(ii) The distance apart of two towns and the time taken to cycle between them

(iii) The distance from a gas fire compared with the temperature

3 This table shows the distances (in miles) to ten towns. Also shown is the cost of a bus ticket (to the nearest £) to each town.

Town	A	B	C	D	E	F	G	H	I	J
Distance	10	16	30	40	48	74	80	88	92	100
Cost	6	7	9	10	12	15	16	17	18	19

(a) Plot a scatter diagram. (Use a scale of 1cm to 10 miles along the horizontal axis and 1cm to £2 up the vertical axis.)

(b) Describe the type of correlation shown.

(c) Draw a line of best fit.

(d) The distance to a village is 66 miles.
What fare would you expect to pay?

(e) How far could you expect to travel for £8?

4 This table shows the batting averages and the bowling averages of eight members of a cricket team.

Player	A	B	C	D	E	F	G	H
Batting	26	65	55	10	21	76	13	56
Bowling	27	14	22	40	35	11	34	13

(a) Plot a scatter diagram. (Use a suitable scale for each axis.)

(b) Describe the type of correlation shown.

(c) Draw a line of best fit.

(d) The ninth member of a cricket team had a batting average of 50 runs. What would you expect the bowling average to be?

(e) The tenth member of the cricket team had a bowling average of 25 runs per wicket.
What would be the expected batting average?

(f) The eleventh member of the cricket team (and the captain) had a batting average of 52 runs and a bowling average of 4 runs per wicket.
Plot this point on your graph.
Comment on this, and give a possible explanation.

Circles and π

In this chapter you will learn:

- → special names for parts of a circle
- → how to find the circumference of a circle
- → how to find the area of a circle

Key fact

diameter = 2 × radius

Starting points

Before you start this chapter you will need to know:

- words associated with circles
- how to measure angles
- how to draw a circle and circle patterns accurately.

Parts of a circle

These diagrams will remind you of some of the names for lengths in a circle.

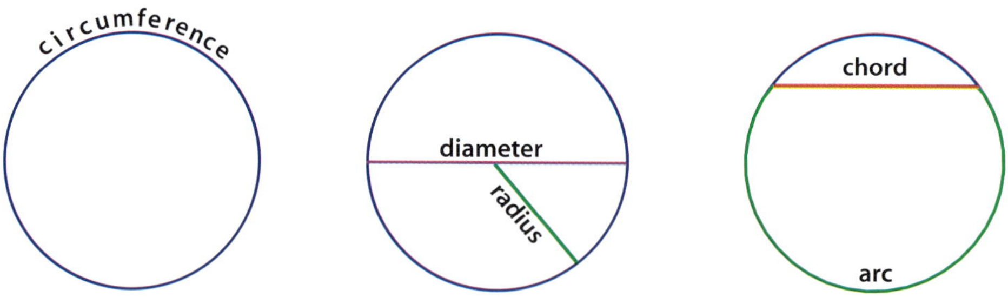

There are other special names for parts of a circle.

This diagram shows a **sector** of a circle.

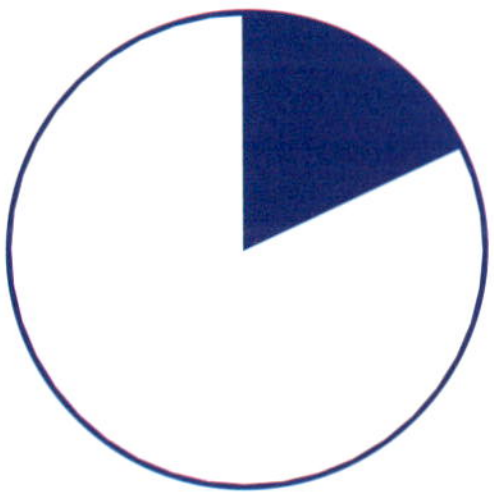

This diagram shows a **segment** of a circle.

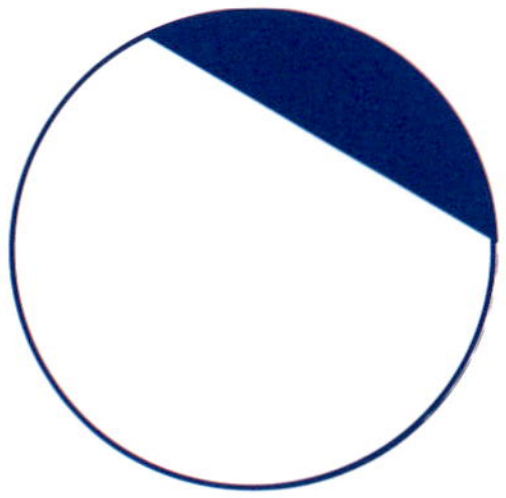

The shaded part is the **minor segment**.

The unshaded part is the **major segment**.

Exercise 1

1 Each of these words describes a length in a circle.

(a) circumference (b) diameter (c) radius

(d) chord (e) arc

Write a sentence to describe what is meant by each of them.

2 Look at these eight diagrams.

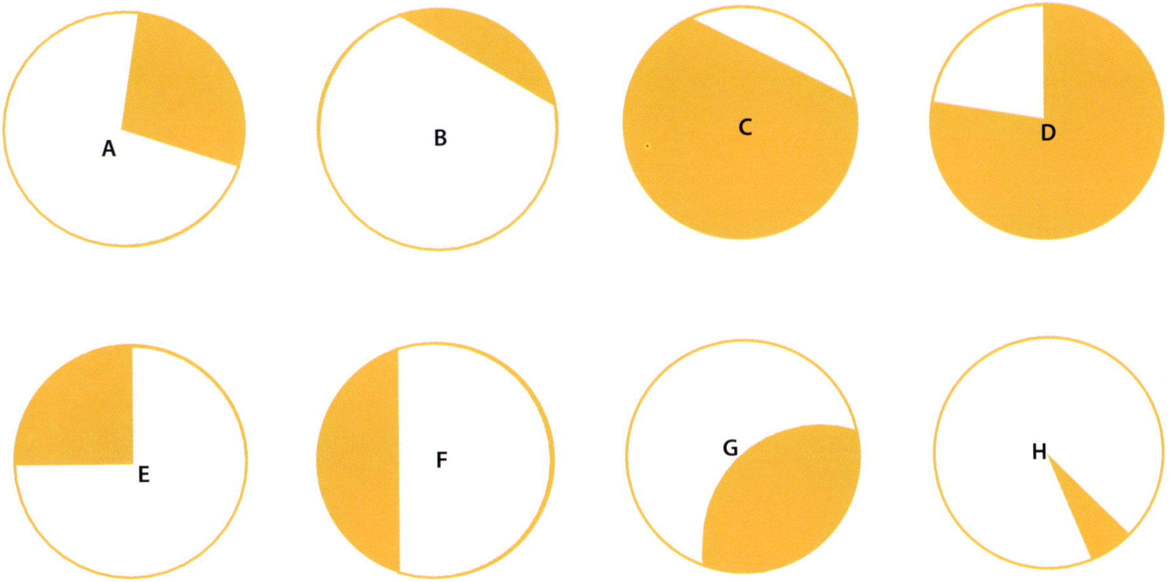

(a) Write down which of them shows sectors.

(b) Write down which of them shows segments.

3 Use a pair of compasses to draw:

(a) a circle which has a radius of 4 cm

(b) a circle with a diameter of 5 cm.

4 (a) Draw a circle with radius 3 cm.

(b) In the circle, draw a chord of length 4 cm.

(c) In the same circle, draw another chord, this time of length 5 cm.

(d) What is the length of the longest chord in this circle? What is its special name in this case?

5 (a) Draw a circle with radius 4 cm, and mark off every 20° around the circumference.

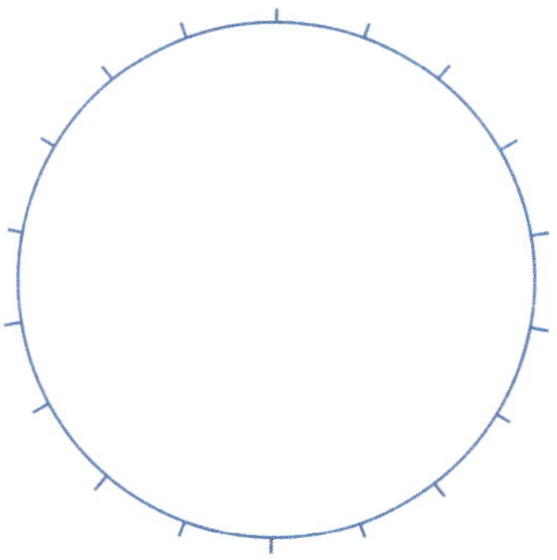

Join each mark back to the centre of the circle.

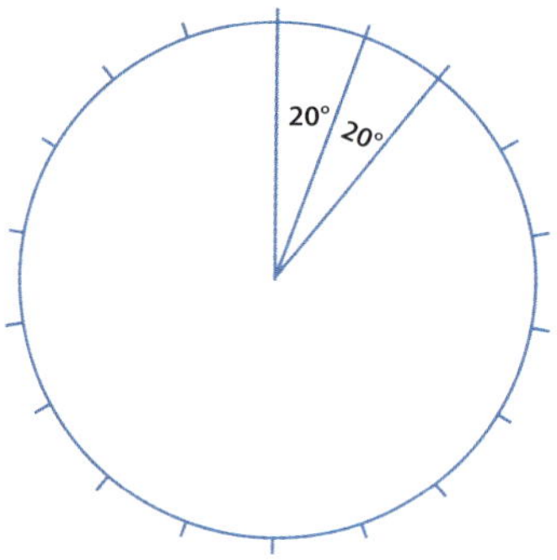

(b) How many sectors has the circle been divided into?

(c) Each sector has an angle of 20°.

How many sectors, each with an angle of 60°, could be fitted inside the circle?

6 (a) Draw a circle with diameter 7 cm.

(b) Mark a point P on the circumference.

(c) Draw a circle which has its centre on the original circle and which passes through the point P.

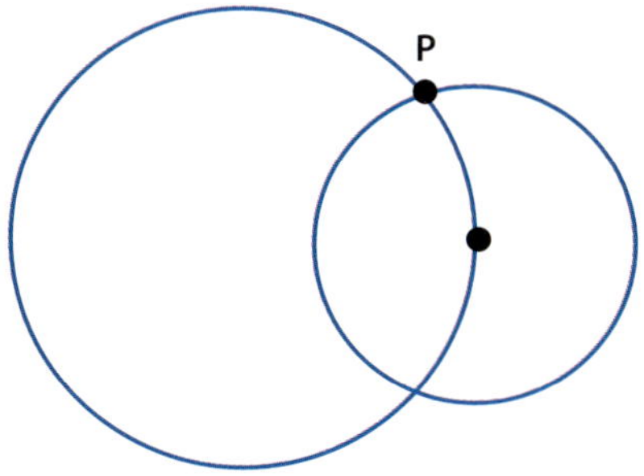

(d) Make a pattern by drawing more circles like this.

7 (a) Draw a circle with radius 3.5 cm.

(b) Mark points every 15° around the edge of the circle and number them from 1 to 24 as shown here.

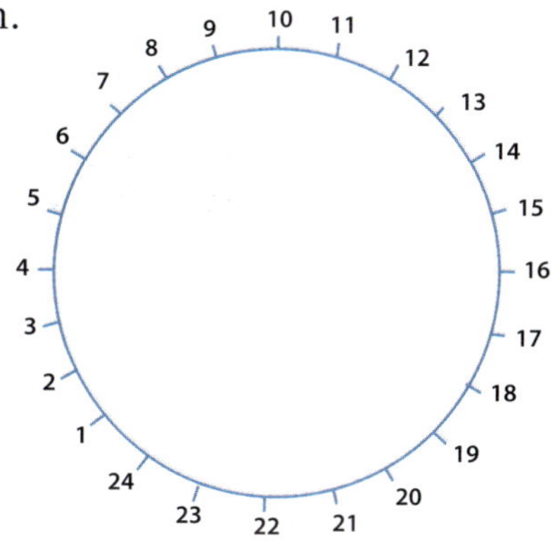

(c) Draw chords from point 1 to point 19, 1 to 18, 1 to 17, ... Continue until you join point 1 to point 2.

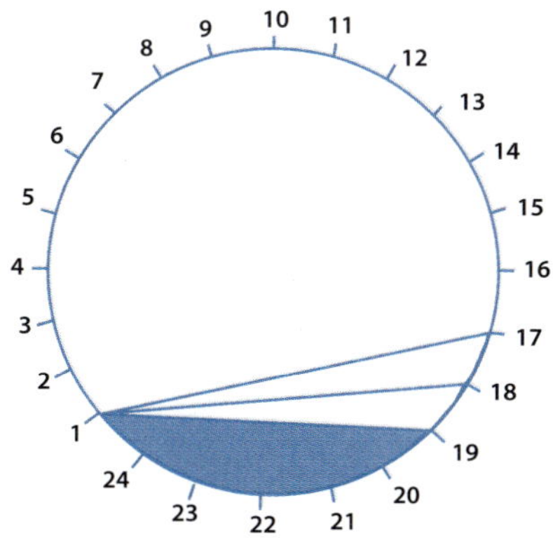

(d) Draw chords from point 19 to point 2, 19 to 3, 19 to 4, ... Continue until you join point 19 to point 18.

(e) How many minor segments are contained in the pattern?

Assignment 1 Centre paths – 1

- Draw two lines, AB and AC, with an angle of 30° between them.
- Draw a circle which has the centre on the line AC and which touches the line AB once only.

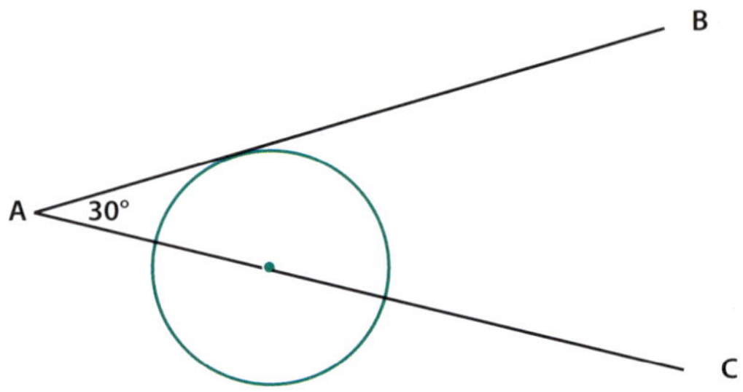

- Draw some more circles which have centres on AC and which touch the line AB.
- Draw another line through A which touches each of your circles once only.
- Measure the angle between your line and the line AC.

  What do you notice?

Assignment 2 Centre paths – 2

- Draw and shade two circles, each with radius 2.5 cm.

  Make their centres 8 cm apart.

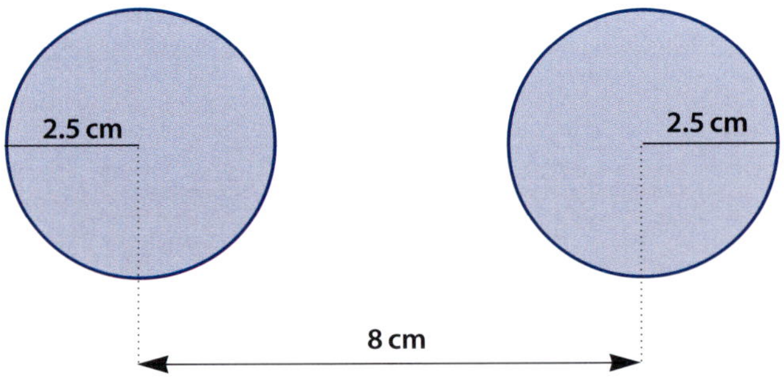

- Draw some more circles that just touch both the shaded circles.

  Join up the centres of these circles.

  What do you notice?
- Investigate what happens if you overlap the original shaded circles.

Measuring the circumference of a circle

Circles can be seen in many everyday objects.

Sometimes it is easy to measure the circumference using a measuring tape or thin string/thread and a ruler.

For very large or very small objects, it is difficult to obtain an accurate measurement of the circumference.

It would be useful to be able to calculate the circumference for a circle with a known radius or diameter.

Assignment 3 Circumference and diameter – a link?

- Make a collection of objects which have a circular cross-section.

  Try to find at least ten objects, each a different size.
- Measure the diameter and circumference of each object as accurately as you can.
- Record your results in a table like this.

Object	Diameter (d)	Circumference (C)
Tin of paint	12.2 cm	37.8 cm

- Draw a scatter graph, plotting the values of the diameter against the circumference.

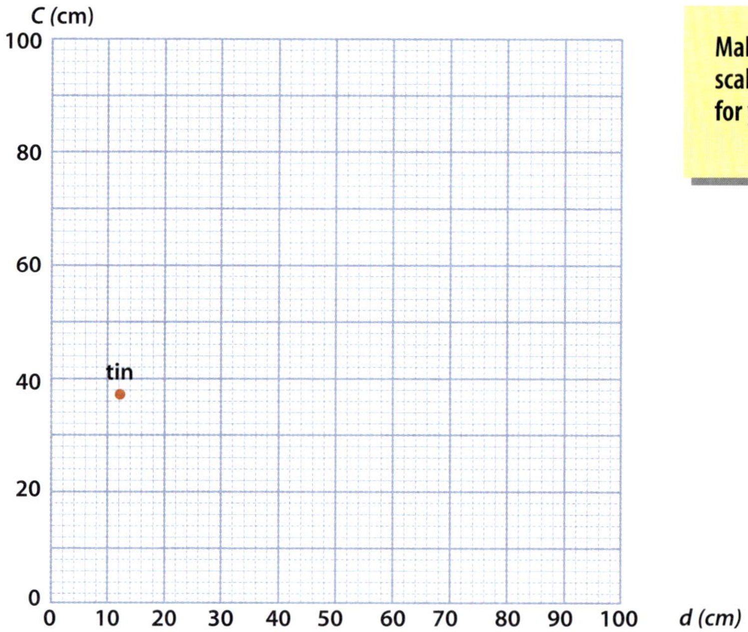

Make sure your scale is big enough for your data.

- Investigate the relationship between the circumference and diameter.

  Try to find a rule that will allow you to estimate the circumference of an object, given the diameter.

The relationship between circumference and diameter

$\frac{C}{d}$ is the same as $C \div d$

By measuring the circumference and diameter of circles of different sizes, you will find the ratio of circumference to diameter $\frac{C}{d}$ is about 3. The approximate rule is: $C = 3 \times d$

Use this rule to answer the questions in the next exercise.

Exercise 2

1 Estimate the circumference of circles A, B, C and D.

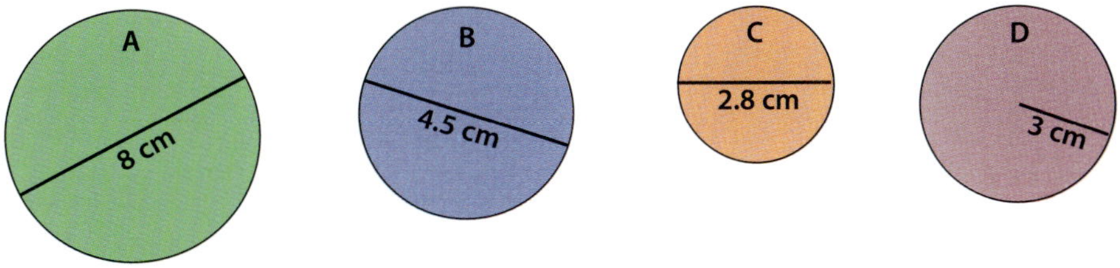

2 A tin of tomatoes has a diameter of 7 cm.
Estimate the circumference of the tin.

3 A bicycle wheel has diameter approximately 57 cm.
Estimate the circumference of the wheel.

4 Oil is stored in a cylindrical tank with radius 2 m.

(a) Write down the diameter of the top of the tank.

(b) Estimate the circumference of the top of the tank.

5 A circular pond has radius 5 m.

(a) Estimate the circumference of the pond.

(b) If tiles 20 cm long are to be placed around the edge of the pond, estimate how many tiles will be needed.

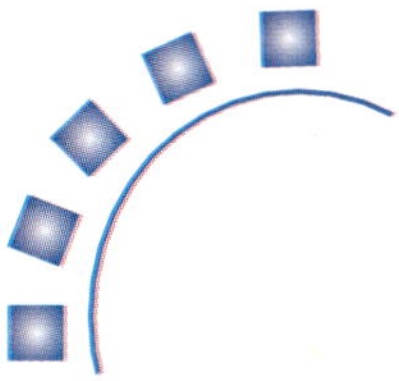

Looking for greater accuracy

By measuring the diameter and circumference of various sized circles, you can see that the circumference is actually slightly more than 3 times the diameter.

The ratio $\frac{C}{d}$ is 3 and 'a bit'

For thousands of years, mathematicians have been trying to find the exact value of the ratio $\frac{C}{d}$.

Over 2000 years ago, Archimedes, a Greek mathematician showed that the ratio of the circumference and the diameter lies between $3\frac{10}{71}$ and $3\frac{1}{7}$.

The ratio $\frac{C}{d}$ lies between $3\frac{10}{71}$ and $3\frac{1}{7}$.

Other mathematicians tried to find an exact value.
Initially, they gave their answers as fractions.

At the end of the seventeenth century, the Greek letter π (pi) was first used as a symbol for the ratio of the circumference to the diameter of any circle. So

$$\pi = \frac{C}{d}$$

Then decimals were introduced, and the value of π was found to an increasing number of decimal places.

Eventually, it was proved that it is impossible to write the number exactly.

Here is an estimate for π to 34 decimal places!

$$\pi = 3.1415926535897932384626433832795028$$

Assignment 4 Estimating

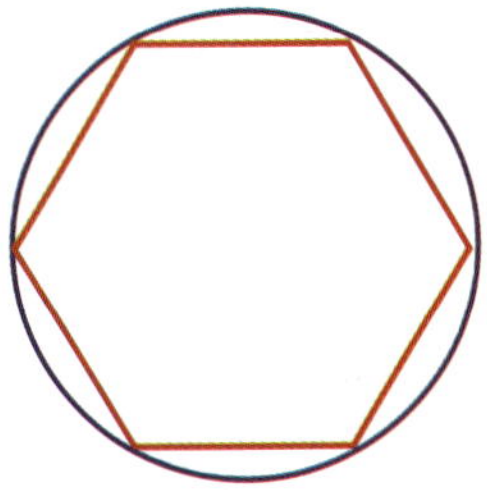

- Draw six circles, A, B, C, D, E and F, each with diameter 10 cm.
- On circle A, use a protractor to mark points every 60° around the edge and join these points to form a regular hexagon.
- Measure the length of one side of the hexagon and multiply by 6 to find the perimeter of the hexagon. Write down your answer.

Measure as accurately as you can.

- On circle B mark points every 40° around the edge and join the points to form a regular polygon.
- Measure the length of one side of the polygon and multiply by the number of sides to find the perimeter of the polygon. Write down your answer.
- Repeat this process on circles C and D, marking off angles of 30° and 20° to create two more regular polygons. As the size of the angle decreases, the number of sides of the polygon increases and the perimeter becomes closer to the circumference of the circle.
- Use circles E and F to find more accurate estimates for the circumference of a circle with diameter 10 cm.
- For each of the six polygons, use a calculator to find the value of the ratio $\frac{\text{perimeter}}{\text{diameter}}$
  Record your results in a table like this.

Number of sides in polygon	perimeter	$\frac{\text{perimeter}}{\text{diameter}}$
6		
9		

You should find you are able to find your own estimate for π in this way. (Archimedes used similar methods to estimate π!)

Key fact

$\pi = \frac{C}{d}$

This can be rewritten as:

$C = \pi \times \text{diameter}$

or $C = \pi d$

A formula for calculating the circumference of a circle given the diameter

When using the formula to calculate the circumference you can use an approximation for π.

Using $\pi = 3.14$ or $\pi = 3.142$ gives reasonably accurate values for the circumference.

Scientific calculators have a π key which gives an approximation to a greater number of decimal places.

Example

Find the circumference of a circle with diameter 8 mm.

$C = \pi d$

Using $\pi = 3.14$ (to 2 decimal places) you can estimate C to 1 decimal place.

A scientific calculator, with the π key, allows you to calculate with a greater degree of accuracy.

$C = 3.14 \times 8$

$= 25.12$

$\simeq 25.1$ (to 1 decimal place)

The circumference of a circle with diameter 8 mm is 25.1 mm (to 1 decimal place).

Using $\pi = 3.142$ (to 3 decimal places) you can estimate C to 2 decimals places.

$C = 3.142 \times 8$

$= 25.136$

$\simeq 25.14$ (to 2 decimal places)

The circumference of a circle with diameter 8 mm is 25.14 mm (to 2 decimal places).

Using the π key on a calculator (3.1415927...) you will get a much more accurate answer.

$C = \pi \times 8$

$= 25.132741$

The circumference of a circle with diameter 8 mm is 25.132741 mm.

Exercise 3

If you do not have a scientific calculator, use 3.142 as an approximation for π and give all your answers correct to 2 decimal places.

1 Calculate the circumference for the circles A, B and C.

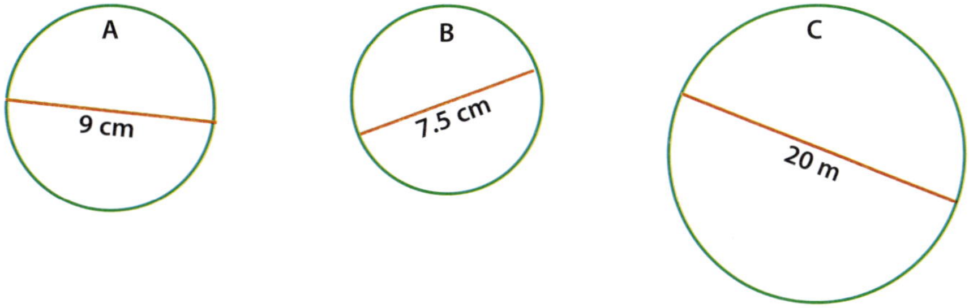

diameter
= 2 × radius
= 2*r*

2 Calculate the diameter and circumference for the circles A and B.

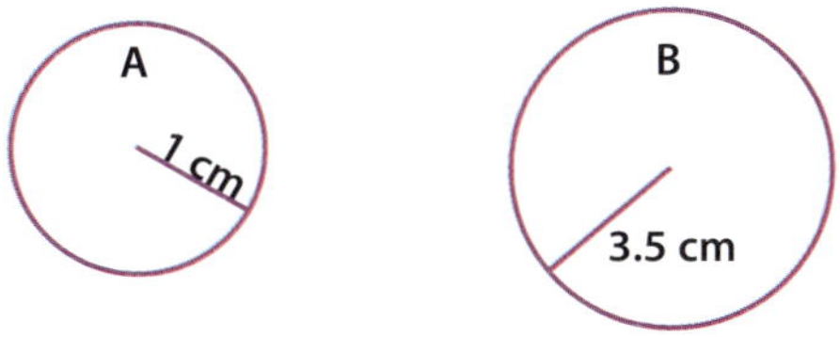

3 Calculate the circumference for each of these circles.

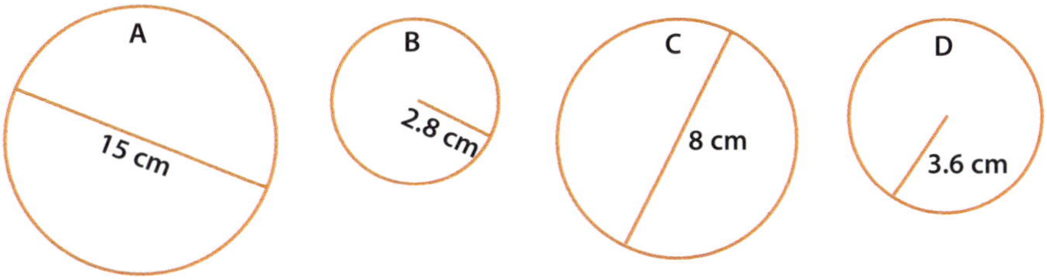

4 A flower bed is circular with diameter 4.8 m.
Calculate the circumference of the flower bed.

5 A wheel has radius 22 cm.
Calculate its circumference.

6 The lid of a tin of paint has diameter 18 cm.
Calculate the circumference of the tin.

The perimeter is the distance all round the edge of the shape.

7 Find the perimeter of this semicircle.

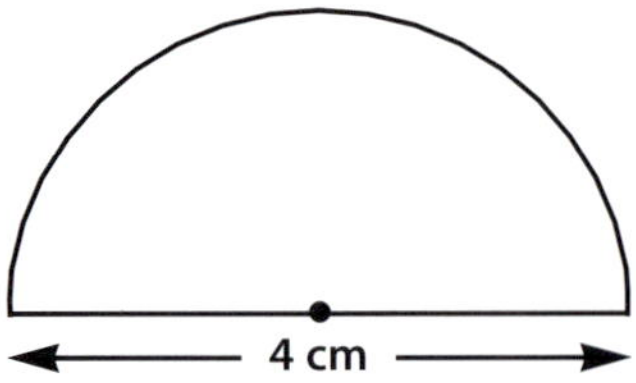

8 A race track has two semicircular ends of diameter 25 m, joined by two straight sections 150 m long.

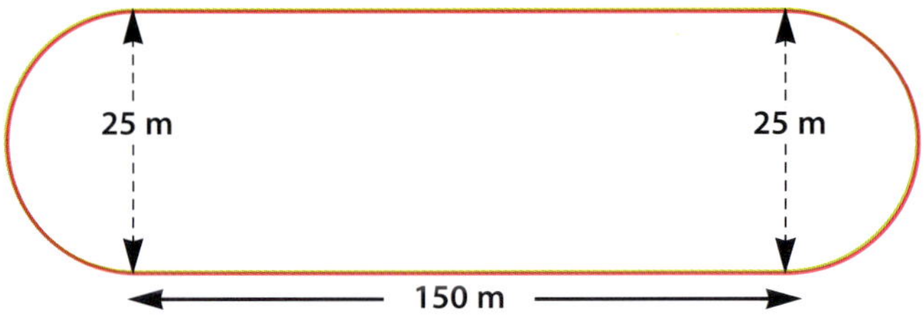

Calculate the perimeter of the running track.

9 A tin of fruit has diameter 8 cm and height 10 cm.

(a) Calculate the circumference of the tin.

(b) If a paper label is to be put around the tin and a 1-cm overlap is needed to secure it, what is the area of paper required? Give your answer to the nearest square centimetre.

$C = \pi d$
So $d = C \div \pi$
or $d = \frac{C}{\pi}$

10 (a) Using the fact that C is approximately $3 \times d$, find an approximation for the diameter of a circle which has circumference 12 cm.

(b) Find a more accurate approximation for the diameter using the fact that $C = \pi d$.

11 Use $d = \frac{C}{\pi}$ to calculate the diameters of circles with circumference:

(a) 30 cm (b) 1.56 m (c) 85.8 cm (d) 45 m

12 Calculate the diameter of a cylindrical vase which has circumference 36 cm.

13 Calculate the radius of a litter bin which has circumference 1.25 m.

14 This diagram shows a quarter of a circle.

Calculate the radius of the circle.

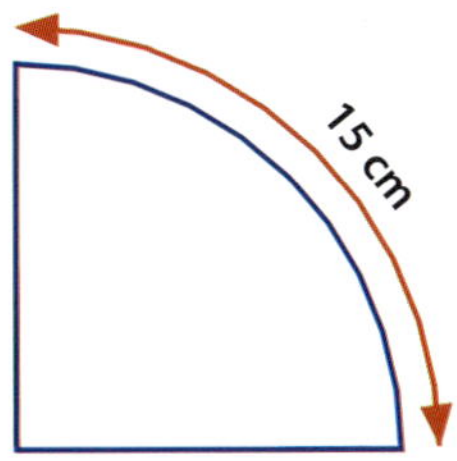

Assignment 5 The history of π

Use CD-ROM, encyclopaedias or books on the history of Mathematics to research the development of estimates for π by mathematicians through the ages.

Make a poster to illustrate your findings!

The area of a circle

Assignment 6 Joining sectors!

You will need paper, scissors and glue for this assignment.

- Draw a circle with radius 4 cm.
- Using a protractor, mark points every 30° around the circumference.
- Join each point to the centre of the circle to form 12 sectors.

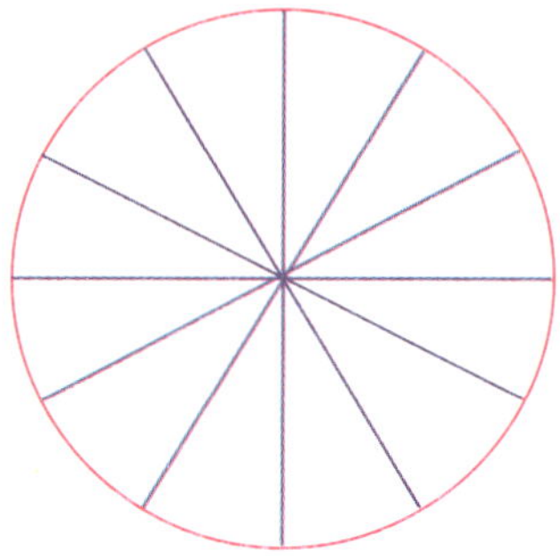

- Cut out all 12 sectors and rearrange them as shown here:

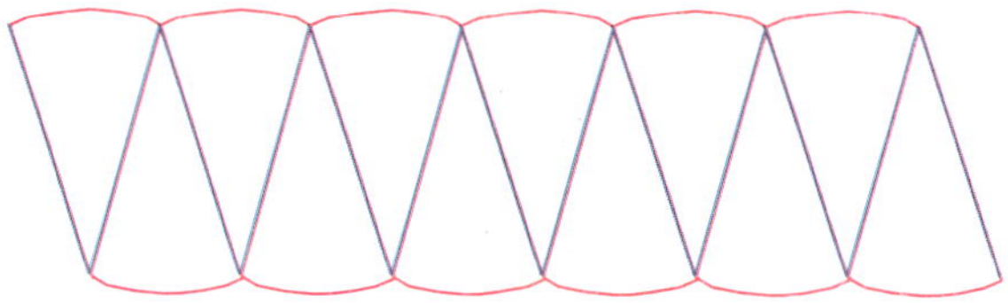

You can see that this arrangement almost makes a parallelogram.

area of parallelogram = base × perpendicular height

- Glue your 12 sectors onto paper.
- Measure the base and height of your parallelogram as accurately as you can.

Calculate its area.

This value is a good estimate for the area of the original circle.

Assignment 7 Plotting radius against area

- Draw a circle, with radius 4 cm.
- Using a protractor, mark points every 20° around the circumference and join each point to the centre to form 18 sectors.
- Repeat the method used in Assignment 6 to find another estimate for the area of the original circle.
- Is this a better estimate than the first one?

  Explain your answer.

  Explain how you could improve the accuracy of your estimate.
- Work in a group to find estimates for the areas of circles with radii 5 cm, 6 cm, 7 cm and 8 cm.
- Display your results in a table like this.

Radius (cm)	Area (cm^2)
4	
5	
6	
7	
8	

- On graph paper, draw a scatter graph plotting radius against area.

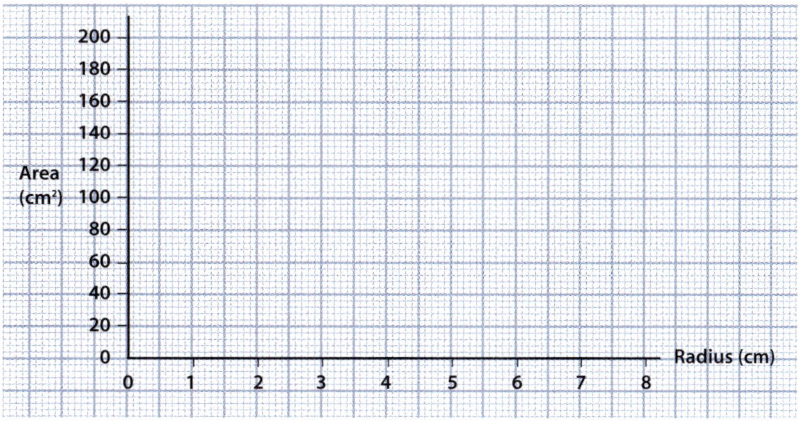

- If possible, find out the results from other groups and add them to your graph.
  Describe the features of your graph.

A formula for calculating the area of a circle

If a circle is divided into a large number of equal sectors they can be arranged to form a parallelogram.

As you increase the number of sectors, the height of the parallelogram becomes closer in length to the radius of the circle and the base of the parallelogram becomes closer in length to half of the circumference of the circle.

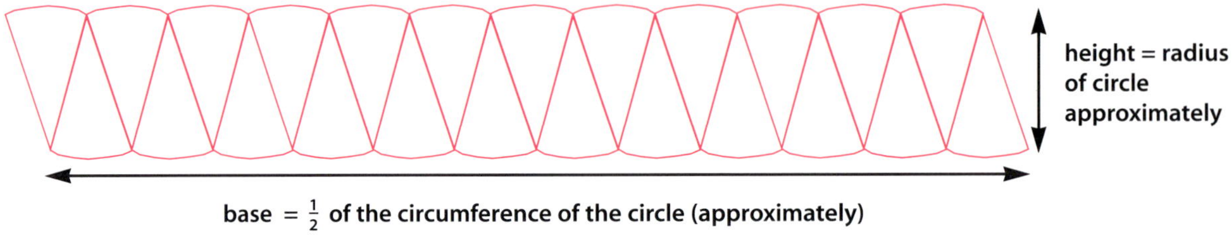

Area of circle = base of parallelogram × perpendicular height

$$= (\tfrac{1}{2} \text{ of } C) \times r$$

$$= (\tfrac{1}{2} \text{ of } 2 \times \pi \times r) \times r$$

$$= (\pi \times r) \times r$$

$$= \pi \times r \times r$$

$$= \pi r^2$$

$$C = \pi \times d$$
$$= \pi \times (2 \times r)$$
$$= 2 \times \pi \times r$$

Key fact

The area (A) of a circle with radius (r) is given by the formula $A = \pi r^2$

Using the formula

Example

Find the area of a circle with radius 3 cm.

Area $= \pi r^2$

$= \pi \times 3 \times 3$

$= \pi \times 9$

$= 28.27$ (to 2 d.p.)

The area of a circle with radius 3 cm is 28.27 cm² (to 2 decimal places).

Find the area of a circle with diameter 20 cm.

$r = \tfrac{1}{2}d = 10$

Area $= \pi \times 10 \times 10$

$= \pi \times 100$

$= 314.20$ (to 2 d.p.)

The area of a circle with diameter 20 cm is 314.20 cm² (to 2 decimal places).

Exercise 4

> **If you do not have a scientific calculator, use $\pi = 3.142$ and give your answers to 2 decimal places.**

1 Use the formula to calculate the areas of circles with radius:

(a) 4 cm (b) 5 cm (c) 6 cm (d) 7 cm (e) 8 cm

If you worked through Assignment 7, compare your answers to this question with those in your table.

How close were your estimates?

2 Use the formula to calculate the areas of circles A, B and C .
(You will need to find the radius of each circle first.)

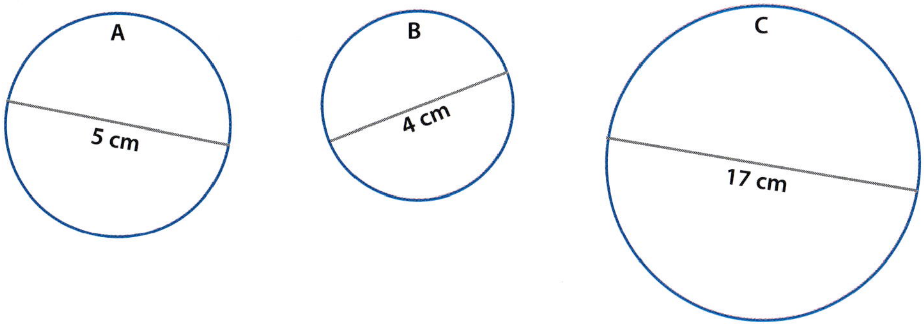

3 A circular table top has a diameter of 1.6 m.

(a) Write down the radius of the table.

(b) Use the formula to calculate the area of the table.

4 A circular flower bed has a radius of 50 cm.
Use the formula to calculate the area of the flower bed.

5 A wooden breadboard is circular, with diameter 30 cm.
Use the formula to calculate the area of the breadboard.

6 A clockface is circular with radius 12 cm.
Use the formula to calculate the area of the clockface.

7 These small cans of juice are packed in boxes of eight.

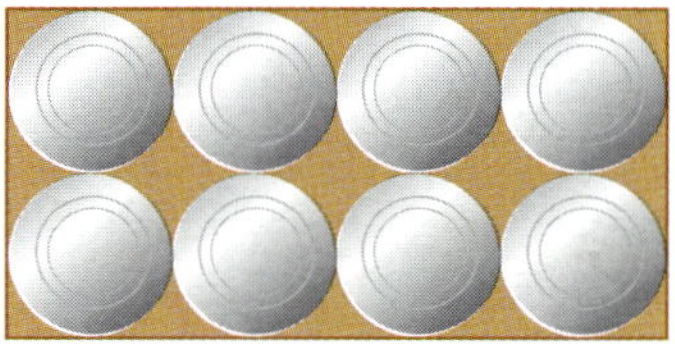

The top of each can is circular, and the diameter of each can is 6 cm.

(a) Calculate the area of the top of one can.

(b) Calculate the length and width of the smallest possible box that could hold the cans in the arrangement shown.

(c) If the height of each can is 10 cm, calculate the minimum area of card needed to make the box.

8 This diagram shows a patio consisting of a semicircle with diameter 3 m and a rectangle measuring 3 m by 2 m.

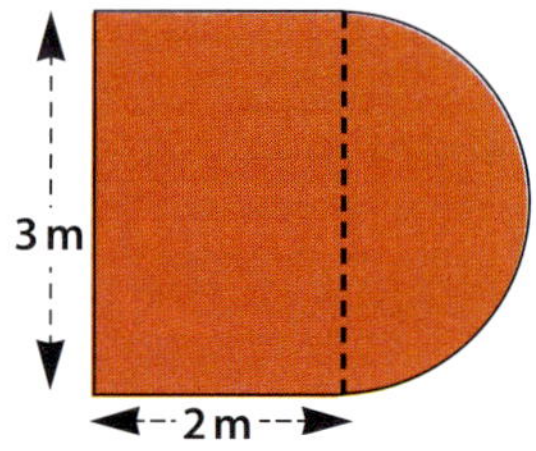

Calculate the area of the patio.

9 This circular pond has radius 4.8 m and a path around it of width 0.8 m.

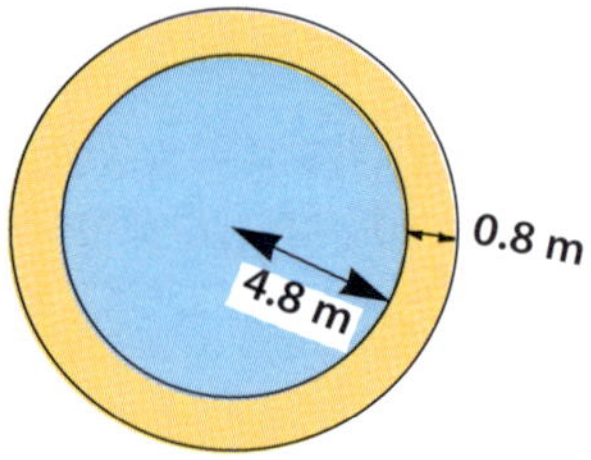

(a) Calculate the area of the pond.

(b) Calculate the area of the path.

A quadrant of a circle is a quarter of a circle.

10 A rectangular garden measuring 8 m by 15 m has two corner flower beds which are quadrants of circles with radius 1.8 m.

The rest of the garden is laid to lawn.

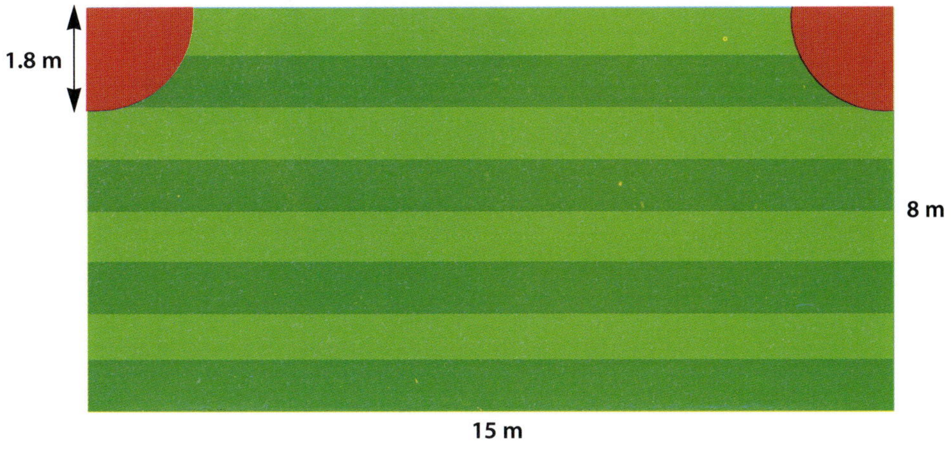

(a) Calculate the area of the whole garden.

(b) Calculate the total area of the flower beds.

(c) Calculate the area of the lawn.

(d) If fertilizer for the lawn costs 28p per square metre, find the cost of applying fertilizer to the whole lawn.

Give your answer to the nearest penny.

11 The formula for the area of a circle is $A = \pi r^2$

(a) Using $\pi = 3$, estimate the area of a circle which has radius 6 cm.

(b) Using the fact that the area is approximately equal to $3 \times r^2$, find an estimate for the radius of a circle with an area of 75 cm^2.

12 Using the formula for the area of a circle and a more accurate value of π, calculate the radius of a circle with an area of 255 cm^2.

Give your answer to the nearest centimetre.

Assignment 8 Area of 100cm²?

For this assignment, you will need four coins: 1p, 2p, 5p and 10p.

- Measure the diameter of each coin in centimetres and calculate the area of each coin.
- By drawing around the coins, create a pattern of circles so that the total area of the circles you use is as close as possible to $100\,cm^2$.

Each circle must touch at least one other circle.

No circles may overlap.

You must use all four coins to make your pattern.

Each coin may be used as often as you like.

- When you have completed your pattern, write down how many of each coin you have used and the total area of the circles in your pattern.

Review Exercise

1 Draw five circles each with a radius of 3 cm and use them to show these parts of a circle:

(a) an arc (b) a chord (c) a diameter

(d) a sector (e) a segment

2 (a) Draw a circle with radius 4 cm.

Using a protractor, mark points every 45° around the circumference.

Label the points, 1 to 8.

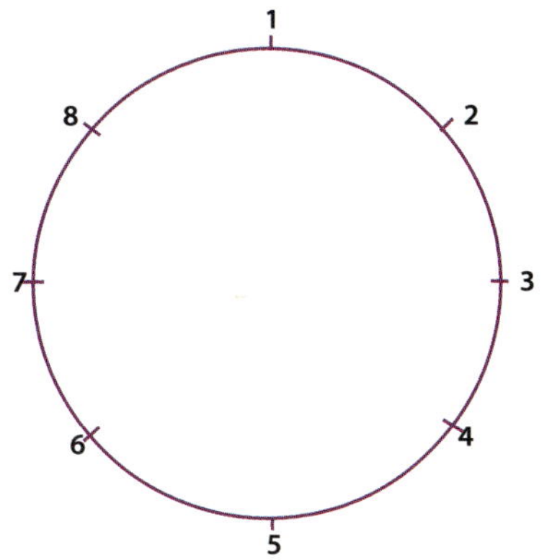

(b) Make a triangle by joining points 1, 5 and 2.

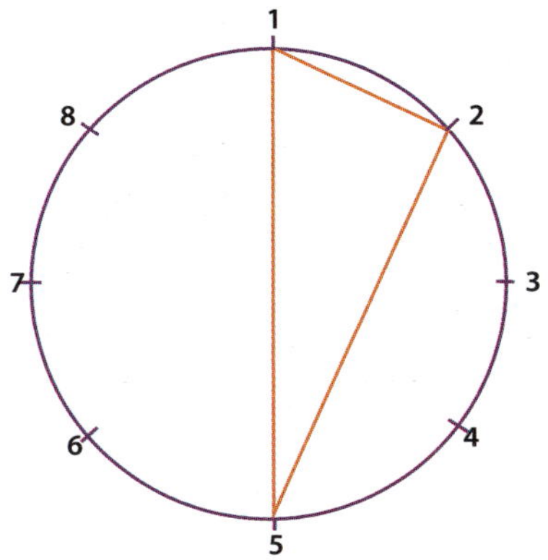

Make another triangle by joining points 1, 5 and 4.

Use points 1, 5 and 7 to make a third triangle.

Write down what is special about these three triangles.

(c) Colour all the minor segments in your diagram the same colour.

You should find the shape left unshaded has four sides.

What is the special name for this shape?

3 Without using a calculator, write down an estimate for the circumference of a circle with diameter 2.5 cm.

4 Calculate the circumference of these circles using $C = \pi d$.
(Give your answers to 1 decimal place.)

(a) Circle, diameter 8.2 cm

(b) Circle, radius 3.9 cm

5 Calculate the diameter of a wheel which has a circumference of 1.8 m.
(Give your answer to 3 decimal places.)

6 Calculate the areas of these circles.
(Give your answers to 2 decimal places.)

(a) Circle, radius 0.5 m

(b) Circle, diameter 2.3 m

7 Calculate the perimeter and area of each of these two shapes.
(Give your answers to 1 decimal place.)

Shape A

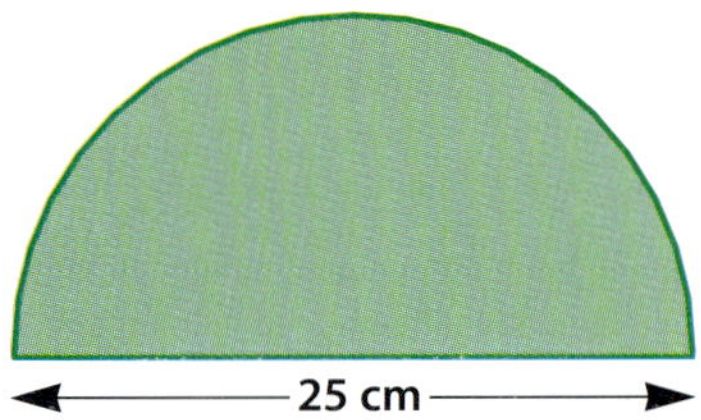

Shape B

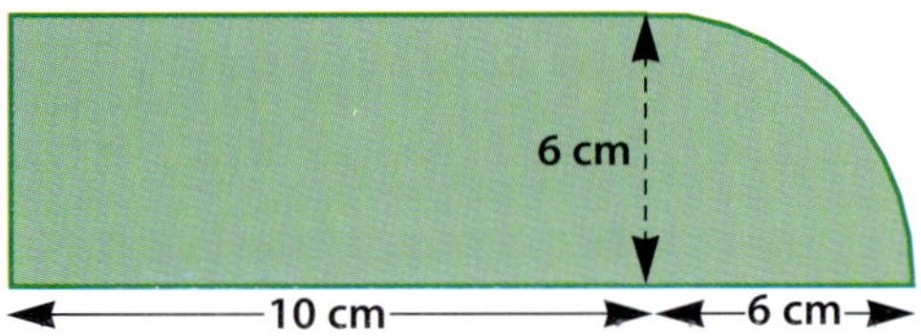

8 A circular pond has an area of 147 m^2.

Using 3 as an approximation for π, estimate the radius of the pond.

Assignment 9 Windows

Many ornate windows in churches and other public buildings are designed to involve whole circles or parts of circles.

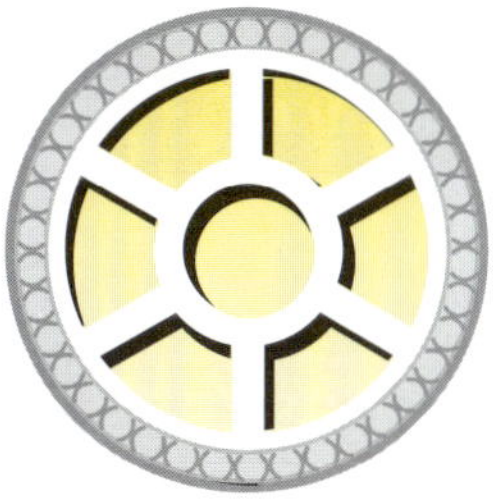

- Make up your own design for a window involving circles or parts of circles.
- Draw your design to scale, using a scale of 1 to 10.
- Write the actual measurements on your scale drawing.
- Which of these can be found in your design?

  chords sectors segments arcs

- Calculate the area of your window.

Straight line graphs

In this chapter you will learn:

- ➜ **how to draw linear graphs**
- ➜ **what is meant by the terms gradient and intercept**
- ➜ **to recognise the graph of a linear equation**
- ➜ **how to form an equation from its graph**

Starting points

Before starting this chapter you will need to:

- know how to plot coordinates in all four quadrants
- know how to substitute into simple expressions
- be able to draw a table of values.

Exercise 1

Your axes should look like this

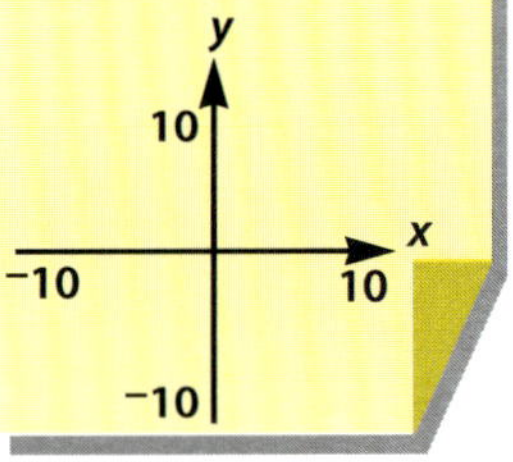

1 On graph paper, draw axes from −10 to 10 for both x and y and then plot these points.

(2, −8) (4, −6) (8, −6) (10, −8) (10, 0) (8, 2)
(8, 8) (6, 10) (4, 8) (4, 2) (2, 0) (2, −8)

Join them up in order.

Reflect your shape in the y axis and write the coordinates of the new image.

2 (a) Write down the coordinates of the points A, B, C, D and E.

(b) The point E will make ABCDEF a symmetrical hexagon.
What are the coordinates of the point F?

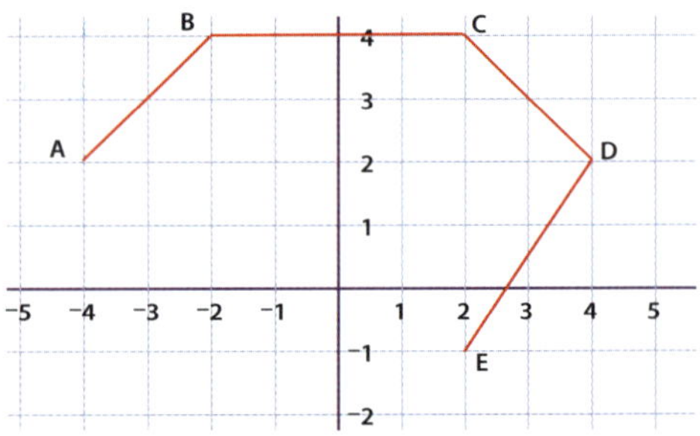

3 If $y = 5x$, write down the value of y when

(a) $x = 1$ (b) $x = 0$

(c) $x = 3$ (d) $x = 10$

4 If $y = 2x + 3$, write down the value of y when

(a) $x = 0$ (b) $x = 1$

(c) $x = 3$ (d) $x = 5$

5 If $y = x + 2$, copy and complete this table to give values of y for values of x from $^-2$ to 4.

$y = x + 2$

x	$^-2$	$^-1$	0	1	2	3	4
+2	2	2	2	2	2		
y	0		2		4		

Write down what you notice about the y values.

6 Copy and complete this table of values for $y = 2x - 2$.

$y = 2x - 2$

x	$^-2$	$^-1$	0	1	2	3
$2x$	$^-4$	$^-2$	0			
−2	−2	−2	−2			
y	$^-6$		$^-2$		8	10

Write down what you notice about the y values.

7 Draw a table of values to represent $y = 3x + 2$ for values of x from $^-2$ to 6.

Write down what you notice about the y values.

Key fact

Linear graphs are straight line graphs.

Drawing linear graphs

Assignment 1 Looking at straight lines

Your axes should look like this

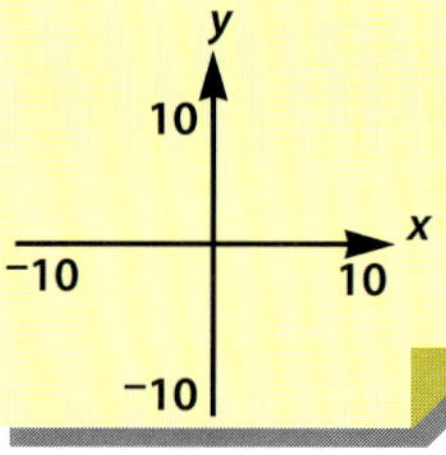

- Copy and complete this table of values for $y = 2x$.

x	$^-2$	$^-1$	0	1	2	3	4
$y = 2x$	$^-4$		0			6	

  On graph paper, draw axes from −10 to 10 for both x and y.

  Plot the points (x, y) and join to make a straight line graph.

  Extend your line as far as possible. Label the line $y = 2x$.

- Draw tables of values for $y = x$, $y = 3x$, $y = 4x$ and $y = \frac{1}{2}x$.

  Draw straight line graphs for each of these on the original grid.

  Extend your lines as far as possible.

  Write down what you notice about your five graphs.

Assignment 2 More straight lines

- Copy and complete this table of values for $y = {^-x}$.

  $y = {^-x}$

x	$^-2$	$^-1$	0	1	2	3	4
$y = {^-x}$			0	$^-1$			

  On graph paper, draw axes from −10 to 10 for both x and y.

  Plot the points (x, y) and join them to make a straight line graph.

  Extend your line as far as possible. Label the line $y = {^-x}$.

- Draw tables of values for $y = {^-2x}$, $y = {^-3x}$ and $y = {^-4x}$.

  Draw straight line graphs for each of these on the original grid.

  Extend your lines as far as possible.

  Write down what you notice about your four graphs.

Key fact
The gradient of a line is its steepness.

The gradient of a line

Consider the line $y = 2x$.

Select a point on the line with a whole number value for x.

Draw a line one unit across and from its end draw a line upwards until it touches the graph.

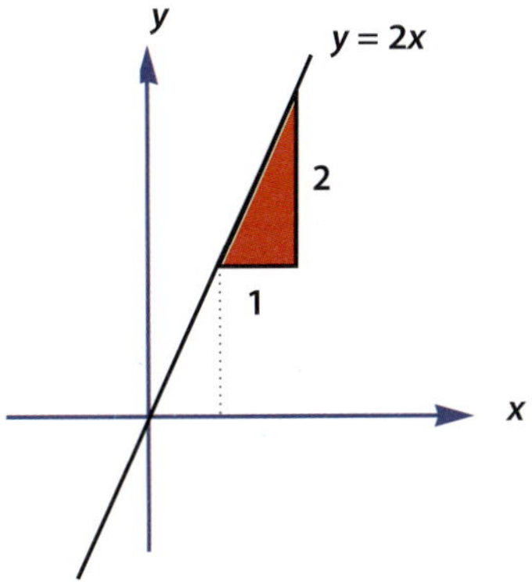

Key fact
The step size gives the steepness or gradient of a line.

For $y = 2x$, the length of the line drawn upwards is 2.

The step size of the line $y = 2x$ is given as

$$\frac{\text{distance up}}{\text{distance across}} = \frac{2}{1} = 2$$

Exercise 2

1 Calculate the gradient of these lines.

(a) $y = x$ (b) $y = 3x$ (c) $y = 4x$ (d) $y = \frac{1}{2}x$

Lines with negative gradient

For $y = {}^-3x$, one unit is measured across and the other unit is measured downwards, that is, negatively.

The stepsize is $\frac{^-3}{1} = {}^-3$

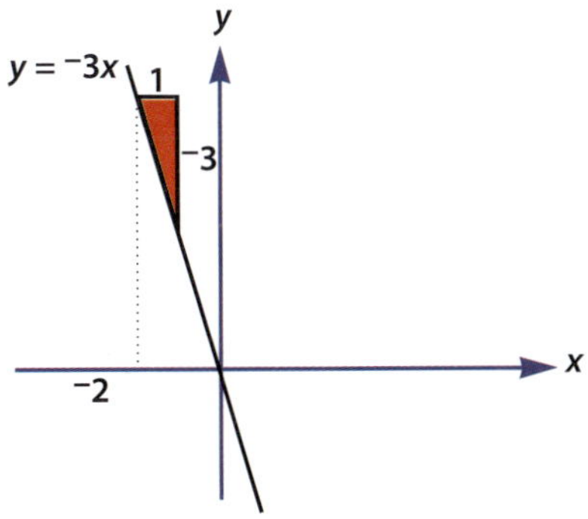

Exercise 3

1 Calculate the gradient of these lines.

(a) $y = {}^-x$ (b) $y = {}^-2x$ (c) $y = {}^-4x$ (d) $y = \frac{^-1}{2}x$

Key fact

The intercept of a line in the value of y where the line cuts the y axis.

Assignment 3 Cutting points

- Copy and complete this table of values for $y = x - 2$.

  $y = x - 2$

x	0	1	2	3			
−2	−2	−2	−2	−2	−2	−2	−2
y	0	−1					

  Using axes −10 to 10, plot the points, (x, y) and join them to make a straight line graph.

- Draw tables of values for $y = x + 2$ and $y = x + 3$.

  Plot the points from each table on the same axes.
  Join each set of points to make a straight line.

  Extend all your lines as far as possible and label each line.
  Write down what you notice.

- On the same diagram, *without* drawing tables of values, draw the graphs of

$y = x - 3$	$y = x + 5$	$y = x + 1$
$y = x - 1$	$y = x - 5$	$y = x - 4$
$y = x + 6$	$y = x + 1\frac{1}{2}$	$y = x$

  Write down what you notice.

- For the equation $y = x + c$, what does the c tell you about the graph?

Exercise 4

1 (a) Copy this table of values and by completing the patterns for x and for y, extend the table to $x = 10$.

x	−2	−1	0	1	2	3	4	5
y				9	8	7		

(b) Write down what you notice about each pair of values.

(c) Using axes from −10 to 10 for both x and y, plot these points on a graph. Write down anything you notice about the coordinates of the points where the line cuts the axes.

2 (a) Write down six pairs of coordinates that fit the equation $x + y = 8$.

Plot them on the same graph.

(b) Which of these points lie on the line $x + y = 8$?

(3, 2) (2.5, 5.5) (1, 8) (10, −2)

Explain how you can tell?

3 The points (3, 4) and (1, 6) both lie on the same line.

(a) What is the equation of this line?

(b) Name four more points which lie on this same line.

4 (a) Which of these points lie on the line $x + y = 5$?

(3, 2) (0, 3) (5, 0) (6, −1) (0, 5) (1, 2) (−1, 4) (1, 4)

(b) On which line do the other points lie?

5 Draw axes from −10 to 10.
Without creating tables of values, draw these lines.

$x + y = 4$

$x + y = 6$

$x + y = 9$

Write down what you notice about the gradient of these lines.

Assignment 4 Computer drawn graphs

- Using either a graphics calculator or software on the computer, try drawing different graphs.
- Investigate the effect of varying the steepness of the line, and the points at which it cuts the axes.

Key fact

Parallel lines have the same gradient.

Exercise 5

1 (a) Draw a table of values for $y = 3x + 2$ and, using axes from $^{-}10$ to 10, draw the graph.

(b) On the same axes, draw four lines of your own choosing which are parallel to $y = 3x + 2$ and label them.

2 These four graphs are parallel.

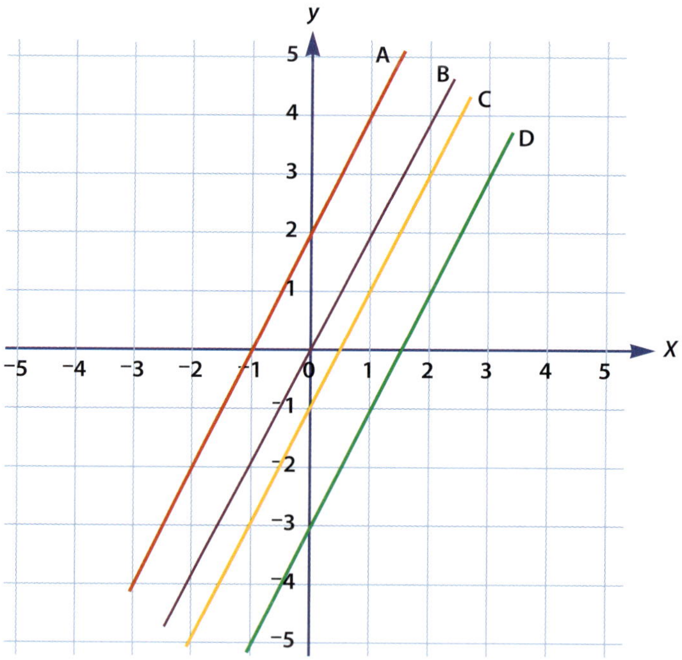

(a) What is the gradient of line A?

(b) Write down the equations of lines A, B, C and D.

Assignment 5 Drawing graphs without a table of values

Look at this equation: $y = 2x + 3$

You know two things about the graph of this equation: the gradient and the intercept.

$$y = 2x + 3$$

gradient = 2 intercept = 3

- Draw the graph, by first marking a point at the intercept (0, 3) on the y axis.

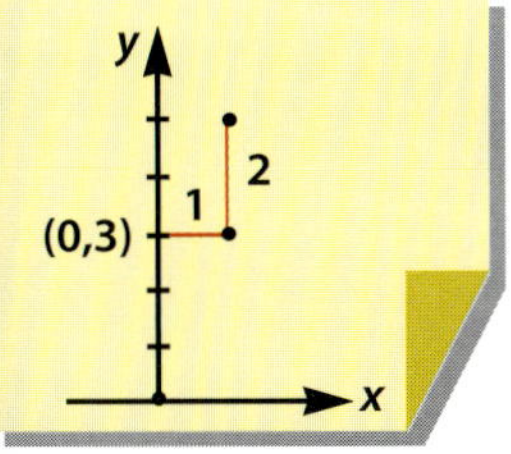

- Then, start at point (0, 3), and move 1 square across to the right and 2 squares up.

  Repeat this movement to mark further points.

  These points can then be joined to give the line $y = 2x + 3$.

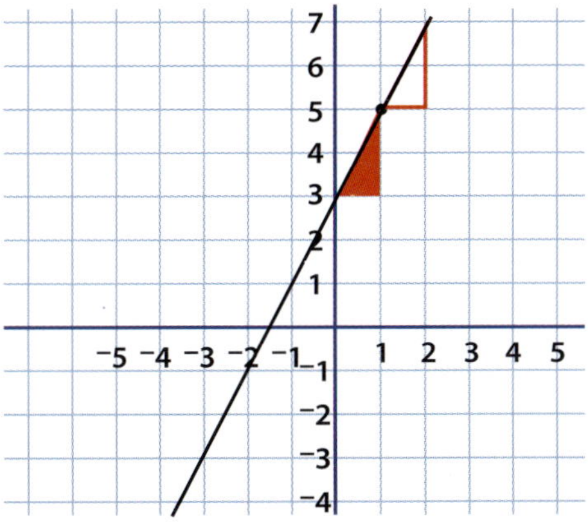

The intercept is 3 so the graph crosses the y axis at (0,3).

The gradient is 2 so the line goes up 2 for every 1 across.

- To make sure that the line drawn is correct, choose another point on the line and check it makes $y = 2x + 3$.

  For example, the point (−1, 1) is on the line.
  When $x = -1$, $y = 2x + 3 = (2 \times -1) + 3 = 1$.

  So, the line is correct.

  Check another point from your diagram.

Exercise 6

1 Using axes from −10 to 10, draw these three lines on the same graph.

(a) $y = x + 2$

(b) $y = 2x + 4$

(c) $y = x + 5$

Label each graph.

2 Using axes from −10 to 10, draw these four lines on the same graph.

(a) $y = x - 4$

(b) $y = 2x - 6$

(c) $y = 3x - 2$

(d) $y = 2x - 1$

For graphs with negative gradients you will need to count down not up.

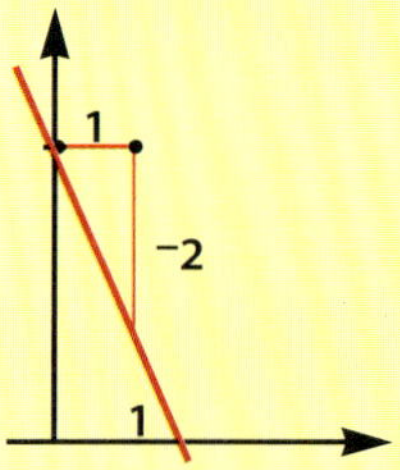

3 Using axes from −10 to 10, draw these three lines on the same graph.

Label your graphs.

(a) $y = {}^{-}2x + 3$

(b) $y = 5 - x$

(c) $y = {}^{-}3x - 5$

4 Draw the graphs of $y = 2x + 3$ and $y = {}^{-}2x + 3$ on one set of axes.

Write down the coordinates of the point where your two graphs cross.

5 Choose your own axes and draw four lines for yourself labelling them with the correct equations.

Swap books with a partner and check each other's graphs.

General equation, y = mx + c

Assignment 6 Reading a graph

- Draw axes −10 to 10.

  Plot one point at (1,6).

  Plot another point at (2, 8).

  Join these two points with a straight line, extending the line to cut both axes as shown.

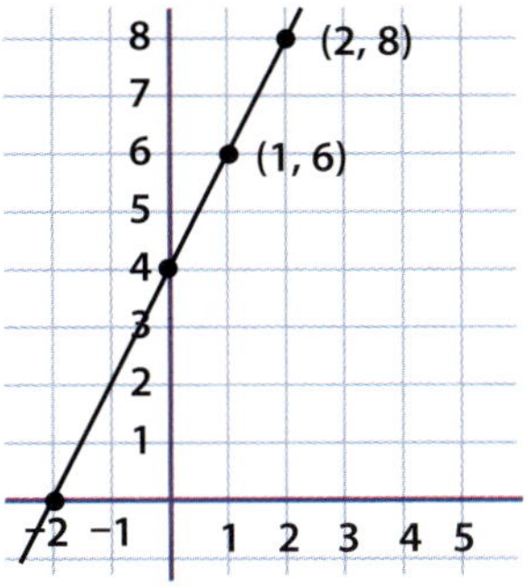

- Where does your line cut the y axis?

  Write down which part of the equation $y = mx + c$ gives you this value.

- On the graph, draw a right-angled triangle from the cutting point on the y axis across 1 square.

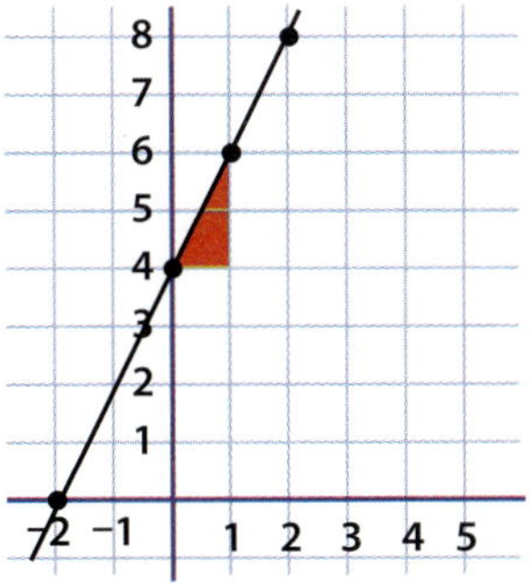

  Count the number of squares up until you reach the line.
  What is the gradient of the line?
  Which part of the equation $y = mx + c$ gives you this value?

- Write down the equation of the line .

Key fact

The line $y = mx + c$ cuts the y axis at $(0, c)$

Key fact

The line $y = mx + c$ has gradient m.

Exercise 7

1 Look at this graph.

(a) Write down the coordinates of the point where the line crosses the y-axis.

(b) Write down the gradient of the line.

(c) Write down the equation of the line.

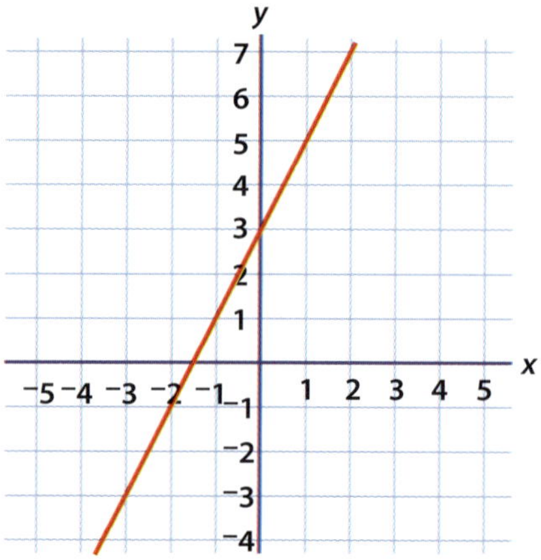

2 For each of these graphs, write down

(i) the intercept, c

(ii) the gradient, m

(iii) the equation of the line..

(a)

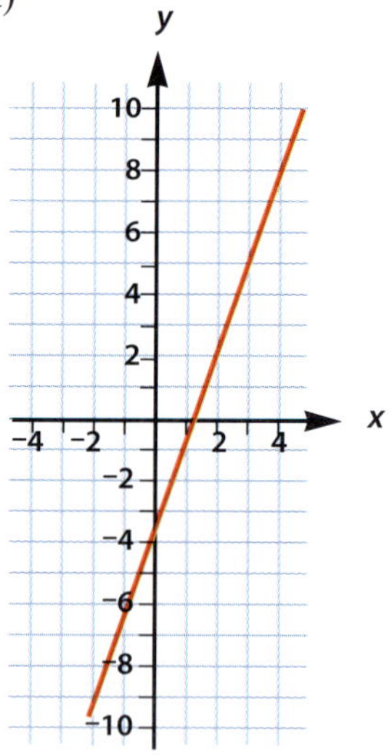

(b)

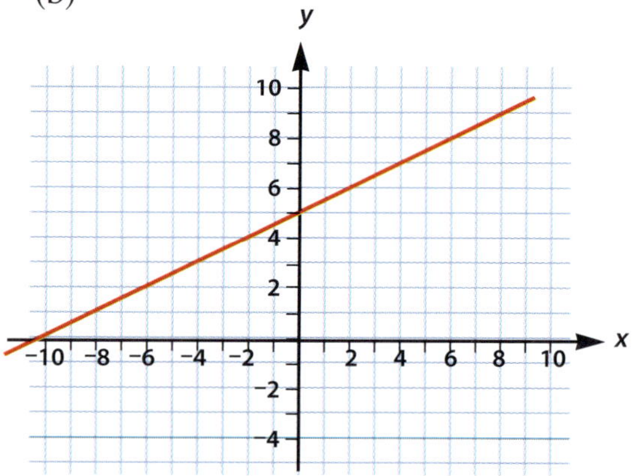

3 Write down the equations of these lines.

(a)

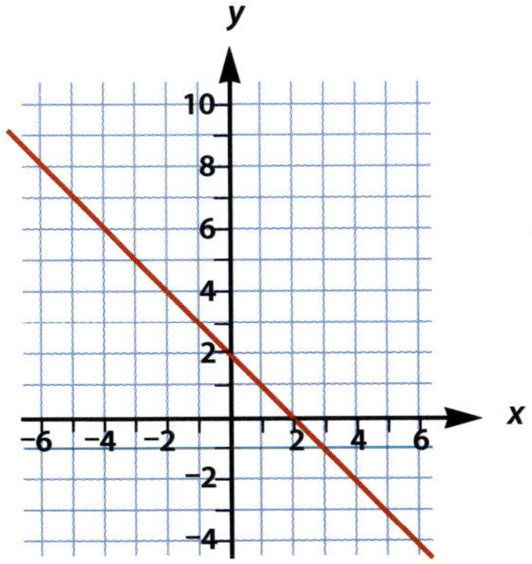

(b)

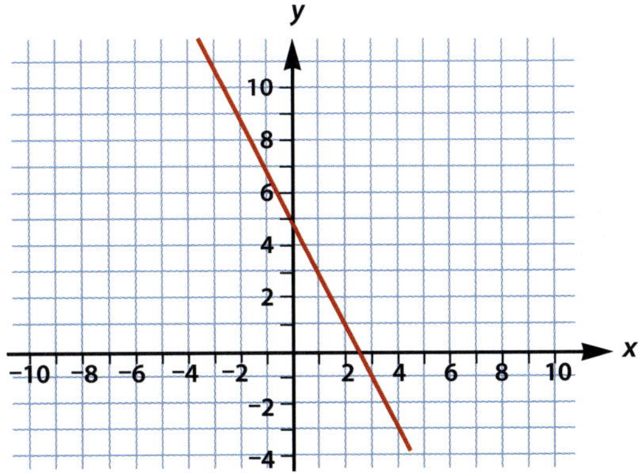

(c)

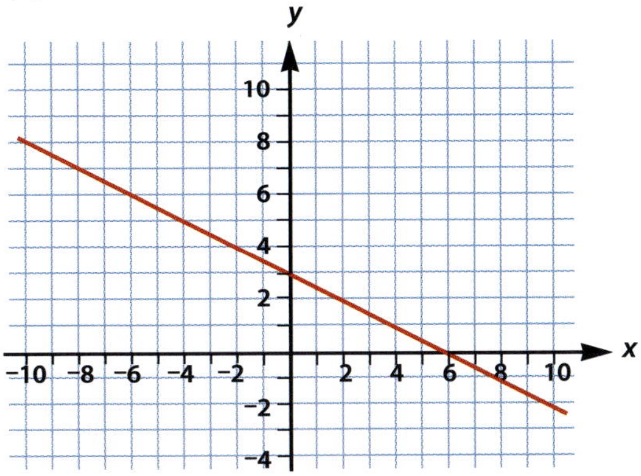

(d)

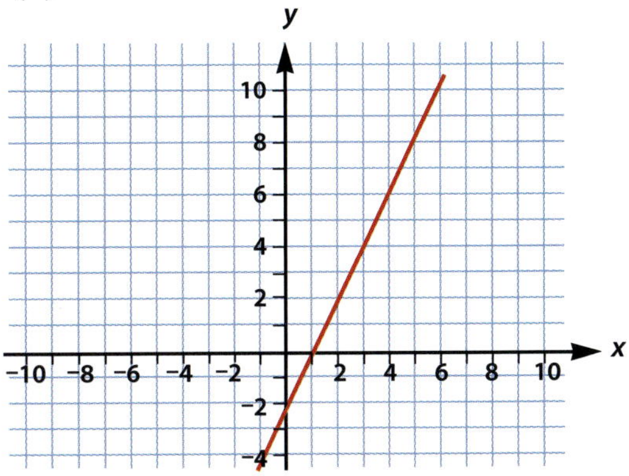

(e)

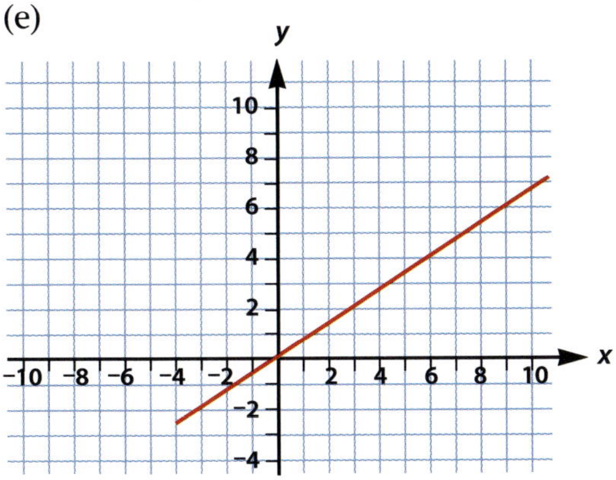

(f)

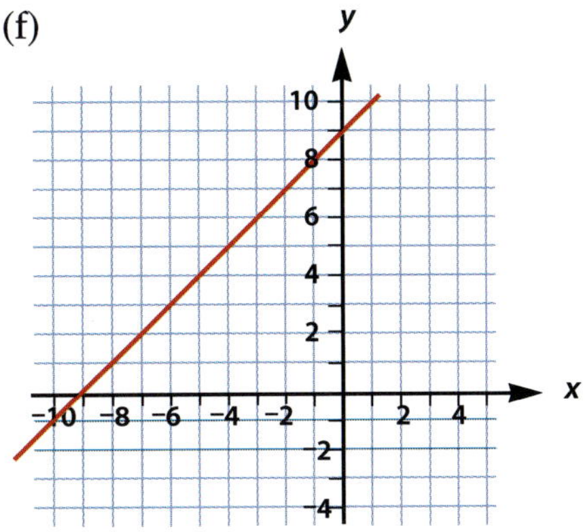

Review Exercise

1 (a) Plot points A(3, 8) and B(4, 11) and draw a straight line through them to cut both axes.

(b) Where does this line cut the y axis?

(c) Work out the gradient of the line.

(d) Write down the equation of the line.

2 Draw the graphs for $y = x + 2$ and $y = x + 5$ on the same axes.

$>$ greater than
$<$ less than
$=$ equal to

3 (a) Draw a table of values for $y = 3x - 2$ for x values from $^-3$ to 5.

(b) Plot the points and join with a straight line using a ruler.

4 On the axes used in Question 3, draw the graphs for $y = 3x$, $y = 3x - 4$ and $y = 3x - 1$.

5 Write down the coordinates of the points where each of these graphs will cross the y axis.

(a) $y = 2x - 1$ (b) $y = \frac{1}{2}x + 1$ (c) $y = 7x - 17$

(d) $y = \frac{1}{4}x + 9$ (e) $y = 8 + 4x$ (f) $2y = 6x + 12$

6 For each of these graphs write down

(i) the coordinates of the point where the line crosses the y-axis

(ii) the gradient of the line

(iii) the equation of the line.

(a)

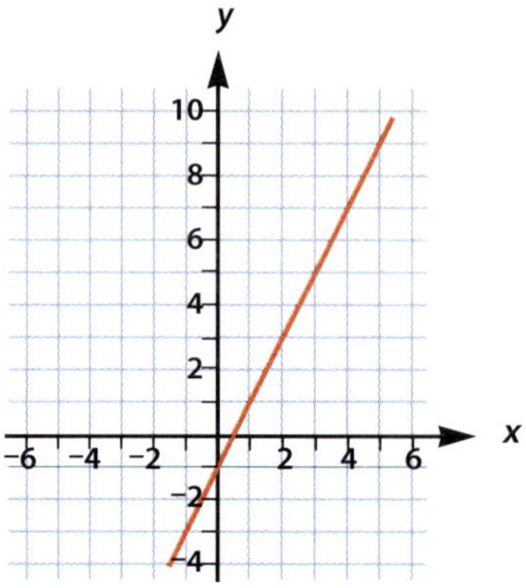

(b)

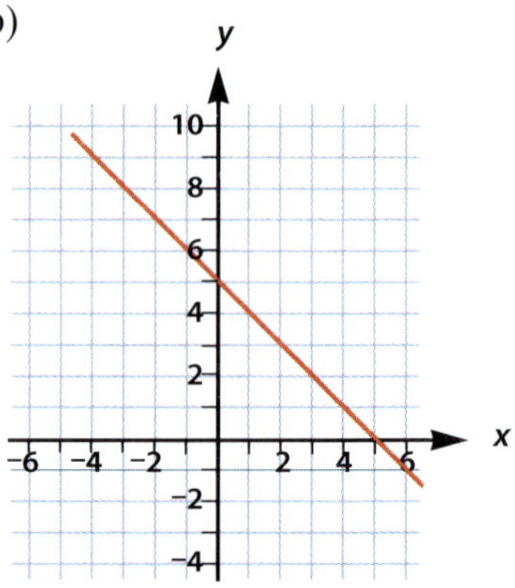

Special triangles

In this chapter you will learn:

- → more about squares and square roots
- → more about triangles
- → about Pythagoras' theorem
- → how to calculate side lengths for right-angled triangles

Starting points

Before starting this chapter you will need to:

- be able to construct triangles accurately
- know how to approximate to a given number of decimal places or significant figures
- know how to find the areas of simple 2D shapes
- be able to recognise different types of triangles
- know the angle sum of any triangle is 180°.

Exercise 1

1 Calculate the third angle in each of these triangles. Write down the value of *a*, *b* and *c*.

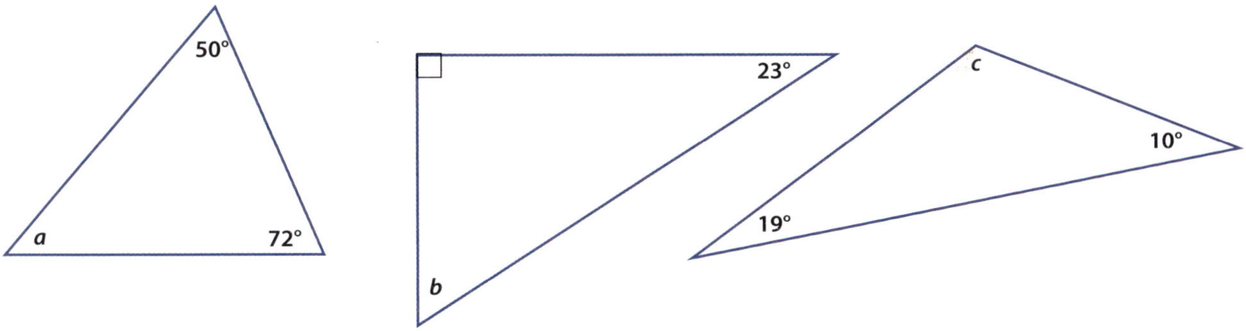

2 Calculate the area of each of these shapes.

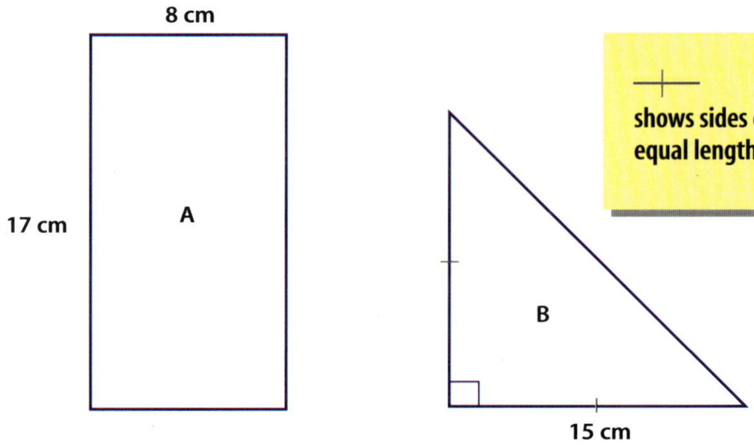

3 Calculate the area of this shape.

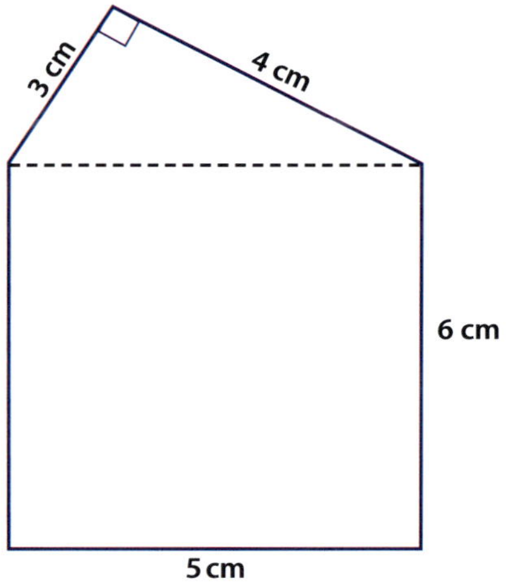

4 Carefully construct these shapes:

(a) A square with sides of 5 cm

(b) A triangle with each side equal to 4 cm

(c) A triangle with sides of length 3 cm, 4 cm and 5 cm

(d) A triangle with sides of length 4 cm, 5 cm and 6 cm

(e) A right-angled triangle with a base of 4 cm and a height of 2 cm

5 Using your constructions in Question 3, answer these questions:

(a) What is the length of the square's diagonal?

(b) What type of triangle is triangle 3(b)?

(c) What is the size of the largest angle in triangle 3(c)?

(d) What is the size of the largest angle in triangle 3(d)?

(e) What is the length of the third side of triangle 3(e)?

6 Using a square dotty grid of 4×4 dots, how many *different* types of triangles can you find? (Remember, no reflections or rotations!)

Is there a type of triangle which is impossible to find on a square grid?

7 Look at these numbers.

(a) 28.34 (b) 205.98 (c) 17045 (d) 2.469

Write each number

(i) correct to 1 decimal place (ii) correct to 1 significant figure.

Squares and square roots

Exercise 2

A number squared is a number multiplied by itself. 'five squared' is written 5^2
$5^2 = 5 \times 5 = 25$

1 Calculate these squares, *without* using a calculator.

(a) 7^2 (b) 4^2 (c) 8^2 (d) 13^2

(e) 11^2 (f) 9^2 (g) 1^2 (h) 12^2

(i) 15^2 (j) 20^2 (k) 100^2 (l) 14^2

$\sqrt{}$ means 'the square root of'.

2 Calculate these square roots, *without* using a calculator.

(a) $\sqrt{64}$ (b) $\sqrt{100}$ (c) $\sqrt{49}$ (d) $\sqrt{36}$

(e) $\sqrt{144}$ (f) $\sqrt{400}$ (g) $\sqrt{81}$ (h) $\sqrt{1}$

(i) $\sqrt{9}$ (j) $\sqrt{225}$ (k) $\sqrt{196}$ (l) $\sqrt{1600}$

More difficult squares and square roots

More difficult squares and square roots need to be found using a calculator. However, estimating the value helps you to check the calculator result.

Estimating squares and square roots needs a knowledge of only simple number operations.

Estimating squares

When estimating the square of a number, follow this procedure:

- Consider the value correct to 1 significant figure.
- Square this approximation.

Example

On a calculator, $32^2 = 1024$. To check this, note that

$32 \approx 30$ (to 1 sig.fig.)

$30^2 = 900$

So $32^2 \approx 900$, and the calculator result is about the same size.

≈ means 'is approximately equal to'.

Example

On a calculator $784^2 = 614656$. To check this note that

$784 \approx 800$ (to 1 sig.fig.)

$800^2 = 640\,000$

So $784^2 \approx 640\,000$, and the calculator result is about the same size.

Notice that the number of zeros is doubled when a number is squared.

Estimating square roots

The same pattern is used when estimating square roots, but the process is reversed.

- Write the value to 1 or 2 significant figures.
- Pair off columns starting with the units, leaving one or two digits at the front of the number.
- Estimate the root of the first one or two digits.
- Replace each following pair of zeros by a single zero.

Example

Calculate $\sqrt{1225}$.

$1225 \approx 1200$ (2 sig.fig. here)

$\sqrt{12} \approx 3$ (1 sig.fig.)

So $\sqrt{1225} \approx 30$.

Example

Calculate $\sqrt{51\,250}$.

$51\,250 \approx 50\,000$ (1 sig.fig. here)

$\sqrt{5} \approx 2$ (1 sig.fig.)

So $\sqrt{51250} \approx 200$.

Example

Calculate $\sqrt{510967}$.

$51\,0967 \approx 51\,0000$ (2 sig.fig. here)

$\sqrt{51} \approx 7$ (1 sig.fig.)

So $\sqrt{510967} \approx 700$.

Exercise 3

1 Estimate these values. Show your working.

(a) 54^2	(b) 382^2	(c) $\sqrt{45}$	(d) 23^2
(e) 81^2	(f) $\sqrt{425}$	(g) $\sqrt{1700}$	(h) 4108^2
(i) $\sqrt{94000}$	(j) 912^2	(k) $\sqrt{232100}$	(l) $\sqrt{807845}$

Assignment 1 Getting to know your own calculator

Calculators can vary from model to model.

- Check your own calculator's manual to find out how to square a number.
- Check that you can find a square root on your calculator as well.
- Use your calculator to answer the questions in Exercise 3 to a sensible accuracy level.

  Use your estimated answers as a check.

Assignment 2 Triangle search

An integer is a whole number.

- How many triangles can you find which have the longest side of length 7 units?

  Take only integer values for side lengths.
- Try other longest side values.

Assignment 3 Dotty squares search

Here is a 4-square drawn on square dotty paper.

The number 4 describes the area of the square.

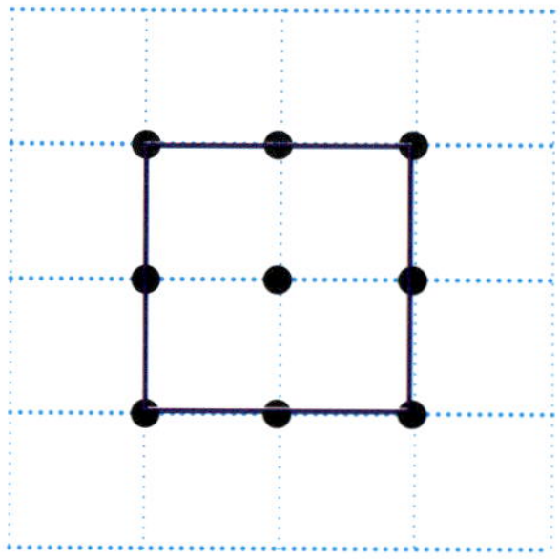

Here is a 2-square:

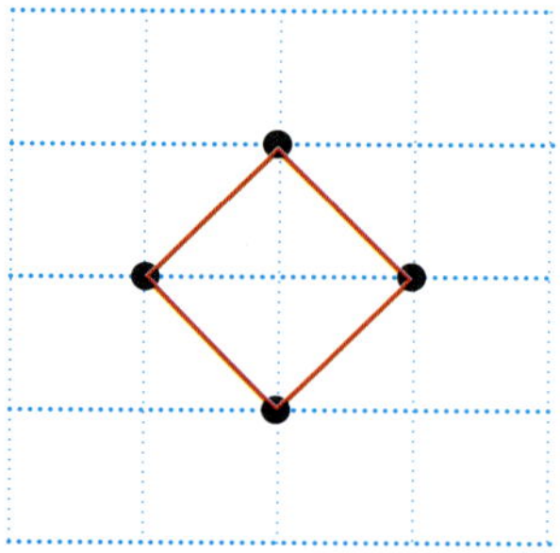

- What area is this square?

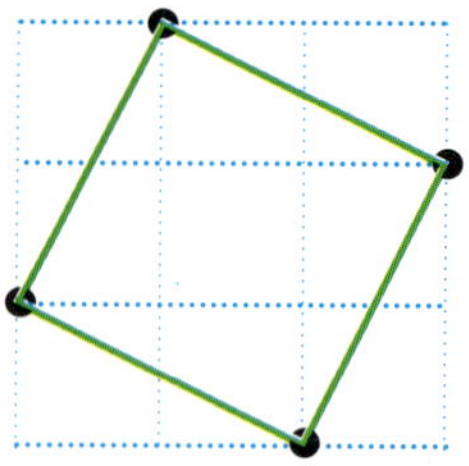

- A 1-square is easy to draw. Starting with this, try to find as many squares as possible up to, say, about 30. You must only join the dots.
- Not all squares are possible.

  How can you tell if it is possible to draw a square or not?

Assignment 4 Triangles from squares

- Cut out a copy of each of the squares drawn in Assignment 3. Label them carefully.
- Take any three squares and join them to enclose a triangle.

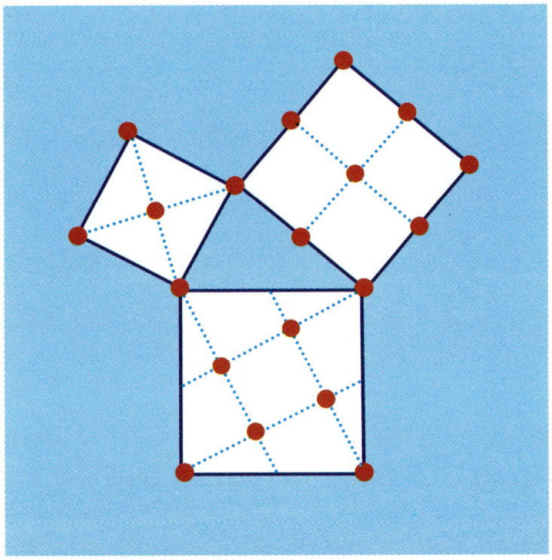

- Classify the triangle as being in one of three groups:

  acute-angled ***right-angled*** ***obtuse-angled***

An obtuse-angled triangle has only one obtuse angle.

- Check that you agree with the entries in this table.

Acute-angled triangles	Right-angled triangles	Obtuse-angled triangles
2, 4, 5	4, 5, 9	1, 5, 9

- Copy the table and add details of your triangle to it.
- Make more triangles. Each time, classify it and record it in the table. You may wish to work with a partner on this, and combine your sets of squares.
  Some triangles will be difficult to classify so take care.
- Can you spot an easier way of classifying the triangles made from squares?
  Write down what you notice.

Exercise 4

1 (a) Using your findings from Assignment 4, decide what type of triangles these squares would make.

A: $5cm^2$, $6cm^2$, $7cm^2$ B: $20cm^2$, $23cm^2$, $24cm^2$

C: $2cm^2$, $5cm^2$, $8cm^2$ D: $7cm^2$, $8cm^2$, $15cm^2$

E: $5cm^2$, $12cm^2$, $17cm^2$ F: $8cm^2$, $8cm^2$, $25cm^2$

G: $2cm^2$, $8cm^2$, $4cm^2$ H: $7cm^2$, $18cm^2$, $25cm^2$

(b) Write down whether the triangles made are acute-angled, right-angled or obtuse-angled

Side lengths of triangles made from squares

To find the side lengths of these triangles, you would need to find the side length of each square used to make the triangle.

Example

A triangle can be made from these three squares:

$7cm^2$	$18cm^2$	$25cm^2$
$\sqrt{7} = 2.65$	$\sqrt{18} = 4.24$	$\sqrt{25} = 5$

So, the triangle has sides of length 2.65cm, 4.24cm and 5cm.

Exercise 5

1 Find the lengths of the sides of the triangles made from these squares.

(a) $5\,cm^2$, $6\,cm^2$, $7\,cm^2$ (b) $20\,cm^2$, $23\,cm^2$, $24\,cm^2$

(c) $2\,cm^2$, $5\,cm^2$, $8\,cm^2$ (d) $7\,cm^2$, $8\,cm^2$, $15\,cm^2$

(e) $5cm^2$, $12cm^2$, $17cm^2$ (f) $8cm^2$, $8cm^2$, $25cm^2$

(g) $2cm^2$, $8cm^2$, $4cm^2$ (h) $7cm^2$, $18cm^2$, $25cm^2$

Pythagoras' theorem

> **Key fact**
> The longest side of a right-angled triangle is called the hypotenuse. It is always opposite the right angle.

The results established in Assignment 4 are the basis of this famous theorem:

The square on the hypotenuse of a right-angled triangle is equal in area to the sum of the squares on the other two sides.

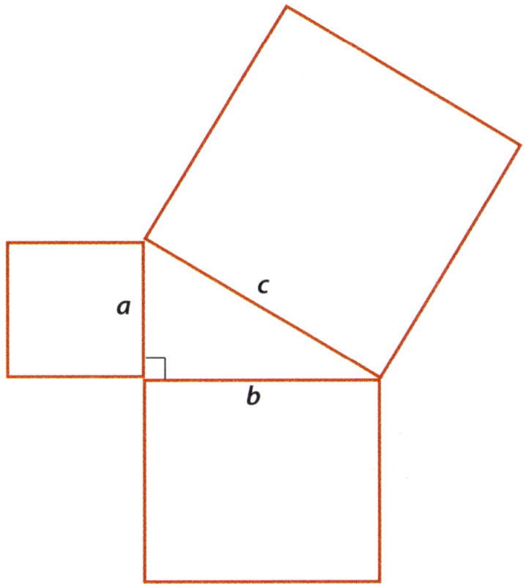

Pythagoras' theorem is often given in an algebraic form:

$a^2 + b^2 = c^2$

Pythagoras was a Greek, living around 540BC.

He studied many aspects of Mathematics as well as other things, for instance music.

However, there is evidence that the link between these areas in a right-angled triangle was known at least 1000 years before Pythagoras lived.

A translation of a clay tablet confirms that the Babylonians knew and used this result. Nevertheless, Pythagoras gave a good proof of the result and his name has been linked with it ever since.

Assignment 5 The life and work of Pythagoras

- Find out about Pythagoras and his many important studies.
- Write an account of his life and work.

Using Pythagoras' theorem to find lengths

This is a right-angled triangle:

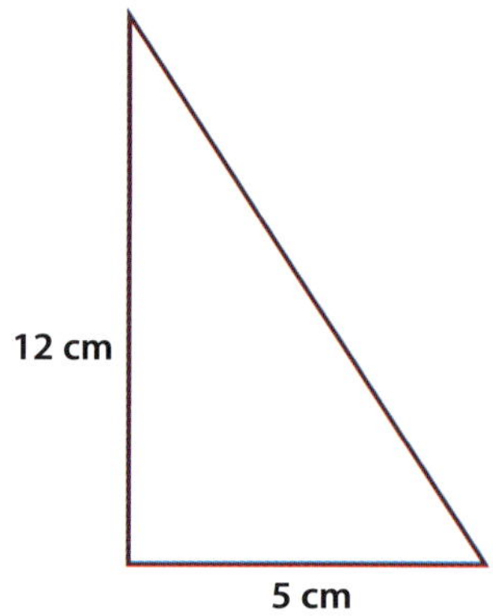

You can find the length of the longest side of this triangle by squaring the lengths of the two given sides and adding.

$$5^2 + 12^2 = 25 + 144$$
$$= 169$$

This means the area of the square on the longest side is 169 cm².

So the length of a side of this square is found by taking the square root of 169 cm².

$$\sqrt{169} = 13$$

The longest side, or hypotenuse, is 13 cm long.

Exercise 6

1 Using Pythagoras' theorem, find the length of the hypotenuse of each of these triangles. Show your working.

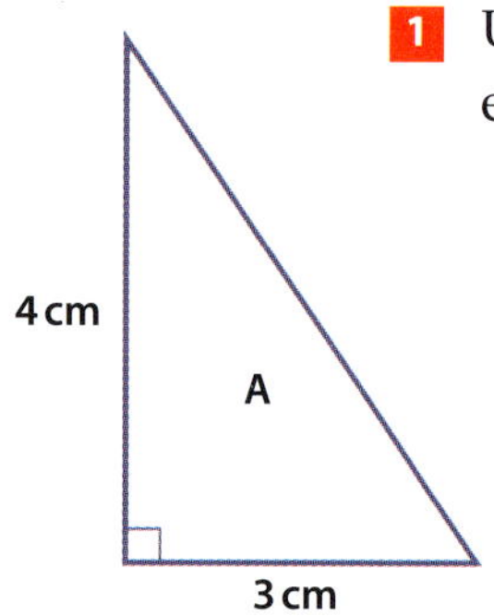

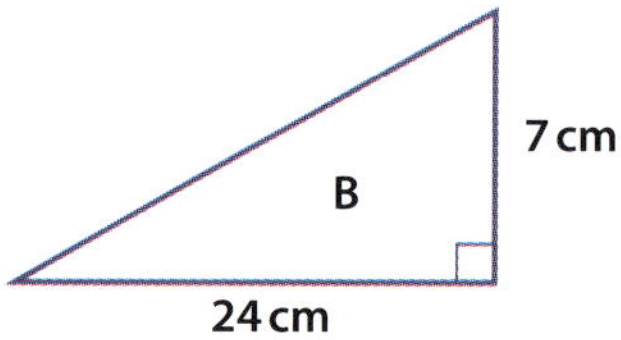

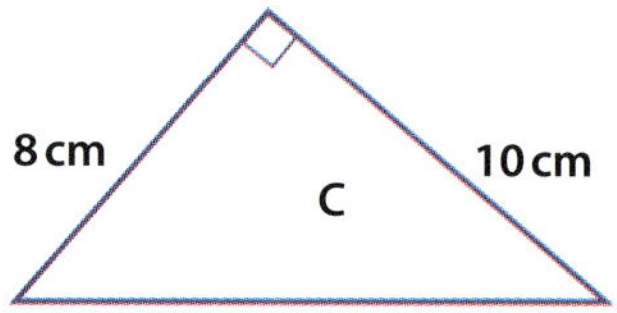

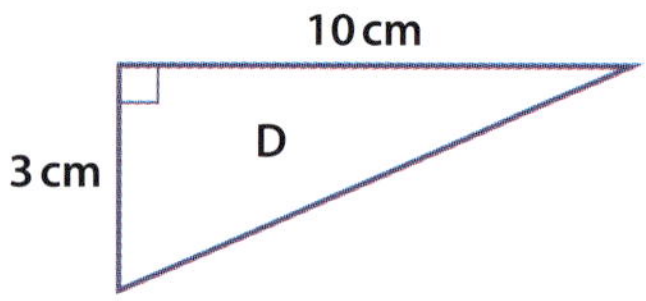

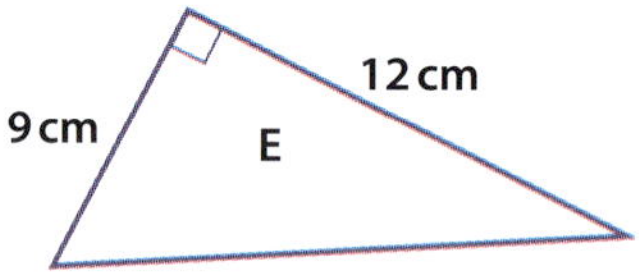

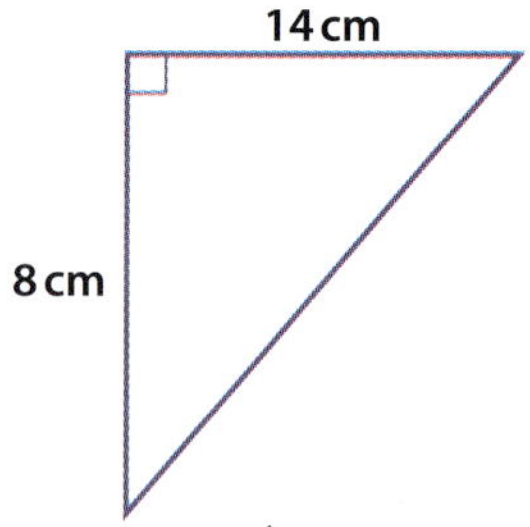

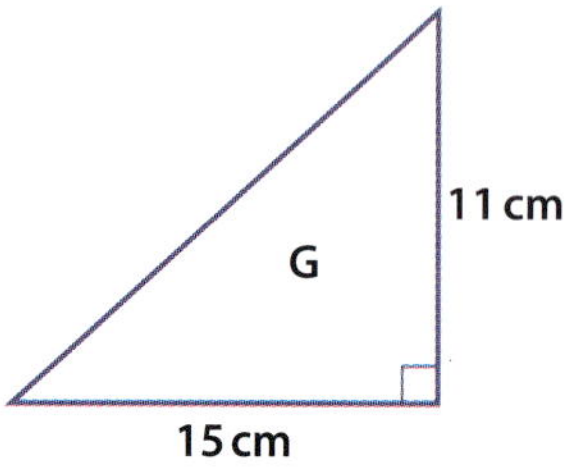

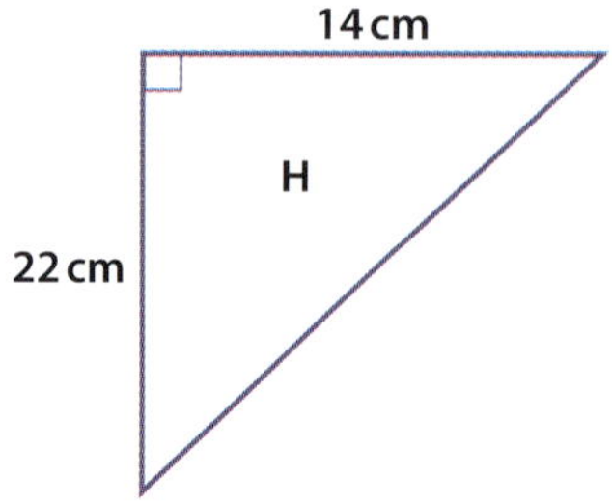

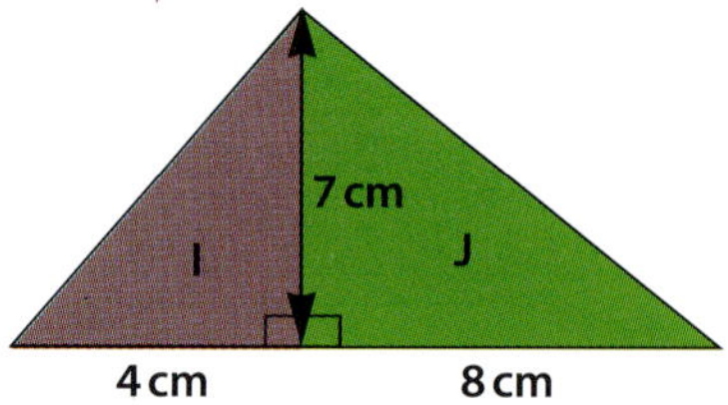

Finding the lengths of sides of a right-angled triangle

In Exercise 6, you calculated the length of the hypotenuse of a right-angled triangle, given the length of the other two sides.

If you know the length of *any* two of the sides of a right-angled triangle, you can calculate the length of the third side using Pythagoras' theorem.

Example

In this triangle, the middle-sized length is unknown.

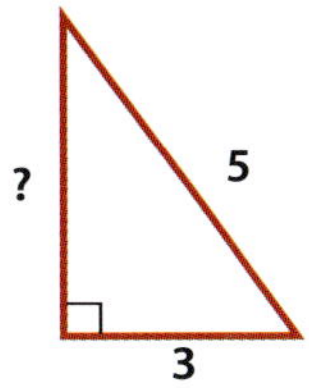

All lengths are in centimetres.

Using Pythagoras' theorem

$3^2 + ?^2 = 5^2$

$9 + ?^2 = 25$

$?^2 = 25 - 9$

$?^2 = 16$

$? = 4$

The length of the middle-sized side is 4 cm.

Example

All lengths are in centimetres.

In this triangle, the shortest side length is unknown.

Using Pythagoras' theorem

$?^2 + 10^2 = 15^2$

$?^2 + 100 = 225$

$?^2 = 225 - 100$

$?^2 = 125$

$? = 11.2$ (1 d.p.)

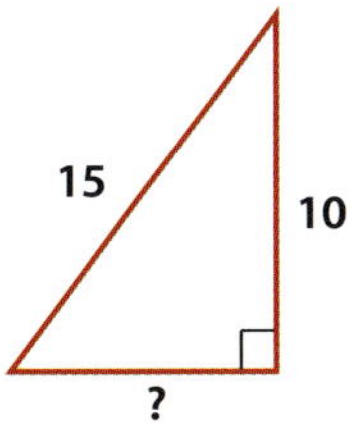

The length of the shortest side is 11.2 cm.

When solving these types of problem make sure that you draw clear diagrams.

Look carefully at the information given to decide whether you need to add side squares or subtract them.

Exercise 7

1 Calculate the length of the third side in each of these right-angled triangles. Write down the values of $a - j$, showing your working clearly.

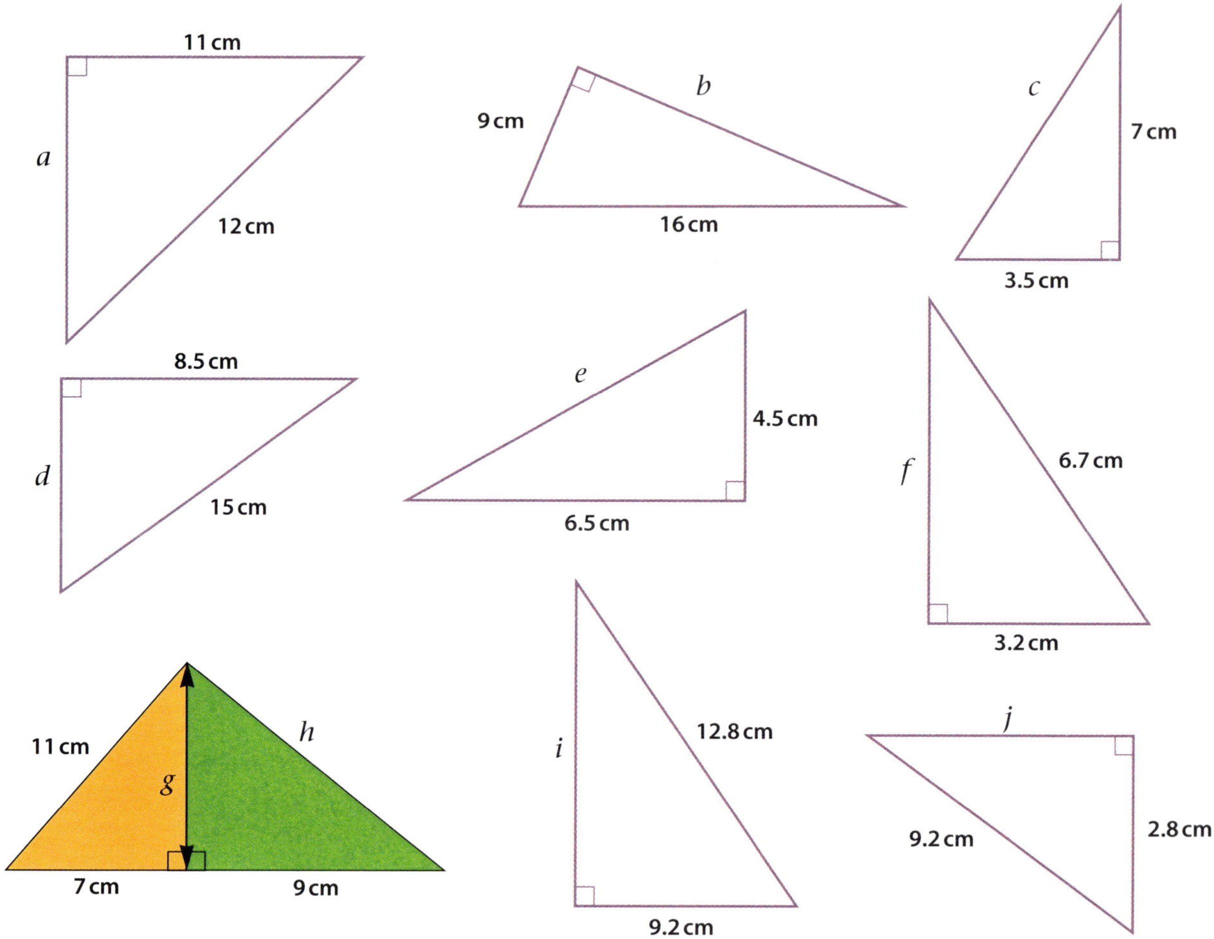

2 Calculate the length of this rectangle, and its area.

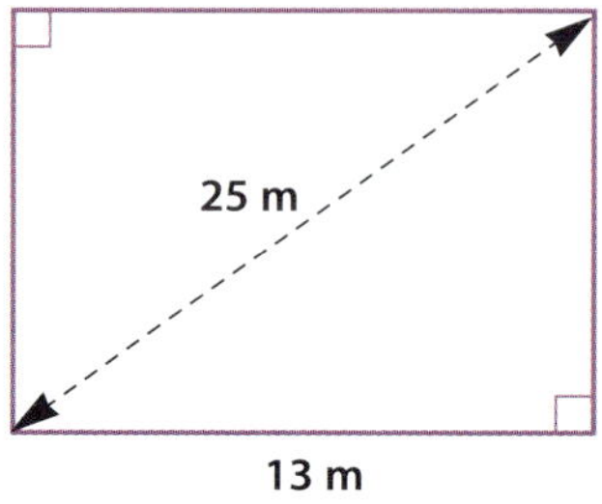

Assignment 6 Computer drawn triangles

Use a graphics calculator or a plotting package on the computer, such as LOGO, for this assignment.

- Draw an accurate right-angled triangle.
- Include accurate squares on each side.

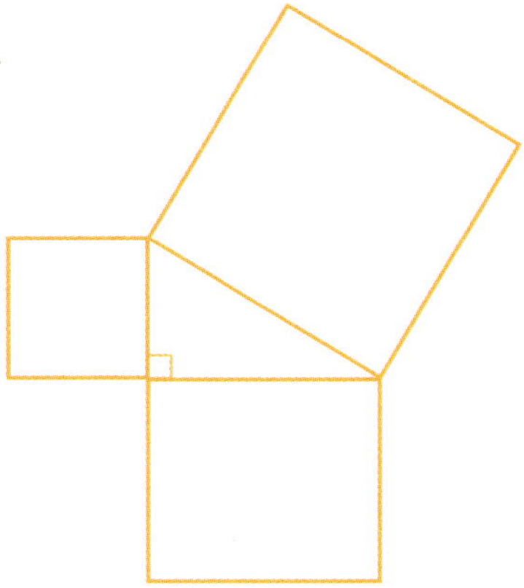

Exercise 8

1 Copy these axes.

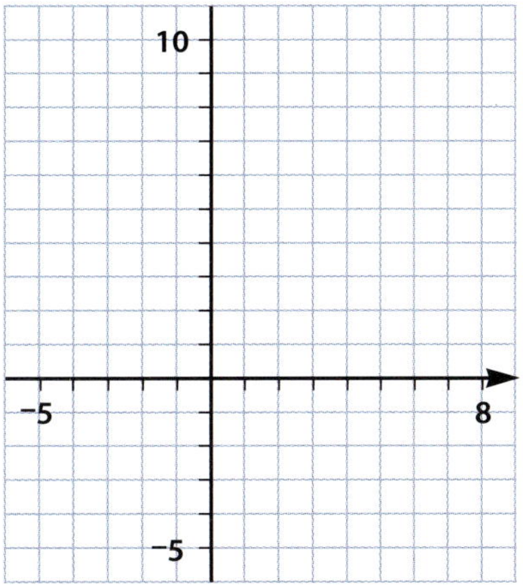

(a) Plot these pairs of points and draw the lines joining each pair.

(i)	(1,2) and (4,5)	(ii)	(1,1) and (5,5)
(iii)	(3,1) and (4,3)	(iv)	(2,0) and (6,1)
(v)	(0,9) and (4,0)	(vi)	(0,3) and (4,3)
(vii)	(2,4) and (−1,4)	(viii)	(1,−2) and (−1,−4)
(ix)	(−2,0) and (−2,6)	(x)	(3,−1) and (4,3)

(b) Calculate the length of each line drawn in part (a).

2 (A challenge!) Write an expression for the distance between any two points.

Call one point (a, b) and the other (x, y).

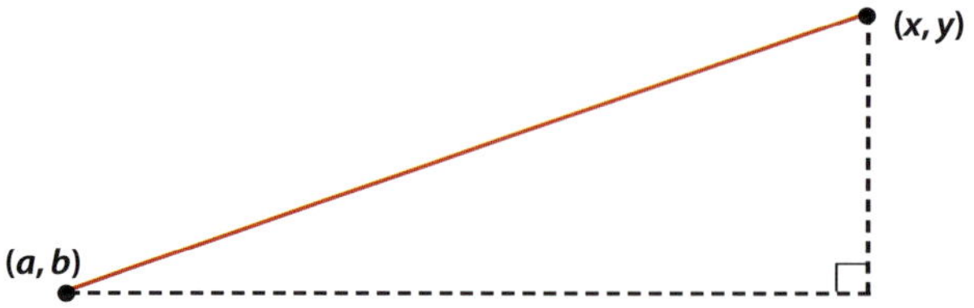

If you manage this, you will have developed a formula for the distance between any two points in two dimensions!

Can you extend this formula to three dimensions?

Assignment 7 Two Pythagorean jigsaws

For the first jigsaw, construct this diagram on plain or squared paper.

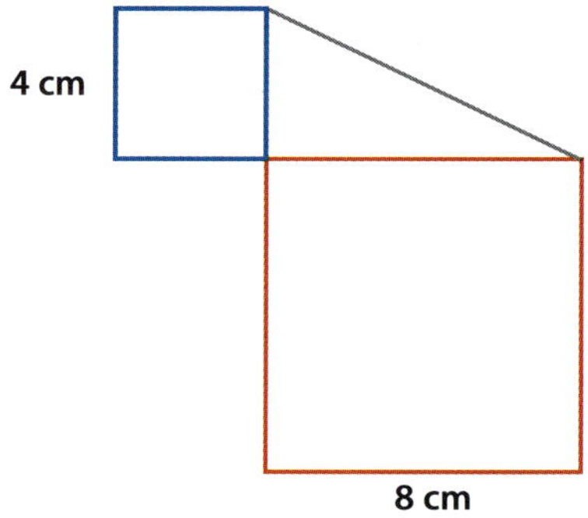

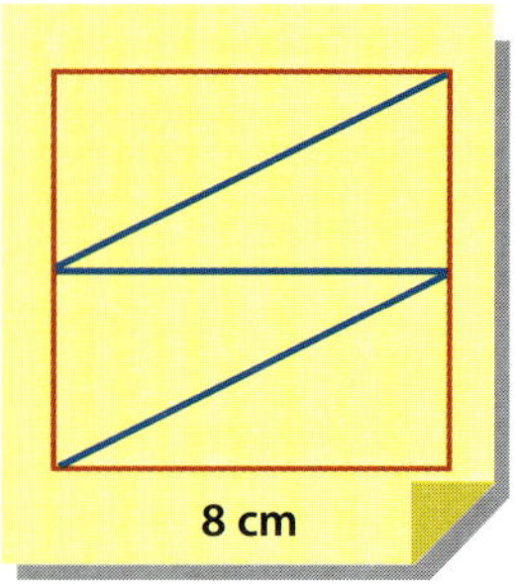

- Draw a line on the bigger of the two squares to divide it into two equal rectangles.
- Draw one diagonal on each rectangle.

  The larger square is now divided into four.
- Cut out these four pieces carefully, together with the smaller square.
- Fit the five pieces together to form one larger square.
  Check that your jigsaw fits exactly on to the longest side of your triangle.

For the second jigsaw, construct this diagram on plain paper. This time, you can choose any size for the triangle.

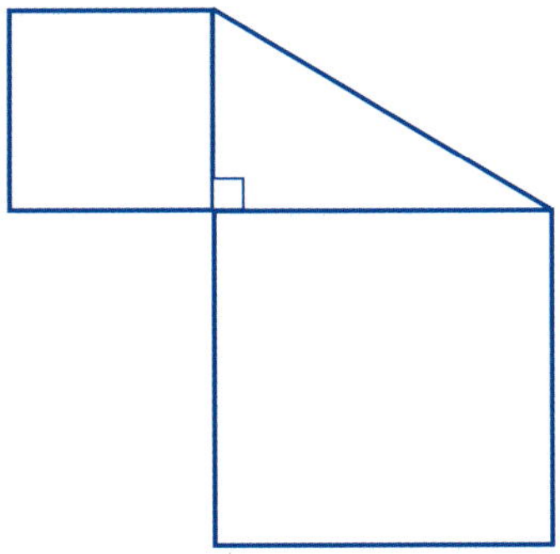

- Check that you recognise the smaller and larger squares.

  If your diagram has two equal squares, this is fine. Either square can be used.

- Find the centre of the larger square by drawing the diagonals lightly.

  Draw a line through this centre which is parallel to the hypotenuse of the triangle.

- Draw a line through this centre which is perpendicular to the last line.

Use a ruler and a set square to draw a parallel line.

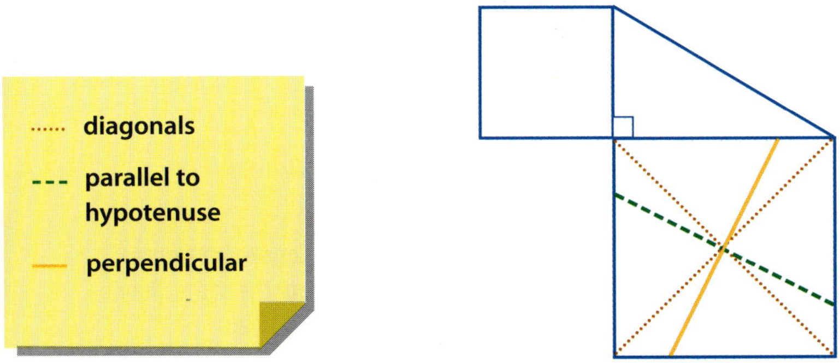

- The larger square is now divided into four.

  Cut out these four pieces carefully, together with the smaller square.

- Fit the five pieces together to form one larger square.

  Check that your jigsaw fits exactly on to the longest side of your triangle.

Assignment 8 Similar shapes

- Construct a right-angled triangle accurately on plain paper, allowing plenty of space around the triangle.

  You may choose any size.

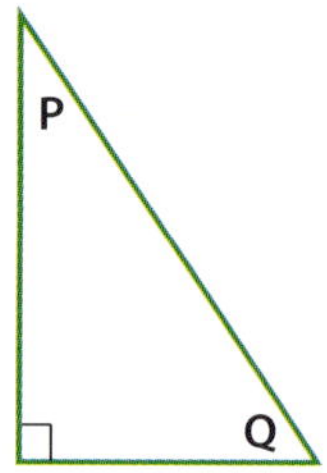

- Measure the angles marked P and Q.

  Use a protractor to draw triangles on each side with angles matching P and Q.

  Your diagram should look something like this:

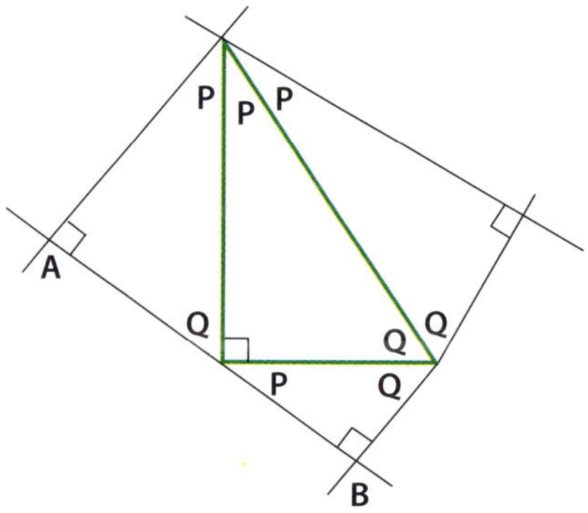

- Notice that the three extra triangles you have drawn are all right-angled.

  Why is this?

- What do you notice about line AB? Can you explain this?

- Note that all four triangles are similar.

  Which two triangles are congruent?

- Now fold the three triangles over along the marked edges.

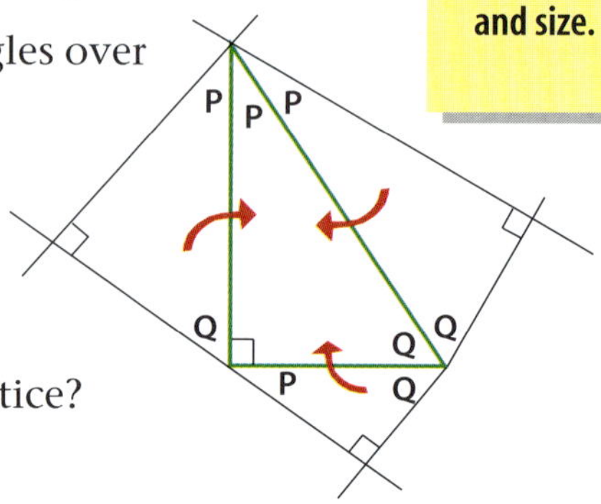

  Write down what you notice?

  What does this show?

Similar shapes are shapes whose corresponding angles are the same. They are enlargements of each other.

Congruent figures are the same shape and size.

Assignment 9 Illustrating Pythagoras' theorem

Assignment 8 shows clearly that it is the *areas* on the sides of a right-angled triangle which are important in Pythagoras' theorem.

Another Greek mathematician, Pappus, used this fact to give another proof of the theorem, around 300BC.

He drew and used parallelograms on each of the sides of a right-angled triangle.

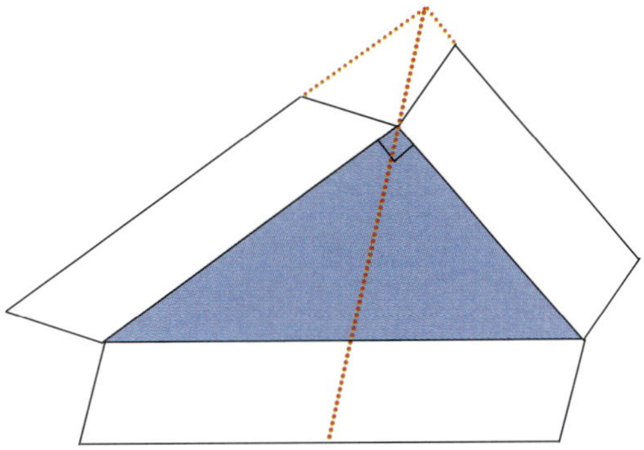

Much more recently, in 1876, President Garfield, who was the 20th President of the USA, used the area of a trapezium to prove the theorem.

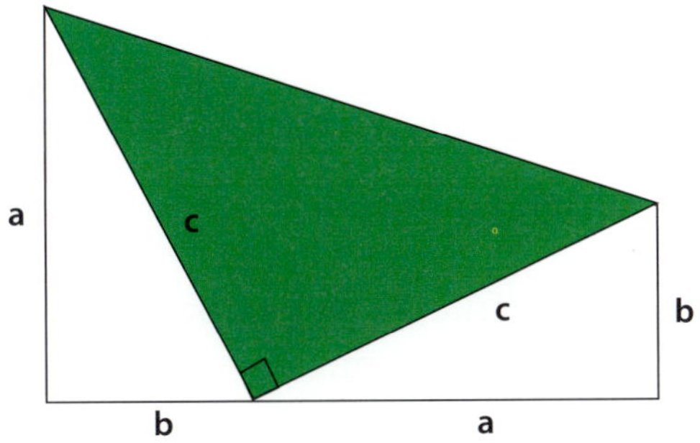

- Construct your own illustration of Pythagoras' theorem by drawing either any regular shape on each side of any right-angled triangle, or any similar shapes on each side of the right-angled triangle.
- The two smaller areas should add to equal the largest area. Do they?

Review Exercise

1 Without using your calculator, for each of these numbers decide which of the estimates is the closest.

(a) 43.2^2 (i) 2500 (ii) 160 (iii) 1600

(b) 289^2 (i) 90000 (ii) 9000 (iii) 900

(c) $\sqrt{562}$ (i) 20 (ii) 25 (iii) 250

(d) $\sqrt{327311}$ (i) 500 (ii) 5500 (iii) 600

2 Using your calculator, find these values.

(a) 14.8^2 (b) 19.8^2

(c) 67.5^2 (d) $\sqrt{572}$

(e) $\sqrt{1000}$ (f) $\sqrt{148.6}$

> **Give your answers correct to 1 decimal place.**

3 These squares are drawn on 1-cm squared paper.

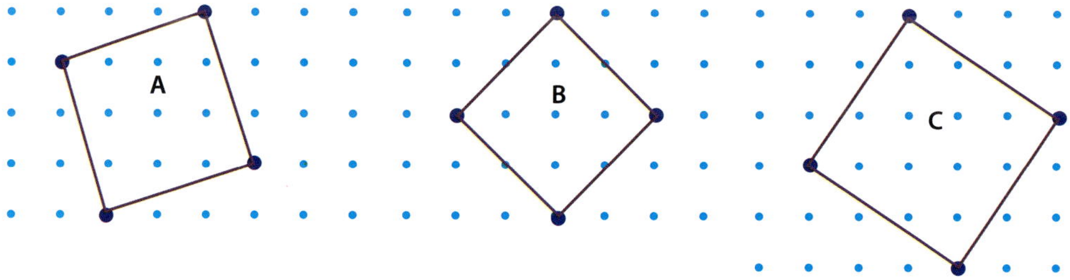

(a) Calculate the area of each square.

(b) Calculate the length of the sides in each of the squares.

4 Construct a triangle with a base of 5 cm and a side, perpendicular to the base, of 3.5 cm.

Measure and record the length of the third side.

Confirm your result by calculation, showing clearly your reasoning.

5 Plot these pairs of points and calculate the lengths of the lines between each pair.

(a) (4,2) and (5,6) (b) (3,3) and (0,0)

(c) (5,1) and (5,−4) (d) (−4,−6) and (2,6)

6 Calculate the length of the third side in these triangles. Write down the values of a, b, c and d.

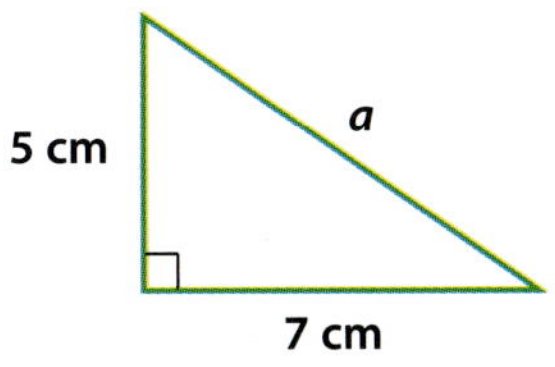

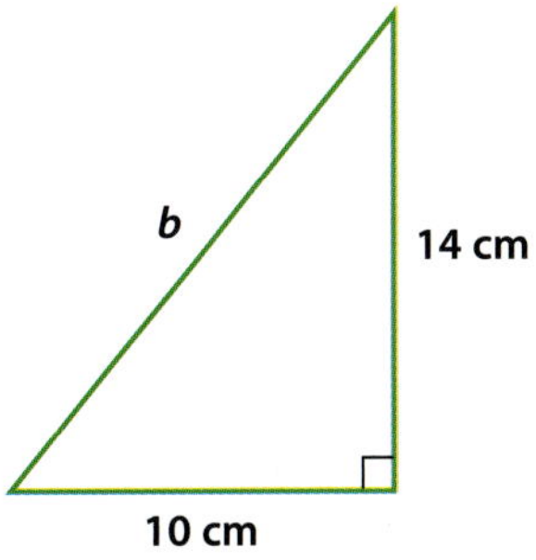

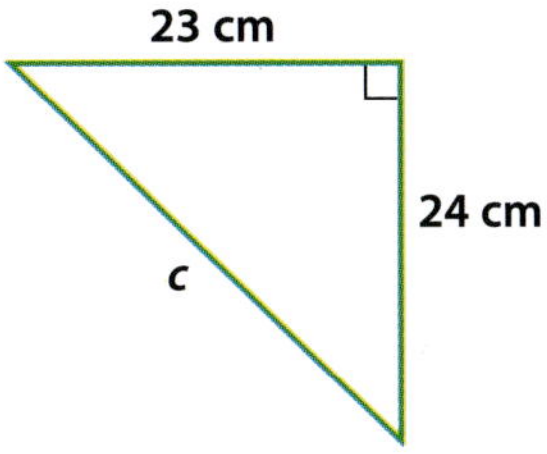

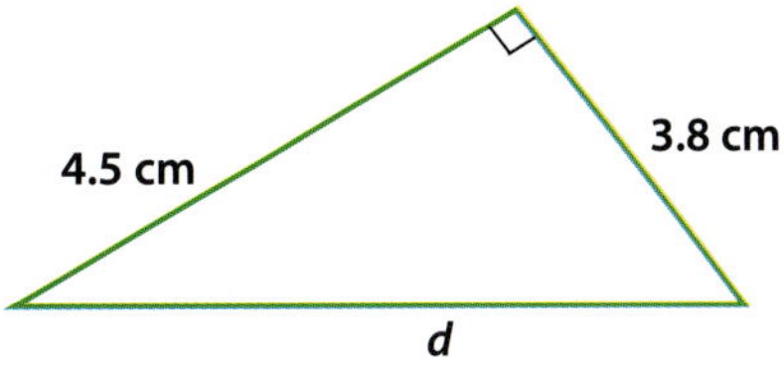

7 Calculate the length of the third side in each of these triangles. Write down the values of a and b.

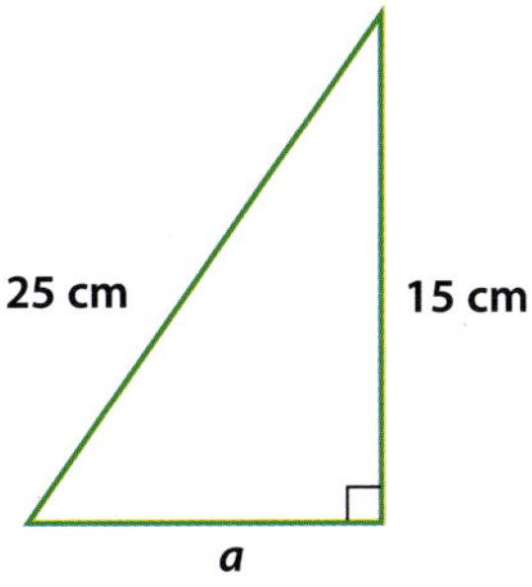

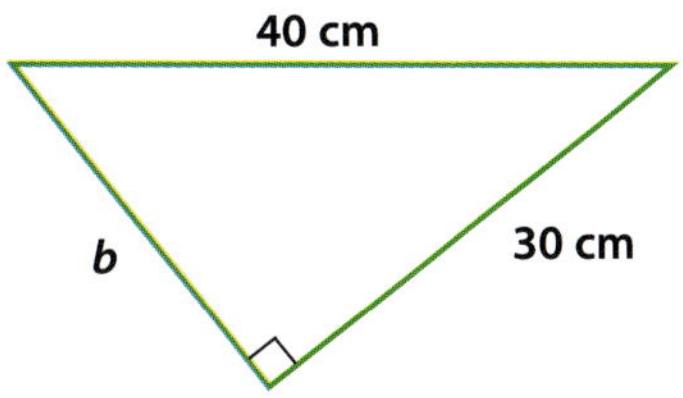

8 Calculate the lengths marked a, b and c. Calculate a first, then b and then c.

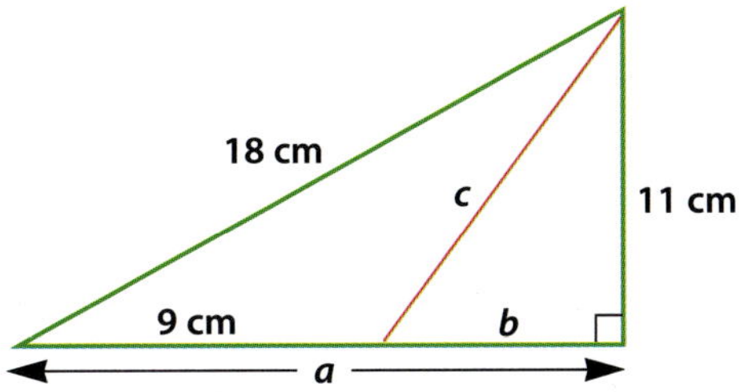

9 A triangle has a 90° angle and is isosceles.
Its hypotenuse is 10 cm long.

Write down the length of the other two sides.

10 Here is the route of a journey.

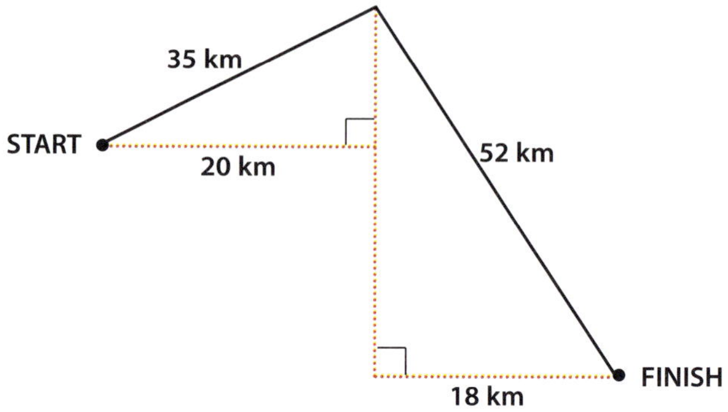

How far due South is the finish compared to the start?

11 Decide by calculation whether the triangle with sides 8 cm, 12 cm and 16 cm is acute-angled, obtuse-angled or right-angled. Show clearly your reasoning.

12 A challenge!

A box is made in the shape of a cube.
Its dimensions are of length 6 cm.

What is the length of the longest pencil which would fit inside the box?

Assignment 10 A puzzle

This is a puzzle for you and your friends!

- Using two straight lines, disect a square into four congruent pieces.

  The lines must not go through the square's corners!

- Cut out the four pieces.

  The four pieces will obviously make one square (your original!), but can you arrange them to make a different square?

Working with equations

In this chapter you will learn:

- → how to solve equations
- → how to form equations

Starting points

Before starting this chapter you will need to know how to:

- simplify algebraic expressions
- multiply out brackets
- solve simple equations.

Exercise 1

1 Simplify these expressions.

(a) $2x + 3x + x$ (b) $5a - 2a$

(c) $3w + w + 2v$ (d) $2x + 5x + 3y - 2y$

(e) $a + b + a + 3b - a$ (f) $3n + 3m - 4n$

(g) $3a + a - 5$ (h) $9 + 3x - x$

(i) $7a + a - 5a - a$ (j) $b + 6b + 2b - 9b$

(k) $2x + 4y + 3x + 2y$ (l) $6n + 3m + 3n + 4m$

(m) $8q + 3r + q - r$ (n) $5f + 4g - 2f - g$

(o) $a + b + a - b + c - a$ (p) $2m + n + p - 2m + 3n$

(q) $8x + y + 6z - 5z + 2y + 3x$ (r) $9a + 7b + c - 7b - c - 9a$

2 Write down an expression for the value of the perimeter (p) for each of the shapes A, B, C, D, E and F.

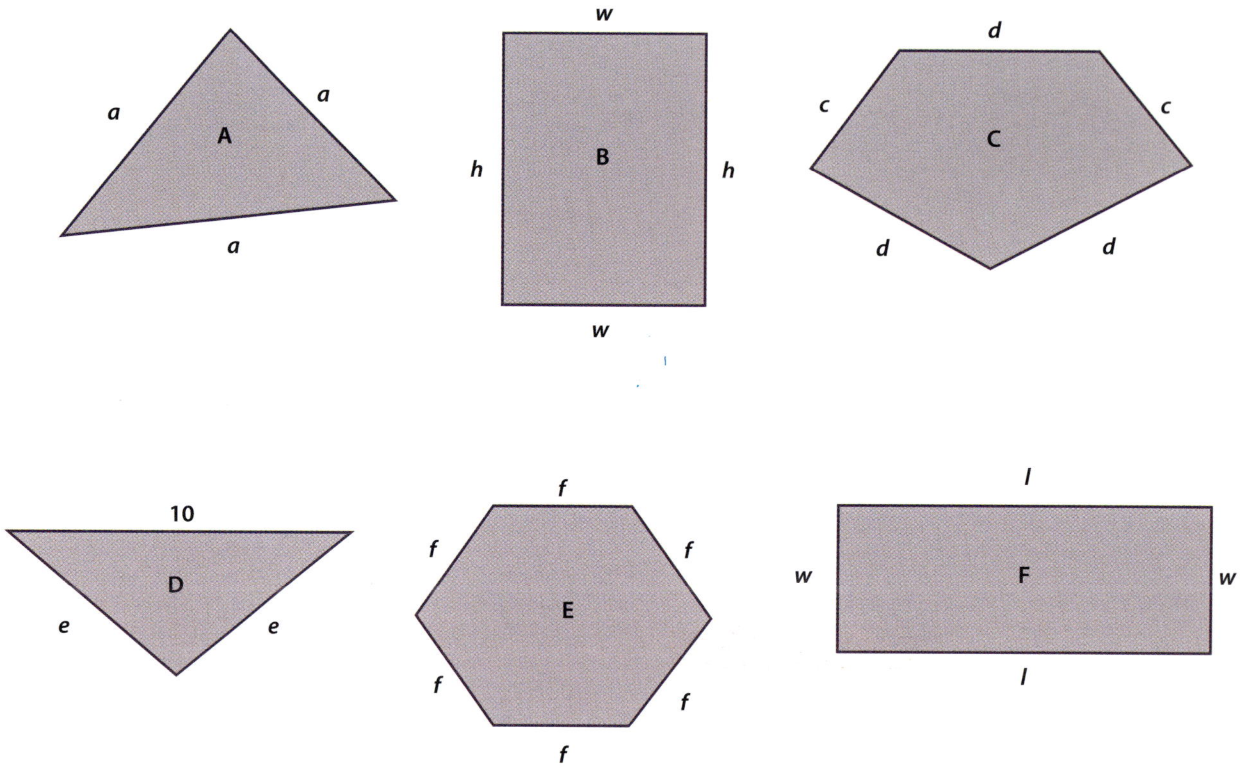

3 Calculate the values of these expressions if $a = 2$, $b = 6$ and $c = 1$.

(a) $2a + b + c$

(b) $5b - 6a$

(c) $2b + c - a$

(d) $4a - b$

(e) $3a + b + 2c$

(f) $3c + 8a - 2b$

(g) $4b + c + 2b + 3c$

(h) $3a + 4b + a + 2c$

(i) $4b + a - 2c$

(j) $2c + 4b + c - 2a$

(k) $5a + b + a - 2b$

(l) $3a + 4c - b$

(m) $6a - 2b + a - c$

(n) $3a + 6c - 2b$

4 The circumference of a circle is given by this formula.

$\pi \times$ diameter = circumference

Calculate the circumference of circles A, B, C and D.

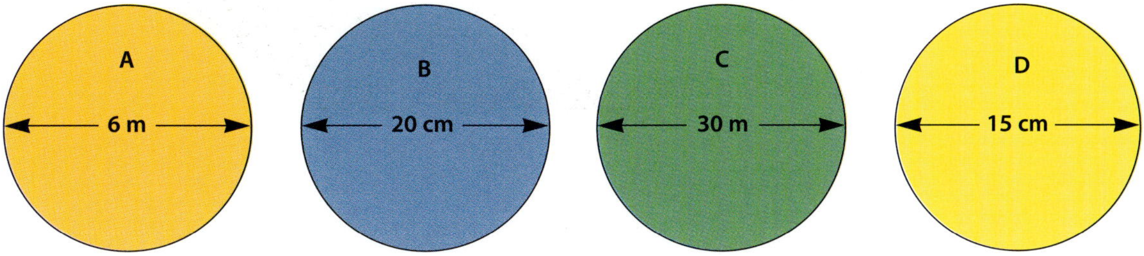

5 The perimeter (p) of a semicircle is given by this formula.

Use $\pi = 3.14$ or the π button on your calculator.

$p = 2r + \pi r$

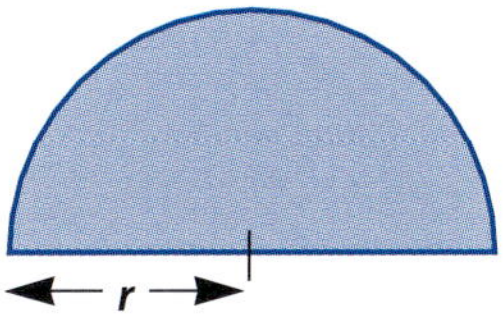

What is the length of the perimeter of a semicircle which has radius

(a) 2 m? (b) 20 cm? (c) 12 m?

6 The distance travelled by a car is given by this formula.

Remember: st means $s \times t$

distance = speed (s) $\times$ time (t)

$d = st$

Use this formula to calculate the distance travelled by

(a) a train travelling at 80kph for 2 hours

(b) a lorry travelling at 60mph for 3 hours

(c) a jet travelling at 550mph for 7 hours

(d) a ship travelling at 36mph for 13 hours.

7 (a) The perimeter of a rectangle is given by this formula.

$p = 2l + 2w$

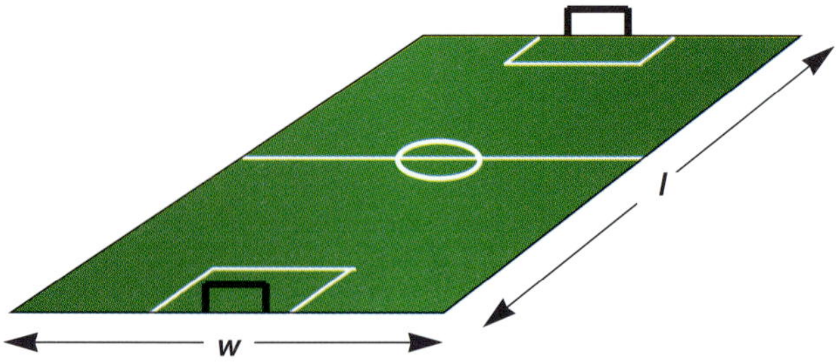

Use this formula to calculate the perimeters of:

(i) a football pitch with $l = 90$ m and $w = 70$ m

(ii) a hockey pitch with $l = 80$ m and $w = 60$ m

(iii) a tennis court with $l = 78$ ft and $w = 36$ ft

(iv) a squash court with $l = 32$ ft and $w = 21$ ft

(v) a swimming pool with $l = 50$ m and $w = 25$ m

(vi) a rugby pitch with $l = 110$ yards and $w = 75$ yards

(vii) a volleyball pitch with $l = 18$ m and $w = 9$ m

(viii) a badminton court with $l = 13.4$ m and $w = 6.1$ m.

(b) The area of a rectangular surface is given by this formula:

area = length (l) × width (w)

$A = lw$

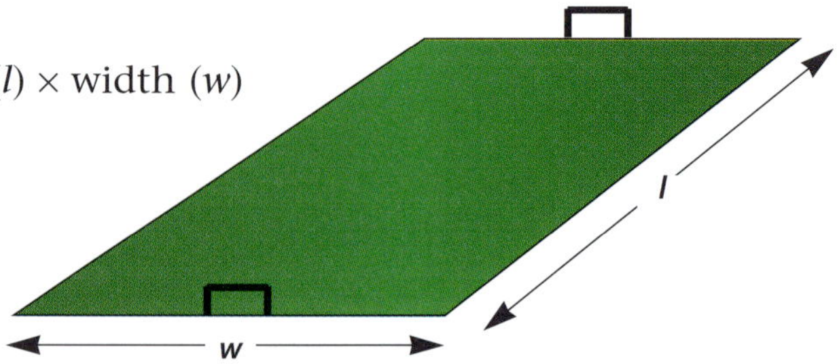

Use the formula to calculate the area of the sports pitches listed in part (a).

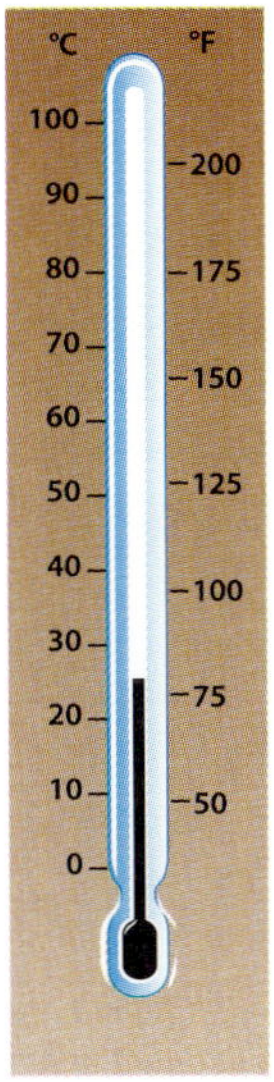

8 The temperature in Europe is usually given in degrees Celsius (°C). In America, it is always given in degrees Fahrenheit (°F).

This formula is used to convert degrees Celsius to degrees Fahrenheit.

> c is the temperature in °C.
> f is the temperature in °F.

$f = 1.8c + 32$

Calculate f when

(a) $c = 20$ (b) $c = 15$ (c) $c = 30$

(d) $c = 12$ (e) $c = 25$ (f) $c = 10$.

One-stage equations

One-stage equations have only one operation and need only one calculation to solve them.

Example

This equation has a subtraction operation:

$15 - a = 9$

What number, subtracted from 15, gives 9? The answer is 6.

The solution is written like this, lining up the 'equals' signs.

$$\begin{aligned} 15 - a &= 9 \\ a &= 6 \end{aligned}$$

Example

Look at this diagram.

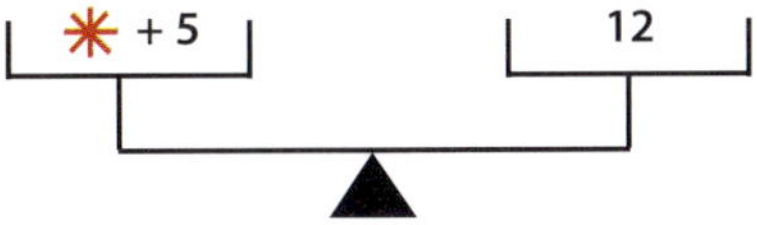

> A single small letter is usually used to represent a value which you do not know.

The diagram can be represented by this simple equation:

$a + 5 = 12$

The letter a in the equation represents the symbol ✳ in the diagram.

The problem can then be solved: What number, added to 5, gives 12? The answer, which balances the scales in the diagram, is 7.

The solution is written like this:

$$\begin{aligned} a + 5 &= 12 \\ a &= 7 \end{aligned}$$

Exercise 2

1 For each of these diagrams, write down the equation represented by the diagrams and the value of each symbol.

(a)

(b)

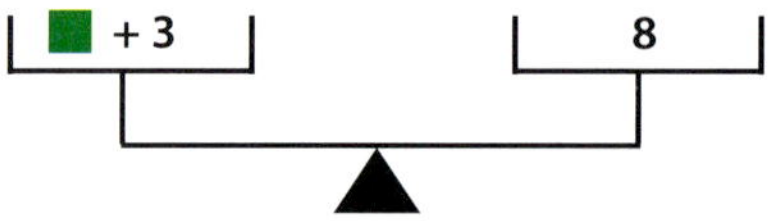

(c)

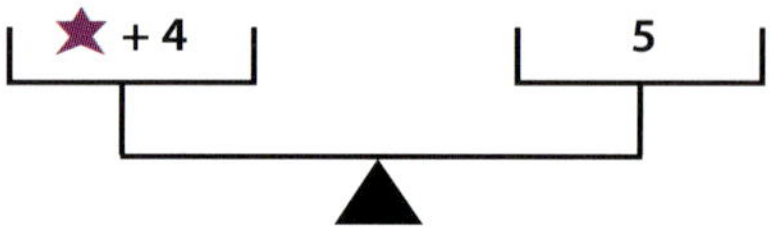

(d)

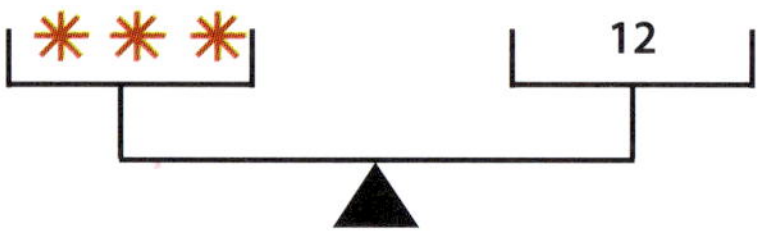

(e)

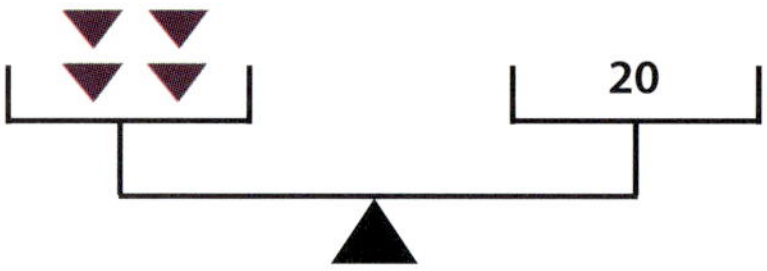

(f)

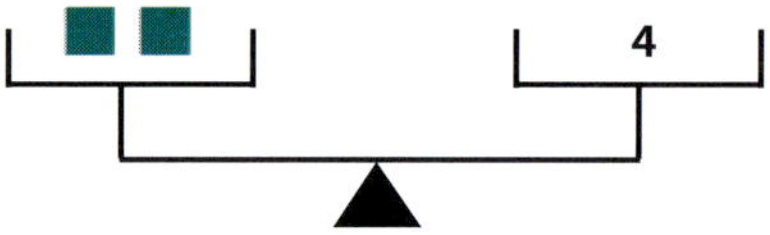

> **Write your solution in full.**
> $4 + x = 8$
> $x = \ldots$

2 Copy each of these equations and write your solution beneath it.

(a) $4 + x = 8$ (b) $5 + a = 8$ (c) $12 + y = 38$

(d) $7 + p = 18$ (e) $15 + b = 26$ (f) $17 + d = 48$

3 Solve these equations.

(a) $14 - e = 2$ (b) $35 - h = 19$ (c) $73 - n = 24$

(d) $43 - c = 27$ (e) $64 - s = 39$ (f) $96 - a = 68$

4 Solve these equations.

(a) $3x = 48$ (b) $5r = 25$ (c) $2j = 24$

(d) $9d = 36$ (e) $3m = 21$ (f) $7q = 84$

5 Solve these equations.

(a) $\frac{1}{2}a = 14$ (b) $\frac{1}{5}b = 7$ (c) $\frac{1}{10}f = 30$

(d) $\frac{1}{4}x = 4$ (e) $\frac{1}{6}y = 5$ (f) $\frac{1}{2}p = 12.5$

6 Solve these equations.

(a) $7 + x = 9$ (b) $15 - a = 8$ (c) $2y = 38$

(d) $p - 5 = 18$ (e) $5b = 25$ (f) $12 + d = 26$

(g) $14 + c = 28$ (h) $78 - h = 39$ (i) $3n = 24$

7 (a) Use your knowledge of angles to write an equation to describe each of these situations.

(b) Solve your equations to find the value of angles $a - f$.

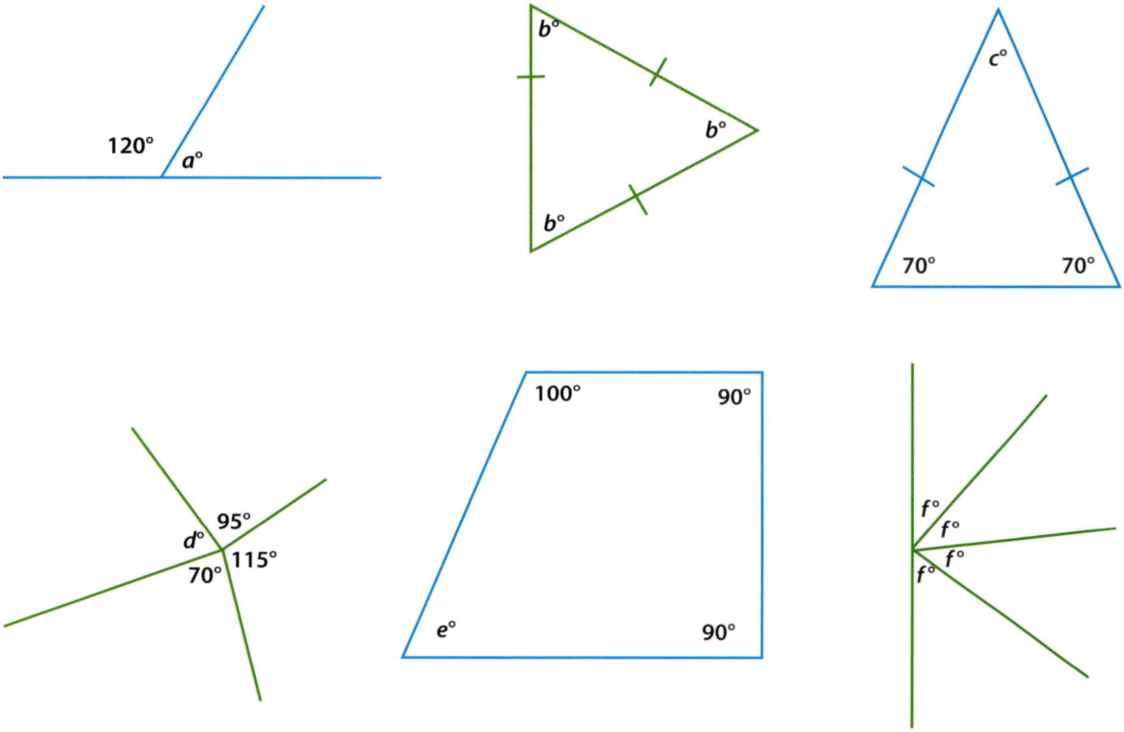

8 Write these sentences as equations using a letter to represent the number. (The first has been completed for you.) Then solve your equations.

(a) Think of a number, add 6 the answer is 8.
This becomes $a + 6 = 8$.

(b) Think of a number, add 2. The answer is 24.

(c) Think of a number, take away 6. The answer is 15.

(d) Think of a number, subtract 4. The answer is 9.

(e) Think of a number, multiply it by 2. The answer is 12.

(f) Think of a number, times by 3. The answer is 30.

(g) Think of a number, divide it by 2. The answer is 8.

(h) Think of a number, share it between 3. The answer is 4.

Two-stage equations

Two-stage equations have two operations and need two calculations to solve them.

Example

Think of a number, multiply by 2, add 3. The answer is 11.

This problem can be written as $2a + 3 = 11$

One way to solve this type of equation is to treat the term 2a as one unknown value. $2a + 3 = 11$

The problem then becomes 'something' + 3 = 11

So 'something' = 8

But 'something' = 2a

So $2a = 8$

You now have a one-stage equation which is easier to solve. The number you thought of is 4.

The solution to this problem is written

$$2a + 3 = 11$$
$$2a = 8$$
$$a = 4$$

Remember to write your solution in full.
$2d + 5 = 13$
$2d = \dots$
$d =$

Exercise 3

1 Calculate the value of the letter in each of these equations. Show all your working.

(a) $2d + 5 = 13$ (b) $8m + 3 = 27$ (c) $2g + 5 = 27$

(d) $5p + 3 = 38$ (e) $3a - 1 = 35$ (f) $4x - 6 = 30$

(g) $9 + 2f = 27$ (h) $20 - 2a = 12$ (i) $36 - 3b = 30$

(j) $2a + 4 = 20$ (k) $3d - 4 = 5$ (l) $8x + 8 = 24$

(m) $4 + 3h = 16$ (n) $3v - 4 = 11$ (o) $4y + 3 = 15$

(p) $4d - 3 = 13$ (q) $7m + 2 = 30$ (r) $8n - 2 = 14$

(s) $2r + 7 = 15$ (t) $2v - 5 = 15$ (u) $3q - 2 = 10$

(v) $5 + 3w = 29$ (w) $50 - 4e = 34$ (x) $4j - 8 = 12$

You need worksheet 12A and counters.

2 Play this matching game with a partner.

Look at worksheet 12A.

$4m + 2 = 10$	$4c + 2 = 18$	$6n + 2 = 32$	$2e + 7 = 15$	$2a + 1 = 7$	
$2z + 7 = 13$	$3n - 8 = 7$	$3a - 1 = 5$	$7b - 20 = 22$	$3v - 12 = 6$	$3f + 7 = 19$
$2m + 11 = 21$	$4g + 1 = 13$	$3a - 1 = 20$	$4y + 7 = 15$	$4z - 8 = 12$	
$5h + 3 = 23$	$5a + 3 = 13$	$3l + 2 = 20$	$5b + 4 = 19$	$2b - 3 = 11$	$3q - 3 = 15$
$8n - 23 = 17$	$2y + 1 = 15$	$8m - 3 = 21$	$2r - 7 = 5$	$12n + 6 = 30$	
$3w - 1 = 8$	$6k - 7 = 17$	$4p - 7 = 17$	$7d - 3 = 11$	$3a - 10 = 5$	$4j - 3 = 13$

Some of the equations have the same solution.

(a) Taking it in turns, choose a hexagon and solve the equation in it.

The winner is the first person to find five equations with the same solution.

(b) There are five sets of six equations with the same solutions to find.

Continue to play the game until all the hexagons have been used.

3 Write down and then solve an equation to represent each of these diagrams.

(a)

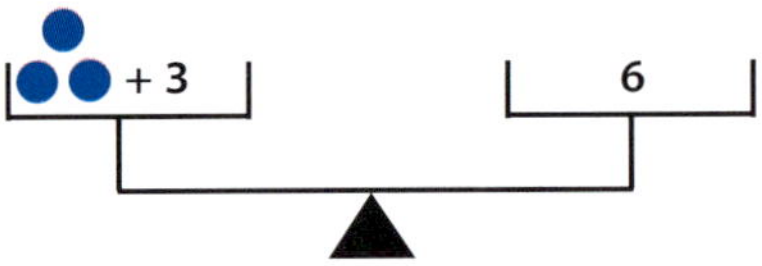

(b)

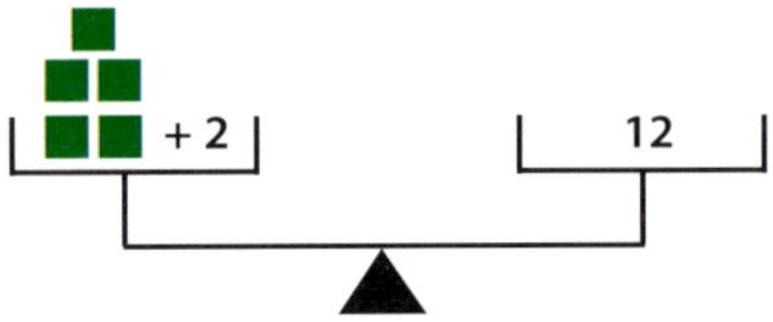

(c)

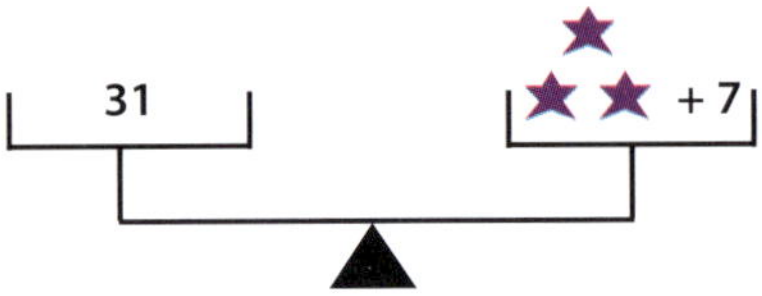

(d)

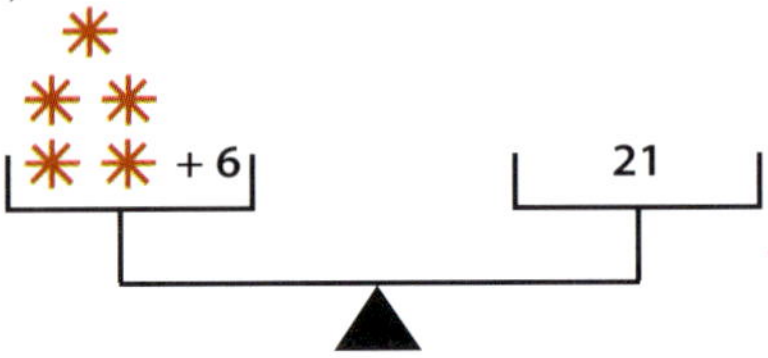

(e)

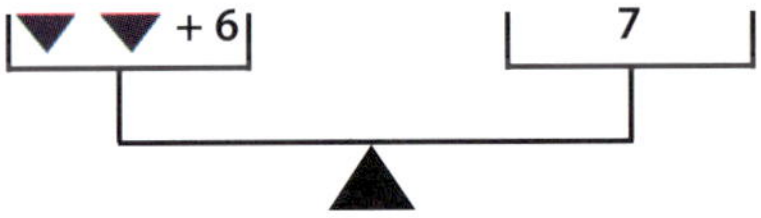

(f)

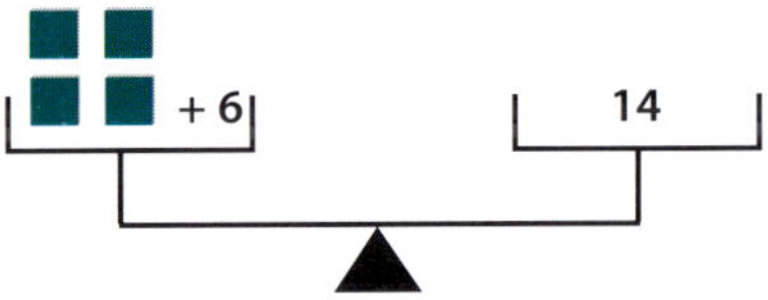

4 Write down and solve an equation to describe each of these situations, and to find the value of a, b, c and d.

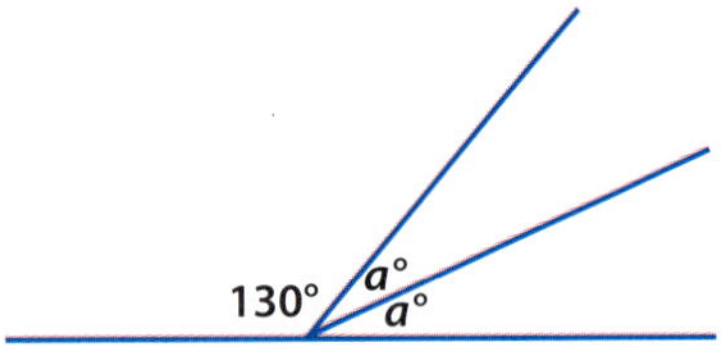

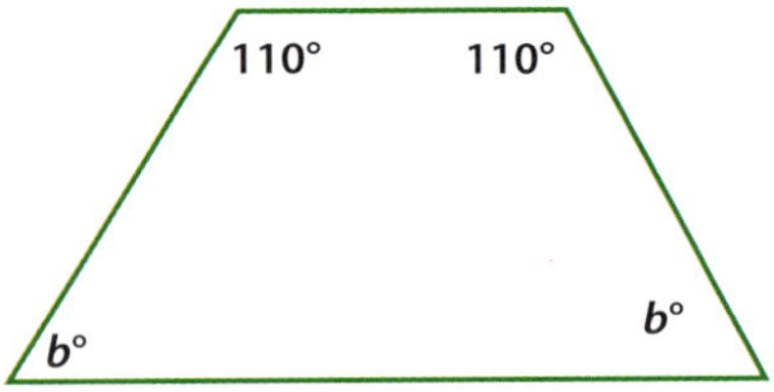

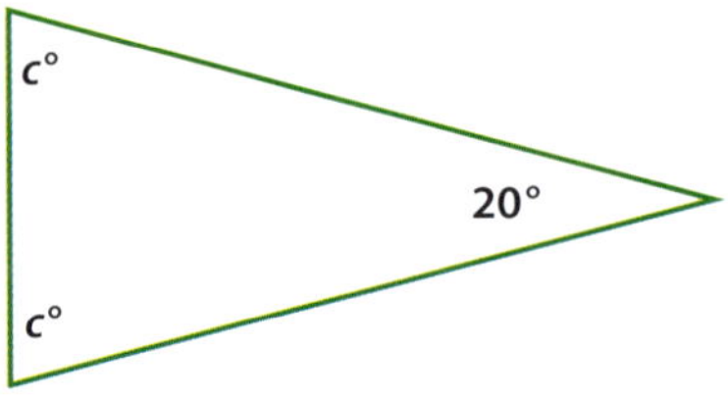

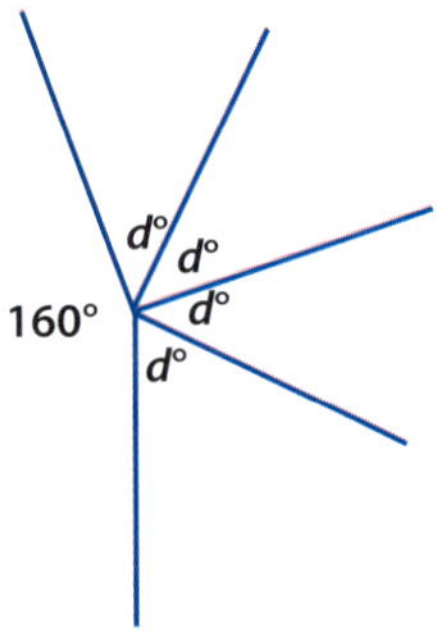

5 Express each of these problems as an equation.
Then solve each equation.

(a) A number is doubled and then 11 is taken away.
The result is 21.

(b) You buy two identical posters and have £5 left.
If you started with £23, how much was each poster?

(c) A number is multiplied by 3 and then 4 is added.
The solution is 13.

(d) You start with £30.
You buy two CDs and have £12 change.
How much did the CDs cost?

(e) Find the cost of five drinks if you have £1.05 change from £5.

(f) Pupils collect 1276 cans for charity in a week.
Four sacks contain the same number of cans and the fifth contains 156 cans.

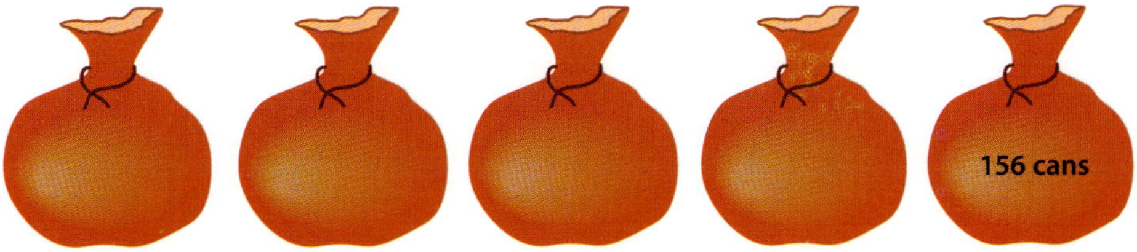

How many cans are there in each sack?

6 Write a sentence to describe each of these equations.

(a) $2a = 6$

(b) $6 + b = 13$

(c) $12 - d = 8$

(d) $5g + 9 = 39$

(e) $10 + 3b = 25$

(f) $2a - 5 + 11$

Equations with brackets

A bracket is like the wrapping on a parcel.

To solve

$4(2a + 3) = 36$

you begin by expanding the bracket.

$4(2a + 3)$

means 4 lots of the parcel $(2a + 3)$

giving $4 \times 2a$ and 4×3

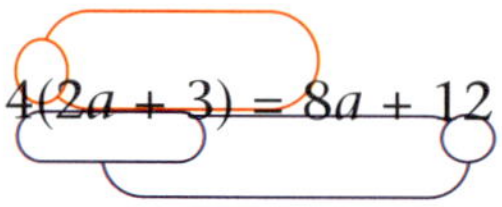

You should then be able to solve the equation

$8a + 12 = 36$

> **'Multiplying out the bracket' is sometimes called 'expanding the bracket'.**

> **Here is how you should write the solution.**
>
> $4(2a + 3) = 36$
>
> $8a + 12 = 36$
>
> $8a = 24$
>
> $a = 3$

Exercise 4

1 Solve these equations, expanding the brackets first.

(a) $3(a - 1) = 3$ (b) $6(2n - 1) = 66$

(c) $2(2x - 3) = 6$ (d) $2(3 + 2m) = 18$

(e) $4(2d + 5) = 36$ (f) $3(3f - 1) = 33$

(g) $4(w - 1) = 16$ (h) $3(2r + 1) = 51$

(i) $2(2g - 5) = 18$ (j) $4(5d - 2) = 2$

(k) $3(7t - 2) = 1$ (l) $3(5p + 1) = 9$

(m) $2(a - 3) = 4$ (n) $6 = 3(b - 4)$

(o) $3(c + 4) + 2 = 29$ (p) $22 = 2(2d + 3)$

(q) $4 + 2(3 + e) = 14$ (r) $8 = 4(12 - f)$

(s) $5(2g + 6) = 10$ (t) $9 = 3(4 - 2h)$

(u) $2(6i - 2) = 2$ (v) $7 = 3(j + 1) - 2(j - 1)$

You will need a partner, worksheet 12B and counters.

2 Play this matching game with a partner.

Look at worksheet 12B.

$3(8-x)=9$	$2(x+2)=8$	$2(2a+1)=22$	$3(m+2)=12$	$3(10-2a)=18$	$2(2a+4)=16$	
$4(3m+2)=32$	$3(4x-1)=21$	$2(2a+1)=10$	$5(3x-4)=55$	$4(2c+1)=20$	$6(8-2m)=12$	$2(20-7a)=12$
$2(2a-1)=10$	$3(5+y)=21$	$4(3n-7)=20$	$5(12-2a)=20$	$5(p+6)=40$	$6(3a-5)=24$	
$6(x+4)=42$	$3(7-2b)=3$	$4(2n+3)=28$	GOAL	$3(2a+7)=33$	$8(9-2a)=24$	$2(3a+10)=44$
$8(7-2x)=8$	$4(3n-2)=28$	$5(2n-4)=10$	$3(x+2)=15$	$2(a+5)=16$	$6(a-4)=0$	
$2(3n-3)=24$	$2(3m-1)=16$	$8(4n-10)=48$	$3(4a-2)=42$	$3(8-2n)=0$	$3(5+2a)=33$	$8(12-2n)=48$
$3(4x+2)=42$	$3(2+3n)=33$	$5(6-m)=15$	$4(4+2a)=48$	$4(1+2x)=28$	$2(2a+11)=38$	

Your objective is to find a route from a hexagon on the outside edge to the goal in the centre of the grid, each equation having the same solution.

(a) Choose any hexagon on the outside edge of the grid as your starting position.
Solve the equation in that hexagon.
Your partner does the same thing, for a different hexagon.

(b) Take it in turns to solve an equation.
If the solution matches your first solution, you can place your counter on that hexagon.
You can *only* place your counters on equations which have the same solution as your first equation.

(c) If you have time, play again starting at a different hexagon on the edge of the grid.

Equations and graphs

Another way of solving an equation is to draw the graph which represents it.

Example

Solve $2x + 2 = 6$

To do this, you let $y = 6$.

Then because $2x + 2 = 6$, it must also be true that $y = 2x + 2$.

Plot the line $y = 2x + 2$ and the line $y = 6$.

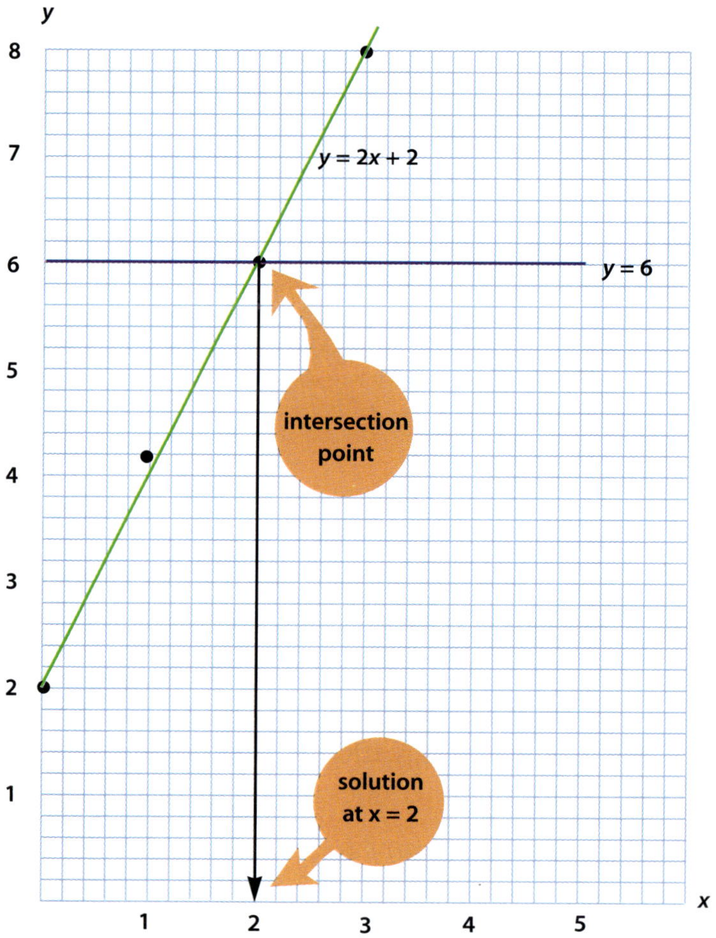

The only place where $y = 2x + 2$ and $y = 6$ is where these two lines cross (their intersection point).

The x-coordinate at this point is the solution to the equation $2x + 2 = 6$.

The solution is $x = 2$.

Exercise 5

1 Look at these four graphs.

(a)

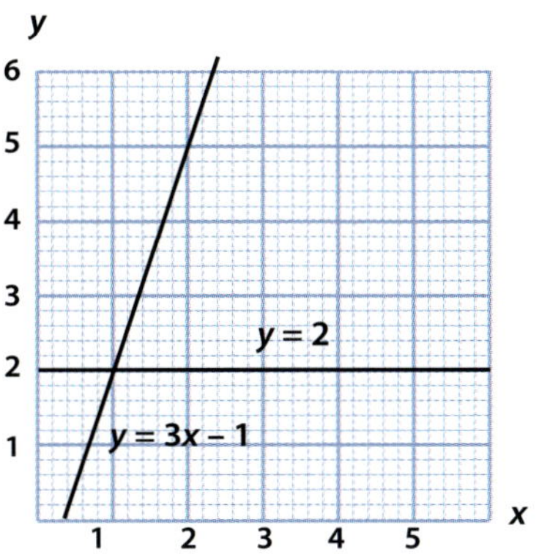

(b)

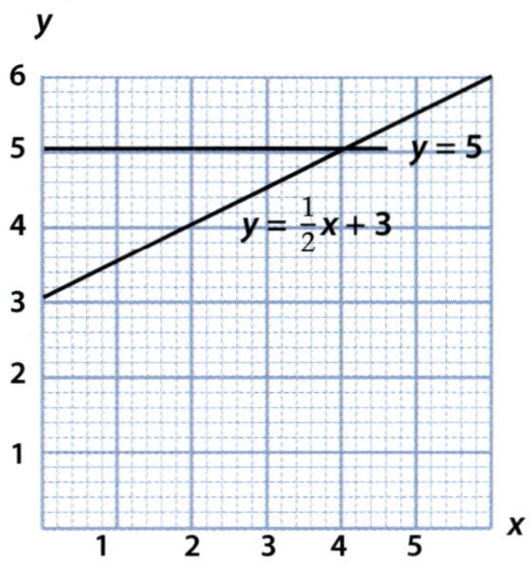

(c)

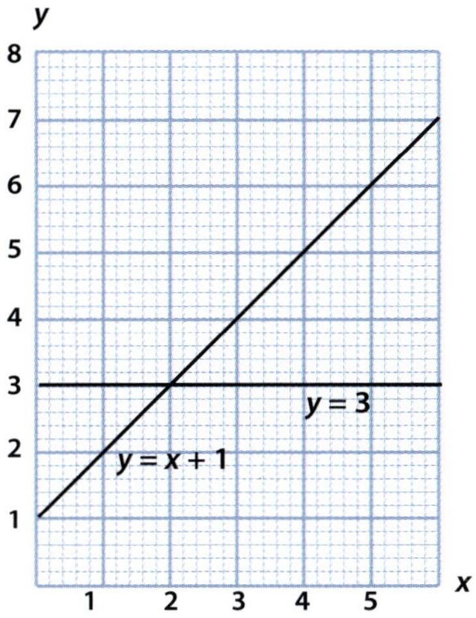

(d)

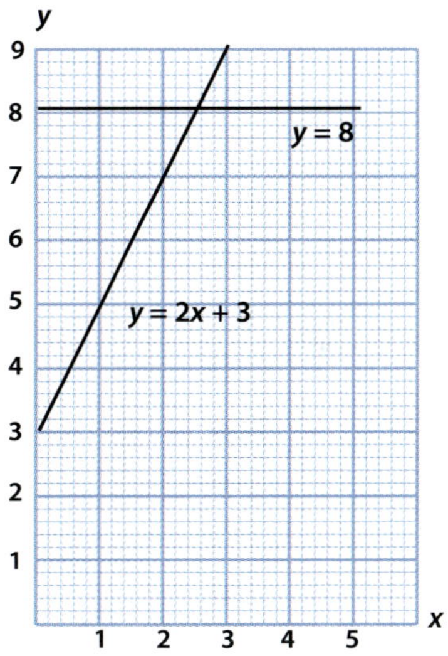

(i) For each of these graphs, form an equation which is true at the point of intersection of the two lines drawn.

(ii) Use the graphs to solve your equations.

> For $2x + 3 = 7$ plot the lines $y = 2x + 3$ and $y = 7$ and see where they cross.

2 Solve these equations by drawing a pair of lines and looking at their point of intersection.

(a) $2x + 3 = 7$ (b) $10 - 2x = 2$ (c) $4x + 3 = 11$

(d) $2x - 1 = 8$ (e) $3x - 1 = 11$ (f) $7 - 2x = 3$

(g) $2x + 3 = x + 6$ (h) $3x - 1 = 2x + 1$

Key fact

In every equation, the equals sign means that the value of one side of the equation balances the value of the other side.

Finding solutions to equations

So far you have looked at one-stage equations like $x + 5 = 8$

two-stage equations like $3a + 1 = 7$

and equations with brackets like $2(b + 4) = 10$

In Exercise 2, Question 2, parts (g) and (h), x appeared on both sides of the equation.

For (g) you should have found that $2x + 3 = x + 6$ only when $x = 3$.

The value $x = 3$ makes the equation balance.

In (*h*) the balancing value of x, which solves the equation $3x - 1 = 2x + 1$ is $x = 2$.

Assignment 1 Unknowns on both sides of an equation

One number can be substituted into both sides of this equation to make it balance.

$3a + 4 = 2a + 11$

- As a first estimate, try $a = 2$.
  If $a = 2$ check that $3a + 4 = 10$ and $2a + 11 = 15$.

  10 does not equal 15, so $a = 2$ is *not* a solution of $3a + 4 = 2a + 11$.

- Try a second estimate of $a = 3$. Check that this gives $3a + 4 = 13$ which is *not* equal to $2a + 11 = 17$.

  Notice that the gap between 13 and 17 is smaller than the one between 10 and 15.

  This suggests that the solution must be even bigger than 3.

- Try the estimate of $a = 4$ and check that this gives $3a + 4 = 16$ which is *not* equal to $2a + 11 = 19$.
  Notice that the gap is smaller still.

- Continue estimating values for a, until you find one which makes both sides of the equation equal.

- Now solve these equations by the same method.

  $2x + 7 = 5x - 2$

  $3y - 40 = y - 4$

  Show all your working.

A systematic approach

Drawing a graph of both sides of an equation is just one way of solving this type of problem.

Another way is to solve the equation by thinking of the two sides of the equations as being in balance.

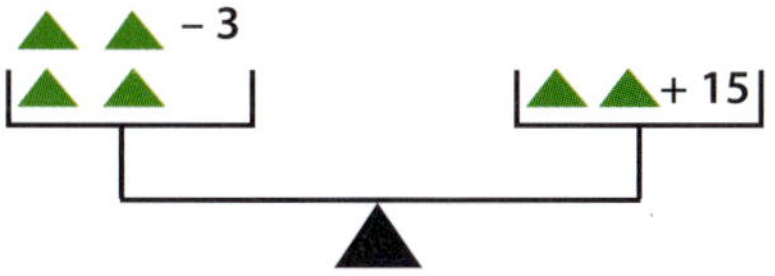

> **Doing the same to both sides of the equation will keep the sides in balance.**

To solve this type of problem you must aim to have the unknown value on only one side of the balance.
Then it will represent a one-stage equation and be easier to solve.

The first step is to remove as many unknown values from both sides of the balance as you can.
It must be the same number of unknown values from both sides, otherwise the balance is lost.

First then, remove ▲ ▲ from both sides.

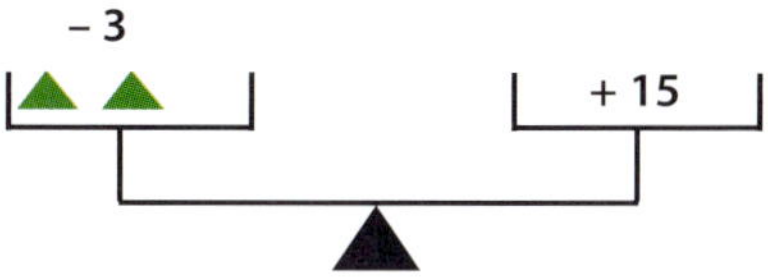

The second step is to isolate the unknown values.
If you add +3 to both sides, this will be the result.

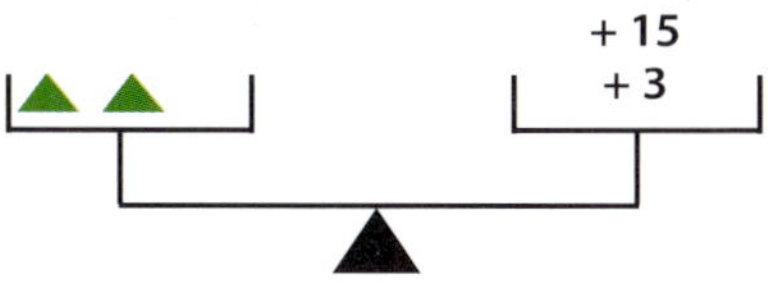

From this, the solution is

2 ▲ = 18

▲ = 9

Exercise 6

1 Look at these diagrams.

(a)

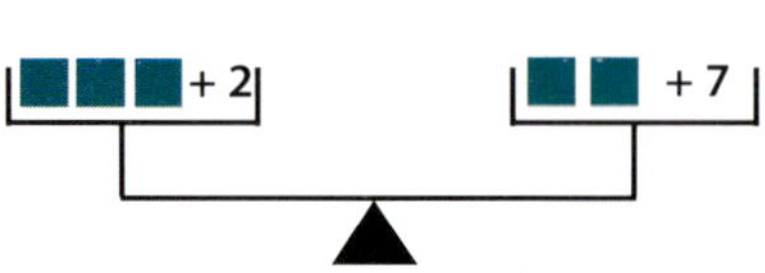

(b)

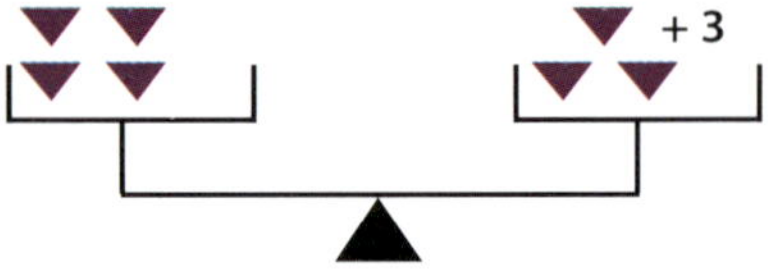

(c)

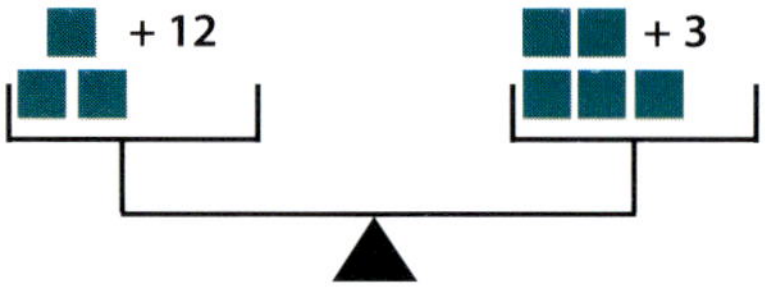

(d)

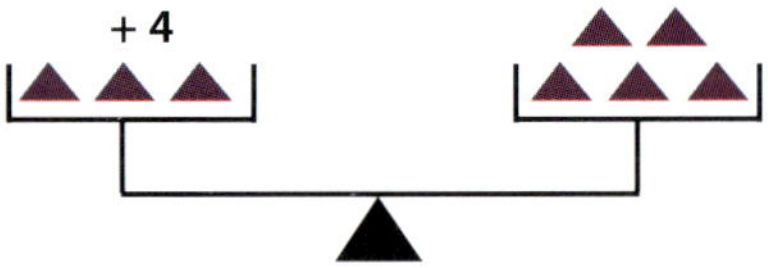

(e)

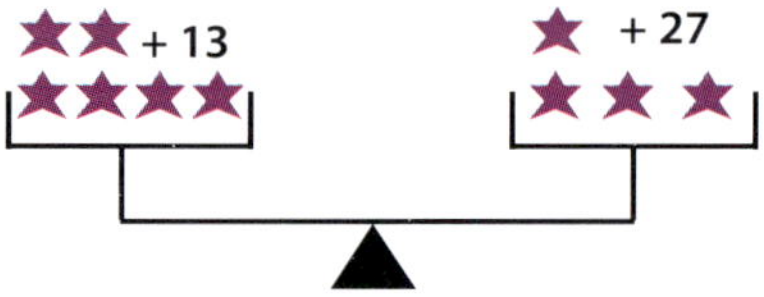

(f)

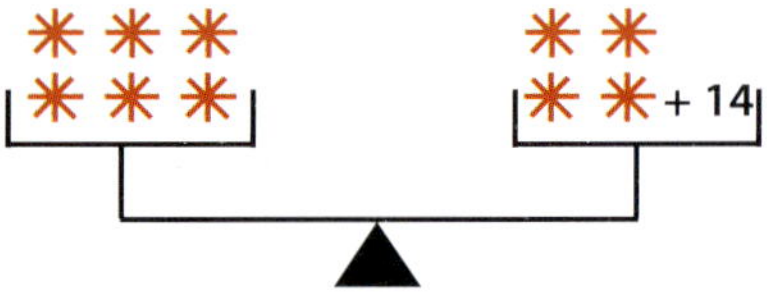

(g)

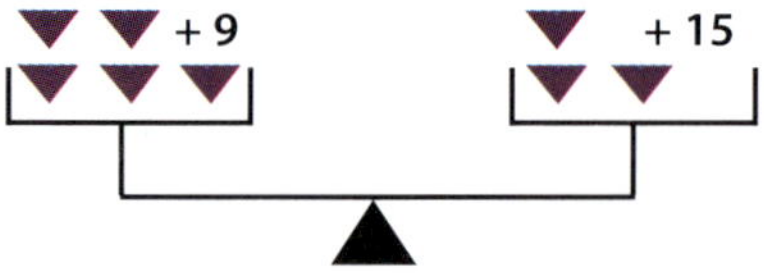

(h)

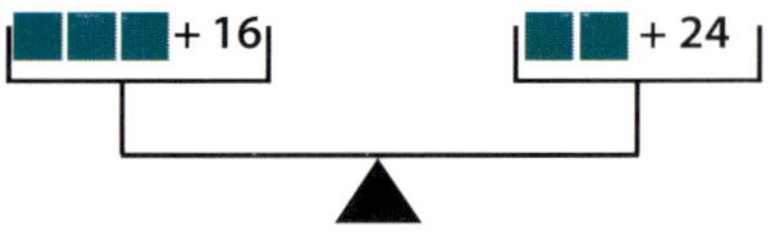

For each diagram:

(i) remove as many unknown values from both sides of the balance as possible

(ii) isolate the unknowns by adding (or subtracting) a number from both sides

(iii) solve the one-stage equations to get the solution to the balance problem.

Always check your solutions by substituting them back into the equations.

Solving written equations by balancing

Written equations can be solved by keeping the balance too.

Example

To solve this equation

4a + 3 = 2a + 13

you can subtract 2a from both sides of the equation and still keep the two sides of the equation in balance.

The process is written like this:

$$4a + 3 = 2a + 13$$

$$4a - 2a + 3 = 2a - 2a + 13$$

$$2a + 3 = 13$$

You can then subtract 3 from both sides.

$$2a + 3 - 3 = 13 - 3$$

$$2a = 10$$

Dividing both sides by 2 gives the solution:

$$a = 5$$

Check:
$4 \times 5 + 3 = 23$
$2 \times 5 + 13 = 23$

Show all your working out and check your answers.

Exercise 7

1 Solve these equations. Hints are given beside each one.

(a) $12x + 17 = 10x + 23$ Hint: Start by taking $10x$ from both sides of the equation.

(b) $6b + 23 = 4b + 27$ Hint: Take $4b$ from both sides so that the b values disappear from the right-hand side of the equation.

(c) $7k + 19 = 2k + 34$ Hint: Take $2k$ from each side this time.

(d) $5s + 17 = 4s + 21$ Hint: Take $4s$ from both sides.

(e) $7r + 12 = 40 + 3r$ Hint: How can you remove all the terms in r from one side of the balance?

(f) $4b + 12 = 8b + 4$ Hint: There are fewer bs on the left-hand side but the process is the same.

Show all your working out and check your answers.

2 Solve these equations.

(a) $3q + 6 = 2q + 9$

(b) $15w + 3 = 5w + 23$

(c) $8e + 7 = e + 14$

(d) $13r - 1 = 5r + 19$

(e) $3t - 7 = 2t - 1$

(f) $2y - 7 = 8 - y$

(g) $7u + 3 = 3u + 11$

(h) $11 - p = p + 5$

(i) $12a + 15 = 15a - 3$

(j) $s + 19 = 5s + 3$

(k) $3d + 1 = 10$

(l) $9f - 4 = 7f + 2$

(m) $12g - 1 = 6g + 17$

(n) $3h + 12 = 40 - h$

(o) $2j + 26 = 4j + 10$

(p) $11k + 8 = 2k + 62$

3 Write down an equation for each of these sentences and then solve your equations:

(a) Multiplying a number by 4 and then taking away 5 gives the same result as multiplying it by 3 and then adding 2.

(b) Multiplying a number by 6 and then subtracting 4 gives the same result as multiplying it by 4 and then adding 4

Equations with brackets

If the equation you need to solve contains a bracket you must multiply out the bracket first.

Example

$4(2a + 1) = 5a + 13$

$8a + 4 = 5a + 13$

$3a + 4 = 13$

$3a = 9$

$a = 3$

Check:

$4((2 \times 3) + 1) = 28$

$(5 \times 3) + 13 = 28$

The solution $a = 3$ is correct.

Exercise 8

Always show all your working.

Remember to expand the brackets first.

1 Solve these equations.

(a) $3(x + 1) = 2x + 7$

(b) $2(3n - 2) = 3n + 5$

(c) $4(a + 2) = 5a + 6$

(d) $2m + 8 = 4(m + 1)$

(e) $2(x + 2) = x + 10$

(f) $4(a - 2) = 3a$

(g) $3(2x + 2) = 5x + 9$

(h) $4x + 10 = 2(x + 9)$

(i) $3m + 13 = 4(m + 1)$

(j) $3(6 + 2x) = 10x - 2$

(k) $3(x - 1) = x + 5$

(l) $4(2a + 3) = 2(3a + 10)$

2 Solve these equations – they may involve negative values.

(a) $3 - 4x = x - 7$

(b) $5 - 8a = 2a + 25$

(c) $5 - w = w - 4$

(d) $2 - d = d - 2$

(e) $5n + 3 = 4n + 2$

(f) $4y + 1 = 2y + 6$

(g) $6t + 5 = 3t - 4$

(h) $7k + 3 = k - 3$

(i) $6(3z + 2) = 4(4z + 7)$

(j) $5(x - 2) = 4(x - 3)$

(k) $2(x - 3) = 3x + 4$

(l) $2m + 3 = 5(3m + 11)$

3 Simplify these equations before you solve them.

(a) $5x + 4 + 3x + 1 = 21$

(b) $6z + 8 + 4(z - 2) = 50$

(c) $3(2y + 1) + 6y + 5 = 44$

(d) $3a + 7 - a + 2a - 4 = 8 - 2a + 10$

(e) $3(5b + 4) - 3b - 10 = 4b - 6 + 16$

(f) $4(c + 3) + 2c + 6 = 5(c + 6) - 2$

(g) $6 - 5(d - 2) = 4 - 3(d + 3)$

(h) $7k + 6 - 3k - 4 = 2k + 6$

(i) $2(3e + 2) + 4 = 4(4e + 1) - 1$

(j) $6(n - 2) = 4(n - 3) + 5$

(k) $3(m - 1) - 2m = 3m + 1$

(l) $4(2r + 3) = 2(3r + 4\frac{1}{2})$

Review Exercise

1 Form an equation to describe each of these diagrams.

Solve your equations to find the values of a, b, c and d.

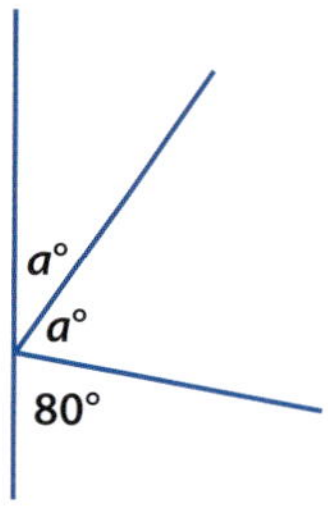

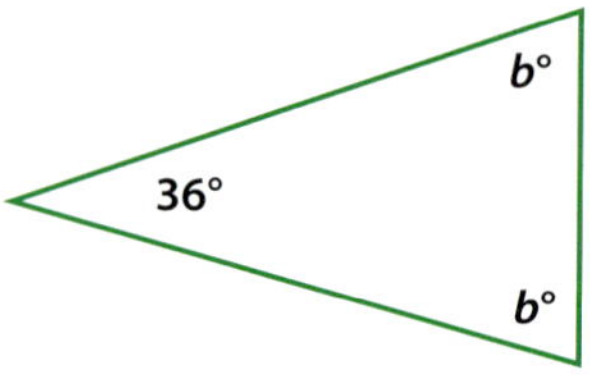

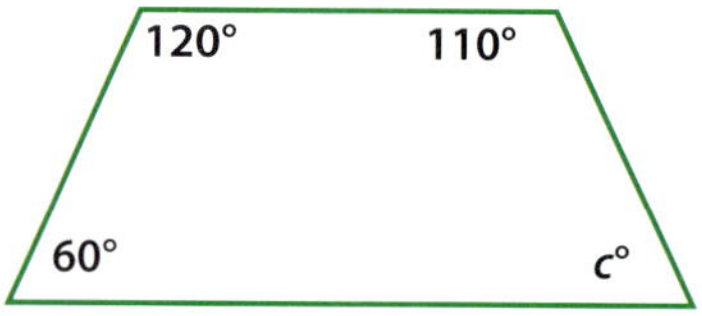

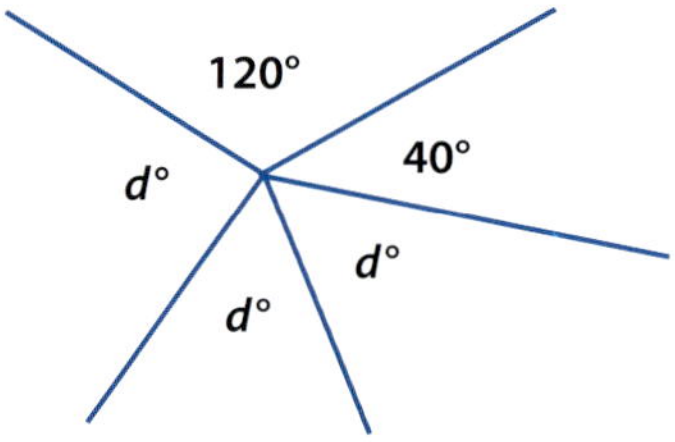

2 Solve these equations.

(a) $5f + 1 = 21$ (b) $2x + 2 = 10$ (c) $6a + 3 = 15$

(d) $2p + 12 = 22$ (e) $4 + 5t = 19$ (f) $11 + 6u = 47$

(g) $2b - 3 = 15$ (h) $3v - 1 = 20$

3 Expand the brackets and then solve these equations.

(a) $4(a + 1) = 16$ (b) $3(x + 5) = 48$ (c) $3(a + 2) = 27$

(d) $3(n - 5) = 18$ (e) $4(1 + m) = 28$ (f) $81 = 9(u - 2)$

4 Solve these equations.

(a) $3x + 22 = 6x + 10$ (b) $5a - 2 = a + 14$

(c) $7d + 2 = 4d + 8$ (d) $9r - 6 = 7r + 4$

(e) $13f - 20 = 3f + 20$ (f) $4x - 25 = x - 1$

5 Simplify and then solve these equations.

(a) $4(5a - 3) = 7(2a + 3)$ (b) $9b + 4 = 3(2b + 3)$

(c) $2(3x - 4) = 4(x + 1)$ (d) $8n - 1 = 3(2n - 5)$

(e) $4(m + 3) - 1 = 3$ (f) $5(2m + 1) + 5 = 7m - 1$

Review chapter

Exercise 1

1 A lottery prize of a million pounds is shared equally among 20 people. How much does each person get?
Show all your working.

2 From this list of numbers, select two numbers so that one is ten times the other. Explain your answer.

3 Roses are packed in bunches of 18 roses.
How many bunches can be made using 630 roses?
Show your working.

4 Calculate the total weight of the six people waiting for the lift
Is it possible for all six to travel in the lift together?
Explain your answer.

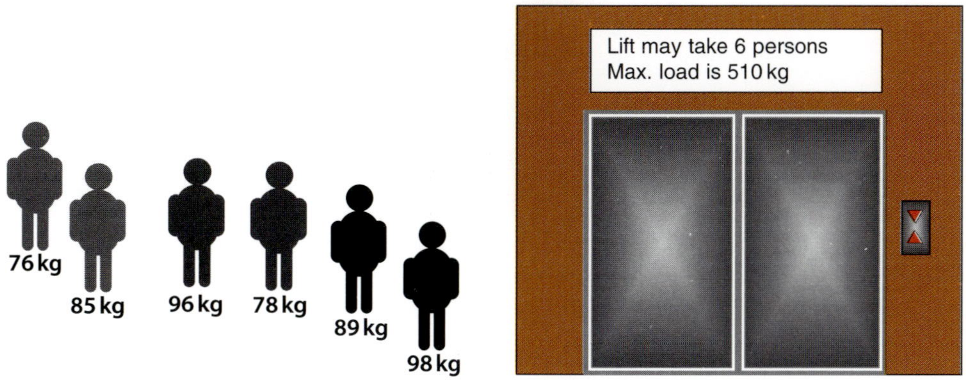

5 This table shows the highest and lowest temperatures in Edinburgh recorded during one week in April.

	High (°C)	Low (°C)
Monday	14	−2
Tuesday	12	−2
Wednesday	12	−3
Thursday	16	0
Friday	15	2
Saturday	13	−4
Sunday	13	−1

(a) Which day had the smallest change in temperature?

(b) Which day had the largest change in temperature?

In both cases, show clearly how you worked out your answer.

6 If 8 kilometres is approximately 5 miles, what is the approximate distance to Bristol in miles?

Show your working.

7

The door is 2 metres high.
What is the approximate height of the chair?
Explain your working.

8 You have to pay a deposit of 20% to reserve a bicycle in a sale.

Show clearly how to work out the amount you have to pay as a deposit on this mountain bike.

9 A piece of string 5.28 metres long is made into a square.

How long is one side of the square

(a) in metres?

(b) in centimetres?

Show your working.

10 In a Maths test, I scored 17 out of 20 marks.

For English I scored $\frac{3}{4}$ of the marks.

For Science my mark was 80%.

Place these examination results in order, giving my best performance first.

Show your working.

Exercise 2

1 A bag of sweets from the Mix & Match contains toffees, coffee creams, eclairs and humbugs.
There are *n* toffees in the bag.

(a) There are the same number of coffee creams as toffees.
Write down how many coffee creams there are.

(b) There are three times as many eclairs as toffees.
Write down how many eclairs there are.

(c) There are two more humbugs than toffees.
Write down how many humbugs there are.

(d) How many sweets are there altogether in the bag?

2 Five bags of marbles each have n marbles inside.
There are three extra marbles not in the bags.

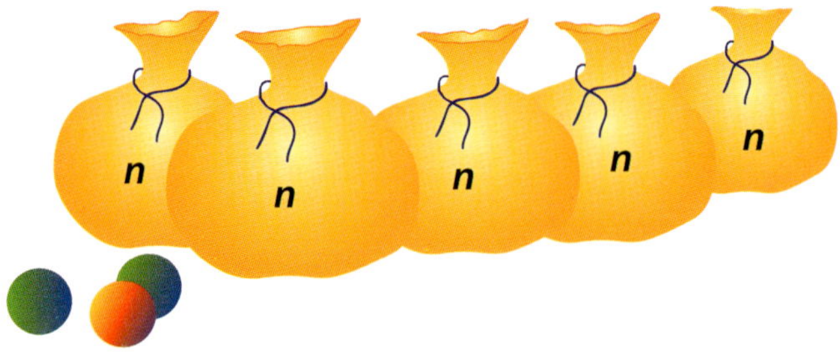

(a) There are at least two marbles in each of the five bags.
Could there be $8n$ marbles altogether?
Explain your answer.

(b) Could there be $3+5n$ marbles altogether?
Explain your answer.

(c) There are 28 marbles altogether.

(i) Copy and complete this equation to describe how many marbles there are.

$$\_\_\_\_\_\_\_\_\_\_\_\_ = 28$$

(ii) Solve your equation to find n, the number of marbles in each bag.

3 Look at this sequence of patterns.

To find the number of triangles you add 1 to the number of squares.

Use T for the number of triangles and S for the number of squares and write a rule connecting the number of triangles with the number of squares.

4 The rule to find the number of legs in a field of ducks and cows is $l = 4c + 2d$.
l stands for the total number of legs.
c stands for the number of cows.
d stands for the number of ducks.

(a) Explain why c is multiplied by 4 in the rule.

(b) How many legs are there in a field containing 8 ducks and 12 cows?

5 Look at this table.

Pattern	Number of dots (d)	Number of lines (l)
●—●	2	1
●—●—●	3	2
●—●—●—●	4	3
●—●—●—●—●	5	4

Write a rule to find the number of dots d from the number of lines l.

6 Three tapes can be bought for the price of one CD.

The rule for this is written as $t = 3c$.
(c is the number of CDs and t is the number of tapes.)

(a) How many CDs can be bought for the same amount of money as nine tapes?

(b) How many tapes can be bought for the same amount of money as twelve CDs?

7 A pencil case holds red, green, blue and yellow pencils.

The number of red pencils is n.

(a) There are twice as many green pencils as red pencils.
Write down how many green pencils there are.

(b) There are three more blue pencils than red pencils.
Write down how many blue pencils there are.

(c) There are the same number of yellow pencils as red pencils.
How many pencils are there altogether in the pencil case?

8 The rule for the number of sticks of chewing gum in a pack is $s = 5p$ where s stands for the number of sticks and p stands for the number of packs.

(a) Use the rule to find the total number of sticks in 7 packs.

(b) Use the rule to find how many packs 30 sticks make.

(c) A number of packs are bought.
Some sticks are eaten and 18 sticks remain.
At least how many packs must have been bought?

Explain your answer.

9 Each carriage on a train can seat 60 passengers.

(a) If there are n carriages, write a rule for the number of passenger seats on the train.

(b) An extra coach is added to the train which can seat 80 passengers.

How many passengers can be seated on the train altogether?

10 The perimeter of this shape is $2a+3b$.

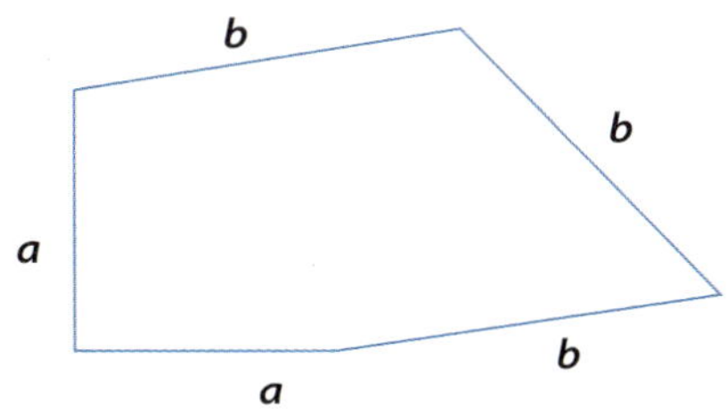

This statement can be written as $p = 2a + 3b$.

Write an expression for the perimeter of each of these shapes.

(a)

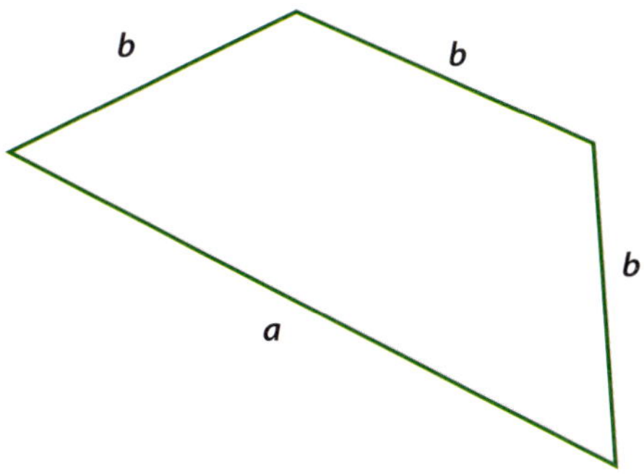

(b)

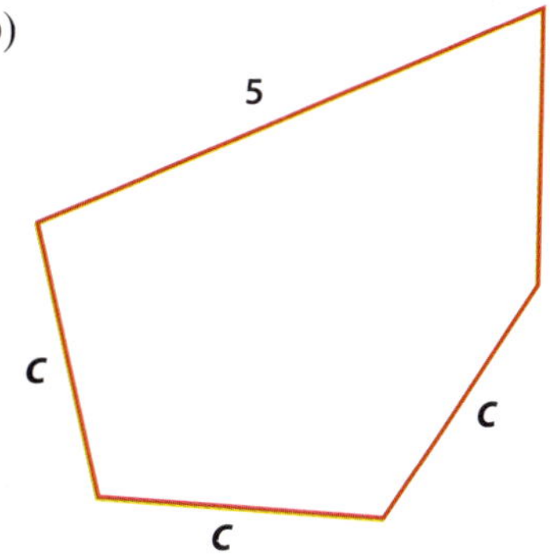

(c)

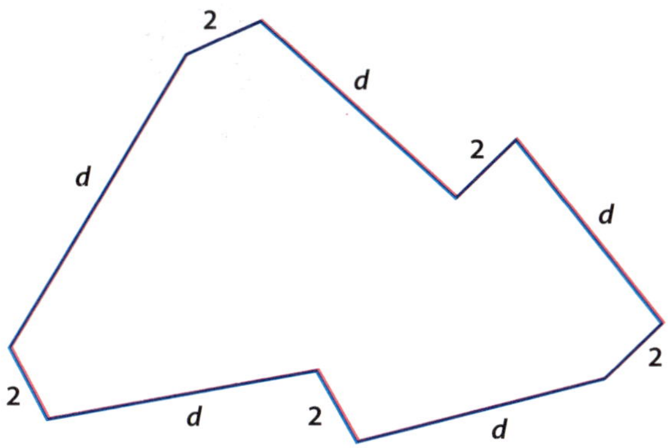

(d)

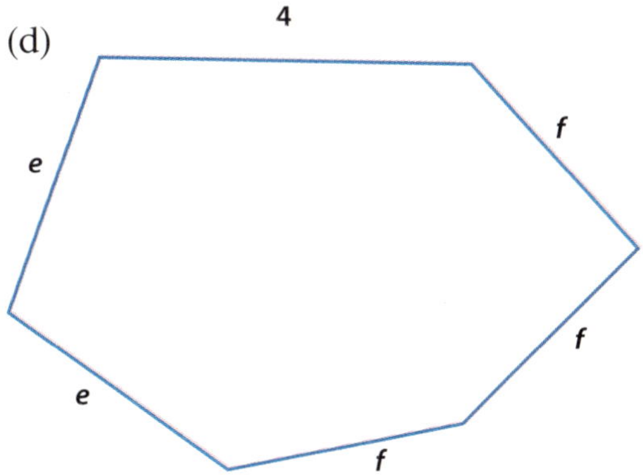

Exercise 3

1 Measure the angles a, c and g in this shape accurately using a protractor.

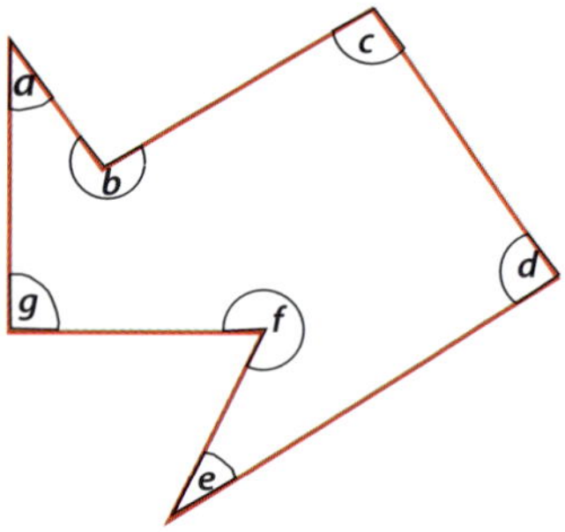

2 Copy and complete this table for the angles in the shape in Question 1.

Angle	acute	obtuse	reflex	rightangle
a				
b				
c				
d				
e				
f				
g				

3 Make an accurate copy of this diagram. (It is not drawn to scale.)

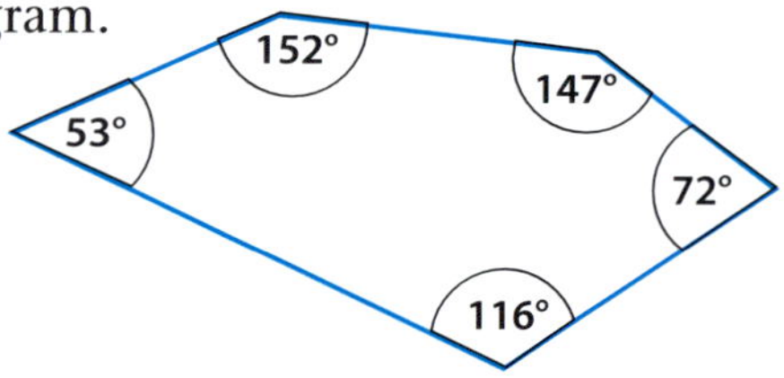

4 Look at these diagrams.

(a) Which of these shapes have exactly one line of symmetry?

(b) Which shape has the greatest number of lines of symmetry? How many are there?

(c) Which shape has rotational symmetry of order 2?

(d) What is the order of rotational symmetry of shape E?

5 In France, I saw a road sign which said the distance to the next town was 8 km. I thought this was about 13 miles, but I was wrong.

(a) Explain how you know that I must have been wrong.

(b) About how many miles do you think it was to the next town?

6 Copy these statements and complete the units used in each. Choose between feet, metres, miles and kilometres.

(a) A pupil's height is 1.48 ____

(b) When I take 10 paces, I walk about 30 ____

(c) From London to Birmingham, it is about 120 ____or 190 ____.

7 Copy and complete these statements.

(a) 5 m is the same as ___ cm.

(b) 3 kg is the same as ___ g.

(c) 3000 ml is the same as ___ litres

(d) 200 mm is the same as ___ cm.

8 This diagram is a sketch of the net for this box.

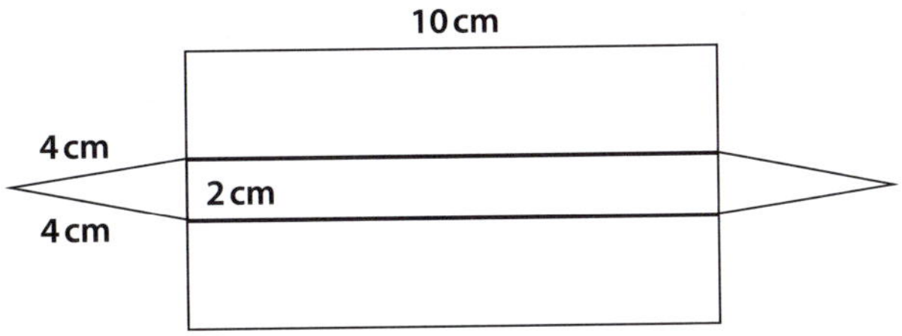

Make an accurate drawing of the net.

9 Draw a separate diagram to show each of these angles.

(a) A right angle (b) An obtuse angle (c) An acute angle.

Label the angles in your diagram.

10 (a) Draw a shape which has exactly four lines of symmetry.

(b) Draw a shape with rotational symmetry of order 4.

(c) Draw a shape with exactly two lines of symmetry and rotational symmetry of order 2.

Exercise 4

1 Here are the shoe sizes of twelve people in Year 9.

7 4 5 3 4 4 5 6 4 7 5 4

(a) Write down the modal shoe size.

(b) Write down the median shoe size.

(c) Calculate the mean shoe size.

(d) Of your answers to parts (a) (b) and (c), one average is less useful when considering shoe size.

Which one is it? Explain your answer.

2 This table shows the number of goals scored by Manchester United, Newcastle and Liverpool in their first ten matches of the season.

Manchester United	3	2	0	4	3	2	1	1	3	2
Newcastle	2	1	0	3	1	2	3	2	1	2
Liverpool	3	2	6	1	4	0	3	1	2	2

(a) Calculate the average (mean) score for each team.

(b) Which team has the highest mean score?

(c) Calculate the range of goals for each team.

(d) Which team is performing best? Explain your answer.

3 Here are the ages, in years, of eight people.

15 18 22 16 16 21 19 17

(a) Calculate the mean age of the group.

(b) What is the range of ages of the group?

Two more people join the group. Their ages are 19 and 21.

(c) Calculate the new mean.

(d) Why is the range of the new larger group the same as the range of the original group?

4 Pupils travel from seven villages to their school.

Each village has its own bus.

Here are the number of pupils arriving on each bus, on one Monday morning.

Village	Number of pupils
St Agnes	47
Mount Hawke	37
Perranporth	41
Chacewater	42
Shortlanesend	48
Carnon Down	43
Porthowan	53

(a) Write down the median number of pupils on the buses.

(b) Calculate the mean number of pupils on the buses.

(c) Explain why is it not relevant to find the modal value.

(d) Write down the range of pupils on the buses.

The bus company needs an average of at least 44 pupils per bus per day to make the journeys profitable.
The bus company say the average is only 43.

(e) Which average has the bus company used?

(f) Which average would you use to prove this is not true?

Explain the difference.

5 In a survey, 200 pupils were asked to name their favourite sport.

This pie chart shows the results.

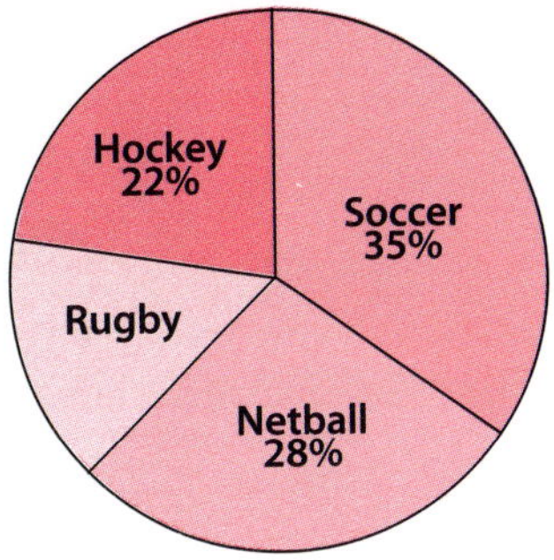

(a) What percentage of the 200 pupils liked rugby best?

(b) How many pupils liked netball best?

(c) Calculate the pie chart angle for rugby.

6 Two dice are thrown.
One dice is an ordinary dice with sides numbered 1 to 6.
The other is an octahedral dice with sides numbered 1 to 8.

Explain why the probability of throwing a six is not the same for each dice.

7 A coin is spun six times.
Here are the results.

Tail Head Head Head Head Head

What is the probability that the next time it is spun it will be a head?

Explain your answer.

8 The arrow on this hexagonal spinner is spun ten times.

Is it possible for the arrow to land

(a) in a white area all ten times?

(b) in a black area all ten times?

(c) in a black then a white area, each five times?

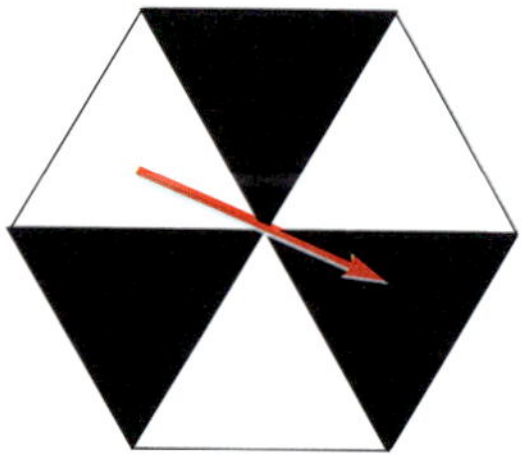

Explain your answers.

9 Explain which of these outcomes is more likely.

A: Throwing an even number bigger than 3 on a fair dice

B: Spinning a head on a coin

10 In a game, you need to throw a six on one dice to get out of jail.

After three attempts to move you are still in jail.

What is the probability that, the next time you throw the dice, it will be a six?

Explain your answer.

Exercise 5

1 I worked out the answer to 374×86 as 5236, but I may have made a mistake.

(a) Make a rough estimate of 374×86 showing all the numbers you use.
Compare your answer with 5236.

(b) Did I make a mistake?
Explain your answer.

2 With 20% off, the price of a mountain bike is now only £300.

(a) I think this means that the original price was £360, but I am wrong.
Explain why I am wrong.

(b) What was the correct original price of this bike?
Show your working.

3 The scale on a house plan is 1:100.

On the plan, the length of a room measures 4.8 cm.

What is the real length of the room?

4 (a) A class has 12 boys and 18 girls.
What percentage of this class are girls?

(b) Boys make up 45% of the whole school population.
If there are 180 boys in the whole school, how many pupils are there altogether?

5 Express 24% as

(a) a decimal number (b) a fraction in its simplest form.

6 At the start of June, the height of a sunflower was 2 metres. During the month it increased its height by 30%.

The ratio of the height of the sunflower at the end of the month to that at the start of the month can be written in the form 1:h.

What is the value of h?

7 The colour 'sea green' is obtained by mixing blue paint with green paint in the ratio 2:3.

(a) How much green paint should be mixed with 1 litre of blue to obtain 'sea green'?

(b) How much blue paint will be needed to make 5 litres of sea green paint?

8 The photograph in the picture frame measures 12 cm by 24 cm and has a border of 5 cm all around it.

(a) What are the dimensions of the picture frame?

The photograph is enlarged to make it twice the original size. The border remains the same in the new picture frame.

(b) What are the new dimensions of the photograph?

(c) What are the dimensions of the new picture frame?

9 This recipe will make enough scones for four people.

Rewrite the recipe, to make enough scones for six people.

RECIPE FOR SCONES

8 oz (225 g) flour

1 tsp baking powder

$1\frac{1}{2}$ oz (40 g) butter

1 oz (25 g) caster sugar

2 eggs

$\frac{1}{4}$ pint (150 ml) milk

10 A standard can of cola contains 330 ml of drink.
A can which is marked 'extra 25% free' contains 415 ml.

Is the label correct?
Explain your answer.

Exercise 6

1 What is the next number in this sequence?

1 4 7 10 13

Explain how you found your answer.

2 A music shop sells tapes for £8 and CDs for £30.

You can calculate the amount of money the shop receives (£A) by using the formula $A = 8t + 30c$.

(t is the number of tapes sold and c is the number of CDs sold.)

(a) Work out how much the shop receives when $t = 15$ and $c = 12$.

(b) On a particular day, $A = 940$ and $t = 50$.
How many CDs were sold on that day?

3 Look at this table.

Position	1	2	3	4	5	…	…
Value	5	7	9	11	13		

(a) Write down the value at position 10.
Explain how you reached your answer.

(b) Write down the value at position 45

(c) Write down the value at position n.

4 (a) Some sheets of paper are pinned to a noticeboard using four pins on each sheet like this.

How many pins would be needed for n sheets of paper?

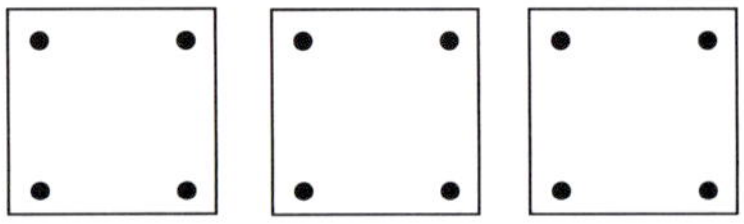

(b) To save pins the sheets can be overlapped like this.

How many pins would be needed for n sheets of paper using this method?

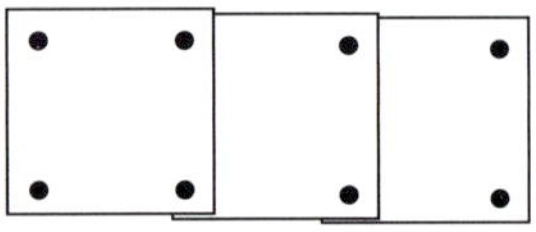

(c) How many sheets of paper can be pinned up with 16 pins

(i) using the first method? (ii) using the second method?

5 This diagram shows the mapping $x \longrightarrow x+3$

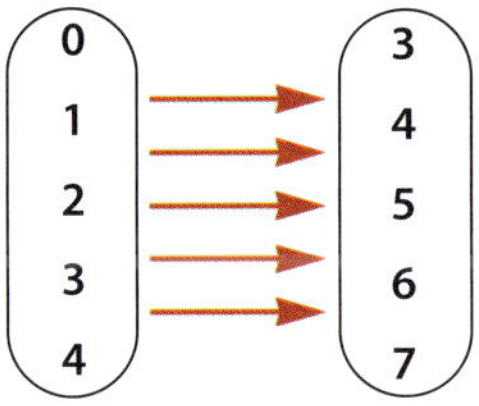

Draw mapping diagrams for these:

(a) $x \longrightarrow x+5$

(b) $x \longrightarrow x-3$

(c) $x \longrightarrow 2x$

(d) $x \longrightarrow 3x+2$

(e) $x \longrightarrow 5-x$

6 Here is the graph of $y = x + 2$.

Make one copy of these axes and draw these graphs.

(a) $y = x + 5$

(b) $y = 2x$

(c) $y = 2x + 5$

Label your graphs.

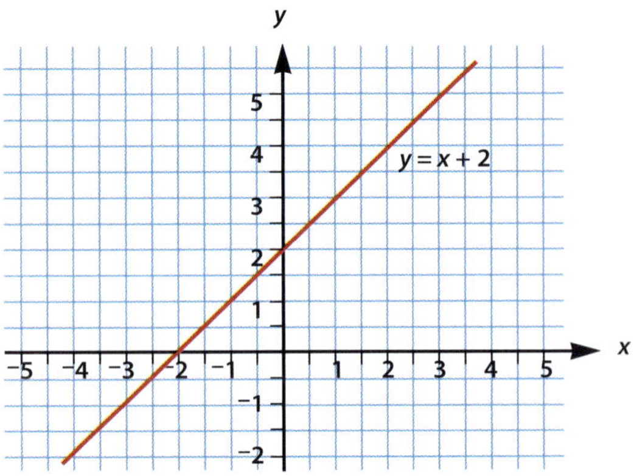

7 Look at this graph.

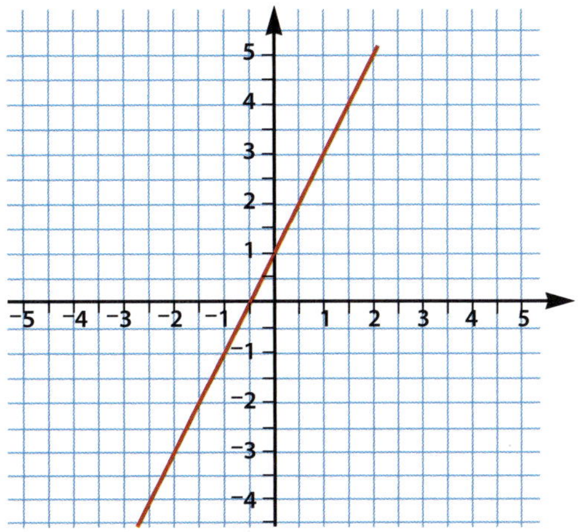

(a) Copy and complete this table for points on the line.

x	−2	−1	0		
y				3	5

(b) Write down the equation of the line.

8 (a) Write down the next three numbers of this sequence.

2   5   8   11   ...

Explain how you found your answer.

(b) What is the 10th number in the sequence? Explain how you found your answer.

(c) What is the 100th number in the sequence?

(d) Write down a rule to find the *n*th number in the sequence.

9 Find a value of x which makes this equation true.

$x^2 - 7 = 18$

Explain how you found your answer.

10 A computer prints out these three pairs of numbers.

2, 7   4, 13   5, 16

(a) Write down three more pairs which the computer might produce. Explain your answer.

(b) Using letters write down a rule connecting the two numbers in each pair. Explain your rule.

Exercise 7

1 Look at this drawing of a 3D shape.

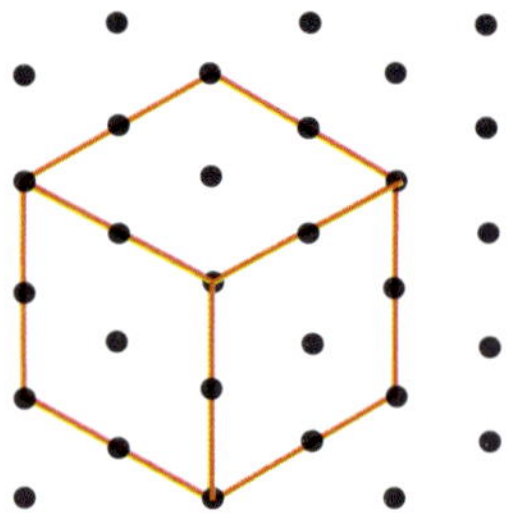

When asked to describe this shape, I called it a square, but was wrong.

(a) Explain why I was wrong.

(b) What is this shape called?

2 On triangular dotted paper, draw a 2D representation of this tower of blocks.

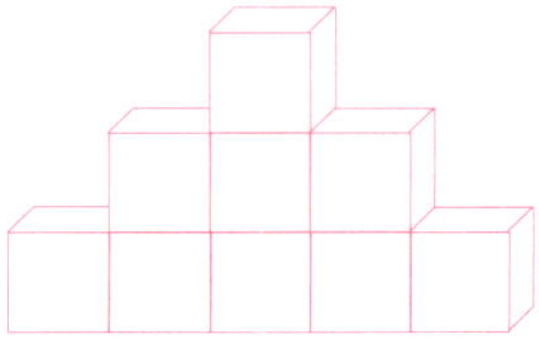

3 Look at these quadrilaterals

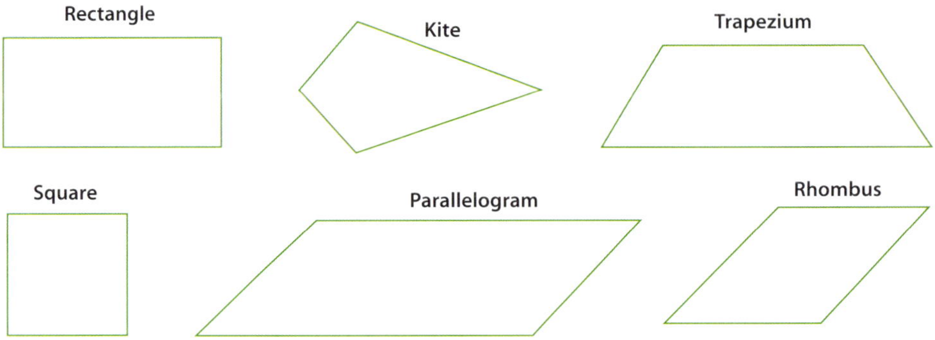

(a) Write down which quadrilaterals have sides which are parallel.

(b) Write down which quadrilaterals have at least two angles which are equal.

(c) Write down which quadrilaterals contain at least one right angle.

(d) Write down which quadrilaterals have adjacent sides equal.

4 Look at this diagram.
The angles marked a and b are 90°.
The angle marked c is 50°.

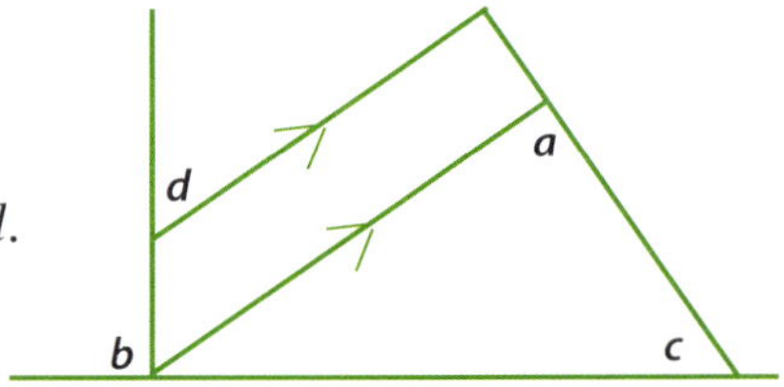

Work out the size of the angle marked d.
Explain each step you take.

5 This picture shows a table set for tea.

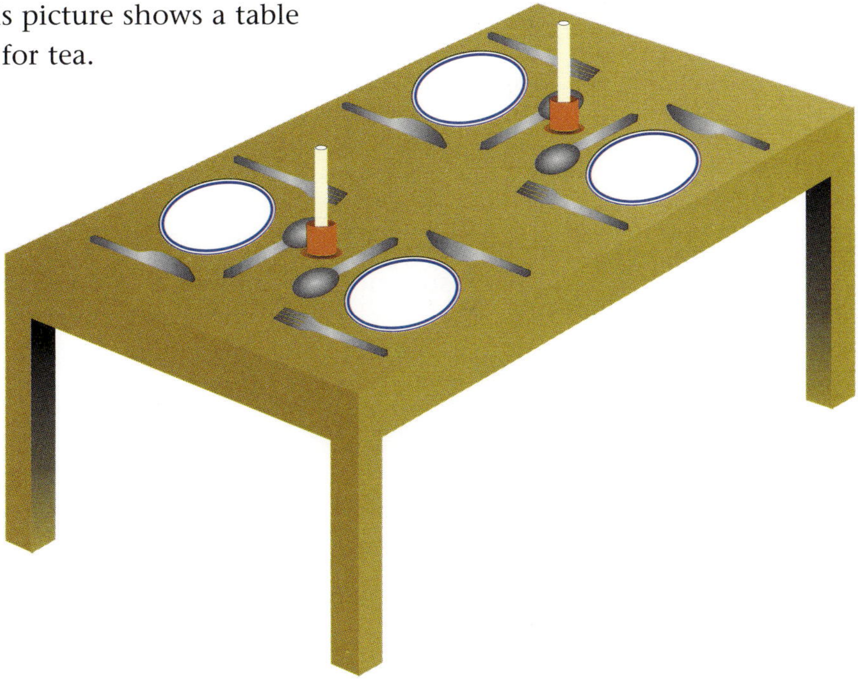

Which of these pictures are plan views of the table?

(a)

(b)

(c)

(d)

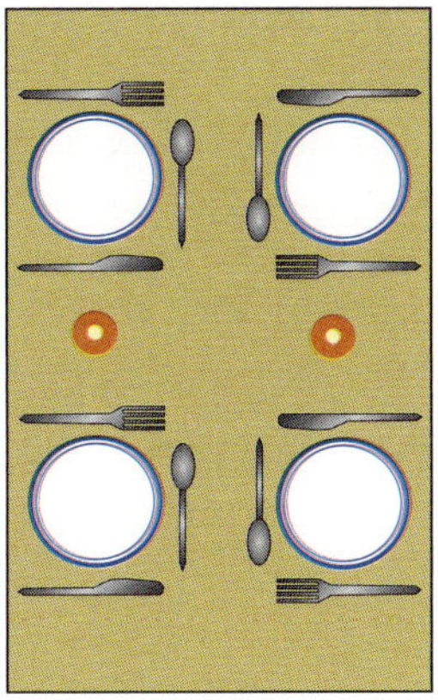

(e)

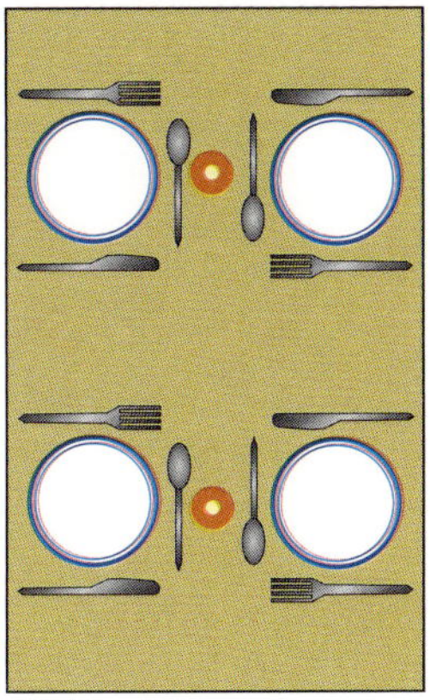

6 Shape A is a square. Shape B is a rhombus.

Shape A

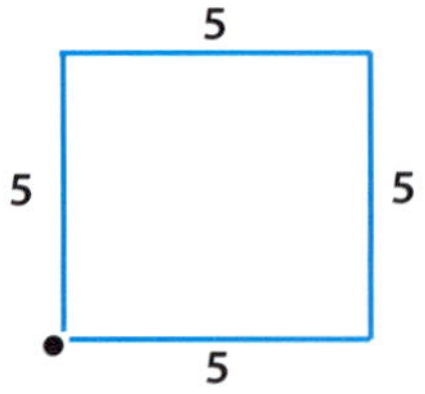

Shape B

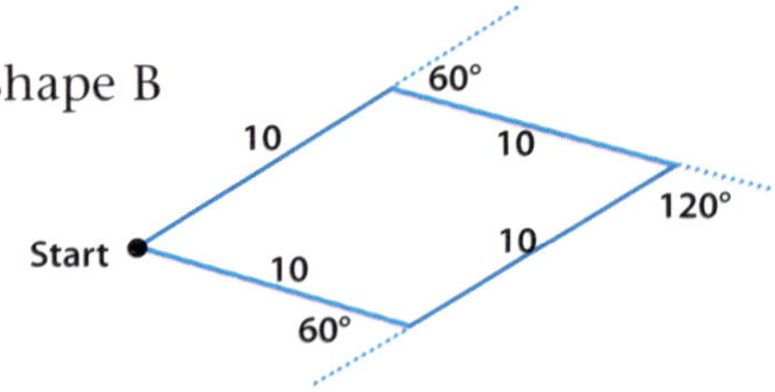

These instructions will draw square A on a computer.

FORWARD 5
RIGHT 90
FORWARD 5
RIGHT 90
FORWARD 5
RIGHT 90
FORWARD 5

(a) Write the instructions to draw another square, this time with sides of length 8.

(b) Write instructions to draw shape B, the rhombus.

7 (a) Find the circumference of a circle which has a radius of 5 cm using π as 3.14 or the value given by your calculator.

(b) I calculated the area of the same circle as 246.5 cm². Explain how you can tell this is wrong. Calculate the correct answer.

Area of a circle, $A = \pi r^2$.

Circumference of a circle, $C = 2\pi r$.

8 This model of a skyscraper is made from three plastic containers.

The plastic containers are all cuboids. What volume of clay would be needed to fill the model with clay? (All measurements are in centimetres.)

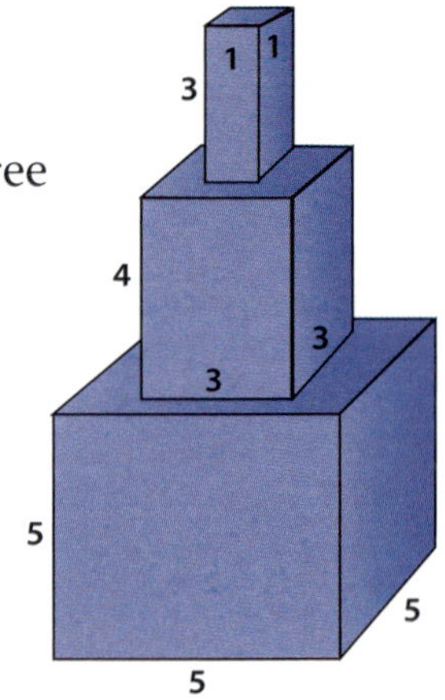

Area of a triangle
$= \frac{1}{2}bh$

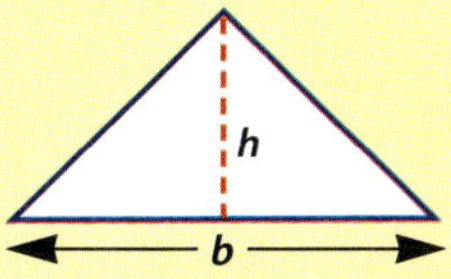

Area of a trapezium
$= \frac{1}{2}(a+b)h$

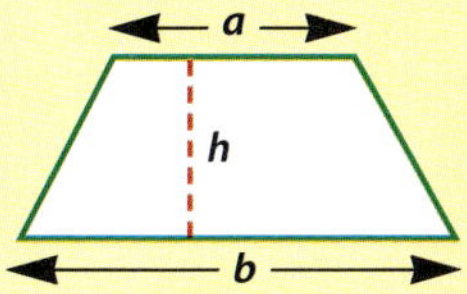

9 Find the area of this shape. Show all your working.

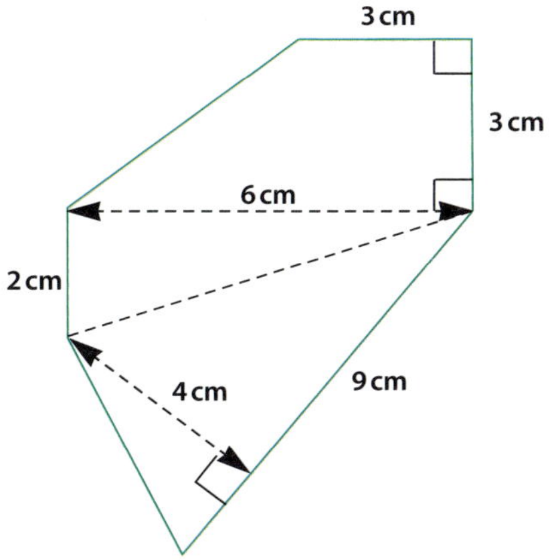

10 The quadrilateral in the diagram is enlarged with a scale factor of 2 using (0,0) as the centre of enlargement.

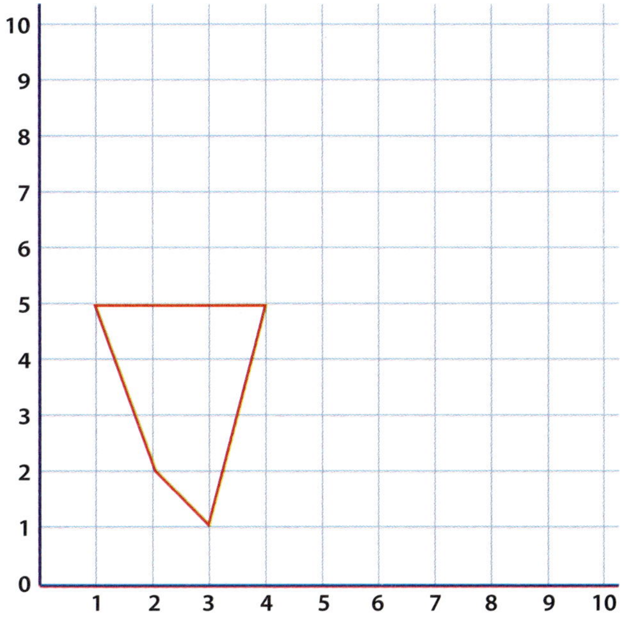

Write down the coordinates of the corners of the enlarged shape.

Exercise 8

1 The weight of 25 pupils is measured to the nearest 0.5kg. The results are shown in this frequency table.

Class Interval	Frequency
30.0 – 32.5	1
32.5 – 35.0	3
35.0 – 37.5	4
37.5 – 40.0	2
40.0 – 42.5	5
42.5 – 45.0	6
45.0 – 47.5	4
47.5 – 50.0	0
	25

(a) What is the range of weights?

(b) What is the size of the class interval used to produce the frequency table?

2 Use the information given in the frequency table in Question 1 to draw a frequency diagram.

3 This table gives the raw data obtained from measuring the heights of 100 pupils.

112	167	115	119	197	179	136	147	188	150
186	155	120	174	113	142	137	175	179	165
176	137	145	128	182	138	176	186	112	165
154	165	133	135	125	134	143	169	142	121
145	120	179	117	127	179	186	145	115	177
115	168	139	151	154	142	187	150	122	119
119	142	118	169	121	126	170	160	160	150
159	135	130	125	130	158	119	159	178	150
169	135	130	125	130	158	119	159	178	150
120	126	164	169	136	131	150	166	185	178

Use the data to construct a frequency diagram with 10-cm intervals.

4 In a survey, 90 Year 9 pupils were asked to comment on this statement:

Fox hunting should be banned.

Here are the results of the survey.

Answers	Tally	Frequency
Strongly agree	卌 卌 卌 卌 卌 卌 III	33
Agree	卌 卌 卌 卌 IIII	24
Disagree	卌	5
Strongly disagree	II	2
Don't know	卌 卌 卌 卌 卌 I	26
Total		90

Use the data to complete this pie chart.

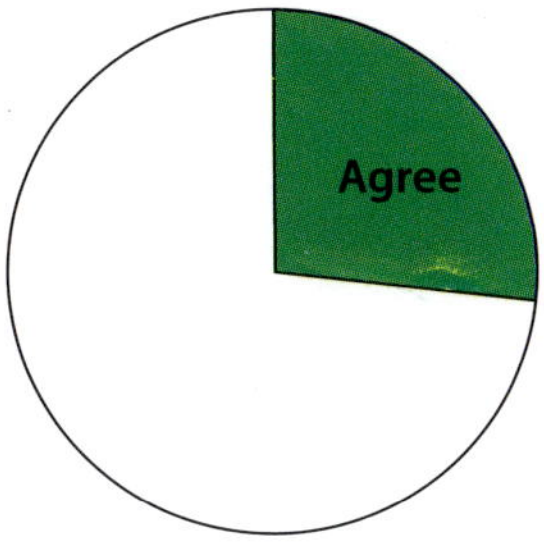

5 In a survey, 200 pupils were asked which television channel they watched the most.

This pie chart shows the results.

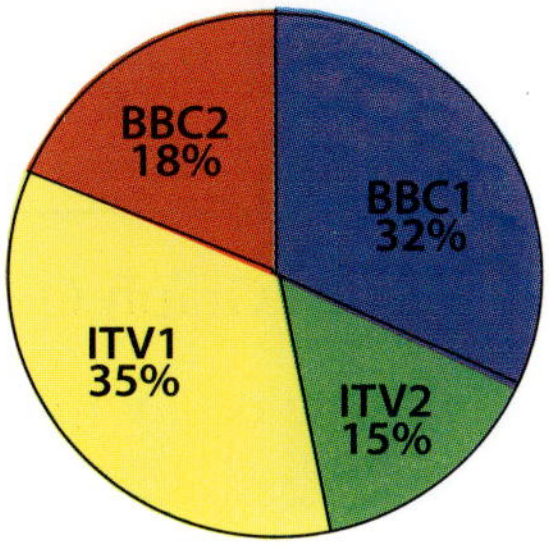

(a) How many of the 200 pupils watched BBC1 the most?

(b) What size is the angle for ITV2?

6 This table shows the height and shoe size of twelve Year 9 pupils.

Height (cm)	172	180	168	168	168	168	168	168	177	182	178	176
Shoe size	7	9	$8\frac{1}{2}$	8	$7\frac{1}{2}$	9	$8\frac{1}{2}$	$7\frac{1}{2}$	$8\frac{1}{2}$	10	$9\frac{1}{2}$	8

(a) Copy this grid and draw a scatter graph to represent the data.

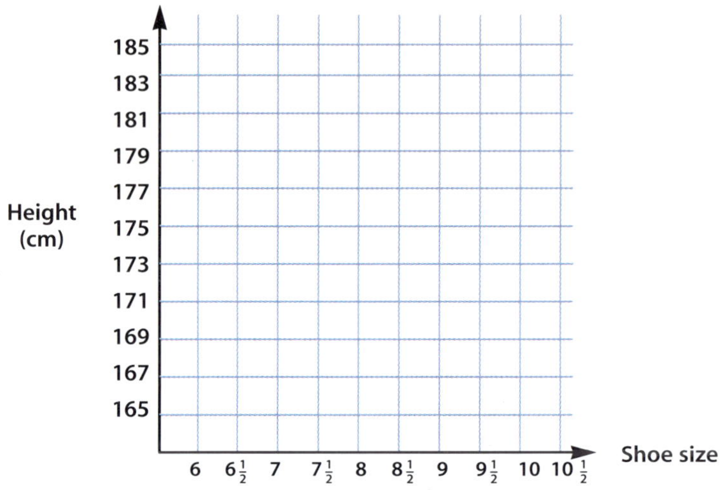

(b) Comment on the trend shown by your scatter graph.

7 Look at these two scatter graphs.

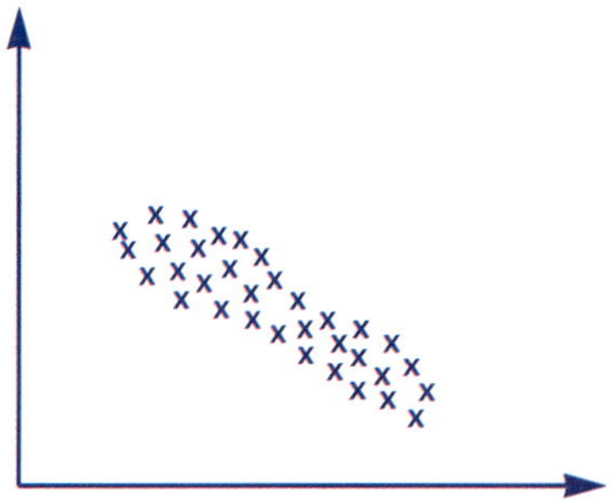

Graph P

Graph Q

From these three titles, choose the one which best matches each graph.

A: Shoe size against the number of letters in the pupil's first name

B: Age of pupil against height of pupil

C: Cost of car against age of car

8 This grid shows all the outcomes fom throwing two dice.

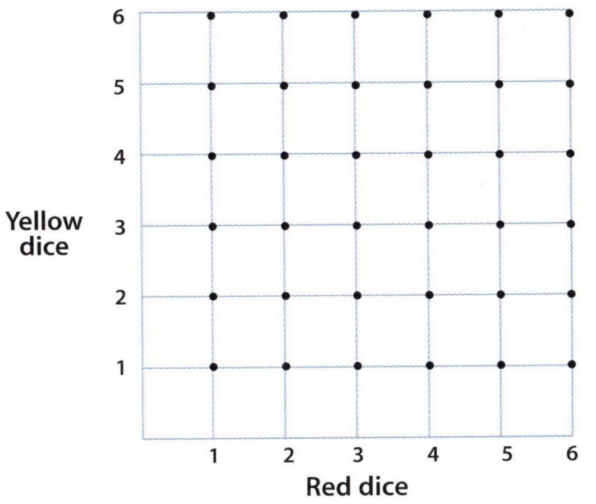

(a) Copy the grid and circle all the points which represent throwing a score of less than six.

(b) Express this outcome as a fraction.

9 One evening, the weather forecast predicts that:
The probability of rain tomorrow is 70%.

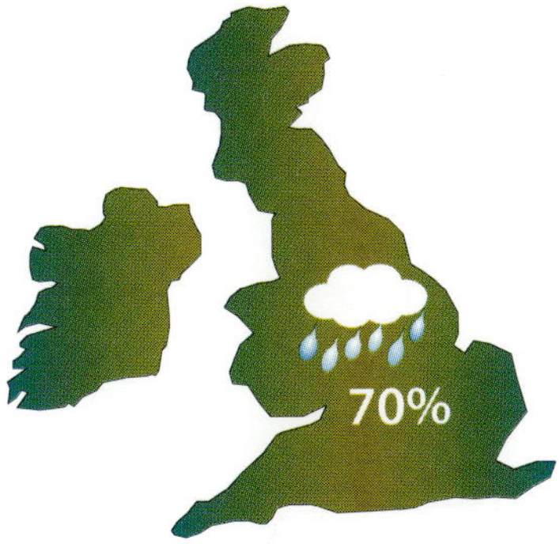

Write as a decimal the probability that it will *not* rain tomorrow.

10 Construct a table to show all possible outcomes from spinning these two spinners.

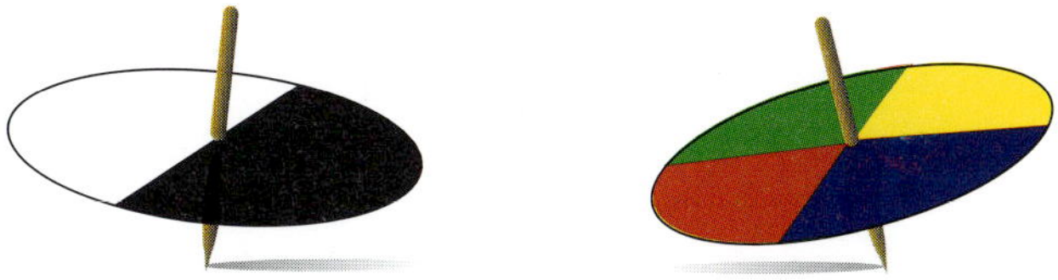

Exercise 9

1 Which of these two has the larger answer?

13×13 $\qquad$ 168×0.98

Explain why.

2 Which of these two has the larger answer?

$81 \div 0.81$ $\qquad$ 8×10

Explain why.

3 Arrange these four calculations in order, giving the one with the largest answer first.

Show clearly the estimates you used.

$241 \div 0.79$ $\qquad$ 241×0.81

241×0.09 $\qquad$ $241 \div 0.03$

2 Kitchen worktops cost £19.75 per metre length.

(a) Make an estimate of the cost of 2.57 m of worktop. Show your working.

(b) How much does the worktop actually cost? Give your answer to a reasonable degree of accuracy.

1 mile = 1.609 km (to 3 d.p.)

5 A road sign in France gives the speed limit as 90 kilometres per hour.

What is this speed limit in miles per hour?

6 Credit card conditions state:

You must pay either £5 or 5% of the balance, whichever is the greater.

If the balance on an account is £157.45, how much is the minimum payment?

1 yard = 36 inches

7 A cricket pitch is 22 yards long.

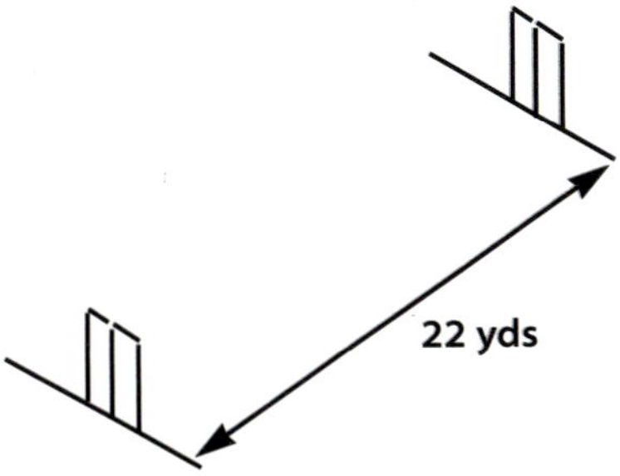

1 inch = 2.54 cm (to 2 d.p.)

What is the length of a cricket pitch in metric units?

Give your answer to the nearest 10 cm.

8 On one day in April 1996, the rate of exchanging US dollars ($) for pounds (£) was $1.47 = £1.

The bank charges 2% commission for changing money.

At the end of your holiday, you have $450 to exchange back to pounds.

How much will the bank give you for this amount of money?

9 To calculate $(2.45 \times 1.3)^2$ you can press these calculator keys.

(| 2 | · | 4 | 5 | × | 1 | · | 3 |) | x^2 | =

Write down which calculator keys to press to calculate these.

(a) $\left(\frac{41.2}{3.4}\right)^2$ (b) $\frac{63.7}{6.4^2}$ (c) $\frac{18}{6.4 + 3.7^2}$

1 mile = 1760 yards
1 inch = 2.54 cm
(to 2 d.p.)

10 In athletics, the distances of 1 mile and 1500 metres are regarded as similar lengths to race.

By converting these distances, decide whether 1 mile is approximately the same distance as 1500 metres.

Explain your answer.

Exercise 10

1 Look at this sequence of patterns.

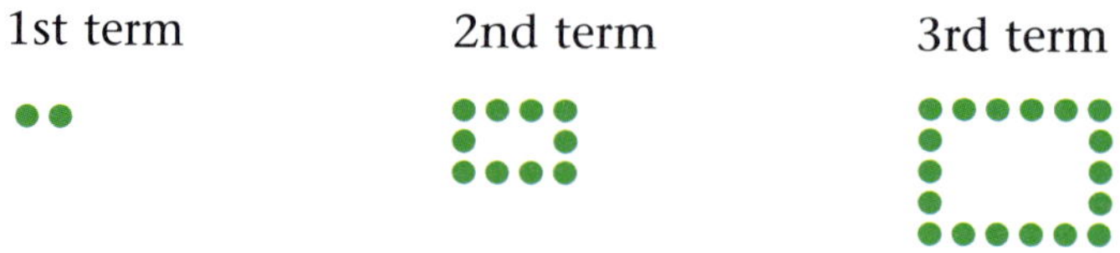

(a) How many dots are needed for the 4th term?
Explain how you found your answer.

(b) How many dots are needed for the 10th term?
Explain how you found your answer.

(c) How many dots are needed for the nth term?

2 Find two values of x which make this equation true.

$x^2 = 5x - 4$

3 Look at this sequence of numbers.

2 6 12 20 …

(a) What is the next number in the sequence?
Explain how you found your answer.

(b) What is the nth number in the sequence?
Explain how you found your answer.

4 Two shops offer bikes for hire.

The first shop uses the formula $c = 2t + 5$ to calculate the hire charge.

(c is the charge in pounds and t is the time in hours.)

The second shop uses the formula $c = 3t$.

For what number of hours do both shops make exactly the same charge?

Show your working.

5 Look at this graph.

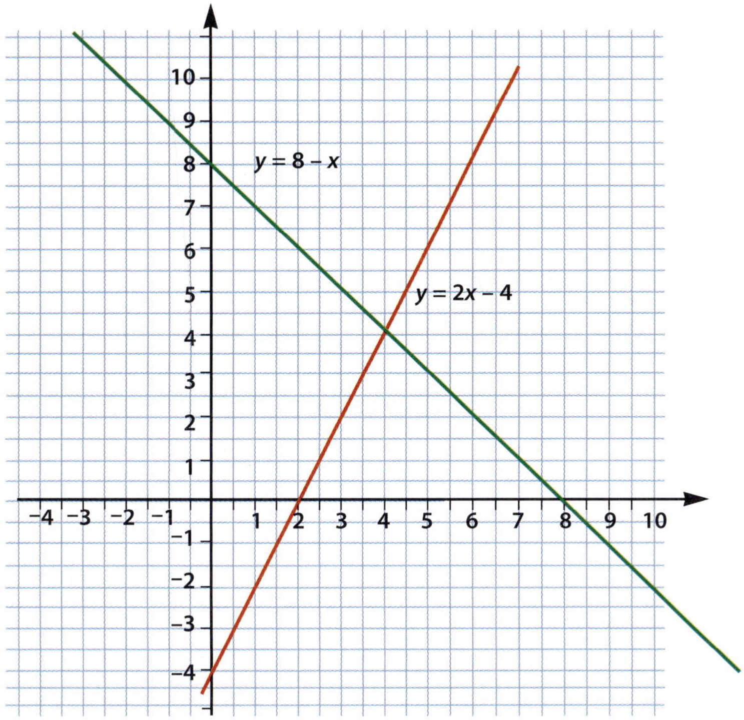

(a) Use the graph to help you to find the value of x for which $2x - 4 = 8 - x$.

(b) Explain how you used the graph to find your answer.

Your axes should look like this.

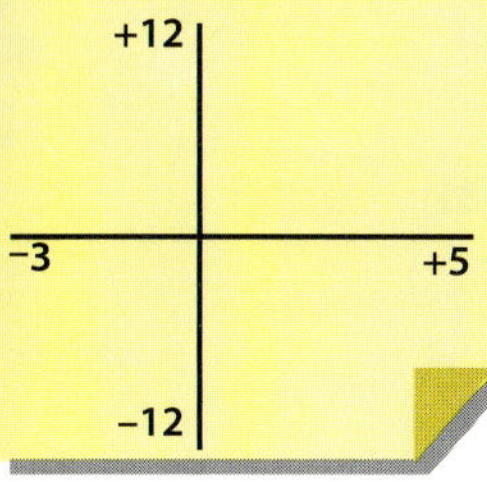

6 Draw axes showing x from $^-3$ to 5 and y from $^-12$ to 12.

On these axes, draw the lines $y = 3x - 4$ and $y = 4 - 2x$.

Use your graph to find the value of x for which $3x - 4 = 4 - 2x$.

Show how you can check your answer.

7 Write down two integer values of x which satisfy this inequality.

$2x - 4 > 6$

8 Look at this sequence.

(a) For the next term in the sequence

(i) how many blue triangles are needed?

(ii) how many yellow triangles are needed?

(b) How many triangles *altogether* are needed to make the 10th term in the sequence?

(c) To make the nth pattern in the sequence

(i) how many blue triangles are needed?

(ii) how many yellow triangles are needed?

(iii) how many triangles altogether are needed?

9 I plan to buy some chocolate bars and packets of sweets.

Chocolate bars cost 15 pence. Packets of sweets cost 10 pence.

I want to buy at least three chocolate bars and three packets of sweets.

I must not spend more than 90 pence in total, but want to buy as many items as possible.

How many of each should I buy?

Explain your answer.

10 What value of x makes both of these equations give the same value of y?

$y = 3x + 4$ $\qquad$ $y = x + 7$

Exercise 11

1 In a bedroom, the bed is positioned as shown in the diagram A.

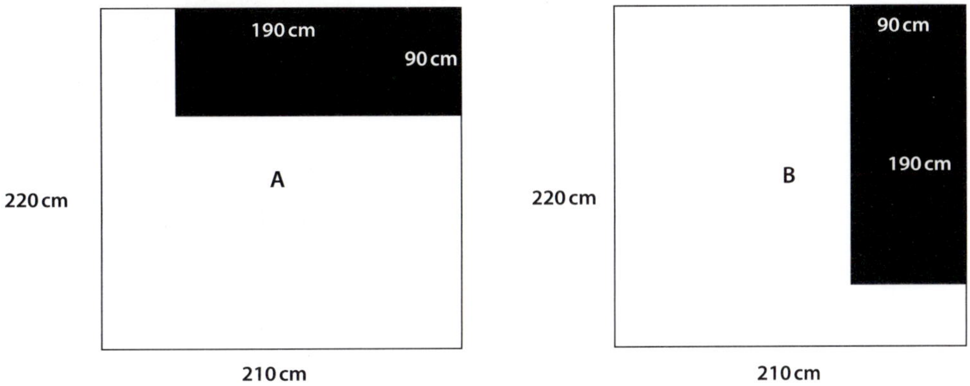

Is the room large enough to turn the bed into the position on diagram B without tipping it up?
Explain your answer.

2 This diagram shows the base of two round cake tins.

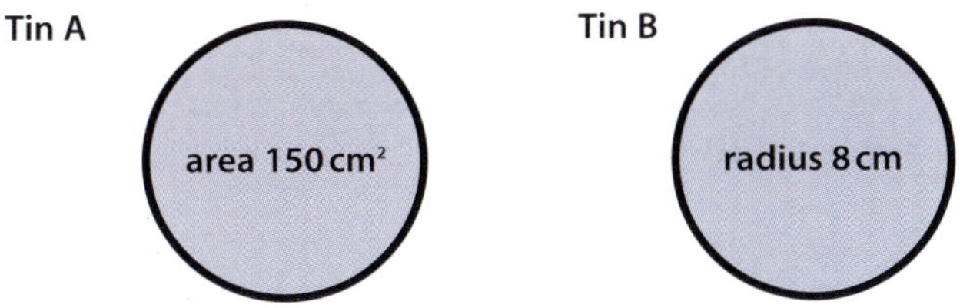

(a) Which tin has the larger base?

(b) When fruit cake mixture is put in tin A, it is 8 cm deep. If the same amount of mixture is put in tin B, how deep will it be?

3 A candle is 9 cm tall and has a hexagonal base with an area of 48 cm^2.

The candle is melted down and reformed into a cuboid.
The base of the new candle measures 3 cm by 4 cm.

How tall is the new candle?

Show your working.

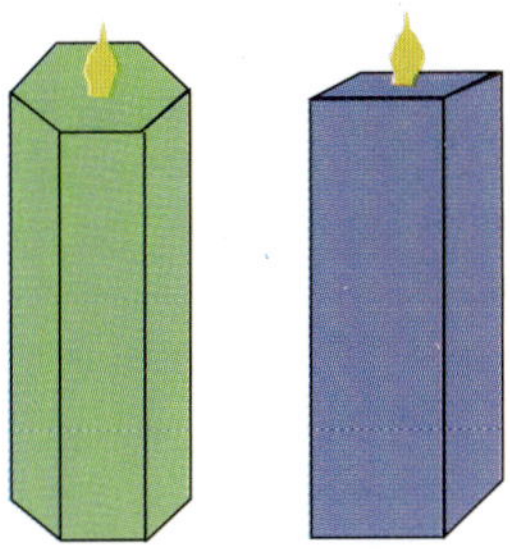

4 These three blocks of wood are all cuboids.

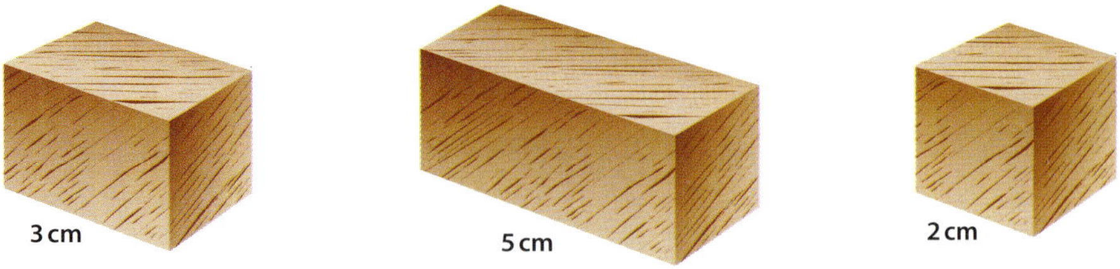

The length measurements are correct to the nearest centimetre.

(a) If the blocks are placed end to end, explain why their total length could be as much as 11.5cm.

(b) What is the least length they could measure in total?

5 The school caretaker plans to dig flower beds beside some of the walls of the school buildings.
The caretaker know that if the flower beds extend more than 50 cm from the wall, pupils are likely to tread on them.

Here is a plan view of part of the school buildings.

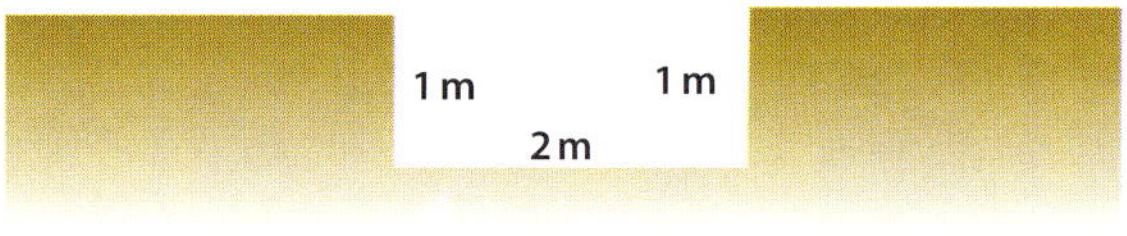

School buildings

Draw a sketch to show where the caretaker should dig the flower beds to make them as big as possible.

6 Copy this diagram on to triangle dotted paper.

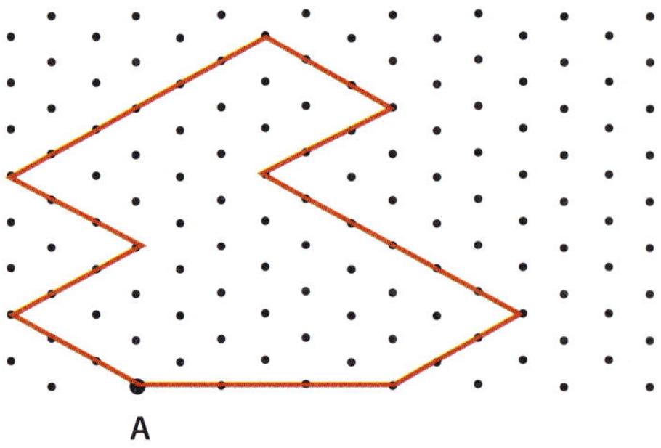

Enlarge the shape with a scale factor of $\frac{2}{3}$ using point A as the centre of enlargement.

7 On a journey, the first 100 miles took $1\frac{1}{2}$ hours.

The next 90 miles took 2 hours 40 minutes.

The last 10 miles took 50 minutes.

Calculate the average speed for the whole journey.

Explain your answer.

8 In the park, the gardener uses a sprinkler to water the flowers.

The sprinkler is made from a piece of hosepipe with holes in it. It manages to reach all the ground up to $\frac{1}{2}$m from the hosepipe.

The hosepipe is $1\frac{1}{2}$ metres long.
Calculate the area of garden it can water.

Give your answer in square metres and show your working.

9 In a science experiment, I placed a box on a pressure mat. The reading from the pressure mat was 8g/cm²

I thought that this meant that the mass of the box was 8 g, but I was wrong.

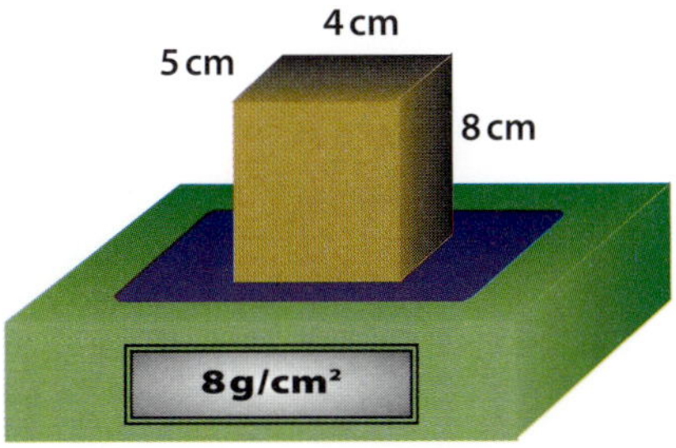

Explain why I was wrong and show how to calculate the mass of the box.

10 On an orienteering course, a group of people start by running 1200 metres on a bearing of 200°.
Then they turn onto a bearing of 110° and run 500 metres.
Finally, they return directly to the start position.
How long is the final part of the course?

Exercise 12

1 Some pupils in Year 9 think they do too much homework, so they decide to do a survey. This is the first question they ask:

Do you think you get too much homework?

The question is too general and will not result in a clear response.

Design a new question for the survey to find out how much homework the pupils in Year 9 do.

2 Some girls in Year 9 believe that girls are more intelligent than boys.
To test this hypothesis, they ask all the pupils in the year this question:

Do you agree that girls are more intelligent than boys?

(a) Explain why this question is not suitable to test their hypothesis.

(b) What data should be collected to check the hypothesis?

3 This box of matches contains approximately 60 matches.

Here are the results of a survey of 30 boxes.

Number of matches	57	58	59	60	61	62	63
Frequency	4	4	8	4	5	4	1

(a) Write down the modal number of matches.

(b) Write down the median number of matches.

(c) Calculate the mean number of matches.

(d) Is the claim about the number of matches a fair one?

Explain your answer.

4 These charts show the scores obtained by 70 pupils in the end of year Mathematics and Science tests.

Mathematics results

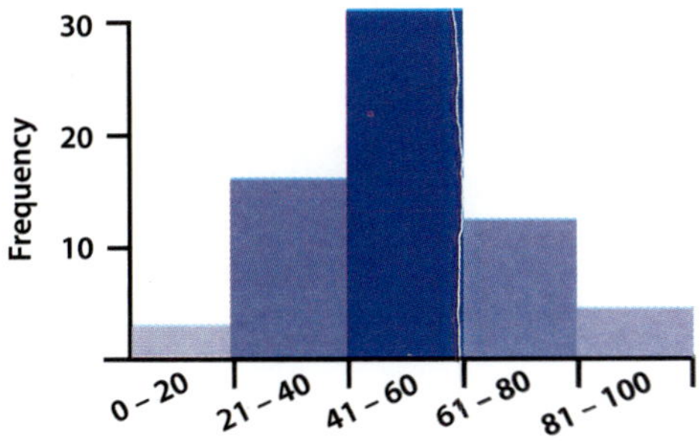

Science results

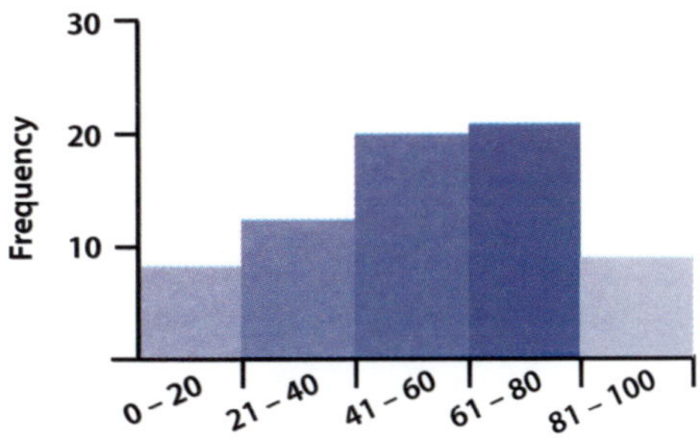

What do the charts suggest about the two tests?

5 The weights of 40 pupils are measured to the nearest kilogram.

The information is recorded on this frequency diagram.

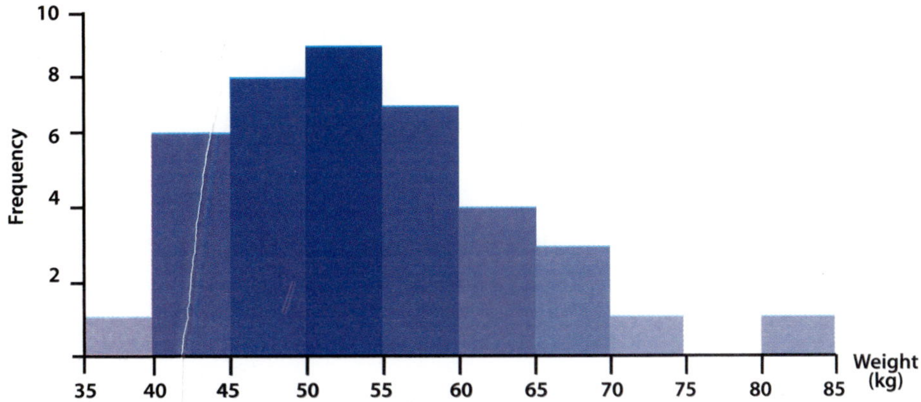

(a) Write down an estimate for the median weight.

(b) Estimate the mean weight.

6 A firm employs seven people. Their salaries are

£21 500	£25 050	£25 050	£28 000
£28 900	£32 000	£85 300	

(a) What are the modal, median, and mean salaries?

(b) Which of these three averages does not give a fair average value for the salaries earned?

Explain your answer.

7 One day, a survey was made of the cars passing a school in each five-minute period.
This frequency diagram records the results.

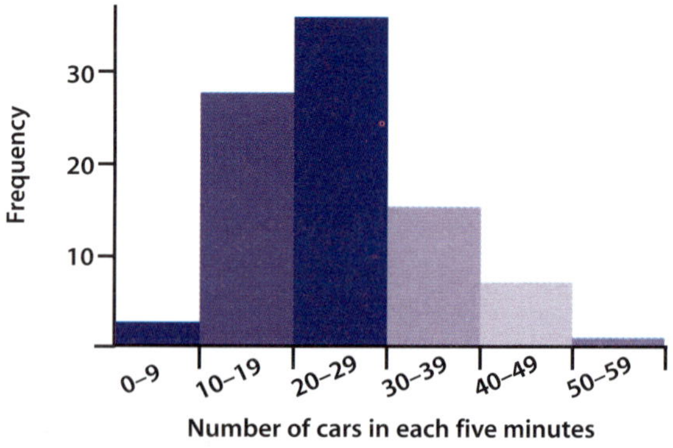

Estimate the total number of vehicles that passed the school that day.

8 Here are the marks obtained in two examination papers.

Pupil	1	2	3	4	5	6	7	8	9	10
Paper 1	17	20	24	31	40	48	52	65	78	92
Paper 2	15	19	20	28	40	46	47	52	71	83

Your axes should look like this.

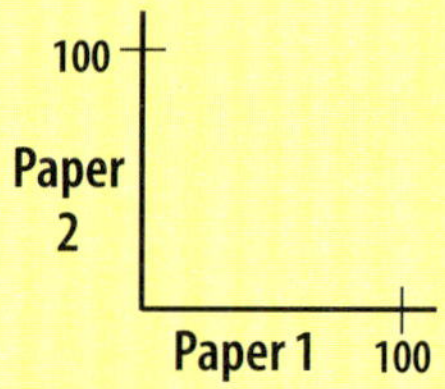

(a) Draw a scatter graph to show these two sets of marks.

(b) Draw a line of best fit.

(c) A pupil scores 45 in the first paper.
What would you expect the score for paper 2 to be?

9 You throw a normal dice 1200 times.
How many times would you expect to throw

(a) a 6? (b) a number greater than 4?

10 A normal dice is thrown a different number of times by four different people, A, B, C and D.
This table shows the number of sixes thrown by each person.

Person	Number of throws	Number of sixes	Relative frequency
A	36	5	0.139
B	120	18	0.15
C	600	124	0.207
D	1200	206	0.172

One of the four wrongly recorded the results of the experiment.
Which one do you think it was? Explain your answer.